R&D DECISIONS

R&D Decisions: Strategy, Policy and Disclosure explores how research and development decisions affect all of us. They are linked inextricably to the performance of firms and of economics as a whole. Their importance means that they are of concern to a large number of practitioners, policy-makers and researchers. This book demonstrates the range of issues and perspectives which R&D can encompass and at the same time brings out the elements which unite them.

The papers in this book are organized into three main sections:

- **Strategy and organization** explores the importance in R&D of the structures and strategies of individual organizations. The impact of the emerging 'core competence' paradigm is given particular prominence.
- **Policy and performance** looks at what new thinking on R&D more generally implies for government policy and the performance of industries, regions and economies.
- **Disclosure and the market** examines issues raised by changing regulations on the disclosure of R&D expenditure.

Contributors to the book include researchers and practitioners in the disciplines of economics, business strategy, organization theory, technology management, finance and policy studies.

Alice Belcher is Senior Lecturer in Law at the University of Dundee. She was previously part of a team researching various market-related aspects of R&D at Keele University.
John Hassard is Professor of Organizational Behaviour and Head of the School of Management at Keele University. His books include *Towards a New Theory of Organization* (1994) and *Sociology and Organization Theory* (1993).
Stephen J. Procter is Lecturer in Human Resource Management at the University of Nottingham. He is the author of a forthcoming book on the performance of British industry and has published widely in the areas of technology management and human resource management.

ROUTLEDGE RESEARCH IN ORGANIZATIONAL BEHAVIOUR AND STRATEGY

1 R&D DECISIONS
Strategy, Policy and Disclosure
Edited by Alice Belcher, John Hassard and Stephen J. Procter

R&D DECISIONS

Strategy, policy and disclosure

Edited by Alice Belcher,
John Hassard and Stephen J. Procter

ROUTLEDGE
London and New York

First published 1996
by Routledge
11 New Fetter Lane, London EC4P 4EE

Simultaneously published in the USA and Canada
by Routledge
29 West 35th Street, New York, NY 10001

Routledge is an International Thomson Publishing company

Typeset in Baskerville by
J&L Composition Ltd, Filey, North Yorkshire

Printed and bound in Great Britain by
Mackays of Chatham PLC, Chatham, Kent

British Library Cataloguing in Publication Data

A catalogue record for this book is available from the British Library

Library of Congress Cataloging in Publication Data

R&D decisions: strategy, policy, and disclosure/edited by Alice Belcher, John Hassard, Stephen J. Procter.
p. c.m. – (Routledge research in organizational behaviour and strategy)
Includes bibliographical references and index.
1. Research, Industrial–Decision making. 2. Research, Industrial–Government policy. I. Belcher, Alice, 1959– . II. Hassard, John, 1953– . III. Procter, Stephen J., 1961– . IV. Series.
T175.5.R23 1996 658.5′7–dc20 95–50137 CIP

ISBN 0–415–13777–2

CONTENTS

List of figures vii
List of tables ix
Notes on contributors xi
Acknowledgements xvi

INTRODUCTION: R&D DECISIONS IN STRATEGY, POLICY AND DISCLOSURE 1
Stephen J. Procter, John Hassard and Alice Belcher

Part I Strategy and organization

1 CORE COMPETENCIES AND THE STRATEGIC MANAGEMENT OF R&D 25
Rod Coombs

2 R&D INITIATIVES AND THE DEVELOPMENT OF STRATEGIC ADVANTAGE 41
Ken Clarke and Martyn Pitt

3 THE ROLE OF COMPLEMENTARY ASSETS IN TECHNOLOGY STRATEGY 64
Julian Lowe and Peter Taylor

4 R&D STRATEGY AND THE IMPLICATIONS FOR MANAGEMENT CONTROL 78
Keith Randle and Frank Currie

Part II Policy and performance

5 NEW VIEWS OF INNOVATION AND CHALLENGES TO R&D POLICY 101
Keith Smith

6 FROM COMMON SENSE TO SHORT-TERMISM: REFLECTIONS ON R&D MANAGERS' PERCEPTIONS 125
Istemi Demirag

7 HIGH TECHNOLOGY EMPLOYMENT AND THE ACHIEVEMENT OF R&D SPILLOVERS 154
Zoltan Acs, Felix Fitzroy and Ian Smith

8 PERFORMANCE IMPLICATIONS OF PATENT FAMILY SIZE 169
Gavin Reid and Colin Roberts

9 CONFLICTS OF INTEREST IN R&D COLLABORATION: NEGOTIATING THE FUNCTION–PERFORMANCE LINK 189
Nikos Kastrinos

Part III Disclosure and the market

10 R&D DISCLOSURE: THEORY AND PRACTICE 203
Alice Belcher

11 R&D IN UK QUOTED COMPANIES: THE EFFECTS OF DISCLOSURE AND FINANCE 224
Jonathan Seaton and Ian Walker

12 THE DECISION TO DISCLOSE R&D EXPENDITURE 241
Alice Belcher

13 THE IMPACT OF R&D KNOWLEDGE ACCUMULATION ON WAGES: EVIDENCE FROM EUROPEAN CORPORATIONS 259
Stephen Machin and John Van Reenen

14 REAL R&D OPTIONS 273
David Newton, Dean Paxson and Alan Pearson

Index 283

FIGURES

1.1 Core competencies 27
1.2 Paradigm 1 30
1.3 Paradigm 2 30
1.4 Paradigm 3 31
1.5 Technology exploitation through core competencies 33
4.1 A linear model of innovation 80
4.2 The 'chain-linked model' 82
7.1 Industry groupings 158
7.2 Plot of aggregate high technology employment, 1989 and university research expenditure, 1985 159
7.3 Plot of the high technology employment–population ratio, 1989 and university research expenditure, 1985 159
7.4 Plot of aggregate high technology employment and the number of scientists and engineers per 100 workers, 1989 160
7.5 Plot of employment ratio against the proportion of scientists and engineers in each MSA, 1989 161
8.1 Histograms of ownership for patent-active and patent-inactive firms 182
11.1 The financial pecking order 229
11.2 The financial pecking order with higher costs 230
11.3 R&D sales by proportion of firms, USA, 1976 231
11.4 R&D sales by proportion of firms, UK, 1990 232
11.5 Average proportion of finance type over sales pre-SSAP 13 (1983–88) 232
11.6 Average proportion of finance type over sales post-SSAP 13 (1989/90) 233
11.7 Sales v. R&D (voluntary/involuntary firms) 235
11.8 Profits v. R&D (voluntary/involuntary firms) 236
11.9 Debt/equity ratio v. R&D (voluntary/involuntary firms) 236
13.1 Disclosure rates across countries 261
13.2 Average real wages: all firms 266
13.3 Average real wages: firms who disclose R&D 266

13.4 Average R&D per worker: firms who disclose R&D 267
14.1 Real R&D option discovery value 279
14.2 R&D option volatility sensitivity 280
14.3 R&D option: volatility and correlation 280

TABLES

3.1 Competition and internal organization: estimated coefficients of logistical regression models 71
3.2 R&D and complementary assets: estimated coefficients of logistical regression models 73
3.3 Probability levels for the change in the χ^2 statistic when complementary asset variables are added to the main models 75
6.1 Pressures from capital markets 142
6.2 Evaluation of R&D projects 146
7.1 Correspondence of university departments and industries 162
7.2 Summary statistics by variable 163
7.3 OLS employment equation estimates with industry, region and time fixed effects 163
8.1 Size, capital structure and financial performance for patent-active and patent-inactive firms in the UK scientific instruments industry 173
8.2 One-way and two-way fixed effects models 177
8.3 Ownership pattern in the UK scientific instruments industry (1983–90) 183
10.1 Accounting treatment and disclosure: FAS No. 2 and SSAP 13 210
10.2 Disclosure categories 213
10.3 Disclosure of R&D amounts 215
10.4 Place of disclosure 215
10.5 Compliance with schedule 7 para 6 (c) Companies Act 1985 by reference to R&D in directors' report 216
10.6 Repetitions of text in directors' report 217
10.7 Accounting policies on R&D 219
11.1 R&D versus non-R&D companies 234
11.2 Of R&D firms, voluntary versus involuntary disclosers 234
11.3 Tobit estimates – R&D equation 237

12.1	Hypotheses and variables used in the logit model showing the predicted sign for the coefficients	246
12.2	Independent variables: definition and descriptive statistics	249
12.3	Cross-correlation coefficients for the independent variables	250
12.4	Logit model of the decision to disclose	251
12.5	Frequencies of actual and predicted outcomes	252
12.6	Probit model of the decision to disclose	253
12.7	Size and predictive accuracy	254
12.8	Predictive accuracy over time	254
12.9	Distribution of observations by time	255
13.1	R&D per employee and average wages by country	260
13.2	Sample characteristics	265
13.3	Probit models of disclosure of R&D data in company accounts	268
13.4	The relationship between firm wages and R&D intensity in four European countries	269
14.1	Real R&D option discovery value and 'moneyness'	279
14.2	Real R&D option: discovery volatility sensitivity	280

CONTRIBUTORS

Zoltan Acs teaches at the Merrick School of Business, University of Baltimore, Maryland. He specializes in small firm research and is editor of an international journal, *Small Business Economics*. As well as numerous journal articles, he has written several books including *Innovation and Small Firms* (1990, MIT Press) with David Audretsch.

Alice Belcher is Senior Lecturer in law at the University of Dundee. She was previously a lecturer at Keele University where she was part of a team researching various market-related aspects of R&D. This work was supported by an ESRC grant under the Functioning of Markets Initiative. Her Ph.D. thesis was on 'Company Reporting of R&D: The Decision to Disclose and the Market's Reaction to Disclosure'. More recently her research has been mainly in the area of corporate governance.

Ken Clarke lectures in strategic management at the University of Portsmouth, formerly at the Universities of Bath and Aston. He presently has two strands to his research interests and publications. One is how managers perceive technological change, and how they manage the introduction and strategic consequences of technologies new to them and their organizations. The second strand concerns managerial attitudes toward environmental issues, how far managers and firms can presently be characterized as green, and with what repercussions. He is presently exploring the interaction of these themes, and in particular the question of whether green issues act as a spur or a block to technological innovation by firms.

Rod Coombs is Professor of Technology Management at the Manchester School of Management, UMIST. He is director of the Centre for Research on Organisations, Management and Technical Change (CROMTEC) in the School, and is also co-Director (with Stan Metcalfe) of the Joint Manchester/UMIST ESRC Research Centre on Innovation which begins in late 1996. He has researched and published extensively on many aspects of innovation and technical change.

Frank Currie is Senior Lecturer in Economics at the University of Hertfordshire Business School. His research interests are the economics of technical change and organizational economics.

Istemi S. Demirag is Reader in Accounting at the Management School, University of Sheffield. His research interests focus on the interface between management accounting and financial management. In particular, these include performance evaluation and control in multinational companies; global competition; the management of innovation; short-termism; and corporate governance. He is the co-ordinator of an international project on short-termism and a co-founder and director of the Centre for Research on Innovation and Technological Change (CRITEC) based at Sheffield University. He is also an associate editor of *The European Journal of Finance.*

Felix Fitzroy is a reader in Economics at the University of St. Andrews. He was previously a Senior Research Fellow at the Science Centre in Berlin and a Visiting Professor of Economics at the European University Institute, Florence. He has published articles on work sharing, profit sharing, wage determination, and urban transport.

John Hassard is Professor of Organizational Behaviour at Keele University, England. He previously taught at the London Business School and Cardiff University. His publications include *Time, Work and Organization* (Routledge, 1989, with others), *The Theory and Philosophy of Organizations* (Routledge, 1990, co-edited), *The Sociology of Time* (Macmillan, 1990, edited) and *Sociology and Organization Theory* (Cambridge, 1993). His research interests lie in organization theory, industrial sociology and the management of R&D.

Nikos Kastrinos is a Research Fellow with the Programme on Policy Research in Engineering, Science and Technology (PREST) at the University of Manchester. He has carried out research for the European Commission and various UK government departments on issues related to technology policy and industrial innovation. His current interests lie with technological innovation in services with particular emphasis on environmental services sectors.

Julian Lowe is Professor of Strategic Management at the Bristol Business School, University of the West of England (Bristol). He was previously foundation chair in management at the University of Wollongong, Australia and has held tenured positions at the Universities of Bath and Nottingham. His main research interests are in technology transfer and the strategy of medium-sized enterprises. Recent publications have appeared in *Strategic Management Journal, International Journal of Technology Management, International Journal of Small Business and Technology*

Analysis and Strategic Management. He has also written books on technology transfer, environmental management and the commercialization of university research.

Stephen Machin is a reader at University College London and Senior Research Assistant in the Centre for Economic Performance. He has published widely in the field of labour economics, industrial economics and industrial relations. He gained his Ph.D. at the University of Warwick.

David Newton is Lecturer in Managerial Finance at Manchester Business School. His experience in R&D decisions includes some years as a research chemist with an MA from the University of Cambridge, a Ph.D. from the University of Salford, as well as an MBA from MBS. His research interests are in mathematical analysis of financial options and futures and in the analysis of stock market behaviour.

Dean Paxson is Professor of Finance at Manchester Business School. He received a BA from Amherst College, an MA from Oxford, and his doctorate from Harvard Business School. He has published numerous articles on financial theory, and has completed articles on real options in petroleum, power, property, shipping and on emotional and career developments.

Alan Pearson is Professor of R&D Management at Manchester Business School, Director of the R&D Research Unit, and editor of *R&D Management.* He gained industrial experience with Pilkington Brothers Ltd and Henry Simon Ltd. He was an adjust programme associate at the Centre of Creative Leadership, North Carolina from 1982–88 and Visiting Professor at the University of Kiel in 1989. He has published widely in scientific and management journals and is co-author of *Mathematics for Economists* and co-editor of *Transfer Processes in Technical Change and Managing Interdisciplinary Research.* In 1984 he was awarded an IEEE Centennial Medal by the Institute of Electrical and Electronic Engineers, Inc. for his contributions to the field of engineering management. In 1992 he was given the Max Planck Research Award from the Alexander von Humboldt Foundation.

Martyn Pitt is Lecturer in Strategic Management and Marketing at the University of Bath. Previously he lectured at Aston University and before that he was involved in business planning in several major companies. His current research interests encompass strategic aspects of entrepreneurship and innovation from the perspective of creative managerial problem-finding and sense-making. He has produced a number of books and articles on these themes.

Stephen J. Procter is Lecturer in Human Resource Management in the School of Management and Finance, University of Nottingham. His research interests are in the areas of organizational change, the management of technology, and their relationship with economic performance. He has published widely in these areas and is at present writing a book on the recent performance of the UK economy.

Keith Randle is a Principal Lecturer in Organisational Behaviour at the University of Hertfordshire Business School. He previously studied at Bath, Liverpool, Brunel and Middlesex Universities. His research interests are in the work, employment and management of highly qualified and professional employees. His current work, which has given rise to a number of papers and publications, focuses on a major research-based pharmaceutical company. His research is informed by a labour process perspective.

Gavin Reid is Professor of Economics at the University of St. Andrews, and Director of the Centre for Research into Industry, Enterprise, Finance and the Firm (CRIEFF). He received his Ph.D. from the University of Edinburgh, and is a specialist in industrial economics. Previously a Reader in Economics at the University of Edinburgh, he has also held visiting appointments in Queen's (Ontario), Denver and Cambridge Universities. He is the author of many articles on small firms, partial monopoly, price leadership, venture capital, business ethics and history of political economy, and has written six books, including *Small Business Enterprise* (Routledge, 1993).

Colin Roberts is Lecturer in Economics at the University of Edinburgh and received his Ph.D. from the University of Warwick. He has previously held posts in Warwick and Southampton Universities. He has been an academic visitor to Monash University and is currently a visitor at Melbourne University. He is an econometric software specialist and the author of articles on applied econometrics. He is joint editor of the *Journal of Economic Surveys*.

Jonathan S. Seaton is Lecturer in Economics in the Department of Economics at the University of Loughborough. His collection of degrees comprises a BA (Hons) Econ. from University of Northumbria (1981), MA Econ. (1982) M. Phil. Econ. (1986) both from University of Essex and a Ph.D. Econ. from Manchester University (1991). His teaching involvement has predominantly been in the field of applied microeconomics, econometrics and quantitative topics. He became interested in R&D investment and firm finance during his time as a Research Fellow at the University of Keele, 1989–91 where he contributed to the functioning of markets project funded by the ESRC.

Ian Smith is Lecturer in Economics at the University of St. Andrews. He received his Ph.D. from the University of Cambridge in 1991. He is an applied econometrician who has published articles on the demand for test match cricket, urban transport systems, European railways, and the Church of Scotland.

Keith Smith is Director of the STEP Group (Group for Studies in Technology, Innovation and Economic Policy) in Oslo, Norway, and Professor of Economics at the Norwegian University of Science and Technology. He has worked extensively on technological change and innovation, particularly from a policy perspective. This has included work for the OECD and European Commission on innovation data and indicators, plus work on service sector innovation, regional innovation issues, and R&D policy evaluation.

Peter Taylor is Lecturer in Strategic Management and a Research Fellow at Bristol Business School, UWE, Bristol, having previously taught economics at Bristol Polytechnic and economics and econometrics at the University of Bristol. He has published numerous articles in two main fields: the econometric modelling of business behaviour and the development of computational methods for the teaching of economics. Current research interests are strategy and capital structure, technology licensing and competition in the UK package tour industry. He has published in such diverse journals as the *Economic History Review, Economics, British Review of Economic Issues, Managerial and Decision Economics, Tourism Economics* and *Strategic Management Journal.*

John Van Reenen is Lecturer in the Department of Economics, University College London and a Project Manager in the Innovation Sector of the Institute for Fiscal Studies, London. He studied at the University of Cambridge, the London School of Economics and University College London where he received his doctorate in 1993. He has published in leading economics journals on the impact of innovation on economic outcomes and the econometric modelling of technological change.

Ian Walker is Professor in Economics at Keele University. He has a BA in Economics from Liverpool and an MA in Economics from Warwick. Before coming to Keele he was a lecturer at the University of Manchester. He is an Honorary Fellow of University College, London, and a Research Fellow of the Institute for Fiscal Studies. He has recently held visiting positions as Professor in Econometrics at Sydney University and Professor of Economics at the Aarhus Business School, Denmark, and he gained a Hallsworth Fellowship at Manchester University for the calendar year 1995. His major research interests are in the econometrics of the labour market and applied aspects of public policy issues, such as the determination of R&D expenditure, taxation and work incentives, social security issues, and the welfare economics of indirect taxation.

ACKNOWLEDGEMENTS

These papers were presented at the 'R&D Decisions' conference at Keele University in September 1994. We are grateful to the ESRC for support in the form of a grant under the Functioning of Markets Initiative (grant L102251012). The conference represented a high point for the Keele team and three of their papers appear in this book. It was also a unique gathering of those involved in research into R&D across a variety of disciplines, and we would like to thank all the participants for contributing to a lively and fruitful conference.

Alice Belcher, John Hassard and Stephen Procter

INTRODUCTION

R&D decisions in strategy, policy and disclosure

Stephen J. Procter, John Hassard and Alice Belcher

Decisions about R&D affect all of us. They are linked inextricably with the performance of firms and of economies as a whole. Their importance means that they are of concern to a large number of practitioners, policy-makers and researchers. Their scope means that their study can be approached from a wide variety of perspectives. It is hoped that this book will demonstrate the range of issues and perspectives which R&D can encompass and, at the same time, that it will bring out the elements which unite them. This introductory chapter is thus in two parts. The first describes the chapters in terms of the three sets of issues around which the book is structured: strategy and organization, policy and performance, and finance and disclosure. The second part addresses the themes which emerge from all this and which bring together contributions from the different sections of the book.

STRATEGY AND ORGANIZATION

In the opening chapter in this section Coombs provides an overview of thinking and practice in the area of the strategic management of technology and R&D. He observes that after the beginning of the 1970s, many British firms took steps towards both making their R&D activities 'market-driven' and integrating them with the broader strategies of the individual business units they served. This has led to a shift in funding away from the corporate level and to a more decentralized R&D effort. While the gains from this have been substantial, argues Coombs, such an arrangement can exacerbate the difficulties encountered by an uncompetitive technological regime, and can make it difficult for an individual business unit to react to the emergence of what have been called 'competence-destroying' technologies. The process of decentralization at the same time weakened the ability of corporate R&D to take up this challenge, a weakness exacerbated by a management style increasingly financially- rather than strategically-oriented. The lesson that market-pull should replace technology-push, argues Coombs, British firms have learnt 'rather too well'.

Coombs' own research reveals that many firms have been taking the action necessary to overcome the disadvantages associated with the decentralized, market-push paradigm of R&D organization. Rather than seeing a return to the centralized, technology-push paradigm which characterized the twenty or so years before the early 1970s, however, Coombs identifies the new policies as representing an emergent 'third paradigm' aimed at transcending the debates between the other two. This involves the creation of a corporate unit for the strategic management of technology whose role is to manage the overall technology portfolio, to co-ordinate the technology activities of the business units and to integrate considerations of technology with the more general strategic management of the company.

It is in this extension beyond its traditional boundaries, Coombs proposes, that the strategic management of R&D can make use of the 'core competence' paradigm which has developed out of the work of Prahalad and Hamel (1990). This holds that technological expertise and organizational capabilities can be combined by a firm into a unique set of core competencies. These provide the basis on which decisions about technology and products can be made. Just as in the case of the management of technology, there is a danger in excessive decentralization: individual business units can take decisions which do not take advantage of and might even be damaging to the company's core competencies.

Linking together the strategic management of R&D and the core competence paradigm, Coombs sees the tasks of R&D managers as being the development of the technological capabilities upon which core competencies are based, the protection of the technological interests of business units when co-operation between them is under financial threat, and the provision of the co-ordination with other functions and other parts of the company which allows the application of the technological capabilities. Thus, argues Coombs, although the R&D function is not the site of the company's core competencies, it acts to invest in them and exploit or 'harvest' their outcomes.

The links with the core competence paradigm in turn allow Coombs to see traditional areas of R&D decision-making in a new light. The evaluation of long-term projects would be based on the criterion of whether the knowledge and skills generated will contribute to the company's core competencies. The model of the organization and funding of R&D would be based on the emergent third paradigm. Long-term elements of the R&D portfolio would be funded centrally and organized around certain technological capabilities, but at the same time this would help determine as well as be determined by the core competencies. Finally, the core competence paradigm would also provide a means by which the effectiveness of R&D could be measured. All in all, Coombs concludes, this kind of approach could be a means by which technological and non-technological aspects of strategy could be linked, allowing R&D efforts to be directed towards rapid innovation and the long-term accumulation of technological strength.

The relationship between R&D and a firm's core competencies is taken up and developed by Clarke and Pitt in Chapter 2 of the present volume. Like Coombs, they argue for an approach to decision-making in R&D based on the idea that any major project should be aimed at both developing particular technologies and, in the longer term, contributing to the firm's competencies. 'For long-run success,' they recommend, 'the firm is well advised to reconcile these goals'. In practice, of course, this can prove difficult. Not only must firms integrate R&D with broader strategic concerns, say Clarke and Pitt, but these must be accompanied by the necessary 'complementary assets' (Teece 1986). It is the synthesis of competencies, technologies and complementary assets which can create the 'architecture' (Kay 1993) essential for long-run competitive success.

At a conceptual level Clarke and Pitt show that it is important to draw a distinction between technologies and competencies. In the case of a license agreement, for example, the same technology enters the repertoire of both licenser and licensee. The competencies the two firms develop, however, may be quite different. An important characteristic of competencies is that they are tacit. In large part the province of individuals in an organization, it is argued, competencies are not always easily transferable between contexts.

Clarke and Pitt apply these considerations to three themes in the strategic assessment of R&D initiatives. The first is the strategic rationale for an innovating project. Again like Coombs, they argue that account must be taken in this of a firm's core competencies. This should go so far as to include an evaluation of the implications for competencies should the innovation fail to achieve its outcomes in terms of technology. The second theme is the trajectories and course of competence development in the firm. Here it is the simultaneous evolution of technology and competence trajectories that is important. R&D must therefore be seen as more than a process of and function for the development of technology. In establishing competencies underpinning the technologies, consideration should be given to their organizational aspects, which may at different levels be essential for the strategic exploitation of R&D. Clarke and Pitt's third theme is the appropriation of returns to innovating. With the firm taking into account returns in terms of learning potential as well as simple economic benefits, the strategic issue it faces is how a long-run stream of competencies can be developed.

In applying this framework and these themes to four case-study companies, Clarke and Pitt show that although in all of them the economic benefits of innovation are likely to be positive, applications of the new technology are seen in rather narrow terms. The development of competencies is thus not a major consideration in decision-making, and where competencies are developed to support the technologies Clarke and Pitt note a reluctance to then redeploy them systematically. Their tentative explanation of this centres on the conflicting interests of different groups within organizations. Though aware of the possible effects on competencies, the uncertainty surrounding this relationship makes it easy for these broader, strategic issues to be downplayed. For firms to develop strategic advantages, conclude Clarke and Pitt, it is essential that these links be made.

In Chapter 3 Lowe and Taylor examine licensing as a means by which technology might be acquired. The key issue they point to is whether this acquisition of knowledge from external sources should be seen as a substitute for or complementary to its internal generation. A second question concerns the importance of a firm's technological and non-technological capabilities in its choice of technology strategy. As Lowe and Taylor show, licensing is undertaken by firms for a variety of reasons. At one level it offers a quick though not costless means of acquiring new technology. It can also be used more broadly as a means of stimulating internal research effort and developing technological collaboration. Its use is likely to depend on certain firm-specific factors, such as the 'NIH (Not Invented Here) syndrome', but also on the nature of competition within an industry and the ease with which the technology can be transferred between firms.

In looking at the factors determining the decision to license technology, Lowe and Taylor show that it might be expected that licensing is more likely to take place where internal research is weak and the 'NIH syndrome' is strong. The overall effect of market structure is not clear at first sight, since an oligopolistic market might be expected to encourage licensing as a means of collaboration but a less concentrated market might demand it for reasons of competition. Within the context of the basic choice between licensing and the in-house development of technology, Lowe and Taylor concentrate on the role played by complementary assets. Like Clarke and Pitt they follow Teece (1986) in arguing that the way in which firms exploit knowledge will be determined by assets in such areas as marketing, manufacturing and market power. Though licensing may be associated with the import into the firm of some of these non-technological assets, Lowe and Taylor make clear that the expectation is that their existence will be positively related to the use of licensing and that they may be more important in a firm's considerations than weaknesses in its internal R&D.

These hypotheses were tested by means of a questionnaire survey of the perceptions of the managers of a sample of 128 companies. Dividing the sample between high- and low- or non-users of licensing, Lowe and Taylor found the size of firm and its sector to be predictors of licensing. Extending the analysis to more fundamental relationships, they first of all confirmed that the competitive environment was significant in explaining licensing, evidence existing for the 'oligopoly effect' described above. Internal structure was found to be of little significance, but licensing activity was found to be associated with an outward cultural orientation and the existence of alliance-type agreements. Weakness in R&D personnel and skills was also identified as a significant factor.

In looking at the question of the effects of complementary assets, the evidence on supplier and distribution networks was quite difficult to interpret, but licensing was found to have a significant relationship negatively with manufacturing strength and positively with marketing. Augmenting the earlier models with variables on complementary assets, Lowe and Taylor show that they increase the use of licensing strategies even with competitive pressures present and that they would enhance the probability of licensing for firms with an outgoing orientation. Not only are complementary assets important in overcoming weaknesses in R&D, it was concluded, but they are important even in the presence of other causes of licensing behaviour.

In Chapter 4 our focus shifts to the development of R&D strategy within an individual organization. Randle and Currie examine R&D strategy and its implication for management control in Glaxo Research and Development (GRD). Looking at the development and exploitation of new biotechnologies, they reject a model based on a division of labour between new, small, creative firms making discoveries and large, incumbent firms exploiting these discoveries commercially. They argue, firstly, that the research process is much more complex and interactive than suggested by this model and the strategy implications are indeterminate, and, secondly, that the problem of reconciling creativity and control cannot be solved by such a strategy.

In considering the nature of the innovation process in general, Randle and Currie show that the division of labour outlined above is based on a conception of innovation as a linear process, beginning with basic research and ending with an innovative product. Such a model is now difficult to defend, they argue, and has been supplanted by models in which the relationship between stages is more complex and the scope of innovation is more widely defined. To illustrate this interactive complexity Randle and Currie draw on Kline and Rosenberg's (1986) 'chain-linked' model of innovation. They reject claims that the abstract nature of the knowledge base in the pharmaceutical and other industries is making them increasingly conducive to an upstream/downstream division of labour, arguing that new firms account for a small part of the industry as a whole and that the fact firms are separate does not necessarily mean they perform different tasks. In place of della Valle and Gambardella's (1993) approach based on economic arguments of efficiency, Randle and Currie argue for a more evolutionary, historical analysis of questions of organization in the industry.

The process of innovation and its implication for organization, it is argued, have in any case to be considered alongside the way in which research is organized and managed within a company. Randle and Currie thus examine the management of innovation in Glaxo Research and Development (GRD). Within GRD research is carried out in multi-disciplinary project teams operating within a matrix structure. The basic problem faced by management is to encourage scientific creativity amongst its staff while at the same time ensuring profitable products are being developed. The latter involves active interaction between the research and marketing functions. The difficulties involved in reconciling creativity and control is well summed-up by a senior manager's references to the activities of the scientists: 'I don't know what it is that they are doing, but I do know that they are doing things that I don't know about.'

This dilemma is illustrated by Randle and Currie in their exploration of two key areas of the employment relationship: working time and the payment system. Seeking to reward performance by means of 'trust time' and performance-related pay, they argue, carries it with the risk of diverting employees from creative activity. Further problems are posed by the planned split of the research and development functions, and the questions this raised about collaboration within external bodies such as universities or new biotechnology firms. The evidence does not suggest, argue Randle and Currie, that the development of informal external links will allow the control/creativity dilemma to be resolved. In place of a general trend either in this direction or towards greater control, they suggest that we are likely to see management shifting constantly between the two.

POLICY AND PERFORMANCE

The introductory chapter in this section is provided by Smith. He points to the key role industrialized countries have identified for R&D policy in their pursuit of a widening range of objectives. At the same time, the nature of R&D policy is changing, and Smith's chapter concentrates on 'the conceptual basis, structure and content of policies directed towards industrial innovation and diffusion policy'. Research in these areas, based on the idea that innovation needs to be seen as a political and a social rather than simply a technical process, has reached the stage, he claims, at which policy can be and should be reappraised.

Smith concentrates on two dimensions of the linear model of innovation which has provided the basis for policy for most of the post-war period in industrialized countries. The first is what he describes as its over-emphasis on research. The basic underlying argument was that because of the risks involved and the 'public good' nature of knowledge, firms in a free market would invest in a socially less than optimal amount of research. Government had therefore either to intervene directly or provide the private sector with the necessary incentives. A second, more neglected dimension of the linear model, according to Smith, was that innovation was seen in purely technical terms – as an act of production rather than a continuous social process. In recent years, as the linear model has come under threat, he argues, these two dimensions have increasingly been called into question. The devotion of resources to R&D has not necessarily resulted in technological or economic development; while successful innovation by firms has come to be seen as the result of organizational as much as technical expertise.

For Smith, it is changing views on the nature of technology that in particular underlie much contemporary research. Rather than as hardware, technology increasingly is seen as involving the integration of knowledge, organization and technique. It also needs to be understood in the context of the social framework which produces it and within which it exists. For the firm, innovation requires an understanding both of the external and internal components of technology and the relationship between them. Drawing on themes developed in the first section of this book, Smith argues that the problem facing the firm is to develop the competencies and capabilities necessary for the creation of a competitive advantage. Innovation can then be carried out with existing skills and knowledge, and need not involve research at all. Although this implies that different firms can produce innovations in different ways, this organization around existing competencies also gives rise to limitations in the form of what Fransman (1990) has called 'bounded vision'. Firms must then look outside their own boundaries for solutions to problems, and it is this combination of internal expertise and external relationships which Smith sees as being at the heart of understanding innovation.

Drawing on these analytical developments Smith identifies five main policy-related issues requiring further research. The first is the basic rationale for public policy. While the economic importance of innovation and technological change has been established, the theoretical underpinnings of this relationship are less well-developed. At present, argues Smith, industrial policy is focused on competition rather than innovation. Given the links with performance, technology policy has to be given a greater emphasis and its relationship with other areas of policy better understood.

His second main concern is that differences in the innovation process between industries have to be understood. Pavitt (1984) has developed analysis in this area which goes beyond a simple consideration of the amount of research an industry requires for innovation. That the difficulties faced by firms in innovation are dependent on the type of industry in which they worked is of enormous importance for government policy. Smith argues that policy should extend even beyond this level, to take account of differences between firms.

Connected with this is Smith's third main point, that as firms increasingly are forced to look outside their own boundaries in solving problems in innovation, this would involve not just a role for government policy but the growth in technological co-operation between firms. This could take a variety of forms which themselves are part of a wider regional or national 'system of innovation'. The development of an understanding of the infrastructure necessary for successful innovation is an area in which much research has still to be done.

These systems of innovation – together with firms' own expertise – have in turn to be considered along with the internationalization of technological change. For Smith, this raises the possibility that the national objectives of government policy may be inconsistent with firms' transnational aspirations. A related problem is that the international nature of much scientific research gives national governments an incentive to shift resources towards more directly applicable research activities. Though this would be to the long-run detriment of all parties, there exist no international mechanisms by which an adequate collaborative solution could be achieved. Further problems are posed by the internationalization of *production* as well as ownership. The idea of nationally-based companies and thus nationally-based policies is thereby called into question. In particular, asks Smith, should policy be concentrated not on support for companies' R&D but on the infrastructure of education, training and basic science?

This brings us to Smith's fifth and final concern, which is the role played by science in the process of innovation. The rejection of the linear model does not imply that science was of no importance, and there are signs, he argues, that the links between innovation and science are in some sense becoming closer. Many of the world's fastest-growing industries are those in which these connections are strongest. However well-founded the links between innovation and performance in this and in other areas, Smith concludes, the policy issues raised by them are still a long way from being resolved.

Demirag's contribution to this volume focuses on the issue of short-termism. Although the failures of British manufacturing are often ascribed to deficiencies in product innovation, and although these in turn are put down to firms' 'short-termism', Demirag points out that there has been no systematic examination of whether managers responsible for R&D feel themselves to be under these kinds of pressures.

Demirag divides the possible causes of short-termism into those external and those internal to the firm. Turning first to the external factors, he finds little evidence that the managers of institutional shareholders in the UK are driven by short-term objectives. More important than this for his own argument is the relationship between shareholders and firms' management. If shareholders do not have or do not understand information on, say, the long-term path of technological development, they are likely to place too great a reliance on measures of short-term performance. Though views on the effect of variations in dividends are mixed, Demirag points to evidence that investment levels in British industry are limited by a shortage of internal funds. Although investment analysts appear not to take a short-term view of R&D, claims of market efficiency are based purely on the information available. In addition to the level of R&D expenditure itself, account needs to be taken of complementary activities in areas such as marketing and training, most of which cannot be capitalized and thus regarded in the same way. Added to this is analysts' lack of technological knowledge. Where the 'visibility' of the innovation process is low, argues Demirag, a stock exchange system like the UK's is likely to generate short-term pressures.

These external factors are considered alongside short-term pressures generated within the firm. Demirag points to the effect of remuneration systems for managers that are based on measures of short-term financial performance. Also important is the relationship between business units and the corporate headquarters. In companies that are 'financially controlled' (Goold and Campbell 1987), it is argued, short-term measures will govern the allocation of resources between business units. Related to the structure of firms is the manner in which they have grown. Financial control is likely to be more suited to firms which have grown by acquisition, Demirag maintains, and acquisition, rather than simply diversification, appears to reduce R&D intensity. He also cites Hoskisson and Hitt's (1988) evidence for the USA that where R&D was centralized, this was taken by financial markets to reflect a search for synergies and was therefore regarded favourably. As Demirag points out, Glaxo and other pharmaceutical companies that have been amongst both the most R&D intensive and financially most successful companies in the UK have been characterized by 'low diversification, organic growth, and centralized R&D'.

Demirag's empirical analysis focuses on R&D managers' perceptions of short-term pressures. Based on a sample of 116 managers, responses to a questionnaire indicated that they did in fact perceive short-term pressures from the capital markets. Significant numbers paid attention to City opinion, felt that they did not generate sufficient funds for investment, and felt vulnerable to take-over. A second group of questions addressed issues of strategic emphasis. This brought out the importance given by R&D managers to the organization of projects around a small number of core competencies, as well as the variety of means by which new products could be developed. The questions relating strategic planning to company structure show how important R&D managers regarded co-ordination with other functions in the organization. With regard to the organizational structure of R&D, around half of the firms were found to have a central laboratory. Finally, on the control and evaluation of R&D projects, the most important factor determining the size of the R&D budget was the company's objectives in terms of growth and market share, and, in evaluation, payback and increased market share proved to be the most important criteria.

In his discussion of these findings, Demirag concentrates on what they reveal about R&D managers' perception of short-term pressures. The first aspect of this is the lack of a long-term strategy for investment and innovation. Support cannot be expected for a long-term strategy, argues Demirag, if no such strategy exists. Coupled with this is a lack of communication between firms' managers and their shareholders. Communication would force top managers into a better understanding of their own firms' technological development and of the relationship between this and wider strategic and organizational issues. Finally, Demirag argues for a reform of firms' performance evaluation and control systems, urging that less emphasis be given to short-term financial considerations. It is the relationship between firms and their shareholders which is given a key role in all this. A closer relationship, it is argued, would change firms' perceptions of capital markets and would lead to the technologies they were developing being more accurately valued. It was government's responsibility to encourage this closer relationship, and Demirag recommends that companies be obliged to disclose more information and that governance structures be moved in the direction of the German 'two-tier' model of control.

In Chapter 7 Acs, Fitzroy and Smith examine the 'spillover' effects which university R&D effort might have on a geographical area. Previous studies, such as Jaffe (1989), have examined the effects of such spillovers on the location decisions of firms and their patenting activity. Acs *et al.* go further than this to look at whether high technology employment is generated. They point to two explanations of the development of high technology 'clusters' around university R&D activity. The first is that university research diffuses informally to firms located close at hand, and although there is evidence from the USA to support this hypothesis, what is not so well-established are the mechanisms by which this process takes place. The second explanation of clusters focuses on the pool of highly-qualified scientists and engineers produced by universities. Either as employees or as entrepreneurs, they provide the mechanism through which knowledge is transmitted.

To examine the spillover effects on employment in the USA, Acs *et al.* selected six R&D-intensive industrial sectors and the 22 most important cities associated with them. Most of the cities also had significant activity in university R&D. Using 15 other cities as well, a preliminary analysis of the data reveals a positive relationship between high technology employment in 1989 and university research expenditure in 1985. Using high technology employment as a proportion of total employment reduces significantly the measure of correlation. Plotting high technology employment against the proportion of scientists and engineers in the workforce reveals there to be little association; using the *share* of high technology employment makes the correlation much stronger.

Acs *et al.* also specify a formal model of high technology employment. University R&D spending is divided according to department, each part being allocated to one of their six industries. The main result is that the coefficient on this variable is positive and significant, thus providing evidence of a spillover on to high technology employment. A positive relationship was also found between high technology employment and real wages, though Acs *et al.* argue this reflects shortages and the lack of mobility of skilled labour. The quantitative confirmation of university R&D spillover effects on employment carries with it implications for policy. It illustrates the importance of high technology clusters in the USA, argue Acs *et al.*, and offers guidance to countries such as the UK where these clusters are not yet so well-developed.

In Chapter 8 Reid and Roberts examine patenting activity in the UK scientific instruments industry. As measures of appropriability, Reid and Roberts note that there is a shift occurring away from patent length – how long a firm should enjoy exclusive rights to an innovation – and towards patent breadth or width – the degree of dissimilarity a rival innovation would have to possess to avoid infringing a patent. Reid and Roberts use Schankerman and Pakes' (1986) idea that the value of the intellectual property protected by the patent can be indicated by the willingness to exploit the monopoly production the patent protects. They put their own interpretation on this idea by looking at the 'patent family' or the 'scope' of patent protection: the extent to which protection is sought across different national regimes. Patent protection, they argue, will be sought in the marginal case only if it generates a positive net present value for the firm. Though this cannot be measured directly, it is indexed by the amount of patenting activity, itself measured by counts of the stages in the regime's 'patenting process'. The variable with which they work measures a firm's total patenting activity in each period across all its patent families and over all regimes in which it is active. Comparing patent-active with patent-inactive firms, Reid and Roberts show the former to be larger and more profitable.

Their broader objective is to develop a model explaining patenting activity. Starting with the Schumpeterian hypothesis that large firms will be more innovative than small ones, Reid and Roberts point to previous work which suggests a non-linear relationship between patent activity and firm size. Rejecting approaches based on market structure and industry characteristics, they consider, along with firm size, a range of financial variables and fixed firm-level effects.

The results from a panel of 92 UK scientific instrument firms over the period 1983–90 show firms becoming more patent-active as they get larger. The proportionate increase in size, however, is not matched by the proportionate increase in patenting activity. This concavity in fact allows a patent-activity-maximizing size of firm to be established. Amongst the financial variables, Reid and Roberts find significant effects for net profit before tax, trading profit margin and gearing, but not for return on capital or liquidity. The findings on profit margins and gearing suggest firms are willing to squeeze margins and allow gearing to rise in pursuit of innovation. In other words, it is claimed, these firms are willing to sacrifice short-term financial performance in this endeavour.

The data on return on capital raise the possibility that patent-inactive firms benefit from spillover effects from patent-active ones. Testing this idea more formally, Reid and Roberts find that there is more direct evidence to support this suggestion for the scientific instruments industry. This in turn, they argue, helps explain why the performance advantage enjoyed by patent-active over patent-inactive firms was found to be so small.

Finally in this section, Kastrinos addresses another form of relationship between firms, collaboration in R&D between users and producers. Incentives for firms to enter into such arrangements, he argues, are most often regarded as being dependent on the novelty and the complexity of the technology they are dealing with. New, complex technologies, however, will not be suitable for all firms, and Kastrinos puts forward the argument that there is a conflict of interest between the producers and users of an innovation. Producers are interested in maximizing the diffusion of an innovation amongst users, while users themselves are interested in minimizing it. The function and the performance of an innovation should thus be seen as the result of negotiation between the two parties. This is particularly important, claims Kastrinos, for public collaborative R&D programmes.

Looking at the relationship between the competitive significance of technologies and their diffusion in terms of an industry life-cycle model, Kastrinos shows how in the later stages of the cycle efficiency in production assumes priority over flexibility in innovation. As a firm becomes more 'mechanistic' (Burns and Stalker 1961), the costs of marrying the organization and the innovation are increased, and to acquire competitive advantage from the use of an innovation requires that the productivity benefits for the firm must be greater relative to the adaptation costs than they are for its competitors. Although in collaborative arrangements users would try to increase the costs of their competitors by building into the innovation certain user-specific assets, Kastrinos argues that for firms in mature industries such assets might be difficult to identify.

The initial concept of an innovation, says Kastrinos, is based on its function. The need for collaboration arises when no means are at hand to perform this function, and such a venture then begins by a process of negotiation between the interested parties. Two issues identified in particular by Kastrinos are intellectual property rights and the division of labour. Over intellectual property rights, while both parties stand to gain if the output of the project can be used immediately, the protection offered to users is of little value if the project turns out a failure. The division of labour is important for two reasons: it determines the level of access each partner has to the knowledge generated, not all of which is accessible on the basis of reports; and it reflects the modular fashion in which the performance characteristics of the 'research prototype' are developed. A trade-off between function and performance, argues Kastrinos, takes place when the prototype does not take into account all aspects of the user environment.

Illustrating his argument with two detailed case studies of R&D collaboration, Kastrinos concludes that this has important implications for the design and management of such projects. Mechanisms must exist to ensure that a mutual interest is in existence throughout, and a key role here can be played by the complementarity of the non-technological assets of the partners. Though technological complexity may provide an incentive for producers to enter into collaborative arrangements, argues Kastrinos, for users it may add to the uncertainties surrounding the performance of the innovation.

DISCLOSURE AND THE MARKET

The final section begins with Belcher's examination of both the theoretical issues surrounding firms' disclosure of information on their R&D and the practices of British companies in this area. In early models of disclosure it was demonstrated that because failure to do so would lead to the belief that they had something to hide, firms voluntarily would disclose all information on their R&D. As Belcher shows, that firms did not in fact act in this manner caused some of the assumptions underlying these models to be relaxed. Some of the later models focused on the actions of managers. If allowed a degree of discretion, for example, it could be argued that disclosure of R&D information would be determined by the prestige attached to it. Other models examined by Belcher relaxed the assumption that the information given out by firms would be correctly interpreted. Against this it could be argued that financial markets suffered from the kind of 'short-termist' views we have already encountered. In the belief that its return would be undervalued, firms might reduce long-term R&D projects. An alternative would be to fail to disclose them, but the hypothesis that perceived short-term pressures have this effect would be a difficult one to test.

Belcher's review shows that a further set of models retained the ideas of efficient markets and managers unable to exercise discretion, but relaxed other assumptions. An important assumption in the original models was that the disclosure of information was costless. Relaxing this assumption meant that firms might withhold information for reasons of cost rather than because they had something to hide. Failure to disclose could not then automatically be interpreted in a negative light. What assumes importance under these conditions is the order in which disclosures are made, the importance of R&D spending being disclosed being more important in some industries than in others. A second departure from the original models Belcher identifies was to allow for those receiving the information to be unsure whether those not disclosing information had information they were withholding. Connected with this are issues surrounding the likelihood of firms disclosing information which is unfavourable and of poor quality. Finally, Belcher shows that consideration has to be given to the possibility that information on R&D might be of a commercially sensitive nature. The costs involved in this have then to be weighed against any benefits of revealing information to shareholders. One potential effect is the entry into the market of a new competitor, though it might also be the competitive threat from firms already in the market that discourages disclosure.

The second part of Belcher's chapter looks at R&D disclosure in practice. In the UK, regulation of R&D disclosure is governed less by legal requirements and more by the self-imposed standards of the accounting profession. These cover issues regarding the definition of R&D, how it should be treated in the accounts – whether as asset or expense, for example – and the amount of detail required in disclosure. Belcher describes how standards on these issues come under Statement of Standard Accounting Practice 13 (SSAP 13). Under this standard, issued in 1977, disclosure of R&D expenditure was at the discretion of firms. Under threat of being superseded by government legislation, it was revised in 1989 so as to make disclosure obligatory.

Against the background of the revision of the accounting standards, Belcher undertook a survey of UK firms' disclosure practices. Looking at 168 firms which, following the revision, disclosed at least that they were performing R&D, she found that only 79 per cent of them were complying fully with the revised standard. An even lower rate of compliance was found for the requirement of the 1985 Companies Act that the directors' report should contain an indication of the firm's R&D activities. Only a very few of the companies not complying with the accounting standard, moreover, fulfilled their obligation to explain in their audit report why they were doing so. Some companies did play up their R&D expenditure, repeating it in the 'glossy' or more public parts of their reports. The diversity in practice Belcher found in her survey led her to the conclusion that it was firm-specific factors that governed the disclosure decision.

In Chapter 11 Seaton and Walker examine the effects of disclosure and of finance on the level of R&D expenditure. The evidence that the stock market undervalues R&D capital gives rise to the ideas that R&D-intensive firms will be less likely to rely on external finance and that the external finance they do make use of will be differently constituted than that used by other firms. The direction of this latter effect, claim the authors, is not clear-cut. On the one hand, banks' demands for collateral for debt may turn firms towards equity; on the other, R&D-intensive firms may use high levels of debt to signal their stability. Seaton and Walker's earlier work in fact found a negative relationship between R&D intensity and the probability of being externally financed and, conditional on being externally financed, a negative relationship with the probability of being debt-financed. It may also be the case, they argue, that if disclosure is made compulsory, firms would be deprived of a signal which allows the market to distinguish between good and bad risks. Three issues are thus addressed: the effect on R&D of the method of finance; the effect on this relationship of compulsory disclosure; and the effect of compulsory disclosure on the level of R&D expenditure.

Seaton and Walker's own model looks at R&D expenditure before and after the introduction of obligatory disclosure in 1989. Using a balanced panel of 457 UK quoted companies over the period 1983–90, the introduction of obligatory disclosure allows them to be divided between non-R&D firms; involuntary disclosers, who disclosed R&D expenditure only after it was made obligatory; and voluntary disclosers, who disclosed R&D in any case. Comparing the types of finance used by these groups of firms before and after the introduction of SSAP 13 (revised), R&D firms as a whole are revealed as becoming more similar to non-R&D firms, but the differences between voluntary and involuntary disclosers are shown to have become more pronounced.

Seaton and Walker also estimate probit equations for the impact of financial variables on the probability of being an R&D rather than a non-R&D firm. These suggest that in finance terms the difference between them is less significant following the introduction of obligatory disclosure. Looking solely at the R&D firms, Seaton and Walker show that following the introduction of SSAP 13 (revised), compared to involuntary disclosers, voluntary disclosers take proportionately less borrowing within one year and use more retained earnings. In terms of the relationships between R&D and sales and between R&D and profits, there is little difference between voluntary and involuntary disclosers. Voluntary disclosers are found to have a higher debt/equity ratio than firms in the other two groups.

In looking at R&D and its disclosure, Seaton and Walker treat financial variables as exogenous and use as their dependent variable the ratio of R&D to sales. Their results show that both before and after the introduction of obligatory disclosure of R&D expenditure, R&D companies faced internal financial constraints. Long-term loans are related positively to R&D expenditure, but the negative financial variables suggest that finance in these areas is bought by reducing R&D. Financial structure, argue Seaton and Walker, does appear to affect the proportion of R&D. In the period following obligatory disclosure, the reduction in the number of significant variables and in the size of coefficients suggests that imperfections in financial markets are diminishing.

Seaton and Walker thus conclude that following the introduction of SSAP 13 (revised), R&D is still sensitive to the availability of internal finance but its sensitivity to financial variables is diminishing. On the whole market failure is reduced, the failure experienced by voluntary disclosers being offset by involuntary disclosers, whose lesser failure was shown in retentions and long-term loans being the main differences between the two groups. Their conclusion that voluntary disclosers respond better to long-term debt lead Seaton and Walker to the recommendation that its provision could increase the rate of R&D investment in the UK.

The decision whether or not to disclose R&D expenditure is the focus of Belcher's second contribution to this volume. Again, it is the introduction of obligatory disclosure which allows some of the motivations underlying this decision to emerge. The theoretical considerations examined in her earlier chapter allow nine hypotheses concerning the decision to disclose to be examined. The first is that because there are likely to be costs involved in not disclosing having once disclosed, previous disclosure is likely to have a strong influence; the second, that as the introduction of compulsory disclosure becomes more likely over time, voluntary disclosure would increase; the third, that there are likely to exist industry norms; the fourth, that a company's visibility will increase the chance of its disclosing; the fifth, that the materiality of the amount of R&D expenditure is important; the sixth, that the costs of producing the figure for R&D expenditure will exert an influence; the seventh, that so too will the proprietary costs associated with competition; the eighth, that the prestige associated with R&D will be a factor; the ninth, that the first disclosure of R&D expenditure will take place when the company has other good news to impart.

Belcher uses a logit model to test these hypotheses. The introduction of the revised version of SSAP 13 allowed firms performing no R&D to be identified and thus excluded from the sample. Analysis could then concentrate on R&D firms and their decision prior to the introduction whether or not to disclose expenditure. A number of the hypotheses were tested by more than one variable, and a number of the variables were used to test more than one hypothesis. Belcher's results show the industry dummies to be insignificant; the lagged dependent variable, positive and significant; the time to 1989, negative and significant; the size of firm, positive and significant; the rating of stock, positive and significant; the R&D/sales ratio, positive and significant; the ratio relative to the industry average, positive but significant only at the 10 per cent level; and an interactive dummy variable representing good news, positive and significant.

The model thus provides Belcher with support for most of the nine hypotheses she examined. The first, the link to previous disclosure, was strongly supported by the significance of the lagged dependent variable. The second, the increasing threat of compulsory disclosure, was supported by the significance of the time between voluntary disclosure and the introduction of compulsory disclosure in 1989. The third, industry norms, received no support from the industry dummy variables. The fourth, visibility, was supported by the significance of both size and whether a company's stock was 'alpha-rated'. The fifth, quality of information, was supported by the materiality variable, which took the form of the firm's R&D/sales ratio for the first forced announcement. The sixth hypothesis, costs of disclosure, was supported by the materiality and size variables but not by the industry dummies. The seventh, proprietary costs, was supported by both the size variable and the relative materiality variable, which was calculated as R&D/sales ratio as a proportion of the industry average. The eighth, managerial prestige, was supported by both the materiality and the relative materiality variables. Finally, the ninth hypothesis, that managers would try to couple the first disclosure with other items of good news, received support from the interactive dummy variable based on the change in firms' profit/sales ratio. It is on this last result and on the effect of proprietary costs that Belcher lays emphasis in her conclusion.

Machin and Van Reenen use changes in rules on disclosure in their examination of the relationship between technology and wage structures in firms in four European countries: the United Kingdom, Germany, Italy and France. The use of R&D spending to model technology effects carries with it the problem that rules on disclosure requirements vary widely between countries. Disclosure rates differ between countries, and Machin and Van Reenen show that because the reasons for the failure to disclose may be correlated with variables in the wage equation, the potential selectivity bias must be corrected for. Looking at changes in accounting practices across the different countries, the authors show these to reveal that under pressure from the EC there have been moves towards greater uniformity but that within the trend towards greater openness, significant international differences can be identified. The variation in the changes in disclosure requirements within and between countries are then used in their selectivity corrections.

In their wage equation Machin and Van Reenen assume wages to be negotiated between managers and 'insider' workers, the outcome being a weighted average of the wage outside the company and – as a measure of insider power – output per worker. They proceed by means of a two-step estimator, estimating first a probit for whether or not a firm discloses its R&D, and then using the Mills ratios from these probits as a regressor in the wage equation. With data from 385 firms and a total of 2,619 observations Machin and Van Reenen find in the first stage that, as expected, the variables which capture changes in accounting regimes have positive coefficients, the most significant increases in disclosure being a result of a change in rules in the UK.

A number of wage equations are then estimated. Without selectivity correction R&D proves positive and significant, suggesting that technologically more advanced firms do in fact pay higher wages. 'According to the central estimates,' say the authors, 'a doubling of R&D per worker is associated with a rise in average wages of the order of 3–5 per cent'. They also take account of the problem of separating R&D effects from the effects of fixed capital. Correcting for selectivity has little effect on the estimated coefficient of the R&D variable but does increase substantially the coefficient on physical capital. The introduction of industry dummies has little effect on the model's results, but the country dummies reveal wages to be very low in the UK and to be highest in Germany. An examination of whether the effect of R&D varies across countries reveals it to be strongest in Germany, followed by the UK, France and Italy, a ranking which Machin and Van Reenen account for in terms of differences in the system of collective bargaining employed in the four countries.

Finally in this section, Newton, Paxson and Pearson examine real option pricing theory as a means of valuing investments in R&D. Any short-termism to which firms are subject, they argue, might be the result of the use of techniques such as net present value and internal rate of return. This would be exacerbated by moves within organizations to the 'contractor–customer' relationships which began to emerge in the early 1970s. In addressing how these kinds of relationships could be managed to ensure long-term benefit, one approach was to focus on the 'relevance' of R&D to the organization (Hubert 1970). The allocation of resources would thus depend on the objectives of the organization.

This relationship between R&D and corporate strategy, argue Newton *et al.*, raises a number of important issues. At the level of the R&D project, the traditional investment appraisal techniques will be of considerable value. However, users may not be able to identify so easily any broader technological development. The function of R&D would then be to identify certain areas and encourage and provide support to business to take a longer term view. The use of corporate funds, however, may diminish a business unit's direct interest in a project. A major role for R&D is to develop technological capability in the organization, which might, Newton *et al.* argue, be seen as part of the development of core competencies. The benefits from this may be quite difficult to quantify, and a final issue is the recognition of the value of 'failed' projects and of work not included within the bounds of specific projects. All this, say the authors, implies seeing R&D as a portfolio, involving different levels of uncertainty, different structures and, with these, different means of evaluating projects and allocating resources between them.

Despite the development of new techniques of appraisal, contend Newton *et al.*, it is still felt that more risky, long-term projects are undervalued. It is to these that the idea of 'real option pricing' can be applied. Illustrating their arguments with examples, Newton *et al.* argue that it can be of real value where the level of volatility is high and where expenditures are difficult to justify on the basis of traditional means of appraisal. At the same time the profitability of an innovation depends as much on how it is exploited as on how novel is its output. The way R&D is organized within a company will therefore also be of greater importance.

THEMES AND ISSUES

Having demonstrated the range of perspectives and approaches covered in this book, we turn to the links which can be drawn between them. Quite aside from the individual contributions of the chapters, four main themes emerge.

The first is the focus on the structures and strategies of individual organizations. Underlying this is the view of the innovation process which lays emphasis on its social and political dimensions. Smith brings this out most clearly, and his rejection of the linear model of innovation is shared explicitly by Randle and Currie.

The focus on structures and strategies is evident not only in the first section of the book. Randle and Currie demonstrate the importance of the way in which research is organized and managed within a company. Demirag points to the influence systems of remuneration can exert. Coombs shows how we might now be entering a 'third paradigm', one which avoids an excessive emphasis on either centralized 'technology-push' or decentralized 'market-pull'. Newton *et al.* also bring out the dangers of too great a reliance on 'contractor–customer' relationships within the firm. Demirag draws attention not only to the structure of firms but also to the manner in which these structures have been developed.

The focus on the strategies and structures of individual firms is found in its most tangible form in the use made by many papers of the idea of 'core competencies'. Coombs deals with this in greatest depth, showing the benefits that can be gained by linking together the core competence paradigm and the strategic management of R&D. Clarke and Pitt take up this theme, and apply the framework they develop to case studies of four companies. Demirag demonstrates how R&D managers perceive the importance of organizing projects around a few core competencies. Newton *et al.* see their development as a major role for R&D within the organization.

Associated with this is the stress laid by a number of papers on the idea of complementary assets. Clarke and Pitt bring out most explicitly the relationship between these assets and an organization's core competencies. Lowe and Taylor show the importance of complementary assets in a firm's decision to license technology. Kastrinos shows how they can play a key role in collaboration between producers and users of R&D.

The second main theme arising from this book is that at the same time as a firm's structures and strategies assume importance, so too do its relationships with other firms and other external bodies. Lowe and Taylor demonstrate why and how a firm can acquire technology through licensing. Acs *et al.* show how high technology employment might benefit from the spillover from the R&D activities of an adjacent university. Reid and Roberts raise the possibility that patent-inactive firms benefit from the spillover from patent-active ones. Kastrinos points up the importance of collaboration between producers and users of R&D. Randle and Currie show the importance in general terms of a firm's external relationships. Demirag argues for a more direct and intimate link between a firm's management and its shareholders. Smith brings these points together with those made in the previous section, seeing the combination of internal expertise and external relationships as being at the heart of an understanding of innovation.

The book's third main theme is the importance which has to be given to the disclosure of R&D expenditure. In her contributions, Belcher brings out clearly the theoretical issues surrounding disclosure, the practice amongst British firms, and the factors underlying their decisions in this regard. Seaton and Walker show that following the introduction of obligatory disclosure, R&D became less sensitive to financial variables. Machin and Van Reenen use changes in rules on disclosure to demonstrate the impact R&D spending has on wage structures.

We turn finally to the book's fourth main theme, the policy implications of the issues we have considered. Smith details the policy agenda given rise to by changing views of innovation. Seaton and Walker suggest that the greater provision of long-term debt could increase the rate of investment in R&D. Acs *et al.* show there are lessons the UK might learn in the encouragement of spillover effects from university R&D. Kastrinos argues that public programmes of collaboration need to take account of the function–performance trade-off in negotiations between users and producers. Demirag sees a role for government in bringing about the structures of corporate governance necessary for a closer relationship between managers and shareholders. Thus just as a firm's core competencies and external relationships give rise to a subtle and complex pattern of innovation, so too do their implications for government policy.

REFERENCES

Burns, T. and Stalker, G. (1961) *The Management of Innovation*, London: Tavistock.

della Valle, F. and Gambardella, A. (1993) '"Biological" revolution and strategies for innovation in pharmaceutical companies', *R&D Management* 23, 4: 287–303.

Fransman, M. (1990) *The Market and Beyond: Co-operation and Competition in Information Technology Development in the Japanese System*, Cambridge: Cambridge University Press.

Goold, M. and Campbell, A. (1987) *Strategies and Styles: The Role of the Centre in Managing Diversified Corporations*, Oxford: Blackwell.

Hoskisson, R. and Hitt, M. (1988) 'Strategic control systems and relative R&D investment in large multiproduct firms', *Strategic Management Journal* 9: 605–621.

Hubert, J. (1970) 'R&D and the company's requirements', *R&D Management* 2, 2: 69–73.

Jaffee, A. (1989) 'Real effects of academic research', *American Economic Review* 79, 5: 957–970.

Kay, J. (1993) *Foundations of Corporate Success: How Business Strategies Add Value*, Oxford: Oxford University Press.

Kline, S. and Rosenberg, N. (1986) 'An overview of innovation', in R. Landau and N. Rosenberg (eds) *The Positive Sum Strategy*, Washington DC: National Academy Press.

Pavitt, K. (1984) 'Sectoral patterns of technical change: towards a taxonomy and a theory', *Research Policy* 13: 343–373.

Prahalad, C. and Hamel, G. (1990) 'The core competence of the corporation', *Harvard Business Review* May–June: 79–91.

Schankerman, M. and Pakes, A. (1986) 'Estimates of the value of patent rights in European countries during the post-1950 period', *Economic Journal* 96: 1052–1076.

Teece, D. (1986) 'Profiting from technological innovation: implications for integration, collaboration, licensing and public policy', *Research Policy* 15: 285–305.

Part I

STRATEGY AND ORGANIZATION

1

CORE COMPETENCIES AND THE STRATEGIC MANAGEMENT OF R&D

Rod Coombs

The purpose of this chapter is to explore the possibility that the core competence paradigm (CCP) has something useful to offer to those concerned with the strategic management of R&D in large firms. Our starting assumption is that there is a *prima facie* similarity between the CCP and the emerging literature on the strategic management of R&D on one crucial issue. This issue is the conceptualization of the diversified firm not as a collection of discrete strategic business units (SBUs), but as a collection of SBUs which draw on certain common corporate resources.

The CCP (Prahalad and Hamel, 1990) argues that corporations can identify core competencies which are firm-specific accumulations of expertise resulting from previous investments and from learning-by-doing. These competencies are seen as longer-lived assets than the particular product-market business units which exploit them. The prescriptive implication which follows is that core competencies become pivots of strategy-making, and that excessive decentralization of control to SBUs can endanger their continued development and value. Comparing this with the field of R&D management, the 1970s and 1980s were decades which were largely dominated by a trend of decentralization of R&D funding and control to SBUs in an attempt to ensure that R&D was market-driven and that innovation success rates would improve. Recently, however, opinion has swung to the view that excessive decentralization has damaged long-term accumulation of technology and reduced effectiveness in the movement of technology skills between SBUs (Coombs and Richards, 1993a; Dussauge *et al.*, 1992). This has led in turn to a growing emphasis on re-claiming corporate control of some aspects of technology management.

The structure of this chapter is as follows. Section 1 presents a brief and selective synopsis of the CCP, drawing out the role of technologies in the construction and application of core competencies. Section 2 reviews some of the recent literature on strategic management of technology, selectively drawing out those issues that relate to the management of technologies that cut across several business units. In section 3 these two themes are brought together to present a simple model of how core competencies can play a role in guiding the strategic management of technology. Section 4 explores the implications of this approach for R&D decision-making in the areas of long-term research programmes, funding regimes, organizational structures, and the measurement of the effectiveness of R&D.

1 THE CORE COMPETENCE PARADIGM

The following compressed summary is based on Prahalad and Hamel's well-known paper in *Harvard Business Review* (May 1990). Some aspects of their approach will be modified as the argument of this paper is developed in later sections.

Core Competencies (CCs) are composed of bodies of technological expertise (both product and process) *and* the organizational capacity to deploy that expertise effectively. Thus they are not simply technological in character, they are also organizational. They are embellished and strengthened through continued use (in other words they are subject to positive returns), and are therefore to some extent firm-specific and non-transferable. Indeed, the definition of CCs given by Prahalad and Hamel insists that not only must they give access to multiple markets, and confer specific advantages to customers, but they must also be difficult to imitate.

CCs are not monolithic. They have an internal structure which is composed of a number of *capabilities*. Thus a CC exists as a specific combination of capabilities. Capabilities are not defined in very great detail but appear to be more disaggregated than competencies and map more closely onto technologically defined domains of knowledge and expertise. The organizational dimension of a CC appears to lie in part in the ability to *combine* appropriate capabilities into specific competencies.

Competencies are given a physical and commercial reality in *core products*, which have a market-leading performance in a specific area of the customer's *functionality* requirements. The often quoted examples here are Canon's laser-printer engines, and Honda's high revving, smoothly performing internal combustion engines. Core products are then deployed in a variety of *end-products*. Thus the model can be represented as in Figure 1.1, which is adapted from the familiar figure in Prahalad and Hamel (1990).

The principle of a variety of technologies (capabilities), being combined in many permutations to create a variety of end-products is not in itself new. The specific feature of the CC paradigm seems to be the

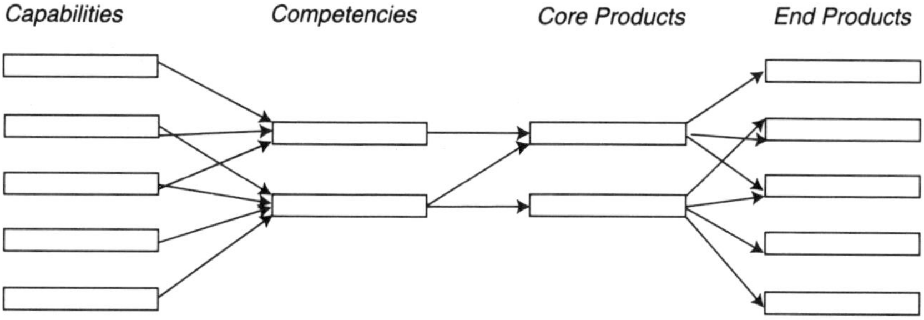

Figure 1.1 Core competencies

emphasis on the intervening concepts of CCs and core products. These are, in essence, *particular* combinations of capabilities, which are robust over time, confer specific advantages to the supplier and the customer, and therefore create a *preferred* and firm-specific migration path from technological knowledge to end-products for the firm in question. Once this is recognized by a firm, it is then argued that it can use its CCs as an 'orientation device' to shape strategic choices about acquisition of new technologies and development of new end-products. Basically, if a technology strengthens your CCs you should acquire it, and if a product exploits your CCs, you should make it. This approach seems to create a need within the company for intelligence and forecasts concerning technical trends and market trends, in order to 'steer' the evolution of the CCs.

Some of the practical implications of this perspective are defined by contrasting the CC paradigm with an outlook based on seeing a corporation as a collection of more or less autonomous SBUs. It is pointed out that a business run as a portfolio of SBUs is in danger of dissipating CCs, or even of inadvertently outsourcing them. CCs can get 'imprisoned' within one SBU and not be made available to other SBUs. The people who are the embodiment of the CCs can be insufficiently *mobile* with respect to the SBUs.

It is clear then, that in the context of large multiproduct firms, the concept of CC is designed to act as a representation of the overlaps and synergies between products. These overlaps and synergies are what make the diversification pattern of the firm *rational* rather than *random*, and in addition, they make the firm capable of specific differentiations of its products which confer competitive advantage. Without the use of CCs a firm's products are less likely to be competitive, and less likely to add new cumulative skills to the firm's armoury.

2 TRENDS IN THE STRATEGIC MANAGEMENT OF TECHNOLOGY AND R&D[1]

For over twenty years Britain's leading R&D-performing firms have been progressively modifying and adjusting their policies with the enduring intention of making their R&D activity market-driven, and integrated into the business strategies of the business units which the R&D serves. This trend is wholly consistent with the received wisdom about what makes for successful innovation. The outcomes of this are complex; some prominent features are as follows:

- Where firms have corporate R&D labs, the balance of their funding has shifted from corporate to business-unit sources, which are more closely monitored through customer–contractor relationships.
- Many corporate labs have either shrunk absolutely, or have reduced in relative importance within the total R&D effort of a company. This is reflected in the growth of decentralized R&D at division or business-unit level. This tendency has been fuelled by mergers and acquisitions which have brought previously separate R&D facilities under one corporate parent. These divisional or business-unit level R&D facilities are by definition market-driven, and do not have a brief to undertake work outside the business areas of their controlling division.
- This decentralization of R&D has permitted new and more intimate arrangements to develop which bring technical, commercial and operations staff together at business-unit level in effective teams for product and process innovation. This is a major historical gain for UK firms, and should not be underestimated.

However, there are also a number of negative consequences that have arisen from this decentralization of R&D, which have been aggravated by other contextual features:

- Business-unit 'ownership' of R&D is very effective at consolidating strength within the existing technological regime applying in that company at that time. If that regime is a competitive one, all well and good. If the technological regime of the company becomes less competitive, the business-unit ownership of R&D could run the risk of digging a deeper hole for the company.
- If new 'generic' technologies emerge which are 'competence-destroying' (Anderson and Tushman, 1990) for such business units (e.g. new materials technologies which render existing manufacturing processes obsolete), their R&D infrastructure may not be able to cope. This has been a feature of the 1980s and the 1990s.

The natural place to look for a compensating source of technical competence in these circumstances is the corporate parent and its

R&D capacity, which will generally be oriented to longer term strategic research. But, for a significant proportion of UK companies, this corporate competence is weak. The weakness at corporate level arises from two principal sources.

- First, the process of decentralization within a flat or slow-growing total R&D-funding regime has weakened both competencies and organizational influence of corporate R&D.
- Second, there is an Anglo-Saxon bias toward corporate management styles[2] which are *financially*-oriented, rather than oriented toward strategic co-ordination of the activities of a portfolio of businesses.

The combination of these two factors has meant that the overall technology and skill portfolio of a diversified corporate structure can often become simply *invisible* to the company. There is no responsible individual or structure to 'own' this problem. Consequently there can be serious deficiencies in transferring relevant technical expertise between member divisions of a large corporate structure, and there can be further deficiencies in assuring sponsorship for new technologies which might be relevant to more than one division.

What these points add up to is a significant shift in the organizational focus of UK R&D organization toward products and markets, and away from technologies. This shift is wholly appropriate at the business-unit level, but wholly inappropriate at the level of a collection of business within a corporate structure. It has led to a relative under-performance of UK firms in identifying, adapting to, and commercializing newer technologies which fall outside the established competencies of individual businesses. At the risk of exaggeration, we might say that firms have learnt the lesson of the 1970s – 'innovations are about market-pull and not about technology-push' – rather too well!

We can summarize this argument by identifying two paradigms of R&D organization: one relates to the early days of organized R&D before the focus on 'market-driven R&D' emerged, and the other captures the 'market-driven' philosophy. These are Paradigms 1 and 2, shown in Figures 1.2 and 1.3.

There is significant evidence, however, that many R&D managers and chief executives have been trying to correct these problems that have emerged as a result of the shift toward decentralized R&D. In the research conducted at CROMTEC for the EC SAST 8 project we found that one favoured method for this is the creation of a corporate unit for strategic management of technology with the following functions:

- To analyse the structure of the overall technology portfolio.
- To ensure that a technological competence in one business is known to and available to other potential user businesses in the group.

Period of dominance:	1950–1970
Characteristics:	Centralization and corporate dominance in some or all of: • funding of R&D • ownership of R&D • control of R&D
Drivers:	Technology-push thinking, relative novelty of R&D in historical terms, and a period of growing R&D spend.

Figure 1.2 Paradigm 1
Source: Coombs and Richards (1993a)

Period:	From 1970 'til the late 1980s
Characteristics:	Decentralization and business unit dominance in some or all of: • funding of R&D • ownership of R&D • control of R&D
Drivers:	Flatter R&D budgets; perceived failure of technology-push thinking; general move in management thinking and practice towards 'market focus'.

Figure 1.3 Paradigm 2
Source: Coombs and Richards (1993a)

- To identify technical competencies which straddle businesses and to take steps to strengthen them through 'horizontal' organizational links and through small special budgets.
- To consider the overall technology portfolio and inject an appreciation of this portfolio into the broader strategic management process of the company.

This trend is an interesting and significant one in our view. It represents a considered institutional response to the challenge of new technologies,

Period:	1990s onwards?
Characteristics:	• Integration of elements from paradigms 1 and 2. • Conceptual separation of technology funding and product funding. • Mixed corporate and business-unit funding with attention to subtle balance of incentives. • Shared corporate and business unit ownership of R&D portfolio and resources.
Drivers:	• Increasing scale and global character of many R&D players: more R&D units to manage. • Perceived negative effects of paradigm 2. • 'Completion' of the institutional learning process through which industrial firms have 'normalized' The management of R&D.

Figure 1.4 Paradigm 3
Source: Coombs and Richards (1993a)

and could enhance the possibilities for UK companies to move towards the practice of their foreign counterparts on the specific issue of commitment to continuous technological renewal. At the risk of over-simplification we can identify it as a third 'emerging' paradigm (see Figure 1.4).

Paradigm 3 is clearly predicated on transcending the old debates about market-pull and technology-push. It aims at combining the market-driven benefits which come from decentralized business-funded R&D with the benefits of corporate sponsorship of the technology base, and cross-fertilization of technologies and businesses.[3] Furthermore paradigm 3 extends beyond 'traditional' concepts of the boundaries of R&D management. It includes 'upstream' issues such as novel modes of technology-sourcing, including collaboration, networks and technology-driven acquisitions. It also includes 'downstream' issues such as concurrent engineering and the use of 'time-to-market' as a competitive weapon. It therefore impinges in a variety of ways on the traditional agenda of strategic management which is the 'home territory' of the core competence paradigm. We can now turn to examine this interaction in more detail.

3 THE LINK BETWEEN CORE COMPETENCIES AND STRATEGIC MANAGEMENT OF R&D

If we now try to combine the language and concepts of these two discourses, we find some initial straightforward results:

- One of the responsibilities of R&D is to acquire, generate and husband the *technological capabilities* which are important building blocks of core competencies.
- Many of those capabilities are relevant to more than one SBU, and R&D managers are often the 'default' location of the responsibility for protecting the technological interests of SBU managers when funding regimes make it difficult for SBUs to co-operate.
- The *application* of the technological capabilities of R&D in specific innovation projects to produce new functionalities in products and processes depends on complex *co-ordination processes* which also involve the marketing and operations functions. These co-ordination processes, which span the whole SBU and often beyond the SBU into other parts of the corporation, are in fact an important part of the *organizational* dimension of core competencies. These co-ordination processes have a firm-specific character which results from the accumulation of specific experience in constrained market and technological domains.

Thus the R&D function is not itself the site of the core competencies of the corporation, but it has two major articulations or points of contact with those core competencies. The first articulation is the *investment* mode, in which a number of R&D and R&D-related activities are concerned with managing and developing a portfolio of technological capabilities in such a way that it directly feeds into the core competencies of the corporation. It follows that this cannot be done adequately unless these core competencies have been identified. The second articulation is the *harvesting* mode, in which the R&D function participates with other SBU functions in the market-driven exploitation of core competencies to produce specific artefacts or services for customers. This approach is summarized in Figure 1.5.

Starting at the top of the figure and working down, we see the following features:

1 The strategic research programme of the corporation is principally responsible for generating and maintaining those technological capabilities which are important components of the core competencies. This strategic research programme will, typically, be managed and funded at arm's length from individual SBUs so that its programme cannot be damaged by short-term pressures from the businesses. However, appropriate organizational structures will be needed to

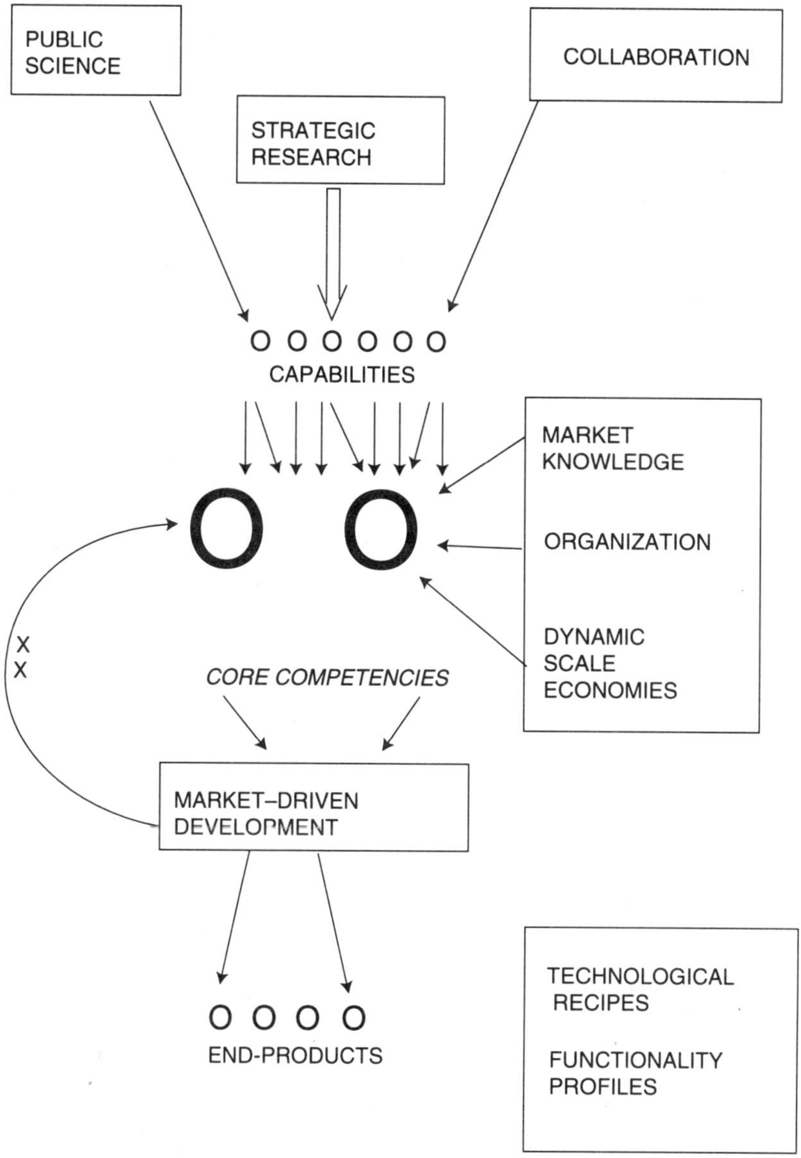

Figure 1.5 Technology exploitation through core competencies

give the technical and business managers from the SBUs the opportunity to participate in the 'steering' of the programme, without actually having direct control of the funding. This funding will typically be a corporate levy on businesses, or a straightforward subvention from corporate profits.

2 Alongside the company's own strategic research programme, another source of input to the key technological capabilities of the company are external linkages to public science, and to the corporate technology assets of collaborators. The role of managing these sources of technology is growing as companies find it harder to cover the whole spectrum of relevant technologies internally.

3 The technological capabilities form one important component of the core competencies. However, they are not sufficient on their own. Three other factors are potential inputs to the core competencies. The first and most important of these is *organizational structure.* In particular the structures which are relevant here are those which link the different functional contributors to the innovation and product development process. These are the linkages at SBU level between technologists, the marketing function and the operations function. Because the core competencies are relevant to more than one SBU it follows that some or all of these functions will have organizational features which allow skills and knowledge to migrate between SBUs or to be shared between SBUs.

The second extra input to the core competencies is *dynamic scale economies.* This refers to the fact that core competencies have to be continually exercised in order for them not to atrophy. Exploitation of the competencies in one product domain actually produces new knowledge which expands and deepens the competence, making it more valuable for future exploitations in other domains. In this sense the competencies have dynamic vector-like properties, whereas the technological capabilities are somewhat more static and scalar.

The third potential input to core competencies is *market knowledge,* defined broadly as the knowledge from all those market domains (which may include supplier as well as customer markets), which are necessary to enable the core competencies to be continually translated into the core products.

4 Summarizing points 1 to 3 then, we can see that the core competencies, whilst they are shaped by many factors which lie well outside the R&D function, do have as one of their determinants the 'technological investment' activity of the R&D function. It follows from this that the identification of appropriate technological capabilities and the management of their accumulation is an activity which can be conceptualized and steered using notions of core competence as a yardstick.

5 Moving now to the 'harvesting' mode of R&D, it is clear that market-focused product development in specific SBUs is an activity in which the firm is exercising its core competencies towards business objectives. However, this does not mean that the activity is depleting the core competencies in any way. On the contrary, because the core

competencies are to some extent the outcome of cumulative processes of exploiting particular skills and structures it is appropriate to identify a positive feedback process from development activities to competencies.

Multiple characteristics of technology

We have used the metaphors of 'invest' and 'harvest' to describe the two principal ways in which R&D is connected to core competencies. Since the principal tangible product of R&D is technology, it is useful at this point to consider the different modalities of technology and their relationship to investment and harvesting. Metcalfe and Boden (1992) make a useful threefold disaggregation of technology into knowledge, skills, and artefacts. Technology as knowledge is the formal abstract representation of technology in a codified form; technology as skills includes the human resources who have specific capabilities to employ technological knowledge as well as the tacit knowledge which is not codified; technology as artefacts concerns the physical objects which embody particular technologies. It is clear that these three dimensions of technology are distinct but related, and that the management and policy issues which attach to them are also distinct. When we take into account the now widely acknowledged firm-specificity of technology which has been referred to earlier in this chapter, it becomes apparent that the notion of technology as artefacts may need further disaggregation. Specifically, we can see in any artefact a *functionality profile* which can be expressed in terms of the services it can provide and the performance levels it is capable of. We can also see a specific *technological recipe* which consists of the particular combination of technologies, design practices, configurations of sub-systems, etc. that actually deliver the functionality. The technological recipe is more likely to be the dimension of the artefacts that is marked by the specific skills and knowledge deployed by a particular firm in its construction.

Using this fourfold conceptualization of technology as knowledge, skills, recipes and functionality profiles we can now re-visit the issues of investing and harvesting, in the context of core competencies. Clearly, the investment mode of R&D is concerned with the first two dimensions: knowledge and skills. Strategic management of these two dimensions of technology therefore needs to be prepared to use performance targets and measures of success which are expressed in terms of knowledge and skills rather than in terms of products or artefacts. This issue is discussed further in the final section of this chapter. In the harvesting mode, the strategic technology management issues revolve around the intrinsic strengths and weaknesses of the technological recipes available to any particular firm. In the 'ideal' state, if these recipes are embedded in core products, which are genuinely derived from core competencies, which in turn satisfy Prahalad and Hamel's criteria of being difficult to imitate, then the firm's recipes will actually define much of what can be achieved in functionality terms in that particular technical area. At the other extreme, if the recipes are based on mature technology with little proprietary content, or if the functionality can be provided by a range of widely differing recipes, then the technologies of the firm are not being effectively deployed in a manner consistent with the core competence approach.

4 R&D DECISIONS AND CORE COMPETENCIES

We can now review some familiar areas of R&D decision-making in the light of the arguments developed so far.

Criteria for longer-term R&D projects

R&D managers often have difficulty deciding on the technical content of the longer term component of their R&D portfolio and justifying their decisions to managers from business units and from other functional areas in the company. There are usually competing demands on limited budgets arising from groups of researchers who are attached to particular technologies, as well as genuine uncertainties about the potential benefits which might be realized from different avenues of investigation and development. However, if the company of which the R&D function is a part has made an explicit identification of its core competencies, then this can help to clarify the choices somewhat. Basically, competing projects or programmes can be evaluated from the standpoint of the question 'does this project offer the prospect of developing existing knowledge or skills, or acquiring new knowledge or skills, *which would contribute directly to any of our core competencies*?'

Of course, it is easy to say this in principle, and much more difficult to do in practice. In some companies, it may be that core competencies will have been defined in a very generic way, making the task of linking technologies to them very difficult. Residual technical uncertainties often will not permit a definite prediction of whether a programme will evolve in the direction expected. However, these difficulties and others are always attached to R&D decisions, especially at the longer term end of the portfolio. What is more certain is that the shape and content of long-term R&D portfolios is no longer something which corporations are prepared to leave solely to the judgement of senior R&D executives. Some sort of transparent and readily accessible set of decision criteria are increasingly required, in order at the very least to enable the R&D programme to have some perceived legitimacy within the wider realms of the company. Thus the use of core competencies as yardsticks for the shape and direction of long-term R&D programmes is a potential source of help, but is as much about process as it is about outcome.

Funding and organization of R&D

The arguments thus far suggest further support and refinement for a model of organization and funding which is beginning to emerge as dominant in many large and diversified R&D-intensive companies. The main features of this approach, which is consistent with the 'paradigm 3' approach described in section 2 above,[4] are as follows:

- Longer term elements of the R&D portfolio funded corporately rather than by SBUs in order to insulate them from short-term pressures, and to reflect the fact that the projects are often relevant to more than one SBU.
- The long-term R&D should be organized not around generic scientific disciplines but around specific technological capabilities which map onto the core competencies.[5]
- Technical and non-technical managers from the business units should be involved in a formal review procedure which enables them to participate in the steering of the long-term R&D, and to learn how it may be relevant to their own SBUs, but with only limited direct authority over the content and management of the programme itself. The aim is to achieve shared ownership and legitimacy without a great deal of detailed horse-trading over specific projects.
- In companies where technology is a frequent source of competitive advantage, the organization and funding of R&D may do much more than simply respond to the strategic agenda and the core competencies defined 'from above'. It may play a very substantial part in the setting of the agendas and the defining of the core competencies and their future evolution. This aspect of strategic technology management is, in general, underdeveloped in the UK.

Measuring the effectiveness of R&D

There is now a rising concern with the need to measure the effectiveness of R&D. This can be seen as a specific instance of the more general trend to tighten management surveillance and control, and to ask searching questions of any functional area about its contribution to the company, and the efficiency of its processes. The problem of measuring the effectiveness and efficiency of R&D has been addressed several times over the years.[6] The prevailing concern of literature has been whether it is possible to identify direct financial benefits from R&D and relate them to the associated programme costs. Whilst this aspect of measurement is clearly interesting, it relates primarily only to the harvesting mode of R&D as discussed earlier. One of the implications of the linkage of R&D to investment in core competencies is that a case can be made for trying to measure the extent to which knowledge and skills are actually accumulated in those technical areas that are agreed as significant contributors to core competencies. These dimensions of technology are even harder to relate directly to financial outcomes than artefacts, and it seems more appropriate to use bibliometric and peer-review styles of measurement in this area.

There is some evidence that this can be done. Lillystone (1993) presents an approach designed to suit the needs of a large industrial gases company. Miyazaki (1993) has shown in great detail how bibliometric techniques applied both to scientific papers and to patents can be used to measure and compare the capabilities of eight large electronics companies in a specific technical field, namely optoelectronics.

The merits of investing significant effort in setting up systems to monitor technology accumulation in this way must obviously be judged on the basis of the scale of the company's investment in competence-building, and on whether the measures would have any operational value in terms of motivation. However, in this area as in many other areas of R&D and technology management, it is hard to escape the view that more performance measurement will be done in future. In part this is an inevitable corollary of the trend to more detailed and careful planning processes at the front end of R&D. The increased linking of post-project evaluations to pre-project benefit statements is likely to be a significant feature of all R&D management in future.

5 CONCLUSION

This chapter has argued that there is an increasing concern amongst R&D managers and their immediate 'customers' and sponsors within companies to have reliable mechanisms to direct R&D simultaneously toward effective rapid innovation and accumulation of long-term technological strength. This is leading R&D managers to seek analytical tools to help them identify technologies which have particular significance for competitive advantage, for multiple SBUs and for longer term strategic positioning, but situate them closer to the core of corporate strategies. An examination of the parallel literature on the idea of core competencies as a new paradigm in corporate strategy has shown that competencies can be useful focusing devices for assisting in the creation of this linkage between the technological and non-technological aspects of the corporate strategy agenda. Further research and case studies on the specific core competencies of particular companies, and on the connections between these competencies and their R&D sub-unit strategies is now required in order to pursue this idea further.

NOTES

1 This section draws heavily on the findings of a research project carried out for the SAST programme of DGXII of the European Commission. The final report has recently been published (Coombs and Richards, 1993b).
2 We are using 'styles' in the sense defined by Goold and Campbell (1987).
3 We have concentrated on presenting these issues as they emerged from the SAST project, and from the earlier work reported in Coombs and Richards (1993a). However, it is clear that the broad approach taken here has significant resonances with other recent work in the field. See for example *Third Generation R&D*, Roussel *et al.* (1991), and Rothwell's 'fifth-generation innovation process' (1992). Rubenstein (1989) also addresses some of these issues.
4 See also 'best practices' numbers 1 to 7 in the list of 13 provided by Krause and Liu (1993).
5 To give an example, a major glass-making company organizes its long-term R&D around a small number of areas such as the 'melting, forming and coating of glass'. These aspects of the manufacture and use of glass are relevant to all of their businesses, and all require the deployment of a variety of scientific and technical skills and specialists.
6 For a review, see Lillystone (1993).

REFERENCES

Anderson, P. and Tushman, M. (1990) 'Technological Discontinuities and Dominant Designs: A Cyclical Model of Technological Change', *Administrative Science Quarterly*, (35), pp. 604–633.

Coombs, R. and Richards, A. (1993a) 'Strategic Control of Technology in Diversified Companies with De-centralized R&D', *Technology Analysis and Strategic Management*, 5(4), pp. 385–396.

Coombs, R. and Richards, A. (1993b) *Research and Technology Management in Enterprises: Issues for Community Policy: Case Study on England*, Report issued as part of EC SAST Project No. 8, EUR-15433-EN, Brussels, October.

Dussauge, P., Hart, S. and Ramanantsoa, B. (1992) *Strategic Technology Management*, Wiley.

Goold, M. and Campbell, A. (1987) *Strategies and Styles: The Role of the Centre in Managing a Diversified Corporation*, Blackwell.

Krause, I. and Liu, J. (1993) 'Benchmarking R&D Productivity', *Planning Review*, Jan/Feb, pp. 17–21.

Lillystone, D. (1993) 'A Review of the Use of Metrics to Measure the Effectiveness of Research and Development', unpublished M.Sc. Dissertation, Manchester School of Management, UMIST.

Metcalfe, S. and Boden, M. (1992) 'Evolutionary Epistemology and the Nature of Technology Strategy' in Coombs *et al.* (eds) *Technological Change and Company Strategies*, Academic Press.

Miyazaki, K. (1993) 'The Dynamics of Competence-Building in European and Japanese Firms: The Case of Optoelectronics', D.Phil. Thesis, University of Sussex.

Prahalad, K. and Hamel, G. (1990) 'The Core Competence of the Corporation', *Harvard Business Review*, May/June.
Rothwell, R. (1992) 'Successful Industrial Innovation: Critical Factors for the 1990s', *R&D Management* 22(3), pp. 221–239.
Rousell, P.A., Saad, K.N. and Erickson, T.J. (1991) *Third Generation R&D: Managing the Link to Corporate Strategy*, HBS for A.D. Little.
Rubenstein, A. (1989) *Managing Technology in the Decentralized Firm*, Wiley.

2

R&D INITIATIVES AND THE DEVELOPMENT OF STRATEGIC ADVANTAGE

Ken Clarke and Martyn Pitt

A firm's R&D initiatives are pursued within a context of strategic influences in and around the firm. This chapter explores the intra-firm relationships between technological innovating and strategic management. In so doing we distinguish between a firm's technologies and its associated, underpinning competences. Particularly as it relates to R&D decisions, this distinction is often overlooked or misunderstood.

We argue that strategic decision-making about R&D initiatives can be improved by recognizing explicitly two interconnected, but ultimately separate goals of any major R&D project. These are (i) to develop particular *technologies* to meet expected market applications in the foreseeable – typically short to medium term – future, and (ii) to contribute constructively to the evolution of the firm's *competences* – as the means to sustain competitive advantage for the long term – a goal to which R&D initiatives can clearly be major contributors. For long-run success the firm is well advised to reconcile these goals.

We explore the implications of these arguments, referring to examples from the literature and our own experience. We consider four cases in which a significant technological innovation is being realized, the strategic rationale for each innovation, the course of competence development associated with it, and issues of appropriability arising. We note a tendency, certainly in the early years, to focus an innovative technology on applications that are rather familiar, narrowly defined and substitutional. Although competences have developed and grown in support of each innovative technology, firms seem generally reluctant to extend the application of these competences systematically throughout the parent organization by seeking collaborations across business units. This seems paradoxical, given that collaboration with customers is an accepted *modus operandi* when developing new applications.

The economic success of a particular R&D initiative is a welcome source of funds for continuing development. In these terms a tight applications focus is justified. But longer term development of associated competences provides the opportunity to direct emerging skills to other areas of potential. This broader, learning priority is evidently difficult to manage systematically, though we suggest that if competences originating via R&D are systematically diffused into the broader organization, the firm is better placed to appropriate the longer term learning potential as well as the more immediate economic returns from a particular technology. Equally, the know-how derived from implementing new products and processes can influence the direction of future R&D activity through a continuing curiosity-driven interchange among technologists and other professional staff beyond the immediate application. In this way the firm makes a strategic progression via a series of parallel (and possibly divergent) developments in technologies and competences which can underpin future strategic advantage.

CORPORATE STRATEGY AND TECHNOLOGICAL INNOVATION

The effective management of technological innovation offers firms in principle a major source of competitive advantage. One would therefore expect research and development to be a significant element in the corporate strategy of the firm. Yet the process of integrating R&D with strategy is frequently problematic, even in successful organizations. Indeed, as Loveridge (1990) observed, strategic managers can demonstrate incomprehension toward technological logics and languages, particularly when they are novel or originate outside the firm.

Many explanations have been offered for this difficulty. Technology commentators emphasize that R&D is a complex, multifaceted activity which, to be successful commercially as well as technically, must be well integrated into the task bases and structures of the firm. For their part, strategy commentators frequently emphasize the goal of enhancing strategic position via generic strategies defined simplistically in terms of technology leadership or early followership; in this respect they are arguably unhelpful in guiding technological development in the firm (Grindley, 1991).

Those who address the 'doing' of technological innovation from a managerial perspective offer structural and behavioural prescriptions which can be categorized into formal, legitimizing approaches (e.g. new venture divisions: Burgelman, 1985; creating an 'office of innovation': Rosenfeld and Servo, 1990) and informal, quasi-deviant approaches (e.g. encouraging competing initiatives by risk-positive, entrepreneurial champions in 'skunkworks' (Peters and Waterman, 1982; Quinn, 1979, 1985). A formal, control-oriented approach can provide adequate resources for approved projects, but it may kill the innovative spirit. So perhaps managers should tolerate, even encourage the informal approaches to technology development characterized by Quinn as 'controlled chaos'. However, informal, emerging initiatives can prove difficult to pursue when inadequate resources have been committed to them, or they become acknowledged as tangential to the firm's declared strategic intent.

This formal/informal dichotomy presents a dilemma for strategists who seek to integrate strategy and technology management in the firm. None the less, the strategic management literature has endorsed the significance of developing and upgrading the firm's competences via technological innovation, as drivers of strategic change and advantage (Porter, 1990; Prahalad and Hamel, 1990; Winter, 1987). Here, the firm's strategic priority is generally not the development and application of an isolated technology but the convergence of multiple technologies underpinned by a set of (ideally distinctive) competences. The parallel development of these technologies and the competences that underpin them form an evolving, long-term, firm-specific (hence difficult to emulate) trajectory (Pavitt, 1986).

Effective technology exploitation requires the establishment and integration of an appropriate set of complementary assets (Teece, 1986), covering both tangible and intangible technological and organizational resources and competences. When this is successful, a firm like Canon creates a powerful presence on a broad competitive front (Prahalad and Hamel, 1990). Conversely, failure to synthesize an appropriate mix of competences leads to relative decline in the marketplace, even abrupt withdrawal. Thus EMI's technical prowess in developing the CAT scanner was not matched by a corresponding broad spectrum of business skills that might have sustained a long-term advantage in medical diagnostics (Spender, 1993); likewise, RCA failed to synthesize a broad base of technological and organizational capabilities into a commercially successful video disc product technology, notwithstanding its long and costly gestation (Graham, 1988).

The synthesis of competences, technologies and complementary assets creates a distinctive, advantage-conferring *architecture* (Henderson and Clark, 1990; Kay, 1993). Thus the value of integrating R&D decisions into broader conceptions of corporate strategy and competence development and exploitation is clear.

CHARACTERIZING COMPETENCES AND TECHNOLOGIES

Winter (1987) noted that it is 'necessary to confront the difficulties that arise from [using] such terms as knowledge, competence, skill, and so forth. When we use such terms, we hardly ever know precisely what we are talking about'. Moreover, the situation is not improved when terms are used inconsistently or given meanings at odds with generally accepted definitions. For example, Teece, Pisano and Shuen's (1992, p. 18) definition of competences as 'firm-specific assets . . . assembled into integrated clusters spanning individuals and groups . . . that . . . enable distinctive activities to be performed' appears to emphasize what is unique to the firm rather than what it has in common with capable competitors. Despite this definition, they reserve the adjective 'core' to those competences deemed necessary for survival, whereas Prahalad and Hamel (1990) use 'core competences' to mean relatively high level skills of integrating or orchestrating diverse resources and functional competences.

However, we agree with Teece *et al.* that to be successful over the long term, a firm needs to renew, augment and adapt its competences. Evolving competences underpin and enable technologies which in turn enable the production of saleable products or services. We suggest that it is useful to consider a particular technology as the outcome of deploying an array of convergent resources and competences. That is, a technology is a *realized configuration* of (scarce) organizational assets, resources and skills (competences) with the potential to create value and advantage through saleable outputs – processes and/or products. Essentially the same set of competences might be subsequently reconfigured to support a variety of related product and process technologies. Whereas a technology tends to exhibit particular features, its supporting competences tend towards generic qualities. Thus the competences of Eastman Kodak are sufficiently broad and generic in character for its management to contemplate a strong presence in digital electronic and chemical imaging technologies.

A process technology is an intra-firm configuration of operating assets, systems and methods, devised with a specific, realizable application in mind. Its characteristics are particular to the application and are generally quite tightly coupled: an automobile assembly line is specified for a limited number of vehicle types for a finite period of time. Products, in their design, encode bundles of realized technological processes linked in complex and subtle ways. The architecture and strength of the linkages are characteristics of the product or product class that enable or constrain its strategic exploitation (Henderson and Clark, 1990).

The qualities of being manifest and particularized render technologies more, rather than less codifiable, though the degree of codification varies from case to case and over time. Greater codification tends to facilitate competitive emulation and even enhancement of a manifest technology, other things being equal. Hence a particularized product or process technology has a finite – and often brief – life span, and the appropriability of returns to a technological innovation is properly a strategic consideration in R&D decisions (Teece, 1986).

A firm's accumulated competence base both underpins and draws on its manifest and emergent technologies. That competences and technologies are distinguishable, however, can be illustrated with the example of a firm deploying production technology acquired under licence from another firm. The terms of the licence provide for the *technology* to enter the repertoire of both firms. However, the form and extent of the *competences* that the licensee acquires from the licenser are limited to what the latter judges necessary for the technology to be exploited for the agreed purpose. Subsequently, both firms will accumulate competences, possibly distinctively so, albeit in very different ways. Whereas the licenser may develop new variants of and applications for its technologies, this option is problematic for the licensee. Conversely, the licensee may develop skills at negotiating and exploiting licence agreements in other fields of technology. So the competences of the two firms start differently and develop in markedly different ways, even though they could appear similar to the casual observer.

A firm's present competences comprise the knowledge and expertise it has learned and accumulated over time. It configures arrays of competences into particular technologies. By exercising and extending its R&D competences the firm also seeks to develop new technologies with distinctive and valuable elements, and to construct linkages among these elements. For example, a manufacturer of automobile engine mounts has knowledge of their physical design and construction, including relevant knowledge of assembly processes. Competitive advantage may derive more from a detailed understanding of the behaviour of elastomeric polymers when supporting a vibrating engine. Proprietary know-how about the blending and moulding of elastomers is less obviously advantageous, though it may also benefit the firm. As it implements each new configuration of competences, the technology thus realized is particularized to the new application, and the competence set becomes ever more idiosyncratic to the firm. This pattern of competences is intrinsic to the firm's current make-up. No other engine mount manufacturer has an identical pattern, making it hard for competitors to emulate an innovation precisely. In being idiosyncratic the firm is also distinctive, though it is not always distinctive in ways that will prove advantageous.

A firm's competences are substantially tacit, uncodified, being possessed – and imperfectly shared – by individuals in the organization (Orr, 1990; Spender, 1993). Leonard-Barton (1992) portrayed individual skills and competences as embedded in technical and managerial systems and in the firm's shared values and norms. Spender (1993, 1994) considered the nature of organizational and managerial knowledge, distinguishing objective and externalized (scientific) knowledge from intuitive, largely tacit (and perhaps personal) experiential knowledge. Whilst it would be convenient if knowledge in technologically developed organizations was primarily of the first type, the facts are somewhat different. Even among trained technologists, the 'knowing of personal experience' is generally significant. For example, one of the authors recalls a leading semiconductor materials firm that sought to document all its manufacturing engineering procedures. Given the fast changing nature of the industry, these documents were invariably obsolescent and in times of crisis the firm turned to its most experienced staff like a primitive drought-stricken community turns to its rain-maker.

Still, in the large or well-established firm a good deal of organizational knowledge will be documented somewhere. But the experienced staff member has a considerable advantage over the relative newcomer in knowing where to look and who to ask, a valuable complement to personal 'knowing how'. Because a substantial part of the cumulative knowledge (hence competences) of an organization is grounded in – and most assuredly enabled by – individuals, frequently there is 'stickiness' in extending competences from one context to another. The translation of what these individuals know into corporate databases and into technologies represents at best a partial codification of their cumulative personal knowledge and at worst a rapidly wasting asset for the firm.

The distinction between the firm's particularized technologies and its broader organizational competences (of which technical competences are an important subset) is important. Ignorance of the distinction may mean that the transfer of a promising technology from laboratory to manufacturing facility will fail. It may result in R&D resources being channelled in directions that prove strategically inappropriate for the firm in the long run. Even worse, it may mean the failure of a major technology in the marketplace and the consequent loss of the firm's competitive standing. We turn, therefore, to the strategic assessment of R&D decisions. We consider three themes: (i) the rationale for a particular R&D initiative expressed in strategic terms; (ii) the course of associated competence development; and (iii) appropriating the economic and other returns from R&D initiatives.

THE STRATEGIC ASSESSMENT OF R&D INITIATIVES

The strategic rationale for an innovating project

Prahalad and Hamel (1990) argued that firms can no longer expect to locate and survive in safe, stable markets. Rather, to succeed in dynamic markets needing rapid responses, strategists must understand the nature of the firm's core competences which transcend and integrate existing businesses, and ask how they may be reconfigured into advantage-creating initiatives. The expected future value of a technological innovation and the attractiveness of a prospective market have to be understood in the light of present and anticipated competence sets. Making decisions opportunistically or in relation to the current business portfolio is inadequate.

Prahalad and Hamel apply a broad definition of core competence. They suggest that core competences of Canon and Honda are the design and manufacture of fine optics and power trains respectively. Their argument underlines the important contribution that R&D can make to the strategic decision process. However, a broad definition may be of limited value when evaluating whether the current competence set can support a specific technological development, and how the latter, if successful, will enhance the firm's future competence set. Moreover, core competences result from years of cumulative experience in developing, manufacturing and marketing specific products. We can agree that strategists should ask how the present competence base will support or stymie a particular R&D initiative. The application of current competences to developing new technologies is a proper component of corporate strategy that can enable the firm to evolve new and upgraded competences, creating a virtuous cycle of progress. But strategists will also do well to evaluate the potential enhancements to the firm's internal routines and core competences deriving from a particular technology innovation *even if it should fail* to achieve all the expected technology outcomes.

Given that competences are refined and extended through being directed at particular technological problems, it is crucial for practitioners with a strategic outlook to define the 'right' problem (Arlin, 1990). For as Schon (1983) commented:

> In real world practice, problems do not present themselves . . . as givens. They must be constructed from the materials of problematic situations which are puzzling, troubling, and uncertain . . . a practitioner must . . . make sense of an uncertain situation that initially makes no sense . . . When we set the problem . . . we set the boundaries of our attention to it, and we impose upon it a coherence which allows us to say what is wrong and in what direction the situation needs to be changed.

Cooper and Schendel (1976) described industry incumbents who solved the 'wrong' problem by directing present resources and competences to sustain current technologies rather than explore alternative means to satisfy known applications, even when novel technologies were clearly on the horizon. Thus in hindsight we know that no restructuring of the US railroads could halt the development of airline traffic. Current technologies derive from a deeply embedded competence set and supporting organizational structures whose obsolescence – and particularly abandonment – are understandably problematic for the firm. As Leonard-Barton (1992) observed, core competences are mirrored by core rigidities. The latter hinder constructive attempts to innovate in respect of new applications as technologists understandably find it easier to solve problems they recognize and have relevant experience of than to address the uncertain and the unknown.

Yet firms also try to solve the 'right' problem with the 'wrong' solution. In the semiconductor industry the performance of photomask alignment equipment has long been central to improving yields. Kasper, once a leading producer of alignment rigs, remained intent on improving rig performance by means of contact alignment procedures. It ignored the significance of proximity alignment even though, according to Henderson and Clark (1990), it was not unfamiliar with this technology. This innovation constituted a change in equipment architecture, the configuration and interaction of components rather than their specification *per se* and Kasper personnel saw little reason to develop proximity alignment technology. Thus they failed to develop associated competences for the future. When Canon, which had acknowledged its potential, introduced an effective proximity alignment rig, the game was up for Kasper.

Changing a technology can of course disrupt the pattern of existing competences and may devalue some entirely (Abernathy and Clark, 1985; Tushman and Anderson, 1986). Not surprisingly, this is an unattractive prospect to a firm like Kasper and goes some way to explain why radical technological changes that diminish the future relevance (real or perceived) of existing competences are often associated *ex post facto* with the emergence of new firms and new product classes. Decisions about particular R&D initiatives therefore need to make reasonable assumptions about their strategic significance in relation to the evolving pattern of competences in the firm if they are to result in a new technology that is successful commercially as well as technically.

Trajectories and the course of competence development in the firm

The existence of identifiable technological trajectories of development is well documented in industries as diverse as automobiles (Utterback and Abernathy, 1978; Whipp and Clark, 1986), semiconductors (Dosi, 1984), process equipment (Henderson and Clark, 1990) and synthetic fibres (Mulder and Vergragt, 1990). The notion that the firm develops a technological trajectory has also been advanced (e.g. Pavitt, 1986; Mulder and Vergragt, 1990). Here we suggest that the joint evolution and interaction of technologies and competences in the firm constitutes its characteristic developmental trajectory (*cf.* Nelson and Winter, 1982).

By way of analogy, the rock climber directs physical and mental strengths to the ascent, but (s)he also needs specific footholds or pegs driven into the rock face (the technologies) to progress upwards, step by painful step. Looking down, the climber sees a line of pegs forming a trajectory of ascent. Just as pegs can be located well or badly, manifest technologies can prove well or poorly directed. Over time the successful firm makes visible progress in some useful directions, yet may be forced to retract from others.

Mulder and Vergragt (1990) show how major firms developing synthetic fibre technologies adopted different postures towards development and commercialization. These differences can be explained by the idiosyncratic firm competences in which the various technologies were rooted. For example, Bayer's trajectory, emphasizing the use of synthetics in textiles, was grounded in its perceived competences as a dye stuffs manufacturer, and its strong skills in marketing to textile companies. Technologies and competences in each firm showed strong interactions. The embodiment of specific competences in a realized technology opened the window to further learning and competence development by exploiting that technology. When a technology was abandoned, learning was stymied or proceeded along a rather different track.

Thus, we argue, technology and competence trajectories evolve simultaneously, pushing and pulling each other. Current competences enable particular technologies that in turn subsequently enable better (different, upgraded) future competences. It is often beneficial to realize a particular technology, even if the commercial return is limited, for the learning opportunities it facilitates. This is demonstrated by Sony Corporation when it continuously reconfigures its competences into new technologies, despite the fact that on past evidence its executives must be aware that a percentage of these initiatives will fail commercially.

The portrayal of R&D as a process of and as a function for technology development is therefore incomplete. Although a large proportion of what an organization 'knows' can be most readily mapped in the form of emergent, mature and obsolescent technologies, a strategic necessity is to establish the core competences in the firm at large which underpin these technologies. This know-how can be classified by extent of codification (explicitness) and extent of diffusion (sharedness): Boisot (1986); Spender (1994). Realized, codified technologies are open to systematic diffusion across boundaries within and between organizations, whereas partially codified personal knowing and competences diffuse haphazardly as knowers make contact across functions and move between firms. Anecdotal evidence suggests that what is known in one firm may prove to be decidedly less valuable in another firm than was anticipated.

Competences exhibit both individual and systemic qualities. Personal skills and expertise develop progressively, though much personal knowledge may remain partially unarticulated in an organization context (Spender, 1994). Enabling and exploiting personal knowledge is a key factor in corporate effectiveness (Nonaka, 1991). In R&D programmes the peer group often plays a major role in activating personal knowledge. Such interaction typically works well among groups of like-minded technologists, but can be problematic in multi-disciplinary project development groups whose members come from heterogeneous backgrounds and share comparatively few interests (Leonard-Barton, 1992). Enhancing the mutual trust and performance of such teams contributes greatly to the firm's strategic effectiveness.

However, there are several foci of skills and know-how for which the organization acts as a kind of umbrella: the individual; the team, work group or task-force; the function; and the business unit as a strategic entity. To these we can add the interface level: between separate business units in the corporation and between the firm and external players. These various foci form nodes of a communications network, and strategic exploitation of R&D will generally require effective interactions among the significant nodes in and around the organization. Indeed, the mobilization of centralized R&D know-how and the diffusion of R&D competences to the wider organization in pursuit of strategic advantage remains a specific and problematic challenge. Graham's (1988) account of VideoDisc development in RCA exemplifies both the failure to translate corporate R&D into commercially successful product technologies, and the very limited injection of new and augmented competences into the organization at large. Such failures, especially those amenable to exploitation in a variety of applications and arenas, constitute a major strategic disaster. They frustrate the installation and application of evolving technologies in the short term, and they diminish the firm's longer term ability to extend and deploy the associated competences, a practice of continuous enhancement analogous to the Japanese concept of *Kaizen*.

The appropriation of returns to innovating

Successful exploitation of an innovation is a function of its appropriability regime determined, according to Teece (1986), by the nature of the innovation and its particularized product and process knowledge, tacit and codified. The form and direction in which a firm's competences and rigidities evolve over time affect its ability to appropriate the benefits of an innovation very considerably, perhaps even more than its competitive environment.

Winter (1987) noted that alternative ways of appropriating returns to innovating differed in their efficacy. Knowledge embodied in product technology is better articulated and observable and therefore more open to emulation, despite patent protection. Process innovations are less open, yet generally less patentable, and patent application may expose the underlying competences that the firm would prefer to keep hidden. To realize the full potential of an R&D initiative the firm has to recognize its limited rights of ownership in and control of personal knowledge. This problem becomes acute in rapidly evolving industries where competences have not yet crystallized into standardized products and the knowledge base remains largely in the minds of R&D actors.

A clear requirement in the strategic management of R&D initiatives, then, is good anticipation of risk regimes and the ability to cope with uncertainty in both markets and operations. Innovating rarely impacts existing production technologies without also having an impact on the firm's marketing context (Clark, 1987). Firms can adopt systematic strategies for coping with these difficulties, for example Sony's stream of new products based on incremental changes to its basic technologies and production competences has primarily been about creating (in Clark's terms) new *niche* market segments, whereas Pilkington's float glass innovation was a *revolutionary* strategy.

When the appropriability of returns to innovative activity is judged not purely in economic terms but also in respect of learning potential, the strategic imperative for the management of R&D initiatives is likely to shift from developing a single technology to the development and effective exploitation of a continuing stream of innovations. This requires that R&D managers are fully involved in evaluating how the firm can best appropriate the long-run returns to innovating. However, we want to reverse the emphasis of the appropriability question by suggesting that the strategic issue is how to foster and exploit a long run stream of valuable *competences*. From this perspective the commercialization of a particular technology is a legitimate, but limited vehicle for exploiting emergent competences. The secret is to ensure that learning derived from exploiting today's technologies will lead to emergent competences being applied in new directions, a process of related diversification arguably of great strategic significance for long-run success. This is the lesson from successful Japanese corporations as articulated by Prahalad and Hamel (1990).

FOUR EMPIRICAL CASES

We discuss the foregoing issues with reference to four case studies of strategic technological innovation. The firms involved are quasi-autonomous divisions of large companies with multinational operations.

The firms

Firm A is a world leader in making aircraft propeller blades, though not the biggest. Its innovation is a moulded carbon composite blade. Moulding technology enables a complex profile and heterogeneous structure to the blade, which is potentially very durable, easily repaired and aerodynamically effective. Jet-prop aircraft using this blade should enjoy a combination of higher speed, greater fuel economy, and lower noise compared with a forged metal alloy or wooden blade.

Firm B is a major producer of motor vehicle components and systems. Its innovation is an electronically controlled diesel engine fuel injection system (FIE). Conventional FIE comprises a remote high pressure fuel pump (there are two dominant design configurations) linked to a set of fuel injectors, one per cylinder. The amount and timing of fuel pumped into the cylinders is controlled by mechanical and hydraulic means. In the new design a very high pressure pumping mechanism and injector are combined in a single device, one per cylinder, fed by a remote low pressure distributor pump. The amount and timing of fuel injection is under very precise electromechanical and electronic control, hence the name 'electronic unit injector' or EUI. EUI offers an improved combination of engine power, reduced fuel consumption and less exhaust gas pollutants.

Firm C is a major producer of computer equipment and dedicated software for sale under its own name, and of peripherals for incorporation into its own and others' equipment. Its innovation is a computer data storage device based on a consumer technology (digital audio tape recording and playback: DAT). DAT technology offers gigabyte storage capacity with high rates of data transfer in a compact format. The basic technology is cheap, well proven and in this form very reliable by virtue of its error diagnosis and correction features.

Firm D is a major manufacturer of copper wire harnesses for automotive uses. Its innovation is a multiplexed structure combining signal and power cables around the vehicle. Such a harness could ultimately integrate the management of various engine, braking and other active subsystems. Only recently have all the relevant technologies including fibre optics emerged to realize this innovation. In its ultimate form the benefits will be reduced weight and greater reliability, as well as enhanced control of the vehicle functions including error diagnosis and driver warning.

The nature of and rationales for the innovations

In all four cases the rationale for the innovation appears to have been constructed around technology development in relation to defined applications, rather than around competence development. Firm A's composite propeller initiative was justified on the grounds that by substituting conventional metal blades it could make Firm A the undisputed market leader. Conversely, Firm A would be severely disadvantaged if competitors pursued the innovation and it did not. Firm A might also establish a technology with considerable licensing potential, and the moulding know-how gained from the project could be applicable to other areas of corporate business, offering potential to extend competences on a broader front.

Firm B's engineers were convinced that FIE technology was approaching its theoretical performance limits and needed a radical design reconfiguration. Only a handful of specialist world suppliers, of which Firm B is one, could realistically achieve this since FIE is a specialist product manufactured to the highest engineering standards. Like Firm A, the innovation was seen as an opportunity to secure a dominant future position but a threat if it was ignored. FIE is a major determinant of engine power, fuel economy and exhaust gas pollutants. Increasing concerns over air pollution spurred Firm B to press ahead with EUI, helping to ensure a positive reception from engine and vehicle makers. Despite potential for cost reduction, EUI is fundamentally more costly than current designs. Thus it was introduced first in large engine applications and only in recent times is it being applied to motor cars.

Firm C perceived a market opportunity for a high capacity, fast access storage device necessitating a new technology configuration. A DAT based device was seen to address the need and would be consistent with its existing product portfolio and reputation. Firm C lacked know-how in some vital areas, and since it was convinced that timing was of the essence, it sought to exploit the opportunity via a joint venture with a leading Japanese manufacturer of consumer and professional tape drives. It hoped to create saleable technology in the short term, and to acquire new competences in the design and construction of data storage devices for future exploitation in other forms.

Firm D foresaw that current wiring harnesses have very limited potential in relation to the increasing use of electronics in cars. The latter, it thought, will require and enable fully integrated vehicle management systems in the not too distant future. Such an innovation constitutes a major change in the technological trajectory of OEM suppliers of traditional harnesses. In principle it could see a major opportunity for a current OEM supplier – particularly one like Firm D with long experience of wiring harnesses – to occupy a much more influential position as a prime systems specifier, enjoying greater bargaining power *vis à vis* the major vehicle OEMs. But like Firms A and B, this innovation constitutes both a perceived opportunity and, if mishandled, a serious threat in the longer term.

To summarize, for three of the four firms technology development was seen both as an opportunity to enhance long-term competitive standing, and a potential threat if it was ignored, since current technologies were maturing fast. Firm C, in contrast, saw its innovation as a clear opportunity, but one it was unable to exploit for lack of critical know-how. The firm's entrepreneurial outlook created a sense of urgency which led to an external collaboration. This aimed to exploit the specific opportunity and in so doing establish expertise which Firm C could then deploy in other, novel directions. The prospect of developing a technology whose associated competences were relevant to other applications also motivated Firm A to some degree. In contrast, Firms B and D were motivated principally by the felt need for a technology to satisfy specific product/market applications; in so doing they would develop new competences, but there is little evidence that this was a strategic consideration in deciding to proceed.

The course of competence development to date

Firm A is conservative and respects engineering excellence. It prefers in-house development and expects long time horizons. Despite the parent company's broad competence base, Firm A needed various new skills in design, manufacturing and materials to realize the new product. There was a high level of technical uncertainty in the early stages. Composite moulding techniques were drawn from external sources and new facilities were established. Enhanced computer-aided design competences had to be implemented before it could achieve the complex profiles needed to create the new blade. The relevant learning was accomplished by Firm A's own R&D staff. This policy was justified on the grounds that competitive advantage would lie in being seen to have all the relevant competences in house. The development of the new competences was protracted. Since a propeller has to be customized to the engine/airframe combination the firm has collaborated with an engine maker, extending the diffusion of know-how beyond the firm to some degree.

Firm B has a pragmatic, patient engineering culture. Like Firm A, it has long time horizons. Historically, it tended to purchase technologies externally and then develop highly efficient manufacturing competences. This changed in the 1950s when its design competences had advanced to the point that it originated rotary pumping technology. Knowledge of complex combustion processes and fuel flow under high pressures can also be traced over decades. Skills transfer from corporate R&D into Firm B has been limited. EUI development was protracted, drawing on a wide range of engineering competences and involving lengthy experimentation with alternative design configurations, including an interim design that ultimately proved fruitless.

Firm B has unquestionably enhanced its competences through EUI, which has required specific new skills in electronics and electromechanics. Existing skills were supplemented by imports – hiring appropriately skilled staff from outside the group. Learning was enhanced by sharing applications development with a trusted engine manufacturer. EUI also required Firm B to develop new design and work organization competences. It chose to locate EUI manufacturing facilities on a green field site remote from existing centres of production. Whilst collaboration is also benefiting some engine and vehicle manufacturers, the lessons from EUI appear unlikely to diffuse widely in the parent company nor, so far as we are aware, to be directed towards non-FIE developments. Indeed, the separation of EUI from other FIE manufacture may indicate that know-how transfer even within Firm B will be constrained.

Firm C has a reputation for defining its own technology solutions. The DAT collaboration meant that its engineers had to reach compromises with counterparts in a company with a very different outlook. Firm C has developed a comparatively successful new product technology and associated facilities. However, its partner cleverly defended its proprietary know-how in miniature electromechanical assemblies by providing its technology essentially as ready to install 'black boxes'. Thus Firm C was denied easy emulation of its partner's competences, and its strategic goals were somewhat stymied in the short term. Firm C encourages a corporate culture where pooling know-how across operating units is accepted behaviour; for this reason it appears to have misread the intentions of its partner. Still, it has achieved new design skills, in manufacturing, and access to useful contacts in a new market sector. Longer term, there is every reason to think that it will have gained significantly from this initiative. Other divisions of the parent company have already benefited indirectly from Firm C's initiative and one anticipates that this process will continue.

Firm D and its OEMs are fairly clear as to the required performance characteristics of a new wiring harness technology, but great uncertainty exists over the exact technological configuration(s) that will dominate in years to come. Technology choices will probably be dictated by the OEMs, but they are uncertain whether or not to push for an industry standard. Firm D's relationships with OEMs have been comparatively distant since its current products do not need the kinds of interactions exhibited by, for example, FIE. Thus Firm D cannot 'read' the development of the prospective technology trajectory with real confidence.

Yet the ultimate impact on the firm's competence base may be dramatic. New harness technology will require more refined skills in electronics and in fibre optics. Dedicated assembly facilities and skills can be anticipated, though the precise form is still unclear. Firm D also needs software skills, though these do not confer advantage *per se*. It has been able to locate relevant know-how elsewhere in the parent company, though the historical precedents for competence transfer are limited, given the structural, historical and cultural pressures encouraging business unit autonomy. Though products are now starting to emerge, this innovation is still at a comparatively early stage. The major new competences are widely found among electronic component manufacturers which could imply that Firm D will face a variety of new competitors including vehicle OEMs in the future.

To summarize, Firms A and B felt the need to develop requisite know-how internally and to maintain a tight control of the competences, drawing expertise from outside only as needed. The nature of the innovations has necessitated that both collaborate with customers, so that some know-how has diffused beyond the firm. Firm D can make little progress without substantial external collaborations, too, given the systemic nature of its innovation. Although each firm has potential access to know-how elsewhere in its parent company, the prevailing history and attitudes favouring autonomy discourage this kind of enquiry except in Firm C. However, the lack of corporate know-how in key areas obliged Firm C to look to an outsider with whom it engaged in a trusting collaboration that proved problematic.

We foresee that in Firms B and D competence development will continue to be seen principally as the means to enable their new technologies in applications they perceive to be consistent with the firms' existing market specialisms and strategic position. These competences are unlikely to be applied on a broader (related–diversified) front, and we suspect they will not diffuse rapidly throughout the group. For Firm D the need for inward competence diffusion may present particular difficulties in relation to other divisions of the parent company. However, if the harness innovation is fully realized it will affect other group members that make components that must link to the harness. Thus there will be pressures on Firm D which could make for a turbulent future. In contrast, Firm A does appear to conceive of extending its new competences in composites moulding elsewhere in the group, though this has not yet occurred. In Firm C's parent there is considerable interfirm communication which makes the diffusion of know-how almost inevitable. In what form Firm C's acquired competences will find application we are not in a position to say.

Appropriability of the innovations

Here we present a brief account of appropriability issues in the four case studies. We distinguish the appropriation of economic returns through developing and exploiting a new technology from the realization of learning potential through deploying a new competence set on a broader stage.

Firm A judged that patent cover for its moulding process was infeasible, and unlikely but not impossible for blade design. First mover advantage was therefore important, given high perceived risks and uncertainties. Proprietary standards are unlikely to be a major issue, since the propeller blade has to be developed to the application. The central issue of the extent to which composite technology will substitute for metal blades in the long run, whether for higher performance or lower cost, is yet to be resolved. Lower cost will arguably not create greater usage, whereas lower noise and better fuel economy implies an opportunity on short haul inter-city routes with new turboprop aircraft. This could be a small niche, or demand could escalate. There could also be potential in applications such as hovercraft.

Passenger airline operators and manufacturers remain cautious about the reliability of a plastic propeller: no one wants to be the first to have a major accident attributable to the failure of a novel component, however unlikely. This slowed the adoption of the technology, increasing the risk of competitive emulation. As an upstream supplier Firm A needs to maintain good relations with engine manufacturers, but has relatively low bargaining power. Thus far it has achieved moderate short-run financial returns and in the longer term things look promising, if uncertain.

Firm A's perceived need to control the composite blade technology has driven the development of an associated competence set. It is now in a position to appropriate additional returns to these technologies, for example by designing and manufacturing complex panel shapes for aerospace use. This is a significant step and will extend competences further. But as yet there is little evidence of a drive to extend the know-how underpinning these technologies in a systematic way. Thus the learning potential will probably not be fully realized.

Firm B has acquired various detailed patents, but system architecture is the key to its innovation and here it is unlikely to prevent emulation. Given the extra cost of EUI over conventional technology, and uncertainty over market receptiveness, Firm B focused initially on the large diesel engine niche. Following success here, it has begun to exploit smaller designs of EUI for the automobile market. Other FIE manufacturers are known to be working on equivalent product technologies. The lack of accumulated FIE-related competences and the need for massive capital investment to produce FIE will deter most would-be entrants, though major vehicle manufacturers could probably produce versions for car engines at some time in the future. History suggests that first moving will be important but not crucial, since FIE is customized for each application. Thus a new design is commercially viable when accepted for a new engine, whereupon it will normally be the preferred lifetime choice.

We predict the continuing development of EUI technology for specific applications for many years to come. Uncertainty remains over some aspects of the preferred technological configuration and over the rate at which EUI will cannibalize Firm B's old FIE technology. Parallel evolution of the competences underpinning EUI will also continue, though establishing a remote green field production site for EUI seems to be a conscious effort to isolate EUI from Firm B's conventional technologies and know-how. Firm B has extended its design and manufacturing expertise with EUI, but it can be far from confident of appropriating the full potential of EUI technology. Whilst its extended competences can theoretically be deployed in new areas of precision engineering, the rather conservative culture of the firm suggests that this is unlikely to happen. As in Firm A, we think that the process of competence development is seen as relevant primarily for the contribution it makes to EUI technology development.

Turning to Firm C, its formal collaboration agreement left both partners free to make and sell competing products using shared DAT technology. Neither secured new patents from the joint project, so first moving was seen as important. The positions of the firms proved asymmetric. Firm C recognized the need to establish rapidly an industry standard by offering low cost licences, but it was confronted by other players offering alternative technological configurations. Its partner also introduced a second generation technology sooner than was anticipated. Thus from the start Firm C has experienced a comparatively weak appropriability regime. Its failure to establish a dominant technology standard in the short term made its financial returns disappointing. In a dynamic industry it is always hard to know how long a standard will survive. The current evidence is that the strength of the parent company's name allied to determined and continuing enhancement of the technology has won over the doubters.

Still, new configurations involving optics and disks are now in play. Though Firm C has extended its technologies and its competences in design and manufacturing with DAT, we doubt that its long-run financial returns will be as good as was originally envisioned. Yet we have little doubt that the firm will exploit its enhanced competences from this project in new technology directions. One suspects also that important lessons have been learned in managing collaborations that will enhance future commercial skills. This will benefit the firm in its dealings with future partners, within the parent company and without. It seems fair to conclude that competence development has been deliberate, allied to a particular technology only insofar as the latter was a pragmatic route for making progress.

Firm D's envisioned new harness technology will be transparent to the car driver. From a technical perspective Firm D has a weak appropriability regime. At the present time uncertainty is still high (e.g. over technology standards) and Firm D's main opportunity for appropriation lies in its scope to convince OEMs to give it the lead role in development. This role could propel Firm D into a revitalizing strategic change process in which it becomes a major producer and/or licenser of high value-added technology. In so doing it will have to secure an extended set of competences for which it will need the unqualified support of other group companies. Otherwise, it risks being relegated to the status of a commodity component supplier as a new sector trajectory unfolds. Some of its managers perceive this innovation as a major source of learning potential; most probably do not see it in this light. We foresee that Firm D's appropriation of the potential returns, economically and in terms of new competences, will be limited, although other firms within the parent group may benefit from interacting with Firm D.

CONCLUSIONS

There are too many imponderables to make confident predictions that the four firms will extract a major proportion of the economic potential of their respective technological innovations. However, in all cases, the returns are likely to be positive.

As regards the learning potential of the innovations, Firm C in particular seems set to appropriate a good deal of the potential of its DAT project. In practical terms this means seeking to deploy new know-how (technical and otherwise) in other areas of its business and probably in other divisions too. We would expect Firm A to extend the competence set of the division by extending its composites moulding technology to a relatively narrow range of other applications familiar to the parent company. Likewise Firm B may be expected to extend its range of EUI applications and associated competences. However, it is probable that neither firm will go beyond what its managers see as 'obvious' applications in aerospace and diesel engines respectively. Thus the full learning potential for the business units or for the parent companies may conceivably not be fully realized.

On the evidence here, when innovating firms develop a novel technology there is a tendency to envision applications that are rather familiar, narrowly defined and substitutional in kind. Competence development does not appear to be the key drive. When associated competences develop to support the new technologies, there is often a reluctance to redeploy them systematically on a broader front, whether in related product categories or new products and markets. Only in one instance here is there much enthusiasm for collaborating with other divisions of the parent company, even though trusting, applications-specific *customer* collaboration is accepted as normal behaviour to get a technology accepted in the marketplace.

It is beyond the scope of this paper to explain why this should be so, though we incline to the view that explanations are likely to be firm-specific and probably non-technical. As Jones, Green and Coombs (1994) acknowledge, technologists operate in the same politicized in-firm environment as everyone else, so that motives may be fragmented and interests divergent. There is a tendency for firms to centre their competence development on the individuals and task groups directly charged with developing a new technology. With the possible exception of Firm C here, they have not sought deliberately to diffuse a new competence widely across the firm, let alone the parent company, appearing to be governed by an implicit 'no need to know' principle. So there is little evidence of a systematic drive to exploit new competences beyond the technology applications with which they are presently associated.

The strategic issues relating to the management of R&D projects, however, are clear, even if generalized prescriptions are problematic. Many firms seem to interpret the development of new technologies largely in relation to their expectations of future threats and opportunities. When they conclude that the forecast trajectory of an existing technology is unattractive, competitively and commercially, technological innovations may offer the prospect of defending or enhancing the firm's market position. It is then a temptation for managers to construe an R&D initiative as being to develop a particular technology (or set of convergent technologies) for specific, identified applications. Indeed, a tight, short-term focus on specific technologies and applications can be desirable, since the early economic success of a particular initiative is a welcome source of funds for subsequent development work. Yet although these same managers most probably appreciate that strategic technological shifts will entail major enhancements to the firm's competences, uncertainty about future technological trajectories can lead them to idiosyncratic decisions about which competences will be most significant, and therefore will need the most immediate attention.

But in the longer term, these choices shape and constrain the future technological trajectory of the firm, its appropriability regime, and the parallel development of associated new competences. The latter process also provides the opportunity to direct skills to other areas of potential. This broader, learning priority is easy to overlook and is evidently difficult to manage systematically. None the less, as is now widely recognized in the strategy and organization behaviour literature, it is an important priority (e.g. Dodgson, 1993; Fiol and Lyles, 1985; Kolb, Lublin, Spoth and Baker, 1986), especially in respect of possible diversification (Pennings, Barkema and Douma, 1994). More specifically, we suggest that competences originating via R&D initiatives – especially where these are conducted at a distance from operations – can be systematically diffused into the broader organization, enabling the firm to appropriate the potential learning as well as the economic returns from exploiting a particular technology. Managers do well to recognize that decisions about new technologies entail a responsibility to consider how they will enhance the firm's future competences. Equally, the know-how derived from implementing new products and processes in production can be systematically diffused back into future R&D activity. There can be a continuing curiosity-driven interchange between technologists and other professional staff that goes beyond the most obvious and immediate applications development. All parties have the opportunity and arguably the responsibility to extend the firm's strategic progression through parallel (albeit possibly divergent) developments in technologies and competences. Unfortunately, cultural norms seem often to militate against this kind of process.

Our four cases indicate that developing a major new technology generally requires some competences that are currently beyond the scope of the innovating firm. Effective strategic development relies on establishing these competences, autonomously or through inward technology transfer. Internalizing, harmonizing and mobilizing the necessary competences in a time frame that offers the firm a realistic prospect of economic returns from a new technology is a crucial strategic challenge. Evidently, it cannot be guaranteed when the need is not envisioned until late in the process. Forward thinking in relation to competence development is therefore important.

Whilst technology and competence development proceed in parallel, strategists would do well to decouple them conceptually so that opportunities to deploy emerging competences are not limited to the technology application immediately to hand. Informed and imaginative judgements have to be made continuously about the competences that the firm must have access to and exploit, and the technological pathways available as conduits for the deployment of these competences. Otherwise, expectations of future strategic advantage will be illusory.

REFERENCES

Abernathy, W. and Clark, K. (1985) 'Innovation: mapping the winds of creative destruction', *Research Policy*, 14, 3–22.

Arlin, P. (1990) 'Wisdom: the art of problem finding' in Sternberg, R. *Wisdom: its Nature, Origins, and Development.* Cambridge: Cambridge University Press.

Boisot, M. (1986) 'Markets and Hierarchies in a Cultural Perspective', *Organization Studies*, 7(2), 135–58.
Burgelman, R. (1985) 'Managing the New Venture Division: research findings and implications for strategic management', *Strategic Management Journal*, 6(1), 39–54.
Clark, K. (1987) 'Investment in New Technology and Competitive Advantage', in Teece, D. (ed.), *The Competitive Challenge*. Cambridge, Mass.: Ballinger.
Cooper, A. and Schendel, D. (1976) 'Strategic Responses to Technological Threats', *Business Horizons*, Feb., 61–79.
Dodgson, M. (1993) 'Organizational Learning: a review of some literatures', *Organization Studies*, 14(3), 375–94.
Dosi, G. (1984) *Technological Change and Industrial Transformation: the theory and an application to the semiconductor industry*. London: Macmillan.
Fiol, C. and Lyles, M. (1985) 'Organizational Learning', *Academy of Management Review*, 10(4), 803–13.
Graham, M. (1988) *The Business of Research: RCA and the Videodisc*. Cambridge: Cambridge University Press.
Grindley, P. (1991) 'Turning Technology into Competitive Advantage', *Business Strategy Review*, Spring, 35–48.
Henderson, R. and Clark, K. (1990) 'Architectural Innovation: the reconfiguration of existing product technologies and the failure of established firms', *Administrative Science Quarterly*, 35, 9–30.
Jones, O., Green, K. and Coombs, R. (1994) 'Technology Management: developing a critical perspective', *International Journal of Technology Management*, 9(2), 156–71.
Kay, J. (1993) *Foundations of Corporate Success: how business strategies add value*. Oxford: Oxford University Press.
Kolb, D., Lublin, S., Spoth, J. and Baker, R. (1986) 'Strategic Management Development: experiential learning and managerial competencies', *Journal of Management Development*, 3(5), 13–24.
Leonard-Barton, D. (1992) 'Core Capabilities and Core Rigidities: a paradox in managing new product development', *Strategic Management Journal*, 13, 111–25.
Loveridge, R. (1990) 'Incremental Innovation and Appropriative Learning Styles in Direct Services', in Loveridge, R. and Pitt, M. (eds) *The Strategic Management of Technological Innovation*. Chichester: Wiley.
Mulder, K. and Vergragt, P. (1990) 'Synthetic Fibre Technology and Company Strategy', *R&D Management*, 20(3), 247–56.
Nelson, R. and Winter, S. (1982) *An Evolutionary Theory of Economic Change*. Cambridge, Mass.: Belknap Press of Harvard University.
Nonaka, I. (1991) 'The Knowledge-Creating Company', *Harvard Business Review*, Nov.–Dec., 96–104.
Orr, J. (1990) 'Sharing Knowledge, Celebrating Identity: community memory in a service culture', in Middleton, D. and Edwards, E. (eds) *Collective Remembering*. Newbury Park: Sage.
Pavitt, K. (1986) 'Technology, Innovation and Strategic Management', in McGee, J. and Thomas, H. (eds) *Strategic Management Research: a European perspective*. Chichester: Wiley.
Pennings, J., Barkema, H. and Douma, S. (1994) 'Organizational Learning and Diversification', *Academy of Management Journal*, 37(3), 608–40.
Peters, T. and Waterman, R. (1982) *In Search of Excellence*. New York: Harper and Row.

Porter, M. (1990) *The Competitive Advantage of Nations*. New York: Free Press.
Prahalad, C. and Hamel, G. (1990) 'The Core Competence of the Corporation', *Harvard Business Review*, May–June, 79–91.
Quinn, J. (1979) 'Technological Innovation, Entrepreneurship and Strategy', *Sloan Management Review*, 20(3), Spring.
Quinn, J. (1985) 'Managing Innovation: controlled chaos', *Harvard Business Review*, May–June, 73–84.
Rosenfeld, R. and Servo, J. (1990) 'Facilitating Innovation in Large Organizations', in West, M. and Farr, J. (eds) *Innovation and Creativity at Work*. Chichester: Wiley.
Schon, D. (1983) *The Reflective Practitioner*. New York: Basic Books.
Spender, J.-C. (1993) 'Competitive Advantage from Tacit Knowledge: unpacking the concept and its strategic implications', *American Academy of Management Best Paper Proceedings*, 37–41.
Spender, J.-C. (1994) 'Knowing, Managing and Learning: a dynamic, managerial epistemology', *Management Learning*, 25(3), 387–412.
Teece, D. (1986) 'Profiting from Technological Innovation: implications for integration, collaboration, licensing and public policy', *Research Policy*, 15, 285–305.
Teece, D., Pisano, G. and Shuen, A. (1992) 'Dynamic Capabilities and Strategic Management', Unpublished Working Paper, University of California at Berkeley.
Tushman, M. and Anderson, P. (1986) 'Technological Discontinuities and Organisational Environments', *Administrative Science Quarterly*, 31, 439–65.
Utterback, J. and Abernathy, W. (1978) 'Patterns of Industrial Innovation', *Technology Review*, 7, 41–7.
Whipp, R. and Clark, P. (1986) *Innovation and the Auto Industry: product, process and work organization*. London: Pinter.
Winter, S. (1987) 'Knowledge and Competence as Strategic Assets', in Teece, D. (ed.) *The Competitive Challenge*. Cambridge, Mass.: Ballinger, 157–84.

3

THE ROLE OF COMPLEMENTARY ASSETS IN TECHNOLOGY STRATEGY

Julian Lowe and Peter Taylor

Technology strategy is defined as the acquisition, management and exploitation of knowledge in the firm. We examine here the alternative routes (make v. buy) in the acquisition of technology and know-how and the role played by the existing asset base of the firm in choosing appropriate strategies and determining successful outcomes.

Technology licensing and in-house R&D are viewed in this chapter as the 'buy or make' decisions. Whilst technology licensing is strictly concerned with trade in technology, it is also usually the basis of a wider technological collaboration, which underpins broader alliances between organizations (Lowe and Crawford, 1984; Lowe and Atkins, 1991). However, the extent to which firms see the internal and external acquisition of knowledge as alternatives and the extent to which they are complementary strategies seem to vary across industries and by type of firm. Lowe and Atkins (1991), for instance, found a close correlation between firms purchasing and selling technology, whilst most research studies have identified the technology and industry specific nature of licensing markets (Teece, 1977; Atuahene-Gima and Patterson, 1993).

The main research question this chapter seeks to answer is how important are technological and non-technological capabilities in the effective choice and implementation of technology strategy. Primary and secondary data collected from a sample of 128 UK manufacturing firms is used to examine some key research propositions derived from the technology strategy paradigm.

The significance of this research lies both in the private and public domain. The impact of a firm's heritage and its stock of technological and non-technological assets on its ability to absorb and appropriate the profits from externally purchased knowledge is of clear interest to public sector initiatives designed to improve local and regional economic development. In addition, it is of obvious benefit to firms seeking to improve performance through an optimum fine tuning of their technology policies.

TECHNOLOGY ACQUISITION THROUGH LICENSE AGREEMENTS

What is licensing and why do firms license?

Licensing is the acquisition, by contract, of product or process technology, designs and possibly marketing expertise. In the context of new product development, it is part of a spectrum which starts with franchising and agency agreements, where the most that is done is a re-badging of a product, continues through assembly from bought-in components, and through to complete manufacture in-house. Ultimately it may result in the development of technology that effectively creates a new range of improved and different products and processes.

Licensing may involve a fee, a royalty as a proportion of sales, or a reciprocal flow of rights and knowledge, and the commitment to obligations by both parties to maintain an agreement over a specified period of time. Whilst the term licensing was originally used for the sale of patent rights, its usage is now more widespread and encompasses the whole range of intellectual property, the rights of which may be established by statute, by common law, or by some form of secrecy and confidentiality agreement.

Licensing effectively separates acquisition and exploitation activities from those concerned with the management and development of the technology, and so has been viewed by strategists either in the context of the firm's strategic focus, or in the context of the individual costs and benefits associated with its implementation. The strategic focus can be considered at the business, corporate and collective levels. At the business level a deepening of competitive advantage is required, at the corporate level the focus is to capitalize on synergy, and at the collective level, technology collaboration helps broaden and form networks and alliances.

A firm may choose to acquire technology, through licensing, for a number of short-run tactical and strategic reasons. Licensing provides a quick way to acquire new technology (Mahajan and Wind, 1988; Lieberman and Montgomery, 1988) although Mansfield (1985) has estimated that the costs of development through imitation and technology transfer can still be substantial. Licensing also allows a firm to 'unlock' the potential of its in-house research through the availability of complementary technology or products (Crawford, 1985; Svenson, 1984) and to develop new strategic directions and partnerships. The acquisition of an industry standard and as a complement to unlock existing technology

(Lowe and Crawford, 1984) are also important strategic levers for the use of licensing.

Typically the use of licensing to acquire technology has been contingent on certain firm-, technology- and industry-specific factors. Obvious issues at the firm level concern the extent of the 'NIH syndrome' (Ford, 1988), prior licensing experience (Lowe and Crawford, 1984) and the existing asset base (Cohen and Levinthal, 1994). At the industry level, the oligopolistic nature of the market has been identified as a driver of licensing (with licensing effectively facilitating wider alliances), whilst industry and technological maturity might influence the extent of licensing (Porter, 1985). At the technology level, the transferability of the knowledge and intellectual property will limit the extensiveness of licensing (Pavitt, 1991). In pharmaceuticals and chemicals, for instance, the nature of knowledge may relate and be described easily by formulae and blueprints, whilst in other sectors, e.g. mechanical engineering, key aspects of knowledge may include shop floor know-how and firm-specific factors which are difficult to transfer (Teece, 1977). The extent to which the overall technology package embraces this tacit knowledge may exacerbate the transfer process, particularly if there are asymmetries in the stock of knowledge or know-how.

A contingency approach is necessary if we are to identify the key determinants of technology acquisition through licensing. The firm/organization, technology, industry and sometimes the individual manager will drive acquisition strategies. However, whilst a contingency approach suggests a complicated framework, some specific relationships do emerge that can be examined through reasonably large data sets.

Some basic propositions

An examination of the impact of complementary assets on the technology strategy of the firm can be undertaken only within the context of the choice between in-house development and the external acquisition of technology.

The initial thread of this investigation is the extent to which licensing is a way of acquiring technological assets. *A priori* it might be expected that weakness in research increases the probability of a firm acquiring technology through licensing. In addition, the level of competition and perceived risk in the market might influence the use of licensing. In oligopolistic markets licensing can be used as a basis for strategic alliances and collusive agreements, while in dynamic markets the drive to keep ahead or catch up might increase the use of licensing. This leads to competing propositions concerning the impact of competition on licensing. Finally we also conclude that via the 'NIH' syndrome an inward-looking orientation and conservative hierarchy might also be expected to reduce the likelihood of technology acquisition through licensing.

So far we have ignored other 'non-R&D' assets. We need now consider how these might influence the relationships we have identified. Teece (1986) identified the important role of complementary assets in determining the pathways firms might take in the exploitation of their knowledge. A firm in possession of these assets, such as marketing channels, manufacturing capability, brand image and market power, can use these to ensure that it appropriates the benefits of its intellectual property and other rights. Thus in the pharmaceutical industry, Swann and Gill (1993) explain the success of small biotechnology firms in the diagnostics sectors compared to the therapeutics sector, in terms of the lower entry barriers and reduced requirements for complementary assets in manufacturing and regulatory access.

Complementary assets have value when they are associated with differentiated skills and routines that provide the basis of a firm's competitive advantage. Their value is intimately linked to the way in which a firm competes, and thus they provide the basis for competition in an industry. The significance of these assets, in the context of technology strategy, is that they need to be nurtured in order to assist in the appropriation of other technological assets.

Complementary assets constrain the exploitation of technology in exactly the same way that path dependencies do. The success of an in-house innovation is likely to be higher only if it is closely related to previous technology and to the assets that support it. Licensing may in fact bring in assets other than technology and design; most studies suggest that only about 30 per cent of royalty payments are for technology, the rest being for manufacturing, marketing and engineering support. Nevertheless, we would expect that the existence of complementary assets would play an important role in determining both in-house R&D investment and technology acquisition through licensing. In particular their role in the appropriation of profits from technology might mean that not only should we expect them to be positively related to licensing as a source of technology acquisition but we might also expect that non-technological complementary assets may be potentially more important as determinants of licensing than weakness in R&D.

RESEARCH DESIGN AND METHODOLOGY

Our research design was based on a number of premises which related to the theoretical and empirical determinants of make v. buy decisions. Firstly, it was necessary to have a sample of firms across a spectrum of licensing use – including not licensing. Secondly, these should be from industries with different technological environments. Thirdly, the sample would require firms of different sizes and operating in different market structures.

Data need to be comparable across firms in very different environments, and whilst the extent to which firms license is quantified cardinally, most of the data collection follows the approach of Reid and Reid (1988) and Atuahene-Gima and Patterson (1993) and is based on ordinal measurement. Thus the motivations underpinning licensing, the competitive environment and relative strength in complementary assets are measured using Likert scales of an individual firm's perceptions. For strategic decisions these perceptions might be more appropriate than other cardinal data (e.g. numbers of firms in an industry, number of sales personnel) because they can be measured in terms of the respondents' perceptions of their *relative* position in their product/markets. Such an approach is well founded in strategy research with its roots in the early work of Bourgeois (1980).

The bulk of the data was collected by a questionnaire, which followed an initial letter identifying the parameters of the population. Just over 300 questionnaires were distributed and 128 were returned. This represented an excellent response rate but was of course part of an earlier survey which had already filtered out many potential non-respondents.

The questionnaires contained large blocks of questions on:

- the extent of licensing
- strategic motivations
- perceived costs and benefits
- perceived competitive position
- relative strength of technological assets
- relative strength of non-technological assets
- contextual and descriptive factors (identify, size of firm, etc.)

Where there were large groupings of questions, factor analysis was used to distil the key factors. Generally, these matched with our *a priori* expectations. The research proceeded using logistical regression to analyse the impact of the motivation, the asset base and the contextual factors on the extensiveness of licensing. This latter was reduced to a dichotomous variable to indicate whether licensing was an extensive or minor (including zero) component of technology strategy.

Firms were asked what proportion of their previous year's sales turnover was derived from licensed-in products or processes. The lowest category was less than 1 per cent which was felt to be so low that the firm could hardly be considered to have a policy of inward licensing. Thus the sample was split into firms for which inward licensing supported more than 1 per cent of turnover (LICPOL = 1), and those for which it was less than 1 per cent or none at all, i.e. solely in-house R&D (LICPOL = 0). The dummy variable LICPOL thus indicated the extensiveness of licensing and so could be used as the dependent variable in logistical regression models that were subsequently estimated.

The sample had a very large proportion of firms supplying the Ministry of Defence (24/128) of which 14 undertook no licensing at all. The sample was collected both for this and another study which was to examine whether firms faced with a rapid decline in their core market could use licensing to assist in diversification. The 'defence' companies tended to be smaller and licence less than the rest. Although for many of the questions there appeared to be little significant difference, the difference in licensing behaviour between the two sectors warranted further analysis.

A logistical regression model was estimated to investigate the relationship between size and LICPOL using the number of employees and the number of employees squared as independent variables. This was significant at the 4.4 per cent level. DEFENCE, a 0,1 dummy variable denoting whether the firm was a Ministry of Defence supplier and DEFENCE slope dummy variables for both of the employee variables were then added to the model. These significantly improved the model at the 2.5 per cent level. Cross-tabulations indicated that licensing was related to firm size for the non-defence sector firm. Thus larger non-defence sector firms were likely to license more than smaller firms; firms in the defence sector, whatever their size, were likely to licence less. Although size and sector could be used as predictors of licensing, the purpose of the analysis was to investigate more fundamental relationships. An additional problem was that size and sector were found to be associated with some of the variables used in the explanatory models. Their inclusion as conditioning variables in the models would, therefore, be likely to confound the effects of the explanatory variables. As a result, a second stage was added to each of the explanatory models, in which the dummy variable DEFENCE was added to the basic model. This would condition not only for sectoral effects, but, implicitly, also for size effects. Its explanatory power and effects on the estimated coefficients of the other variables were noted, and the significance level for the change in model χ^2 is reported in the tables for each model.

There were a very large number of questions in the questionnaire which were arranged in blocks according to particular topics, and most of the questions were presented for response on a seven-point Likert scale. Factor analysis was used on each block of questions to examine the underlying dimensions. The dimensions derived from the data generally confirmed *a priori* concepts, and so were used to group sets of questions into composite variables. The composite variables were constructed by the simple addition of the individual scales of each of the variables in the group. These composite variables, and not the factor scores, were then used as independent variables in the logistical regression analyses. The one or two dimensions that did not confirm *a priori* concepts were not used as the basis of composite variables.

THE RESULTS

The main propositions identified earlier were that weakness in research *increases* the probability of licensing, and conservative firm orientations *reduce* the likelihood of licensing. Competition in product and factor markets may influence licensing but this would depend on market structure and market dynamics. Finally, strength in non-technological assets may be posited to *increase* the probability of licensing strategies; this proposition being the one dealing centrally with the complementary assets issue.

The results of our analyses are described in Tables 3.1–3.3 which summarize different models used to examine the above propositions. Model I examines the impact of competition; model II the impact of firm organization and culture; model III the impact of research strength/weakness, to which non-technological complementary assets are added in model IV. Model V is the same as model IV but with the addition of the defence sector dummy variable. Table 3.3 is a summary of whether the addition of complementary assets to the earlier models significantly increases the explanatory power of those models.

Model I in Table 3.1 investigates the effects of competition on inward licensing, which was measured using six questions that approximated to Porter's five forces model (Porter, 1985). Only the variable COMPET (competitive environment) has any notable statistical significance (5.5 per cent) and seems to refute the proposition regarding oligopoly. It is composed of rivalry within the industry, buyer power and supplier power. The addition of the DEFENCE dummy variable has a very significant effect on the overall explanatory power of the model, but reduces the statistical significance of COMPET to 10 per cent. The addition of the firm size variables, instead of DEFENCE, had little effect on the significance of COMPET (5.8 per cent instead of 5.5 per cent).

In addition, although firm size may sometimes be used as a proxy for competitive pressure, it was unlikely to be of such use here as the firms in the sample generally did not operate in the same markets, and the DEFENCE firms were significantly smaller than the rest of the sample which would confound the effects.

As the DEFENCE dummy variable is such a blunt instrument and implicitly includes characteristics of the competitive conditions, which probably differ between the two industrial sectors, its effect of reducing the significance of COMPET is to be expected. It is therefore reasonable to conclude that firms that face horizontal and vertical competitive pressures are less likely to undertake inward licensing. Although the

Table 3.1 Competition and internal organization: estimated coefficients of logistical regression models

Independent variables	*Model*	
	I	*II*
COMPET	−0.0977	—
	(.055)	
POTENT	0.0752	—
	(.248)	
FOREIGN	0.0756	—
	(.491)	
CONSV	—	−0.0502
		(.319)
OUTGO	—	(0.0451
		(.280)
OFFERSIN	—	0.2086
		(.044)
CONSTANT	0.3321	−0.8972
	(.721)	(.301)
Model χ^2	4.887	8.531
Degrees of freedom	3	3
Significance level	0.1802	0.0362
Correct predictions (0)	57.38%	60.66%
Correct predictions (1)	52.38%	60.66%
Number of observations	124	119
Significance level for change in model χ^2 when DEFENCE added	0.0187	0.0389

Notes: Dependent variable: LICPOL
Figures in parentheses are probability levels at which coefficients become significant

sample was constructed of firms that operated generally in dynamic markets and were not oligopolists, the results do not support the proposition that licensing is a way of keeping up with the competition. In addition there is no evidence of potential competition or competition from overseas having an effect on licensing behaviour.

Model II in Table 3.1 analyses policy and cultural aspects of the internal structure of the firm, rather than the structure itself. Models containing variables that indicated the formality of the internal structure and degree of staff empowerment were estimated earlier, but had poor overall explanatory power, and so structure, *per se*, does not seem to be important. In model II CONSV is a composite variable measuring the degree to which the firm is conservative relative to the rest of the industry in which it is located, while OUTGO measures the degree to which the firm is involved in outward going activities, such as joint ventures and overseas distribution agreements, and scanning of the external environment. Originally, OUTGO had included the scale for a question about receiving unsolicited offers for inward technology licensing, but this appears to have been the main reason for OUTGO being statistically significant in the models tested. In model II this question is included as a separate variable, OFFERSIN. The signs of the estimated coefficients of CONSV and OUTGO are as we would expect but both have very poor levels of statistical significance, which reinforce the earlier results relating to internal organization. The estimated coefficient of OFFERSIN is both positive and significant at the 4.4 per cent level. This could indicate an information problem whereby potential licensees do not become actual licensees because they lack the necessary information. Licensers would, therefore, be missing opportunities by not sending unsolicited offers to firms not already undertaking licensing. Alternatively, licensers may be very efficient when targeting such offers and so send only to firms that they recognize are likely to undertake inward licensing. Either way, there is no evidence that this is a matter of internal organization.

A subsequent regression which excluded OFFERSIN was significant at the 10.57 per cent level and OUTGO became significant at the 7 per cent level. All in all, there is little evidence that internal structure or conservative orientation have any influence on licensing policy but that an outward cultural orientation and the existence of alliance-type agreements are associated with inward licensing activity. Although the addition of DEFENCE improved the model's explanatory power at the 3.62 per cent level, the significance levels of the other independent variables did not change much.

Model III in Table 3.2 addresses the proposition regarding weakness in research. Initially a single composite variable was used to measure research capability, but this had a very low level of significance. The variable was made up of questions relating to research skill, research personnel and patents.

Patents seemed different in kind to the other two strengths as it represented not only research capability, but also a stock that was easily tradeable, and experience in technology transfer, which was likely to include outward technology licensing. The result of making strength in patents separate from strength in research skills and research personnel was to make the explanatory power of the model significant at the 8 per cent level. The negative sign of R&D confirms the weakness in R&D (skills and personnel) proposition at the 8.6 per cent level. The fact that PATENTS has a positive sign and is significant at the 3.6 per cent level lends weight to the idea that skill in technology transfer is an important capability. For this model the addition of DEFENCE not only improved the explanatory power of the model, but also improved the significance levels of R&D (6.8 per cent) and PATENTS (3 per cent).

In model IV the complementary assets necessary to exploit the attributes of the licence are added to model III. The complementary asset

Table 3.2 R&D and complementary assets: estimated coefficients of logistical regression models

Independent variables	*Model* *III*	*IV*	*V*
MKTING	—	0.0875	0.0958
		(.106)	(.097)
MANUF	—	−0.1883	−0.190
		(.014)	(.018)
WIDTH	—	0.0534	0.1110
		(.581)	(.280)
SUPNET	—	0.2836	0.3452
		(.170)	(.104)
DISTNET	—	−0.2830	−0.3793
		(.144)	(.0613)
R&D	−0.1564	−0.0739	−0.1145
	(.086)	(.505)	(.326)
PATENTS	0.2871	0.2761	0.3038
	(.036)	(.068)	(.060)
DEFENCE	—	—	−1.4131
			(.017)
CONSTANT	0.3535	−0.4002	−0.4228
	(.622)	(.783)	(.784)
Model χ^2	5.085	13.805	20.148
Degrees of freedom	2	7	8
Significance level	0.0787	0.0548	0.0098
Correct predictions (0)	51.67%	60.38%	67.92%
Correct predictions (1)	63.33%	64.15%	66.04%
Number of observations	120	106	106
Significance level for change in model χ^2 when DEFENCE added	0.0128	0.0118	—

Notes: Dependent variable: LICPOL
Figures in parentheses are probability levels at which coefficients become significant

variables were created from a series of fifteen questions relating to the firm's strengths and weaknesses. The groupings were confirmed by factor analysis. One of the original variables, NET, signifying the firm's supplier and distribution networks, had very poor explanatory power. However, when split into SUPNET and DISTNET respectively, the two variables not only had much better significance levels, but also had opposite signs. This was rather unexpected, especially as the two variables were positively correlated with each other. An explanation could be that inward licensing may be a way in which a firm can exploit its supply chain if it has a weakness upstream, as licensing may bring marketing and other upstream support. This interpretation is supported by the fact that in both models IV and V the two variables not only have opposite signs but are also very close to each other in terms of magnitude. This implies that equal strength in supplier and distribution networks has a neutral effect on licensing behaviour.

The signs and significance of the other coefficients have intuitive appeal. Manufacturing strength has a negative sign and is highly significant, in fact it is the most significant coefficient. Thus a weakness in manufacturing is associated with a higher level of licensing behaviour, presumably the licensing of manufacturing processes. Strength in marketing is positively associated with licensing at the 10 per cent level, presumably product licensing. The variable WIDTH measures the width of the product line and breadth of market coverage. Its sign is positive as expected, but it has a very poor level of significance.

It can be seen that the significance level for R&D weakness in model IV is very much lower than in model III. This is probably due to correlation between R&D and the five complementary asset variables added in model IV. R&D was significantly correlated with MANUF, WIDTH and PATENTS. The addition of DEFENCE to model IV has a significant impact, and the full results of the augmented model are presented as model V. The effect is to improve the significance levels of all the independent variables, except for MANUF, which is still significant at the 2 per cent level. We can conclude that the proposition that weakness in research acts as a spur to inward licensing is sustained by our results, and that complementary assets, including the ability to manage the activity of technology transfer, are important in determining the use of licensing.

In order to analyse the proposition that strength in non-technological assets may increase the probability of adopting a licensing strategy, models I–III were augmented with the complementary asset variables, as were models based on size and defence. This essentially involved adding model IV to each of the other models, and testing whether the χ^2 statistic improved significantly. Table 3.3 shows the probability level of the improvement in the χ^2 for each of the augmented models. Although it may be argued that we have only five complementary asset variables as regards the exploitation of technology, the PATENTS variable, as discussed above, indicates the firm's ability to manage technology transfer. Thus PATENTS can be considered to indicate a complementary asset for the successful use of licensing. In addition, the R&D variable also has to be included with the complementary assets variables, either because it represents the level of technology that licensing can supplement (providing complementary assets exist in sufficient quantities), or because it may itself be considered to be a complementary asset (in a looser conceptual framework than that put forward by Teece (1986)).

Above, it was concluded from model I that competitive pressures seemed to have had the effect of reducing the use of licensing. The augmentation of model I with the seven complementary asset variables

Table 3.3 Probability levels for the change in the χ^2 statistic when complementary asset variables are added to the main models

Model I	0.0539
Model II	0.0679
Model III	0.0533
Model III & DEFENCE	0.0258
Size, size-squared	0.0078
DEFENCE	0.0241
(Model IV	0.0548)

Note: Model III and model III & DEFENCE have only five complementary asset variables added as model III is composed of two of the complementary asset variables. All the other equations are augmented with the full seven complementary asset variables.

indicates that the additional effect of complementary assets is significant at the 5.4 per cent level. Thus complementary assets increase the use of licensing strategies even in the presence of competitive pressures, which would otherwise reduce it. The augmentation of model II is also significant, but only at the 7 per cent level. This indicates that although the openness of the firm to unsolicited licensing offers and an outward orientation were important, complementary assets were also necessary. In the cases of model III and model III with the DEFENCE dummy variable, only five complementary asset variables were used as two were already present. Again, the complementary asset variables made a significant improvement to both of these models.

In addition to the main models, the model that had been used to investigate the relationship between licensing and the size of the firm in terms of employees (a quadratic function) was also augmented. The augmentation was significant at the 1 per cent level. This may indicate that it is not only the *existence* of complementary assets that is important, but also the *amount* of complementary assets. Further analysis would be necessary to determine this. Finally, a model that simply had the DEFENCE dummy as the independent variable was augmented. Complementary assets improved this at the 2.5 per cent level.

Thus we can conclude that complementary assets are very important not only in the successful use of licensing to overcome a weakness in R&D and indeed are likely to be necessary, but also when other causes of licensing behaviour are present. The existence of complementary assets would seem to enhance the likelihood of licensing behaviour even though competitive pressures were reducing it. We also find that complementary assets enhance the probability of licensing for firms with an outgoing orientation. Complementary assets would also seem to enhance the likelihood of licensing that is related to firm size or industry sector.

CONCLUSION

This chapter has assessed the nature of 'make v. buy' decisions in a technology context. Whilst policy and external conditions can be seen as important determinants of licensing, it is also possible that technology markets exert their own important endogenous influence on whether a firm licenses. However, the initial focus of this chapter was to examine whether competition, weakness in research and cultural influences within the firm might influence the use of licensing as a strategy. There was some support for these factors influencing licensing in this study.

The role of complementary assets in technology strategy has been identified as an emergent and important theme in the research literature. Our research gives strong support to these effects. For inward licensing to be an effective strategy in the development of new products and processes, it seems to be important for there to be complementary assets which can assist the licensee in the transfer of technology and its effective appropriation. These assets effectively 'drive' policy towards technology acquisition as firms recognize, through experience, their importance in the exploitation of intellectual property. A focus on this and the whole issue of the absorptive capacity of organizations is clearly an important area for future research.

REFERENCES

Atuahene-Gima, K. and Patterson, P. (1993) 'Managerial Perceptions of Technology Licensing as an Alternative to Internal R&D in New Product Development: An Empirical Investigation', *R&D Management* 23 (4), pp. 327–336

Bourgeois, L.J. (1980) 'Strategy and Environment: A Comparative Integration', *Academy of Management Review* vol. 5, pp. 25–39

Cohen, W.M. and Levinthal, D.A. (1994) 'Fortune Favours the Prepared Firm', *Management Science*, vol. 40(2), pp. 227–251

Crawford, N.C. (1985) 'Small Firm Technology Licensing', unpublished Ph.D. thesis, University of Bath

Ford, I.D. (1988) 'Develop Your Technology Strategy', *Long Range Planning*, vol. 21(5)

Jordan, J. and Lowe, J. (1995) 'Innovation and Technology Acquisition: Characteristics of Strategic Decisions', *Discussion Papers in Business and Management*, Bristol Business School, UWE (Bristol)

Koberg, C.S. (1987) 'Resource Scarcity, Environmental Uncertainty and Adaptive Organisation Behaviour', *Academy of Management Journal*, vol. 30(4), pp. 798–807

Lieberman, M. and Montgomery, D. (1988) 'First Mover Advantage', *Strategic Management Journal*, vol. 9, pp. 41–58

Lowe, J. and Atkins, M. (1991) 'Australian, US and UK Technology Transactions', *Prometheus*, vol. 9(1), pp. 138–146

Lowe, J. and Crawford, N. (1984) *Innovation and Technology Transfer for the Growing Firm*, Oxford: Pergamon Press

Mahajan, V. and Wind, Y. (1988) 'New Product Development Processes: A

Perspective for Re-examination', *Journal of Product Innovation and Management*, vol. 5, pp. 304–310

Mansfield, E. (1985) 'How Rapidly does New Industrial Technology Leak Out?', *Journal of Industrial Economics*, December, vol. XXXIV(2), pp. 217–223

Pavitt, K. (1991) 'Key Characteristics of the Innovating Firm', *British Journal of Management*, vol. 2, pp. 41–50

Porter, M.E. (1985) *Competitive Advantage*, New York: Free Press

Reid, S.D. and Reid, L. (1988) 'Public Policy and Promoting Manufacturing under Licence', *Technovation*, vol. 7, pp. 401–414

Svenson, B. (1984) 'Acquisition of Technology through Licensing in Small Firms', unpublished Ph.D. thesis, Linkoping University

Swann, P. and Gill, J. (1993) *Corporate Vision and Rapid Technological Change: The Evolution of Market Structure*, London: Routledge

Teece, D. (1977) 'Technology Transfer by International Firms: The Resource Cost of Transferring Technological Know-How', *Economic Journal*, vol. 87, pp. 242–261

Teece, D. (1986) 'Profiting from Technological Innovation: Implications for Integration, Collaboration, Licensing and Public Policy', *Research Policy*, vol. 15, pp. 285–305

4

R&D STRATEGY AND THE IMPLICATIONS FOR MANAGEMENT CONTROL[1]

Keith Randle and Frank Currie

The impact of the new biotechnologies upon the developed economies is likely to be substantial. Technological change of such magnitude will redefine industrial structures, creating and destroying jobs in the process. In time new industries may emerge, whereas major existing sectors will have to adapt. The particular interest of this chapter is the effect these radical technologies will have upon the structure of the pharmaceutical industry and specifically the way that research is organized therein. However, whether advantage is gained through the organization of research depends upon what impact choices about this have on the research scientists themselves. How scientists are managed thus represents a further concern. Both are vital and necessarily interrelated in delivering successful, innovative products for the firm.

The pharmaceutical industry is highly profitable. It is argued that this is a result of its innovative record which is founded upon considerable spending on R&D. The latter, it is also suggested, is reliant upon these high profit levels to provide both the requisite funding and appropriate incentives. It is the case that bringing a drug to the market is an expensive[2] and uncertain activity. Anything which promises to alleviate these factors can expect a welcome embrace from the industry. The new biotechnologies offer this potential through enabling a more rational approach to drug discovery and development.

However, the key repositories of these biotechnology skills are the universities and the small, new biotechnology firms (NBFs) (Kenney 1986). These must, therefore, be engaged in some way by the established pharmaceutical firms if the latter are to access such expertise. What is more, it is posited by della Valle and Gambardella (1993) that such relationships should generally not take the form of integration as this would strangle the creativity of the NBF. In fact, these authors suggest that a division of labour in innovative activity is opening up in this area.

Implicit in this suggestion is that NBFs enjoy a comparative advantage in terms of rational drug discovery, perhaps because they possess the skills and, being small, are more creative than their large counterparts. Skills apart, creativity presumably derives from flexible organizations with good communication. Both are more likely with the small firm rather than the large with its inevitable bureaucracy. Further, the incentive structure is likely to be more conducive within the small firm.

The large, incumbent firms, however, are still advantageously positioned with respect to the assets and resources required for the commercialization of viable potential drugs. As well as deep pockets, this process requires expertise and capabilities in development and, further down the line, marketing and distribution: all of which will have been accumulated over many years. The upshot, for della Valle and Gambardella (1993), is that the generation of new chemical entities is a task more efficiently undertaken by the NBFs, whereas the subsequent commercialization is more effectively undertaken by the established pharmaceutical giants.

This vision would seem to imply a fairly simple conception of the innovatory process, where 'upstream' and 'downstream' research activities can be readily separated and effectively conducted by independent organizations. It suggests something akin to a linear model of innovation. Such a simplistic view of innovation ceased to enjoy currency in the literature some time ago.[3] More plausible models of this process tend to be concerned with its complexity and uncertainty and the need for continual interaction.

Within the context of a large firm, the division of labour described above offers clear guidelines as to, generally, which activities are best conducted in-house and which are best conducted externally. Following on from this we could expect to read off the appropriate strategies for the management of the research process within the company. Once the 'creative' element of research has been hived off into small, flexible organizations subject to loose control, the more routine, downstream research can be managed using tighter forms of control to assure rapid progress towards the market.

Employing an interdisciplinary approach which draws from economics and the behavioural sciences, this chapter disputes the validity of both the theoretical and empirical foundations for this argument. Firstly, we suggest that the research process is highly interactive and complex. This is inconsistent with such a deterministic, prescriptive managerial strategy. Indeed, no generic strategy implications are obvious. Secondly, the dilemma posed by trying to elicit creativity while maintaining control cannot be resolved by such a managerial strategy. Both arguments are further supported by the empirical evidence from Glaxo Research and Development (GRD).

The chapter begins by providing a fairly detailed consideration of the nature of the innovatory process and the implications this has for the organization of research. Next, we look at the management of research within GRD and the role of their external links. Our conclusions are then presented.

THE INNOVATORY PROCESS

The notion of a division of labour driven by specialization according to the theory of comparative advantage is 'one of the most venerable concepts in the intellectual history of economics' (Arora and Gambardella 1993: 1) and, as such, is an attractive one for the economist. Of course, it also permits a fairly simple and deterministic framework to be applied to the organization of the activity in question, and it would appear to be a relatively straightforward matter to test.

The feasibility of a division of labour in the research process would seem to imply a series of readily identifiable tasks which mesh together fairly easily. The 'deconstruction' of research is thus enabled with the various activities being assigned to those agents who can undertake them most efficiently. The communication and aggregation of all the results from these different sources must, we suggest, be unproblematic for such an approach to be tenable. The conception of the innovatory process which is implied by these remarks is the linear model. Figure 4.1 represents this approach.

This model postulates a sequential and reductionist process. More recent approaches present a more plausible conception of the innovatory process, viewing it as a wide and complex phenomenon. Comparatively, such approaches can be depicted as being parallel models in that the essential, pervasive role of feedback is emphasized. So, for instance, development does not exclusively flow from applied research in any straightforward manner but rather basic research may flow from development. Also, the scope of innovatory activity has to be seen as wider than simply what is conventionally perceived as R&D. Innovation does not cease with the introduction of a novel product. Further innovations are likely to be spurred by, *inter alia*, interactions with users and experience of production. Thus, Anderson and Braendgaard (1992: 253) comment, 'The process of innovation-diffusion is just as much a process of innovation as a process of diffusion.'

The complexity of a plausible model can be demonstrated with

basic research ⟶ discovery/invention ⟶ applied research ⟶ development ⟶ innovative product

Figure 4.1 A linear model of innovation

reference to the linear schema illustrated in Figure 4.1. This does highlight some of the key elements of the process but as what is involved at each stage is 'fleshed-out' the crudeness of abstraction becomes clear. First, while ideas may act as the inspiration which stimulates basic research, they can also usefully occur at, and impact upon, any stage of the innovatory process. The pool of potential ideas is, of course, infinite although the ability of different individuals or firms to tap into this pool will be variable.[4] Only ideas which satisfy the relevant selection criteria will therefore be pursued further. There will be a variety of such selection devices involved at each and every stage, from individuals considering the worth of an idea to consumers actively buying (or not) the relevant products. It should immediately be clear, therefore, that the linear depiction presents one specific sequential example of the innovatory process but in no way is this a general representation. As Professor Rod Coombs pointed out to us:[5] if the linear model was ever relevant, it was in the pharmaceutical industry. In a comparative sense at least, there is something to this. However, we should note that the impact of biotechnology would be to erode this linearity. In terms of della Valle and Gambardella's thesis, such a division of labour between firms should now be less likely, therefore two-way arrows ought to run from idea to every other element in the schema. The same could be said for the other elements and their interaction. To an extent, and this may differ among industries and technologies, a parallel process is suggested.[6] Thus, Kline and Rosenberg (1986), acknowledging this interactive complexity, suggest the 'chain-linked model' of innovation (Figure 4.2).

Understandably, in the literature, the respectability of the linear model has been stripped away. Jorde and Teece (1988: 9) provide an apposite summing-up, arguing that, 'Innovation is an interactive and reiterative, interdependent process in which design, manufacturing, and product development all drive and, at the same time, are highly dependent on research.'

This discussion would seem to be fairly damaging to della Valle and Gambardella (1993), however, to be fair, their discussion does attempt a more sophisticated view of the innovatory process. Further, they make reference to and align themselves with the earlier related work of Arora and Gambardella (1993). It is useful, therefore, to consider the argument presented in Arora and Gambardella for it is consonant with the approach of della Valle and Gambardella, in a sense providing the theoretical foundation for the more empirical orientation of the latter. The main point of the former paper is that the increasingly general and abstract nature of the knowledge base in the pharmaceutical industry (among others) permits a division of labour between firms, with the smaller firms specializing in 'upstream' activities and the multinationals in 'downstream'. They conclude with the following:

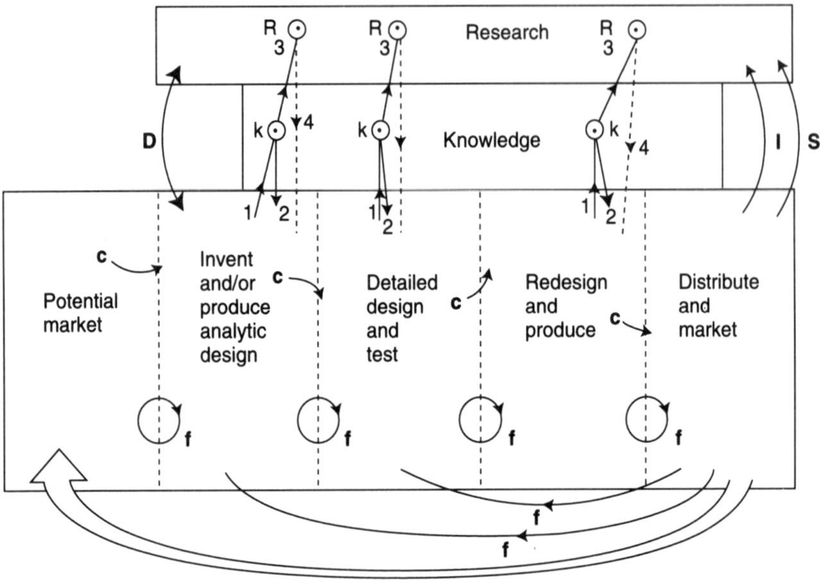

Figure 4.2 The 'chain-linked model'
Source: Klein and Rosenberg 1986. Reprinted with permission from *The Positive Sum Strategy: Harnessing Technology for Economic Growth*, National Academy Press, 1992.
Notes: Symbols on arrows: *C* = central-chain-of-innovation: *f* = feedback loops; *F* = particularly important feedback. *K–R*: Links through knowledge to research and return paths. If problem solved at node *K*, link 3 to *R* not activated. Return from research (link 4) is problematic – therefore dashed line. *D*: direct link to and from research from problems in invention and design. *I*: support of scientific research by instruments, machines, tools and procedures of technology.

> Thus far, the so-called "high-tech" industries, biotechnology, new materials, and semi-conductors, have shown the greatest extent of specialisation. These are sectors where the technology has changed quite rapidly and thus the accumulated knowledge of the large incumbent firms has not been a decisive advantage. These are also sectors where use of abstract and general knowledge has been the greatest and where intellectual property rights are well-defined. If our argument is correct, then the patterns of specialisation in these sectors are harbingers of the future.
>
> (Arora and Gambardella 1993: 26)

In response, the first point to consider is the extent of this 'specialization' or rather how structurally significant the NBFs actually are. We can begin to analyse this by looking at their contribution in terms of market valuation, turnover, research and, perhaps, significant new drugs. At the end of 1991, the whole US biotechnology industry ('capitalized NBFs') had peaked on the stock market at around $60 billion (*Financial Times* 1993). This value is slightly less than the value of Merck, one of the world's largest ethical drugs companies which commands just 4.5 per cent of the world market (Sharp 1991). Turnover for the US biotechnology industry in 1992 was $8.1 billion of which product sales accounted for $5.9 billion (*Financial Times* 1993). In 1989, the global pharmaceuticals market was worth $192 billion (Allen 1990). The research spend of the US biotechnology industry in 1992 was $4.9 billion, whereas that for the pharmaceuticals sector was reckoned to be $26.5 billion (*Financial Times* 1993). As a significant proportion of this could justifiably be considered biotechnological, then the total spend by the established companies probably surpasses that of the NBFs.[7] The quality and range of the innovative research and potential products of the latter may still surpass that of the established firms. However, continual claims of imminent takeoff notwithstanding, the market is far from awash with big-selling products[8] which would lend credence to the views of Gambardella and his co-authors. What these figures do indicate is how much the NBF sector is dwarfed by its established counterparts. Enthusiastic claims about its significance should always be tempered with this in mind.

There is no convincing evidence that NBFs are assuming a permanent role of research provider for the industry. It is the case that many of them have been involved in and continue to be involved in various forms of research collaborations with established firms. This does not necessarily imply a specialization in a particular stage of research but simply a knowledge of a particular area or possession of certain skills distinct from the competences of their partner. To look at this from a different angle, the NBFs obviously cannot hope to compete with the established companies as integrated pharmaceutical firms. Regardless of expertise, they do not possess the financial muscle to get drugs approved. The regulatory barriers and costs deny them a role in this area. A niche which is available is innovative research. The NBFs have thus emerged in one of the few areas open to them.

This 'division of labour' need not suggest that discrete organizations perform the different tasks, just that they are separated. Of course, there may be other organizational costs to having these activities occur within a single organization but such considerations should be recognized as being quite distinct from the notion of a division of labour. While Arora and Gambardella (1993: 6) dismiss the transaction cost approach, this would seem an obvious contender for its application as it represents the classic 'make or buy' scenario. Della Valle and Gambardella (1993: 291–92) suggest that scientific knowledge, 'unlike scale and experience . . . can be divided into "pieces", which can be composed in a modular fashion to define "larger" pieces of knowlege. With suitable contracts and property rights, the pieces of knowledge can be bought and sold.'

From a general transaction costs perspective this provides several points with which to take issue. Economies of scale could be captured without requiring unified ownership if suitable contracts could be devised. It is this very contractual difficulty which often necessitates integration (Williamson 1975). Similarly, contracting for experience, a knowledge-based asset encounters similar if not more acute difficulties. As a general rule, it seems dubious that knowledge can be divided into pieces, especially where some of these pieces will inevitably be experience-based and tacit. Suitable contracts and property rights, even in the realm of the strong pharmaceutical patent, are unlikely to exist for such knowledge trade. Such a view is a misconception of the trade of knowledge and fundamental difficulties inherent in the market for what is obviously a peculiar economic good (Teece 1988; Casson 1987).

Arora and Gambardella (1993) contend that the use of abstract and general knowledge in biotechnology has been great and that this facilitates such a division of innovative labour. They do not offer convincing evidence for this contention. Abstract knowledge itself is 'knowledge that is representable in a universal form' (1993: 7), whereas generality 'means that the outcome of a particular experiment can be usefully related to outcomes of other, more distant experiments' (1993: 7). They would seem to mean that in biotechnology some fundamental principles are now usefully understood and can be articulated to a fairly wide audience using an abstract language. The latter, however, may or may not adequately represent the knowledge in question. Further, all science and knowledge is essentially 'working knowledge', it is continually evolving – on this even Feyerabend (1975) and Popper (1972) would agree. Science today is certainly not close to discovering all there is to know whether in biotechnology or any other area.

While the recent progress in the biological sciences is undeniable, spurred by key breakthroughs in the understanding of fundamentals, there is no inevitability about the pace of advance being maintained. If research avenues turn into blind alleys it could slow down. Nor is there any inevitability about the NBFs and universities remaining the repositories of 'leading-edge' science. The established companies are in alliances precisely because they do not know how to do certain things which they hope to learn from their partners. Once they learn them will they still need the alliance? It would seem not, if the argument is to be based upon the notion of abstract, generic knowledge.[9] Otherwise, we are saying that the large firm possesses just enough knowledge to understand what its partner tells it but not enough to do it itself. It is both 'bright' and 'stupid' at the same time.

The discussion above has presented several reasons for caution in accepting the thesis of della Valle and Gambardella. In general they do not provide a plausible economic conception of knowledge and its 'trade'. While they claim to appreciate the limitations of the linear model of innovation, they implicitly invoke such a conception. Their notions of abstract and generic knowledge and its increasing relevance in biotechnology are unconvincing. It also makes one wonder why other functions such as marketing and distribution, where surely the knowledge involved can be no less abstract and generic, cannot be similarly conducted by entities external to the firm. Simply pointing to the existence of research networks entangling established firms with NBFs and universities is insufficient to validate their argument. In any case such 'evidence' is consistent with alternative views such as providing complementary assets or that an alliance represents the most efficient way of transferring knowledge. Further, this 'division of labour' need not suggest that discrete organizations perform the different tasks, just that they are separated. Of course, having these activities occur within a single firm may entail other organizational costs but these must be significant to outweigh the disadvantages of disintegration in such circumstances – *inter alia*: communication difficulties; the threat or actuality of opportunism. Della Valle and Gambardella, by glossing over organization detail, that is, that there are many distinct forms of collaboration, and by inadequately considering the managerial implications, have missed much of what is relevant.

It is unlikely that there is a general organizational imperative that the pharmaceutical industry is being compelled to follow. Gambardella and his colleagues are right to focus upon knowledge and its trade, however, they present an 'efficiency' argument when an evolutionary/historical approach is more appropriate.[10] As our experience with GRD also shows, in pursuit of their strategy, established firms will attempt to access relevant knowledge wherever they can find it. This, more than the position of the innovation on any notional spectrum, will determine the organizational structure adopted. Universities and NBFs currently possess knowledge and skills of relevance to the large pharmaceutical firms whose extant knowledge and competences are partially and probably temporarily outmoded.

While a consideration of the innovatory process and its organizational implications is obviously necessary, it is only one side of the matter. An effective research effort by the firm is also reliant upon how its own research scientists perform and how managers can influence this. Thus, in the next section we attempt to provide an empirical element to the discussion through considering the organization and management of research at GRD. It is essential to consider the total research effort of this division because this is how managers will approach the issue and because it makes little sense to focus on particular elements in isolation. Thus, we begin by looking at Glaxo, the company, and the organization of its principal R&D division. Next, the problem of attaining both creativity and control within the research process is discussed, and GRD's move to 'trust time' and performance related pay are referred to in this context. Finally, we discuss the role that external links and alliances play in the division's overall research strategy.

THE MANAGEMENT OF INNOVATION AT GLAXO RESEARCH AND DEVELOPMENT

Change, the pharmaceutical industry and GRD

A series of linked forces are having important effects on the pharmaceuticals industry; these are detailed elsewhere (Sharp 1991: 219). Green (1994a) has argued that four main corporate responses are emerging in response to these changes including a redirecting of research programmes away from 'me too' drugs towards innovative and high selling drugs. In addition there is a growth in strategic alliances between the major players themselves, between the major players and small biotechnology companies, and between the major players and generic companies, concentrating on the over-the-counter (OTC) market.

One noticeable effect of these pressures is an increasing concentration within the industry. In 1989 the top twenty-five companies accounted for 50 per cent of worldwide pharmaceutical sales. By the year 2000, fifteen companies will account for the same proportion.

Competition, it is argued, is based on M&D (marketing and development), meaning the ability to develop and bring drugs to the market quickly and then sell them successfully (Cookson 1994). The world's drug companies spend at least £34.2bn a year on sales and marketing, more than twice as much as they spend on research and development (Green 1994b).

In the financial year to June 1992, Glaxo was claiming to be the second largest pharmaceutical company in the world, with sales of over £4,000m. The company had grown rapidly from being a medium-sized UK company in the late 1950s and early 1960s to its present stature. Growth had been largely on the back of two drugs: firstly, Ventolin (an asthma treatment) launched in 1969, and secondly Zantac (an anti-ulcerant), launched in 1981 and now the biggest selling prescription drug in the world. Zantac accounts for around 43 per cent of Glaxo's turnover.

Since the early 1970s, expenditure by Glaxo on R&D has grown from around £8m per annum to a projected spend of £850m per annum in 1994. The growth in R&D spend is being driven by the search for blockbuster drugs, with only one in every ten thousand compounds investigated ever reaching the market. Glaxo has the second highest research spend of any company in the UK. However, in terms of

R&D per employee and R&D as a percentage of sales it is in the leading position.

At the beginning of 1995 the UK operation of Glaxo Research and Development Ltd will move from its present inadequate, split-site location in Ware, Hertfordshire and Greenford, west London to a custom built site in Stevenage, Hertfordshire. The new site, currently the highest value construction project in the UK, will cost about £700 million to construct, providing a 'campus' style environment for in the region of 1,000 scientific staff as well as around 500 clerical and ancillary workers. The move is being driven by the important changes that are underway in the process of scientific discovery and the pharmaceutical industry and which have been described earlier in this chapter.

Managing research within GRD

Glaxo is a multidivisional organization, with Glaxo Research and Development existing as a Division in its own right. The operating companies of Glaxo employ around 12,000 people in the UK. Glaxo Research and Development employs approximately 3,500 people internationally. In the UK about half of all staff have at least one degree. The research function is international, with major centres in the UK and the USA, and smaller units in Italy, France, Spain, Switzerland and Japan. Glaxo's strategy is to concentrate on patented prescription medicines and avoid becoming directly involved in the development of OTC drugs.

Within GRD there is a matrix management structure. Research is divided into a series of divisions based on scientific disciplines and each is led by its own head of division. Targets for research strategy are divided into therapeutic groups, of which there are currently seven internationally with five represented within Glaxo Research and Development in the UK. Each Therapeutic Group is run by a Research Management Committee (RMC) chaired by a head of division, whose job it is to decide priorities, resource allocation, start up and wind up of projects and membership of project teams. Project teams are increasingly multi-disciplinary, with members drawn from a number of divisions. Teams can vary in size from perhaps ten to over fifty members. The project team is led by a project leader who is responsible for the scientific direction of the project, whilst the head of division retains responsibility for non-scientific managerial concerns.

Observers of the company have commented on the importance of talented scientific staff to its success in innovation:

> Glaxo's R&D is ideas based; that is, there is a high level of creativity involved as opposed to a more rigid or theoretical new product development model. As a result, the company views the limiting

> factor in the rate of drug development as being the generation of this creativity. Not surprisingly, the quality of human resources is seen as the company's most important strength. This quality determines the thinking, the motivation and the work rate. Acquiring the technology or the equipment to take ideas forward is not seen as a problem of costs or availability.
>
> (Taggart and Blaxter 1992)

The suggestion that human resources, in the form of talented scientists, is a critical factor in Glaxo's innovation process is confirmed at the highest levels of management within the company. The management of such talent in the pursuit of innovation is the job of experienced and senior scientists:

> Most of our management is done through science. You don't want a heavily structured or heavily organised environment if you want people to be creative. I always say it's like running an opera house, I see my job as being akin to managing an opera house. You've got to make sure that the toilets are clean, you've got to make sure that the tickets are sold, the ice creams are there in the interval, your gin and tonics are available, but if the fat lady don't sing, it's all a waste of time. And it's generating an environment where ultimately the prima donnas perform, because it's the prima donnas who actually make the invention, who take you to places you couldn't otherwise go . . . but there's a few people out there who are really a bit special, who put things together in a different way . . . what we've got to create is something that allows them to perform, not something that necessarily satisfies the aspirations of the masses, because you can do that by making it run very smoothly. Everyone will enjoy coming to work and say it's a fantastic place to work, but you never make inventions. What the hell good's that?
>
> (Senior manager)

There was general agreement amongst the managers we interviewed that managing research was about allowing scientists the freedom to use their creative skills, as another senior manager put it, 'that's what we try to encourage, an environment where people are happy to bring forward daft ideas'. However, a fundamental tension exists between the nature of scientific research work and the drive for profit. Managers maintain that freedom of investigation, through relatively loose control structures, is vital in promoting an atmosphere within which research can take place. But set against this is the pressure to produce profitable ethical drugs. This pressure requires careful monitoring of projects to make sure, firstly, that sufficient progress is being made, and secondly, that progress is being made in a direction that might produce a marketable molecule.

This second consideration can mean that projects are closed down on the basis of decisions that have little to do with the science involved. Either a rival has got there first, or the marketing people do not feel that the area is of sufficient prospect to warrant further development. Success in pharmaceuticals, it is argued, is based on an ability to combine capabilities such as running clinical trials and marketing with research. Therefore marketing managers talk to researchers to direct them towards the illnesses for which a product could be designed. Developers talk to marketing people and researchers to determine which treatments regulators would approve speedily, and researchers brief marketers and developers on technological possibilities. Management have to balance the perceived necessity of freedom of investigation with market-driven monitoring – reviewing and dropping projects on a monthly basis (*Economist* 6 March 1993).

At the level of the individual it is believed that there is a necessary degree of indeterminacy in scientific research work. To some extent management cannot know what scientists are doing, because by trying to control and codify scientific research work rigorously the risk is run of destroying the spark of creativity, the commitment and the drive. One divisional head explained:

> obviously, it's a question of balance, balancing people's ability to chase their own ideas for a bit, not having to go through a heavy-weight justification for every damn thing that they do scientifically. I mean it's just that open-minded scientific creativity requires you giving people who you think are good the opportunity to express themselves scientifically without having to get full justification.

But the problem of controlling freedom whilst promoting creativity can give rise to unique problems as a senior manager, asked what he expected of his staff, demonstrated:

> they should be chasing down new things, going about the lab, reading the literature, without me saying they should. In fact there's a lot that goes on you don't see. If I don't see it, I'm glad I don't see it, it's sort of skunk working. Stuff should be going on all the time . . . I just need to know it's going on, because if it's not going on then there's something wrong, and I think there's a lot going on that I don't know about, and that's great.
>
> *Interviewer*: If you don't know what they are doing, how do you know that they are doing it?
>
> Well, that's a very good question, I don't know what it is that they are doing, but I do know that they are doing things that I don't know about. No, it's true, it is true, I mean, when I say I don't know about

> them, I don't know the content. I do know they are doing interesting science. I just don't happen to have seen it, so I shouldn't see it either, not until it's ready.

The problem of controlling the unknowable is manifested in the operation both of the system of time management and the reward system, as we hope to demonstrate shortly. However, it is worth noting that initial group interviews with project teams painted a very different picture of the degree of freedom available. They appear to view themselves as being over-managed within a highly bureaucratic system that stifles innovation. Tight control over resources, they argue, meant that it was impossible to build on new or innovative ideas without approval being gained at the level of the Research Management Committee.

Rewarding performance and managing working time

From the mid-1980s, through to the early 1990s, the system of monitoring attendance at work, within Glaxo Group Research (as it was) evolved from flexitime through to what is known as 'trust time'. The system is not unique to Glaxo. Research in the 1980s (WTA 1984: 65) suggested that agreements of this type were fairly common amongst research, scientific, academic and other specialized staff. It may be that Glaxo are relatively late in introducing this form of flexible working.

The original flexitime system allowed employees to bank hours which could then be converted into days off to a maximum of twelve per year. In the late 1980s, Glaxo Group Research reduced the maximum number of flexidays from twelve to six. Flexitime was, however, believed by management to be inappropriate to a research setting insofar as it simply measured attendance rather than activity or commitment.

Under trust, outside of core time, scientific staff are free to come and go as they please as long as they fulfil their commitment of a 37.5 hour week. Managers have the ability to offer 'trust days' (days off) to individuals whose performance warrants them, but these are not monitored and there is no entitlement to days off beyond formal holiday entitlement.

Individual performance is also rewarded through a system of performance related pay (PRP) and is monitored through a pay review and appraisal system. The review is the sole source of annual pay rises. What is considered vital in determining the level of performance is active contribution to the work process, in this case the project team. This cannot be measured either in direct outcome terms (there being no guaranteed product) nor in time spent at work, insofar as attendance at the bench is no measure of what is actually done.

On the whole there is little concrete evidence in the literature that performance pay has any positive effect on employee task performance in organizations where it exists. On the contrary, Kohn (1993) cites a growing collection of evidence that rewards typically undermine the very processes they are intended to enhance. He concludes that, by and large, rewards only secure temporary compliance. On the negative side they discourage risk-taking and creativity (important in scientific research), destroy co-operation (important where work is team-based), and undermine intrinsic motivation (important where tasks are interesting or complicated).

Taken together 'trust time' and PRP offer a way of rewarding perceived performance that is highly subjective and which places control firmly in the hands of line managers. There may be a danger, however, that in seeking to portray themselves as worthy of such subjectively allocated rewards employees are diverted from the task of creative activity.

The role of external links[11]

As mentioned previously, the whole research function of GRD will be moved to the new Stevenage site by 1995. A significant pressure in this respect has been the emergence of biotechnology and with it the need to utilize multidisciplinary teams of scientists to pursue drug discovery and development. Splitting research from development in this manner and providing a common home for all of their research scientists will, GRD believe, facilitate the type of research team demanded by the new environment. It is not envisaged that Stevenage will reduce these external links but rather it will enable GRD to get more out of them. All of which is hardly at odds with della Valle and Gambardella (1993). However, such links still account for a relatively small proportion of the £800+ million R&D expenditure of GRD, albeit development assumes the lion's share (70 per cent) of this in any case. As to the nature of the R&D conducted by external partners, it would seem to be predominantly, though not exclusively, of a more 'basic' and speculative nature. However, the wide and, as we have previously argued, somewhat suspect label 'basic research' aggregates a heterogeneous bunch of activities. For instance, some links represent a focused drug discovery programme founded upon a known new chemical entity (NCE). Others are concerned with 'enabling' skills and technology, where specific drugs are more distant. They are as often about multidisciplinarity as vertical specialization. Still others, such as some university links, are not directly about new drugs at all but are really mechanisms for promoting the corporate image and facilitating future recruitment.

An alliance with an NBF or university, therefore, may provide 'targets and enabling skills' but does not necessarily provide the full complement of such research knowledge and expertise at this level. Rather than simply assuming the basic research function for GRD, their partners are doing so in areas where GRD is weak and areas where essentially the work is of a speculative nature. Primarily, the former is about developing skills and the latter permits greater flexibility and lower risk. Another alliance may actually be concerned with accessing skills which are, and are likely to continue to be, peripheral to GRD's core technology. Categorizing all of this as 'basic research' would be somewhat misleading. Not surprisingly, different collaborations fulfil different roles.

Currently, GRD experiences difficulties with multidisciplinary interaction and ensuring effective performance from scientists within their own division. It is hard to believe that such problems are reduced within a collaboration. A senior manager referred to a lot of 'to-ing and fro-ing' of compounds, test results and studies required for a collaboration to be worthwhile. To reiterate an earlier point, high levels of interaction are required, which in itself can be problematic. However, it is essential for successful innovation and derides the notion of a sequential process.

A senior manager also felt that the NBFs often require direction, and while there is probably some validity to this, it may also be a further indication of the desire to control that is readily apparent with the management of GRD's own scientists. This 'propensity to manage' its own staff does not seem consistent with a free, open and flexible relationship with another company's staff. Indeed, if a fundamental problem facing GRD is how to reconcile creativity with control, it is difficult to envisage how this should be any easier with a collaboration, for the reasons given above. The question of managing informal collaboration is even more problematic. Kreiner and Schultz (1993) point out that strategic alliances and other formalized collaborative structures are emphasized in the literature whilst informal collaborations are 'dramatically under-represented'. The results of their own study show that 'patterns of interaction have an unmistakable character of anarchy and licence. The picture is one in which individual researchers informally appropriate organisational resources and divert these into unauthorised projects and relationships' (1993: 204).

The mesh that is the innovatory process does not allow a deconstruction of R&D according to any simple linear notion. While many of the NBFs involved with GRD may be conducting work which is closer to basic research than GRD's, the latter will also have to conduct similar work or develop the requisite skills to enable understanding and further development. It is envisaged that Stevenage will facilitate this through enabling more effective communication with the biotechnology community. However, ideas, problems and solutions may emerge partially or completely from any of those conducting the research (or other functions for that matter), so that to label any party's contribution as of a particular kind is somewhat artificial. It is akin to Marshall's query as to which blade of the scissors does the cutting. To the extent that NBFs may be pursuing less focused programmes this may be as much a reflection of their youth and commercial inexperience as their basic research specialization. Further, as Teece and Pisano (1987: 28–29) contend, 'value creation comes from building an organisation, rather than simply cashing in on one's technology in the market for know-how'. It is also the aspiration of many of the NBFs to become integrated, pharmaceuticals companies. So, some of the inter-organizational division of labour may disappear when they cease to need the established companies.[12] In the meantime, there is also some learning to be done by the NBF in terms of how to develop and market drugs.

Glaxo has always been 'tapped into' the scientific establishment as it is well aware of its dependence upon it for ideas and people. Previously this meant the universities but now also includes the NBFs, given their emergence in recent times. The NBF, however, are not exclusively the 'hunters/providers' of NCEs, contrary to what might be inferred from della Valle and Gambardella (1993). This is because they do not always conduct this activity on their own – often it is in an alliance with another, where separating the relative contribution is difficult; nor are they exclusively concerned with this activity (Burrill and Roberts 1992). Ultimately the goal of any Glaxo programme is to produce a drug but collaborative activity is undertaken for a variety of reasons. The scope of programmes varies as does the level of a partner's input. The process of drug discovery and development itself is interactive and complex. In other words, della Valle and Gambardella (1993) provide an inappropriate generalization which derives from a simplistic deconstruction of the research process.

CONCLUSION

We recognize that the critical discussion of models of research and development is not matched in detail by any alternative thesis. There is a limit to what any one paper should seek to achieve and establishing the deficiencies of some current approaches and laying some groundwork for future research are both valid exercises in their own right. Further, the presentation of some empirical work should help advance theoretical understanding. In this respect, it is important to consider the whole research activity conducted by the firm to enable a proper understanding of the role of the various elements. This means considering both the innovatory process and the management of scientists. We have achieved this by utilizing an interdisciplinary approach drawing from the literatures of both economics and behavioural science.

We have sought to demonstrate in this chapter that models of research and development that suggest a simple division of labour between firms in the pharmaceutical industry cannot be sustained. Neither can simple models of the division of labour within firms. Furthermore, the role of universities and small biotechnology firms as the sole providers of basic research has been questioned. The research and development process, we maintain, is characterized by a complexity which forbids the easy characterization of pharmaceutical research into a linear, and therefore easily segmented process. Thus, successful innovation requires continual interaction and reiteration.

If the research process is more complex than has been suggested then we can expect the management of the process to be equally complex. Where there is no homogeneity in the task to be performed by scientists within the industry, the search for management prescriptions applicable to all seems bound to fail. The result is an industry which appears to be pushed and pulled in different directions by an underlying dynamic, itself the result of the tension between the need for creativity in research and the need to maximize profitability.

The case study material shows that managers are both aware of the need to give scientists a degree of freedom in research and the need to maintain tight control on that freedom. The former is demonstrated by what managers say about the research process and their attitudes to the management of working time. The latter, in its turn, is demonstrated by the use of a performance-related pay system and its impact on scientists when combined with the trust-time system, and the consequent power to operate subjective control that has been handed to line managers by the two systems. This control/creativity issue is an important dilemma facing GRD, although it is unlikely to be resolved by these managerial approaches. It is equally unlikely that external links or a division of labour between firms can resolve it. The evidence from GRD does not suggest a fundamental shift in this direction. Such links encounter further problems with communication and opportunism. They do, however, provide an essential tap into the scientific community (which now includes the NBFs), and enable the requisite skills and knowledge to be accessed. The history of the development of biotechnology points to this without having to invoke organizational efficiency arguments. To an extent, the established pharmaceutical firms have 'watched' and 'waited' (Sharp 1985) and now they are adapting. The NBFs are an important element in facilitating such a flexible response.

Looked at from an alternative perspective we can argue that staff within GRD need a relatively high degree of autonomy in order to maintain collaborative links with external bodies. Where knowledge cannot be easily codified and the informal network has a vital part to play, scientists must be given the freedom to explore the network in order to gain the intangible benefits that may emanate from it. Again, the tight controls that seem to be reflected in the reward and time management systems may militate against this informal activity, restraining rather than contributing towards the building of effective external links.

The tension between the need for creativity and the need for control is not one which can be resolved easily or permanently. Work carried out more than a quarter of a century ago (Kornhauser 1962; Cotgrove and Box 1970) in both the USA and the UK indicates that the issue is neither new nor transient. It is our belief that we can expect to witness continuing attempts to resolve this tension in the form of pragmatic and shifting tactics by managers. As each one proves unable to provide the overarching and permanent management solution that is sought, we can expect to see it dispensed with or overlaid with further devices (Hyman 1987). In furtherance of this aim GRD can be expected to continue to look both to the management of its in-house science and to its network of external relationships.

NOTES

1 We would like to thank Glaxo Research and Development for continuing to grant access to carry out the study upon which this chapter is based. We would also like to thank our colleagues Jane Hardy and Al Rainnie at the University of Hertfordshire for their comments on earlier versions of this article.

2 For the average new drug this cost is $242m (O'Donnell 1993) and the drug will have been in development for at least ten years before it comes on to the market.

3 As Nathan Rosenberg has said, 'Everyone knows that the linear model is dead' (Hall 1994: 22).

4 However, the task of the innovator should not be conceived as one of simply fishing from such a pool. Knowledge cannot be depleted in the same way as fish stocks. The pool is not fixed; it can expand and contract. The user's knowledge will determine which ideas can be usefully tapped. It is not enough for information to be available, it has to be translated and interpreted.

5 In discussion following presentation of an earlier version of this chapter at the 'R&D Decisions: Policy, Strategy and Disclosure' conference, Keele University, UK, September 1994.

6 Teece (1989) provides a good overview of the various conceptions of the innovatory process.

7 If just 20 per cent of this is biotechnological R&D then at $5.3 billion it exceeds the US biotechnology industry.

8 In this respect, Amgen, the US NBF, has two products, Epogen and Neupogen, which are forecast to be $2 billion plus 'blockbuster' drugs by the year 2000 (*Financial Times* 1993).

9 Walsh (1988) supports this view, noting some of the mergers/buy-outs which have already occurred.

10 Interestingly, in doing so they eschew the most popular of such approaches, that of transaction costs.

11 In addition to secondary source material and the ongoing research into GRD (see, for example, Randle and Rainnie 1994), this section has benefited primarily from an interview with the Head of External Scientific Affairs. It is also our intention to interview project managers regarding the contribution of such linkages but due to practical difficulties these have yet to be conducted.

12 Admittedly, this may imply too optimistic a prognosis for the prospects of the NBFs (Oakey *et al.* 1990).

REFERENCES

Allen, G. (1990) 'Our chemical industry', *Chemistry & Industry*, 4 June, pp. 349–53.

Anderson, E.A. and Braendgaard, A. (1992) 'Integration, innovation and evolution', in Lundvall, B.A. (ed.) *National Systems of Innovation*, Pinter.

Arora, A. and Gambardella, A. (1993) *Division of Labour and Inventive Activity*, H. John Heinz III School of Public Policy and Management, Working Paper Series 93, 3.

Burrill, G. and Roberts, W.J. (1992) 'Biotechnology and economic development: The winning formula', *Bio/Technology*, June, pp. 647–53.

Casson, M. (1987) *The Firm and the Market*, Basil Blackwell.

Cookson, C. (1994) 'Combination of brains and brawn', *Financial Times*, 23 March.

Cotgrove, S. and Box, S. (1970) *Scientists and Industry*, George Allen and Unwin.

Della Valle, F. and Gambardella, A. (1993) '"Biological" revolution and strategies for innovation in pharmaceutical companies', *R&D Management* 23, 4: 287–303.

Feyerabend, P. (1975) *Against Method*, Verso.

Financial Times (1993) FT Survey: Pharmaceuticals: R&D, 22 April, pp. 37–42.

Green, D. (1994a) 'Sweeteners for a bitter pill', *Financial Times*, 31 January.

——— (1994b) 'Economists in the salesforce', *Financial Times*, 24 March.

Hall, P. (1994) *Innovation, Economics and Evolution*, Harvester Wheatsheaf.

Hyman, R. (1987) 'Strategy or structure? Capital, labour and control', *Work, Employment and Society*, 1,1: 25–55.

Jorde, T. and Teece, D.J. (1988) 'Innovation, cooperation and antitrust', Program in Law and Economics, Working Paper no. 88–6, University of California, Berkeley.

Kamien, M. and Schwarz, N. (1982) *Market Structure and Innovation*, Cambridge University Press.

Kenney, M. (1986) *Biotechnology: The University-Industrial Complex*, Yale University Press.

Klein, S.J. and Rosenberg, N. (1986) 'An overview of innovation', in N. Rosenberg and R. Landau (eds) *The Positive Sum Strategy*, Washington DC: National Academy Press.

Kohn, A. (1993) 'Why incentive plans cannot work', Harvard Business Review, September–October.

Kornhauser, W. (1962) *Scientists in Industry: Conflict and Accommodation*, University of California Press, Los Angeles.

Kreiner, K. and Schultz, M. (1993) 'Informal collaboration in r&d. The formation of networks across organisations', *Organisation Studies*, 14, 2: 189–209.

Oakey, R.P., Faulkner, W., Cooper, S. and Walsh, V. (1990) *New Firms in Biotechnology: Their Contribution to Innovation and Growth*, Pinter.

O'Donnell, P. (1993) 'Powerful economic assets protected', *Financial Times* 22 April, FT Survey: Pharmaceuticals: R&D, pp. 37–42.

Popper, K. (1972) *Objective Knowledge. An Evolutionary Approach*, Oxford University Press.

Randle, K. and Rainnie, A. (1994) *Creativity and Control in a Pharmaceutical R and D Company: The Case of Glaxo Research and Development*, University of Hertfordshire Business School Working Paper Series, UHBS 1994: 7.

Sharp, M. (1985) 'Biotechnology: watching and waiting', in Sharp, M. (ed.) *Europe and the New Technologies*, Frances Pinter.

——— (1991) 'Pharmaceuticals and biotechnology: perspectives for the European industry' in C. Freeman, M. Sharp and W. Walker (eds) *Technology and the Future of Europe*, Pinter.

Taggart, J.H. and Blaxter, T.J. (1992) 'Strategy in pharmaceutical r&d: A portfolio risk matrix', *R&D Management* 22, 3.

Teece, D. (1988) 'Technological change and the nature of the firm', in G. Dosi *et al.* (eds) *Technical Change and Economic Theory*, Pinter.

——— (1989) 'Inter-organisational requirements of the innovation process', *Managerial and Decision Economics*, Special Issue, pp. 35–42.

——— and Pisano, G. (1987) *Collaborative Arrangements and Technology Strategy*, School of Business Administration, University of California, Berkeley.

Walsh, V. (1988) 'Desperately seeking solvency: Or external linkages of small UK biotechnology firms', Manchester School of Management, Paper prepared for Workshop on Inter-Firm Technological Co-operation Agreements, Université Paris X Nanterre, November 21–22.

Williamson, O.E. (1975) *Markets and Hierarchies*, New York, The Free Press.

WTA (Working Time Analysts) (1984) *Flexible Working Hours Theory and Practice*.

Part II

POLICY AND PERFORMANCE

5

NEW VIEWS OF INNOVATION AND CHALLENGES TO R&D POLICY

Keith Smith

The field of R&D and innovation policy is of increasing importance in the agenda of government in the OECD countries. Taken together, OECD governments spend approximately $300 billion per year on R&D, which is between 1 and 2 per cent of OECD GNP (European Commission, 1994: Figure 1b.1, p. 15). But although the size of expenditure makes it an important field, it of course remains much smaller than other major areas of public spending; the importance of R&D policy derives not from the scale of expenditure but rather from what is held to be its central role in achieving policy objectives that lie well outside the arena of R&D policy as traditionally conceived. The Maastricht Treaty, for example, specifically mentioned the role of R&D policy in industrial change, regional cohesion and so on; the communiqué from the G7 summit in Detroit on unemployment laid great emphasis on R&D and innovation policies in reducing OECD unemployment, and this theme was repeated in the EC White Paper on unemployment (and it is worth noting that the current OECD work programme on unemployment focuses almost exclusively on technological change issues). This emphasis is reflected in action. Almost the first major policy document from the Clinton administration was on innovation policy, and this has been followed up by fairly significant expenditure decisions – the new National Institute for Standards and Technology has been the only institution in the Federal government to grow rapidly during the first phase of the Clinton administration; in the EU, the budget of FRAMEWORK, the overall R&D programme budget, is one of the few growing areas. Finally, it could be argued that R&D is also being taken more seriously in finance ministries as one effect of the so-called 'new growth theory', which emphasizes dynamic scale economies resulting from knowledge creation.

It is not simply the scale of the R&D policy effort which is changing: policy-makers are also starting to re-examine central issues regarding the scope, foundations and methods of policy. This chapter discusses changes within the implicit and explicit conceptual frameworks which have been used to develop and implement R&D and innovation policies, both at national and supra-national levels, focusing on the policy implications of some significant changes which have occurred in our understanding of the links between science, innovation and technological change over the past twenty years.

When economic performance is seen in terms of search, learning and knowledge accumulation, then a fundamental problem is to explore the policy implications of the move to a knowledge-based economy. This has a number of dimensions, which at a minimum include the following:

- Basic science policy.
- Technology policies aimed at invention and innovation.
- Diffusion policies, and all policies related to the adoption of new technologies.
- Technology policy aspects of industrial and regional policies.
- Human capital, human resoures and mobility, including all aspects of education and training.

This chapter concerns only parts of these issues; it focuses on the conceptual basis, structure and content of policies directed towards *industrial innovation and diffusion policy*, at national and regional levels, and the implications of this for industrial R&D policy.

Over the past two decades, social scientists in a range of fields have in effect carried out a major programme of research on science, technology and innovation. If there is any unity in this research, it is the view that these activities are social and economic processes, not simply technical processes of discovery and invention. The argument here is that this research has reached the stage where it is both necessary and possible to rethink the rationale, objectives and instruments of policies in the general areas of science, technology, innovation and industrial change. At the same time, this background research work opens up new areas of policy-relevant questions. This chapter therefore overviews some of the main themes in modern research in innovation and technological change, focusing on their implications for policy. How does recent research change our conceptions of the appropriate objectives and methods of science and technology policy? Against this background, what are the main unresolved problems facing policy-makers over the next ten years?

THEORY AND PRACTICE OF TECHNOLOGY POLICY IN THE POST-WAR PERIOD

Science and technology policy-makers are engaged in a far-reaching shift away from the ideas which dominated much science and technology policy during the post-war period. Rather than working with oversimplified models of the relationship between science and new technologies, they are seeking to achieve more sharply-defined policy objectives by trying to construct policy measures and instruments which reflect the real characteristics of innovation processes, both in industry and the public sector. What are we moving away from? Here we are not considering government policies aimed at achieving specific objectives (where government is the user of science and technology), but rather policies which aim at the general technological performance of industry, or the technological needs of society as a whole. For most of the post-war period this type of science and technology policy in Europe has been explicitly or implicitly based on some variant of the so-called 'linear model of innovation'; in many policy arenas the linear model remains strong if not dominant.

The linear model had two dimensions, one widely recognized, and one more or less neglected. The first of these dimensions was an overemphasis on research (especially basic scientific research) as the source of new technologies. The belief was that technology or engineering are forms of applied science, dependent on basic scientific advance. From this perspective the task was to fund scientific research, and to 'transfer' its results from laboratory to manufacturing plant. The linear model was present at the creation of post-war science and technology policy: a particularly clear statement can be found in Vannevar Bush's famous 1945 report to President Roosevelt which led to the establishment of the National Science Foundation:

> Basic research leads to new knowledge. It provides scientific capital. It creates the fund from which the practical applications of knowledge must be drawn. New products and processes do not appear full-grown. They are founded on new principles and new conceptions, which in turn are painstakingly developed by research in the purest realms of science. . . . *A nation which depends upon others for its new basic scientific knowledge will be slow in its industrial progress and weak in its competitive position in world trade, regardless of its mechanical skill.*
>
> (Bush, 1980: 19. Italics in original)

However, a second element in the linear model was a technocratic view of innovation as a purely technical act: the production of a new technical device. Technological change was seen as a *sequence of stages*, with new knowledge (usually founded in scientific research) leading to processes of invention, followed by engineering development resulting in innovation (or the commercial introduction of new products and processes). In this framework, technology development and engineering were usually seen as forms of applied science. Finally there was a stage of diffusion, in which the completed product spread into application. The linear model was therefore *research-based*, *sequential* and *technocratic*.

In this perspective the primary constraint on innovation was the supply of R&D. The basic argument for public-sector involvement was that problems of appropriability and risk led to under-provision of R&D (especially at the basic end of the spectrum) in market economies. Because of lack of mechanisms for sharing risk, and because firms could not appropriate all of the economic benefits of research, firms did not have incentives to invest in a socially optimal amount of R&D. The point of departure here is one of the most widely cited papers in modern economic theory, K.J. Arrow's 'Economic welfare and the allocation of resources for invention' (Arrow, 1962). Arrow, like most writers on technology, sees technology primarily as a form of knowledge: it is knowledge related to material transformations. His argument is that knowledge, considered as a commodity, has a number of distinctive characteristics which set it apart from other goods and services. Firstly, a producer cannot convey the economic value of knowledge to a potential user without transmitting the knowledge itself, but once it is transmitted, there remains nothing to sell. Secondly, the cost of transmission of knowledge – once it is produced – is negligible or even zero. Thirdly, costs of production of knowledge do not rise with the number of users; that is, there is non-rivalry in consumption of knowledge with the marginal cost for extra users being zero.

Taken together these characteristics mean that it is difficult or impossible to create a market in knowledge, and the economic benefits of new knowledge are not appropriable by producers. Knowledge is therefore a pure public good, characterized by non-rivalry and non-excludability. Although this means that a competitive market economy is unlikely to produce an optimal level of technological knowledge, it also means that if technological knowledge is somehow produced, then it will convey strong technological externalities; this approach to knowledge externalities has frequently formed the theoretical basis for arguments for public support of scientific and technological R&D.

But what sort of knowledge are we really talking about in the Arrow case? What cognitive or other characteristics must knowledge have if it is to produce these 'public good' effects? I want to argue that implicit in such an approach is a view that technological knowledge has the following attributes:

- It is *generic*. An item of knowledge, or a particular advance in knowledge, can be applied widely among firms and perhaps among industries.
- It is *codified*. Transmittability implies that knowledge is written or otherwise recorded in fairly complete usable form.

- It is *costlessly accessible*. On the one hand this can involve the idea that transmission costs are negligible, but it can also mean that firms do not face differential cost barriers in accessing knowledge or bringing it into production.
- It is *context independent*. That is, firms have equal capabilities in transforming such knowledge into production capability.

Against this background a fundamental task of policy, therefore, was either to provide this research directly, or to construct incentives for private-sector provision. In practice, therefore, in most countries, technology policy came to consist of R&D support measures such as grants, tax credits, infrastructure support (for university research, for example), and so on. Of course there have been differences in emphasis between national research strategies, and also differences over time within countries. None the less, in essence we have had policies based on the idea that innovation rates depended on the volume of research, and that finance for R&D was the fundamental obstacle to innovation by firms or other social institutions.

But, as noted above, the linear model also embodied a second dimension: an implicitly *technocratic* approach to innovation. That is, technology was seen as a technical process of hardware supply, of the development of knowledge related to specific products and processes. Technological innovation was seen essentially in terms of construction of pieces of equipment. It was viewed as an act of production rather than as, for example, a continuous social process involving such activities as management, co-ordination, learning, negotiation and so on. Those aspects of innovation whch involved non-R&D processes, such as exploring user needs, acquiring competence, managing new product development, financial management and so on, were neglected.

It is important to note that the linear model did not confine policy-makers simply to R&D support, or to any particular type of technology development. It was possible, without changing the basic view of how innovation occurred, to focus on a range of technological objectives, military and civil. It was possible also to focus on the diffusion of new technologies, via policies organized around investment incentives, support programmes for the use of specific items of equipment (such as NC machine tools or CAD/CAM), licensing of research results from universities, and so on. But diffusion policies were also seen essentially in a linear way. For example, such approaches have usually been seen either in terms of 'technology transfer', the shifting of results from fundamental research into industrial applications, or – less frequently – in terms of diffusion of allegedly critical items of technology. However, neither of these approaches questioned either the prioritization of research or the technocratic aspects of the linear model of innovation (see Ergas, 1987 for a well-known discussion of some of these approaches).

In recent years, the linear approach has become less secure. It has become very clear that devoting resources to R&D does not automatically mean success in technological development, let alone economic success in the use of technologies. Countries such as Britain, the former Soviet Union and India have maintained large science bases, but have exhibited poor industrial performance, while the countries of the Pacific Rim have strong growth records without large-scale fundamental science or public-sector R&D support. At the same time the technocratic aspects of the linear approach have revealed their limitations. Invention of new techniques by itself guarantees nothing; it has become increasingly clear that the innovation performance of successful corporations owes a great deal to organizational and strategic skills – to the identification of opportunities, to the development of a wider range of competences, rather than to purely technical achievements. Similar points apply to the use of new technologies in such socially important areas as health and education.

THE CHANGED POLICY ENVIRONMENT

Changed views at the present time are not simply a result of a reassessment of the 'linear model', but also relate to more fundamental shifts in the scientific, technological and economic policy environment, which has changed radically over the past twenty years. The primary changes are as follows:

- The emergence of new fields of science, or processes of dramatic advance in existing fields (for example in molecular biology).
- The emergence of new generic technologies, of wide industrial and social significance, which are highly internationalized in terms of their development.
- Profound change in the macroeconomic situation: increased international interdependence, in a context of economic instability, high unemployment and sharper international competition.

In the mid-1980s, following the serious recessionary problems associated with OPEC-I and OPEC-II in the 1970s, science and technology policy-makers began to turn towards industrial competitiveness as an explicit objective, both in national policy thinking and in such transnational arenas as the EU's FRAMEWORK programmes. In many countries this resulted in some sharp policy changes. New roles, forms of organization and levels of support have been defined for such infrastructural institutions as universities, publicly-supported institutes, and research councils. At the same time, price inflation in the context of generally rising unemployment made the control of public expenditure a key issue in many OECD economies during the 1980s: this too had an impact on science and technology policies, producing an emphasis on the need to concentrate resources on areas which were perceived as high priority in innovative terms, or where more or less direct economic results might be achieved. At the present time such issues are sharpened by the existence of extremely high budget deficits in OECD economies generally; in the USA, Germany, the UK and Scandinavia, such deficits are at record levels, and are unsustainable. These issues too feed into the drive for a more 'effective' policy.

What must be said about these policy changes is that they rarely had a coherent rationale; they often had rather narrow approaches to the aims which they sought to achieve. They were certainly not based on superior understandings or consistent analyses of how new technologies are actually innovated and diffused. Broadly speaking, these were changes within the linear/technocratic paradigm, rather than an alternative to it.

However, the linear model has also been shaken by rapidly expanding research on innovation. From the mid-1970s, research on science and technological change has grown very sharply in Europe and the USA, in fields such as history of technology and science, economics of technological change, management of R&D and innovation, and the sociology of technology. Some of the approaches and the broad conclusions emerging from this large transnational programme of research will be discussed below. Here it can simply be said that we now have research results which significantly change our views about the following areas:

- The nature of innovation processes, in particular of the different roles of R&D and non-R&D inputs within them; in particular the notion that innovation processes are in some sense systemic.
- The role of social factors in shaping the evolution of technology and scientific disciplines.
- The nature and importance of technology diffusion.
- The role of tacit knowledge and human skills in innovation, and the nature of the learning involved.
- The role of national and regional knowledge infrastructures and support services, and more broadly of the importance of 'national and regional innovation systems'.
- Creation of new firms and technological innovation.
- The role of technological change in economic growth; in particular the development of at least three significant bodies of theory concerning the role of knowledge creation in growth.

These changed approaches to innovation have also led to changed views about the economic *effects* of new technologies. The theme of the interaction between technological innovation and economic growth is an old one in economic analysis. But it seems clear, in the light of the research of recent years, that there remains much to be said about the causal links between innovation processes, international competitiveness and economic growth in the long run. A particularly important recent development is the elaboration of theories which attempts to explain growth rates primarily on the basis of technological change or externalities arising from R&D.

This combination of changed understandings and new policy objectives has led, for the first time, to rather basic questions about the scope, objectives and instruments of science and technology policy. By far the most important forum for policy-related thinking in this area in recent years has been the OECD's TEP (Technology-Economy) programme (1988–92) which has in effect introduced this body of general research into policy analysis and debate. We turn now to an outline of these 'core ideas', after which the TEP contribution and future directions will be discussed.

MODERN INNOVATION RESEARCH: CORE IDEAS AND IMPLICATIONS

If modern innovation analysis has any one single source, it lies in the work of Joseph Schumpeter. Schumpeter's work is open to various interpretations, but it is based on three central ideas. Firstly, that competition in industrial economies is primarily technological – firms compete not in terms of the efficiency with which they produce given products, but rather by changing products and processes. Secondly, that this dynamic process of change and replacement – 'creative destruction' – is the source of both instability and economic growth in industrial economies. Thirdly, that the generation and management of such change is the primary internal problem in the modern corporation. Each of these ideas has had substantial impacts on modern research, but broadly speaking we can distinguish two main themes deriving from the influence of Schumpeter:

- A theme which attempts to develop the theory of the innovation process itself – to explore how firms innovate, to develop a more subtle understanding of the processes involved.
- A theme which explores how innovation at firm level affects the evolution and dynamics of industrial structures, and general economic performance.

Underlying much modern research is a more nuanced concept of technology itself, in which technology is no longer seen in a technocratic engineering sense, but in its social and economic context. In the following sections we outline this broad approach, and then look at the key problems concerning the nature and effects of innovation which emerge from recent research. The following sections deal with these issues:

- The conceptualization of technology as both a social and technical process.
- Innovation as a non-linear process, involving not just research but many related activities (training, design, marketing and so on). Innovation relies on the creation of specialized competence and results in variety, diversity and 'bounded vision' at firm level.
- Innovation as a process of interaction between firms and their external environment; the conceptualization of this environment in terms of 'national or regional systems of innovation'.
- Innovation as an increasingly globalized activity.
- Technological change as an increasingly science-linked activity, which is central to the growth of output and productivity.

THE NATURE OF TECHNOLOGY

The point of departure for much modern research has been a concept of technology which sees the 'hardware' aspects of technology in a dynamic social and economic context. What is technology? Firstly, technology involves *knowledge* related to production: it implies understanding and competence relevant to material transformations. This knowledge can range from abstract scientific knowledge – codified and widely available – concerning the properties of nature, through to engineering 'know-how' or operative skills. The latter are often tacit, unwritten. Secondly, technology involves *organization*: at the most direct level this means the management and co-ordination systems which integrate individual activities and through which production takes place, or through which public-sector activity is organized. Thirdly, technology involves *techniques*: that is, machines, tools or other equipment with their rules and procedures of operation, and their ancillary activities such as maintenance, repair, training and so on. Technology can therefore be thought of as *the integration of knowledge, organization and technique.* However, there is a further essential aspect: technology is produced by and exists within a *social framework.* The social system makes economic and political choices which influence the development and spread of technologies, and which – through education and general culture – develop the skills needed to operate technologies. Social values and decisions thus shape the path of technological development. It seems apparent that differences in technological performance between societies have at least some of their roots in social structure and cultural forms, although how these differences operate is as yet far from clear. At the same time, technological developments have important impacts on the social world: on the environment, on the way we work, on our general social interrelations.

Against this background, technology can be seen as generic or specific. A key element in modern innovation analysis has been the distinction between the technological knowledge-base of the firm – which is focused on particular products, and therefore highly specific – and the wider set of knowledges which provide the framework within which the firm operates. In referring to the wider dimension of technology, Richard Nelson has suggested that

> a technology consists [in part] of a body of knowledge which I shall call generic, in the form of a number of generalisations about how things work, key variables influencing performance, the nature of currently binding constraints and approaches to pushing these back, widely applicable problem-solving heuristics etc. . . . generic knowledge tends to be codified in applied scientific fields like electrical engineering, or materials science, or pharmacology, which are 'about' technology.
>
> (Nelson, 1987: 75–6).

Closely related to this notion of generic knowledge is the concept of 'technological paradigm': this concept, a key development in modern theory, sees technologies not as individual technical solutions, but rather refers to the whole complex of scientific knowledge, engineering practices, process technologies, infrastructure, product characteristics, skills and procedures which make up the totality of a technology. Technology can be thought of, therefore, at firm level as a highly specific set of skills and competences focused tightly on specific niches and products, but these exist within a wider technological framework, which is evolving over time, and which structures activities inside the firm. In considering the technological performance of firms, we should therefore think of technology as consisting of both internal and external components; innovation always involves an interaction between the two. A principal issue for R&D and innovation policy is to understand the extent to which support for generic knowledge, or a specific technological paradigm, can improve the performance of firms that are users of that knowledge or paradigm.

UNDERSTANDING THE INNOVATION PROCESS

In understanding the process of technological change, modern theory begins from Schumpeter's view that competition is primarily a technological phenomenon. The basis of competition is the quality, design characteristics and performance attributes of products. Firms seek competitive advantage on the one hand by continuous development of technologically differentiated products, and on the other by changing processes so as to generate these products with competitive cost structures. Usually, innovation takes the form of incremental change within fields in which firms have specialized skills and experience; that is to say, firms seek to establish a technically differentiated product range within an established technological paradigm. Alternatively, firms can seek to innovate by changing the paradigm itself; this is less frequent, but it does happen.

What is involved in the innovation process itself? Most modern research sees innovation in the following way:

- Firstly, as an interactive social process which integrates market opportunities with the design, development, financial and engineering capabilities of firms.
- Secondly, as a process characterized by continuous feedbacks between the above activities, rather than by linear transitions.
- Thirdly, as a process characterized by complex interactions between firms and their external environments.
- Fourthly, as a process which is continuous rather than intermittent. (After Kline and Rosenberg, 1986)

The primary problem for the firm is to build a set of technological competences and capabilities which will enable it to create distinctive areas of competitive advantage. Through marketing exploration, and general relationships with customers or product users, firms attempt to identify opportunities for innovation, but this is usually done within the context of an existing set of technical skills, and an existing knowledge base. Research – in the sense of a search for novel technological solutions – is usually undertaken only when firms face problems that they cannot solve within their existing knowledge bases. In other words, research is not necessarily the primary process generating innovative ideas: it is better seen as problem-solving activity within the context of ongoing innovation activity.

A key point is that firms can combine these various components of the innovation process in many ways. Firms not only produce differentiated products, they generate innovations in different ways. This has two important implications.

- Firstly, the process of differentiation generates a high level of variety and diversity among firms. There is no single model of the innovation process: firms can differ very significantly in their approaches to innovation.
- Secondly, the fact that firms attempt to specialize around existing areas of competence means that there are limits to their technological

capabilities and awareness. This leads to a phenomenon which Martin Fransman has referred to as 'bounded vision':

> the field of vision of for-profit corporations is determined largely by their existing activities in factor and product markets, in production and in R&D, and by their need in the short and medium term to generate satisfactory profits. The resulting bounded vision implies that new technologies emerging from neighbouring areas where the corporation does not have current activities are likely to take some time to penetrate the corporation's field of vision. . . . The need to generate satisfactory profits in the short to medium term therefore further bounds the vision of the corporation, contributing in some cases to a degree of 'short-sightedness'. One example is the creation of technologies for 'the day after tomorrow' where the degree of commercial uncertainty is frequently great. In view of their bounded vision, corporations often tend to underinvest in the creation of such technology.
>
> (Fransman, 1990: 3)

'Bounded vision' is a phenomenon of considerable importance for public policy. On the one hand it means that the long-term strategic capabilities of firms can often be limited. On the other, it means that when firms seek to solve innovation-related problems, they must frequently look outside the boundaries of the firm for solutions: they draw in outside information, expertise, and advice. This can of course include inputs directly or indirectly from the public sector – from universities, from libraries and databases, from research institutes, and so on. The point here is that understanding innovation means understanding the internal capabilities of firms – how they are developed, maintained, etc. – at the same time as understanding their relationships with their external environments. The process of technological change, considered broadly, is in part a process whereby technological paradigms develop (to a considerable degree on the basis of publicly-supported science and technology activity), and in part a process in which firms access, develop and refine the elements of the paradigm into specific products.

SOME CORE RESEARCH ISSUES

The only place in which the above issues have been extensively discussed from a policy viewpoint has been the OECD's TEP (Technology-Economy) programme, which consisted primarily of a series of conferences and workshops sponsored by the OECD between 1988 and 1991 (OECD, 1991, 1992). The report which initiated TEP emphasized 'the interdependence of technical, economic and social change', arguing that 'technological change is, in its development and application, fundamentally a social process, not an event, and should be viewed not in static but in dynamic terms' (OECD, 1988: 11). TEP was not in itself a research programme, and consisted essentially of a forum in which state of the art economic research could be presented. However, the following main themes – which emerge also from the analysis presented above – were emphasized:

- The need to rethink models of the innovation process.
- The importance of technology diffusion.
- The neglected role of technology in the analysis of corporate organization.
- The role of networks.
- The role of human resources and intangible investment.
- The role of technology in competitiveness and economic growth.
- The increasing importance of globalization in technology development.

The problem which remains unresolved after TEP is how these areas should be researched in the future, and how such research should be linked with policy measures and instruments; some of these issues are currently being addressed through the European Commission's 'Targeted Socio-Economic Research Programme'. We turn now to a discussion of some of the main problems, looking at the policy issues involved, and some of the key research challenges.

THE BASIC RATIONALE FOR PUBLIC POLICY

The role and significance of technological change and innovation in the 'agenda of government' depends in large part on its importance to the economic, social and cultural development of society. Recent research suggests that innovation and technological change deserve a more central place in the analysis of economic and social dynamics, but this remains an area requiring much more work, and new conceptual approaches.

While a wide body of applied research suggests there can be little doubt about the economic significance of innovation and technological change, there still remain unexplored issues in this field, especially from a policy perspective. Applied economic analysis has demonstrated, for example, that technical change is the most important factor in economic growth, that innovation performance (as measured by science and technology variables) underlies export performance and shares of world trade, that productivity and R&D are closely linked, and that returns to investment in R&D – even basic R&D in the university system – are high (see Freeman, 1987; Fagerberg, 1988; Griliches, 1986; Dosi, Pavitt and Soete, 1990 for examples).

However, two important issues remain unresolved. Firstly, the theoretical bases on which some of these analyses have been made are open to question, and have been the subject of increasing debate in recent years. In some areas – such as growth theory and the theory of trade policy – there have been significant theoretical developments in the past few years. At the same time, the conceptions which underlie analyses of productivity growth and returns to R&D have also been questioned. There is now a real need to analyse the adequacy of our existing techniques for thinking about the social and economic impacts of technological change and innovation.

There are two principal questions here. The first concerns the priority which should be given to technology policy in the general 'agenda of government'. If it really is the case that technological change has the general effects described above, then it should be given a much more central role in public policy, both at national level and at the level of the EU. The immediate question is, what kind of priority should be given to innovation and technology policy within industrial policy? At the moment, we have industrial policies which are organized primarily around issues of competition, rather than around issues of innovation. If we seek an 'innovation-oriented industrial policy' then this should be founded on a more comprehensive view of the role of new technologies in competitiveness, structural change and economic growth. However, this leads on to a second question, which concerns the integration of technology policy with other forms of policy action, especially macroeconomic policy and education policy. Many policy actions in these fields have important consequences for the rate and direction of technological change, yet technology issues are rarely taken into account in decision-making. How can integrated policies, which take proper account of innovation perspectives, be formed and implemented?

What is needed here is not, primarily, new research so much as synthesis of the main themes and results of innovation analysis over the past two decades, and application of these results to a wider set of policy problems. There are two main areas to be analysed. Firstly, we need critical overviews (not surveys) of the state of the art when it comes to the role of technological change in output growth, trade, productivity growth, etc.; these reviews should aim to draw prescriptive conclusions concerning the general policy significance of innovation/technological change issues. As well as providing a basis for policy analysis, such reviews will of course define areas for future research. Secondly, we need analyses which relate existing results to other policy fields, in particular industrial policy, macroeconomic policy, education and infrastructure policies (in particular relating to telecommunications).

UNDERSTANDING DIVERSITY: TYPOLOGIES OF INNOVATION PROCESSES

It is now clear that past models of the innovation process are too narrow and have been generalized across industries in an unrealistic way. Innovation is a complex, highly differentiated process, and the time has come to seek a 'map' of the myriad forms taken by innovation processes, and of how those forms are distributed across industries.

One of the key conclusions which might be drawn from the TEP programme is that policy should take closer account of the real characteristics of industrial innovation processes, and in particular of the differing roles of research in industrial innovation. The interactive approach to innovation emphasized by TEP does not mean, however, that we have adequate alternative models or theories of innovation processes to replace the linear model. What has been achieved through research on innovation and technological change over the past decade is a kind of outline map of the complexity and diversity of innovation processes across firms and industries. Perhaps the single biggest study of innovation processes, the Minnesota Innovation Research Project in the USA, emphasized that its primary result was 'a complicated, somewhat unruly set of empirical observations that described the multi-faceted nature of innovations and that are often beyond the explanatory capabilities of existing innovation theories' (Poole and Van de Ven, 1988: 637). But if there is great variation in innovation processes, in terms of their objectives, organization, cost, use of research, and so on, then it also means that there is variation in the problems and constraints which firms must overcome in order to undertake successful technological change.

How do innovation processes vary between industries? At the simplest level, there are differences in the amounts of research which industries must perform in order to innovate. The variations extend much further than this, however. Keith Pavitt, in a study of UK innovation activity, distinguished between three broad types of technical change processes corresponding to three types of firms: supplier dominated, production intensive, and science-based. The nature of technological change differs sharply between industrial sectors, according to the types of firms within an industry (Pavitt, 1984). The point here is that the main innovation-related problems which occur within a country or region are structure-dependent, and this is vitally important for policy. Firstly, there is no point having a technology policy designed for science-based industries in an economy with predominantly supplier-dominated firms. But then there are wider questions about the links between technology policy and industrial/economic policy. On the one hand, policy-makers may wish to influence the evolution of industrial structure. On the other, there is no special merit in having high-technology (in the sense of R&D-intensive) industries when a country has resource advantages which can be exploited industrially, even if the resource-based industries do little R&D. What matters is that industries are technologically dynamic, even if they do not access their technologies through R&D, but this may involve issues in science and technology monitoring, investment policy (meaning both macroeconomic policies which affect investment, but also tax treatments of investment), infrastructure provision and public investment, education and training, etc. In order to know something about the appropriate balance and structure of policy measures, policy-makers need a more nuanced understanding of the types of innovation processes at industry level.

But recognizing the variety in innovation processes should go further than this, down to firm level. Much economic policy is implicitly based on the economic concept of the 'representative firm', that is the idea that firms are essentially similar, and that they will respond in similar ways to changes in their environment. This includes the environment of policy measures, and it is therefore assumed that any policy measure will induce common responses in firms; thus a subsidy or a tax will cause firms to respond in similar, or at very least predictable, ways. The problem here is that, in practice, firms actually differ sharply in terms of their internal cultures, management systems, explicit or implicit objectives, growth strategies, capabilities in accessing and processing information, technological competences and so on. Policies which assume this diversity away – such as tax-based subsidies to R&D – are likely to founder on the problem of differential response. Of course it is out of the question to design policies which accommodate the multiplicity of company types, especially in economies with hundreds of thousands of companies in existence. But this leads to the question of whether we can construct workable typologies or models of innovation processes which are both descriptively sound and policy-relevant. In my view this is possible, via an appropriate combination of case studies and statistical methods.

At the present time, policy remains more or less based on the idea that firms face only one problem in innovation, namely the finance of R&D. But the extreme diversity of innovation processes at both industry and firm level implies that firms face a variety of quite different problems. Innovation and technology policy should reflect this, with a more subtle and differentiated mix of objectives and instruments which correspond to the real characteristics of relevant innovation processes within the economy or region. The starting point for this can only be a wider range of models of innovation processes, and this is a key task for policy analysts in years ahead.

EXTERNAL ENVIRONMENTS: NATIONAL AND REGIONAL SYSTEMS OF INNOVATION

As technologies increase in complexity, it is more and more difficult for firms to acquire, maintain and develop knowledge bases which cover all of their technological needs. This means that they must look outside the firm to solve some of the problems that they encounter in innovation. On the one hand this opens up questions about the role of the public sector. But firms also look to inter-firm co-operation in problem solving. As we noted above, firms exist, technologically speaking, within networks of equipment suppliers, design specialists, universities and research institutes, customers, consulting engineers, and so on, and they seek to use these networks to resolve problems. Even quite small firms often have extensive formal and informal links with other firms (Hagedoorn, 1991; Håkonssen, 1988). Formally speaking, there are joint ventures, licensing and cross-licensing arrangements, acquisitions, and various co-operative research arrangements. Informally, there is extensive 'know-how trading' (Von Hippel, 1989). On one level these developments raise important questions about the boundaries of the firm, about what it means to speak of a 'firm' at all in the context of networks.

As argued above, a substantial body of modern research emphasizes the fact that firms never innovate in isolation: they do so inside technological paradigms or regimes which are external to the firm. But what is the concrete basis of a technological paradigm or regime? An important body of modern analysis sees this question in terms of more or less complex networks of formal and informal relationships. In part, these are relationships with other firms: suppliers, customers, sources of finance, even competitors. In part, they are relationships with factor markets, especially for skilled labour. In part, they are relationships with the public sector: with universities, technological institutes, standards-setting organizations, regulatory agencies and so on. A final element is the policy environment within which these institutions operate. Together, this complex set of institutions and environmental factors make up a *system of innovation*, which usually has specific geographic and political boundaries. Such systems can be understood either as a *regional system of innovation* (perhaps crossing national boundaries) or a *national system of innovation.*

One way of looking at this body of work would be to see it as an exploration of the problem of infrastructure. It is widely recognized, in public policy terms, that both physical and science-technology infrastructures are a key element in innovative and economic performance. But we have as yet no established theory of infrastructure, nor do we have analysis of how infrastructures work; the 'system of innovation' concept should be seen as a step forward in this area, but there remains much to be done to explore its implications.

INTERNATIONALIZATION IN TECHNOLOGICAL CHANGE

Finally, the firm's capabilities, and national and regional innovation systems, interact with powerful global forces in technological innovation and diffusion. There are those who argue that national borders have become meaningless in this new international context, but this remains an area of considerable uncertainty and debate. What cannot be denied is that rapid acceleration in foreign direct investment, the growth of intra-industry trade, the international movement of skilled personnel, the liberalization of capital and foreign exchange markets all contribute to an increasingly internationalized context for technological change.

Given that firms exist in a wider economic/technological context, how does that context relate to the wider development of the global economy and its changing organization? It seems clear that major changes are happening in this area at the present time, which suggests a final research theme, related to firstly the international distribution of innovative activity, and secondly the speed and reach of technology diffusion processes.

Technology development appears to remain concentrated on specific national environments, while diffusion, like the overall operation of market forces, is more or less global, but policy is national or regional. This raises a number of dilemmas for policy-makers. Many policy systems have as their objective the competitiveness of national industries, an objective which in some cases does not fit with the transnational dimensions of the technological change process. As the authors of a recent study of semiconductor-based industries remarked:

> the model of a battle between distinct and well-defined "national" industries is an inappropriately unsophisticated one in the case of microelectronics. Indeed, we would maintain that it is impossible to come to terms with competitiveness without first recognising and appreciating the international inter-relatedness of the industry.
>
> (Langlois and Nelson, 1988: 3)

On the other hand there are many sectors in which technology creation remains non-internationalized. However, the speed and comprehensiveness of global diffusion processes inhibit the ability of follower regions or countries to create technological capabilities. This means, at the very least, continuing dilemmas concerning the focus of science and technology policy for particular regions or countries. In some cases, arguments for support of specific firms or technologies may remain valid, but these issues also raise questions about the nature and role of infrastructures. For policy-makers concerned with a country or region, what matters for 'competitiveness' is the ability of firms located within the region/country to engage and act within the transnational networks through which technology is developed or diffused. Of course this is in part a function of R&D performance at firm level. But only in part. It also depends on access to skilled personnel, access to the science and technology infrastructure, financial and marketing resources and so on. It is very important for policy-makers to conceptualize and operationalize these wider factors in technological competitiveness if they are to devise appropriate policy instruments in the new international context.

A further international policy dilemma relates to fundamental science. The problem here is precisely the fact that science is, and always has been, international: it is based for the most part on open publication, and results are mostly non-appropriable. At the same time the links between science and technology are often tenuous. These points suggest that, for national policy-makers concerned with economic results, an obvious move is to reallocate resources away from fundamental science towards research which is more or less directly oriented to industrial applications. There is much to be said in favour of this, and certainly there should be nothing sacrosanct about the post-war allocation of scientific resources (which heavily favoured high-energy physics). But at the same time such moves mean that no national system has any incentive to develop scientific fields where there may be long-term opportunities, but no short-run benefits. To the extent that such fields exist – and however sceptical one might be about the linear model, there are many historical examples to show that they do exist – then strategies which are right for individual countries are wrong for the world. From a game-theory perspective, this is a straightforward Prisoners' Dilemma problem. Like the Prisoners' Dilemma, the solution lies in collaboration. But existing international mechanisms for support of fundamental science are either non-existent or inadequate, and an important policy challenge for the future is therefore to build appropriate collaborative institutions which can decide priorities, allocate resources and disseminate results.

The 1980s saw a significant step forward in the internationalization process; in the past, internationalization has been discussed mainly in terms of multinational corporations. But over the last decade, internationalization came to affect almost all aspects of the industrial economy. The most obvious development was the liberalization of capital markets so that the world now has integrated 24-hour capital and foreign exchange markets; one effect of this is that ownership of corporations is becoming more diffused internationally. But production also became much more internationalized: global foreign direct investment grew at

20 per cent per year through the 1980s, which was very much faster than the growth of international trade (which grew at less than 5 per cent per year). Instead of producing from national bases and then exporting, large companies now produce globally: US firms now produce eight times more output outside the USA than they export from the USA. This is not just a matter of multinational companies: in almost every important industry and product group, products are produced through integrated global manufacture. Even a simple product such as a piece of clothing involves primary production, cloth manufacture, design, fabrication, finance and so on occurring in several countries. Most firms, regardless of their size, are involved in complex relationships (including sub-contracting) with suppliers and customers which often go beyond national boundaries. This internationalization process extends into the technological sphere: even small companies in small countries have joint ventures, R&D co-operation, licensing arrangements, technology trade and so on which are international in scope. The technical division of labour involved in the production of industrial products is now thoroughly internationalized. These internationalization processes take different forms in different industries, and are far from complete. But they do form a real and significant trend.

What are the implications of all this? On one level, there are real questions about whether we can think about companies, especially the large companies, as 'national' entities. When the ownership, management, finance and technology of a company are integrated across many national boundaries, it becomes unclear whether there is such a thing as a national company. This has obvious implications for industrial and technology policy. Can we have a national industry policy in the context of internationalized industries and companies? What problems of international policy co-ordination are raised by the internationalization process?

Most of the questions raised in science and technology policy make sense only against the background of these internationalization processes. One critical issue concerns location of industry. Should there be some kind of international 'rules of the game' on incentives for companies to locate in particular countries or regions in order to prevent competitive bidding – in terms of tax breaks, subsidies, etc. – by countries? A second issue concerns public research systems. How should the public support of industrially-oriented R&D be organized in this new international context? What are the appropriate objectives and methods? Is it possible to have a national technology policy of the traditional kind, namely R&D support to national companies? Or should industrial policy be focused on the education/training/basic science infrastructure? In the latter case, there are serious questions about the role of international collaboration and co-ordination. This question also takes us to the second major trend indicated above, namely the role of science in technological change.

NEW TECHNOLOGIES, ECONOMIC GROWTH AND THE SCIENCE BASE

The increasing recognition of research and technology as supports to economic growth has also directed attention to the use of science in industrial innovation. If we reject so-called 'linear' models of innovation, this should not imply that science is unimportant in industrial innovation processes; rather, it is a question of how science fits into these processes. If we take the view that firms do research in order to solve key problems either in existing technologies or planned innovations, then it is clear that many industrial innovation problems require basic science in order to be solved. Nathan Rosenberg has emphasized the fact that we do not possess an adequate scientific understanding of many aspects of advanced industrial technologies. This is often the case with quite fundamental processes: for example, combustion processes, airflow over aircraft wings, and aspects of computer architectures are all areas where technological development lacks a basis in scientific knowledge, and where industrial processes remain based on 'trial and error'.

Technology is not simply applied science, and new technologies do not necessarily flow from previous scientific research. More often, fundamental science has its problems and search areas shaped by practical needs (often military rather than commercial). Since this kind of science is characterized by high levels of uncertainty in research output, and by long time lags between research and identifiable applications, economic evaluation is more or less impossible. But there are plenty of examples of the use of fundamental or university-based research that are relevant in understanding the evolution of industrial innovation, and there is some evidence that this scientific role is increasing. Perhaps the quantitative indicators in this area are the references to basic research literature in patents. A number of writers have shown that patented inventions are increasingly drawing on academic science, as measured by academic journal literature in patent applications (Narin and Noma, 1985; Narin, 1988). But how does this occur? What are the main channels of knowledge flow? What are the main industries whose technological problems now require scientific solutions? There is a serious 'mapping' problem here, which will feed into some of the other problem areas described above, and which is of great importance for policy-makers.

There is evidence that the connections between industrial innovation and fundamental science are becoming closer. Although there is no general or linear relationship between basic or fundamental scientific research, on the one hand, and product or process innovation activity on the other, there are none the less industries and activities where the two are closely related. The fastest growing industries within world trade are without exception research-intensive, and in a number of these industries – chemicals and pharmaceuticals, electronic and photo-optic products, and so on – tight links can be demonstrated between the invention process, and underlying fundamental research. In Europe, Japan and the USA, research policy is increasingly directed towards attempts to enhance competitive advantage in industry, with both companies and policy-makers believing that future competitiveness will spring from the exploitation of results in basic scientific research. So industrially-oriented research at the present time finds its priorities not just in innovations based on reasonably well-understood technological principles, but also in large-scale research programmes in basic science areas such as recombinant-DNA, biotechnology, superconductivity, new materials and so on. Whatever the long-run historical relationship between science and technology in the development of the West, there can be little doubt that at the present time the links are close.

The following problem arises. If countries concentrate their science policies on 'oriented basic research', aimed at areas where specific industrial applications are envisaged, what happens to more general areas of science where results are not easily appropriated or linked with industrial applications? Science is a 'public good', in the sense that it is non-marketed and that published results are easily transferred. This gives countries an incentive *not* to provide basic research, but to utilize the results of research carried out by others. If everyone takes this perspective, there will be a general underprovision and underfunding in scientific areas where results are not easily appropriated. The only way around this problem is some general international commitment to co-ordinated funding of such scientific areas. There are obvious problems concerning levels of funding, selection of research areas and institutions.

TECHNOLOGY AND THE ENVIRONMENT

A key current policy issue concerns the technology policy aspects of environmental change. Apart from natural shocks such as volcanic eruptions, environmental problems generally stem from an interaction between population increase, economic growth, and the underlying technologies on which economic growth is based. In the case of greenhouse gas emissions, for example, we are dealing with the effects of long-term use of core industrial technologies related to energy supply and use, and reducing the scale of emissions must involve either a significant reduction in the scale on which these technologies are used, or their more or less complete replacement. In either case, a move towards environmental stability must entail large-scale technological change. For environmental policy the understanding of technological change in systems of energy supply and use becomes a key issue. The question of environmental stability and sustainability is therefore central to modern technology policy, both nationally and internationally.

CONCLUSION

The recognition that innovation and technological change are central to economic development is a firmly-founded one, but the policy implications are far from clear at the present time. In part the future of R&D and innovation policies depend on quite fundamental political debates about the role of government, which are as yet unresolved in a number of OECD economies. But this chapter has tried to demonstrate that there is also a rather comprehensive set of theoretical and empirical issues as well, which will require both serious research and reflection before a really adequate approach to policy emerges in this critical field.

REFERENCES

Arrow, K.J. (1962), 'Economic welfare and the allocation of resources for invention', in R. Nelson (ed.) *The Rate and Direction of Inventive Activity*, Princeton: Princeton University Press, pp. 609–625; republished in N. Rosenberg (1974), *The Economics of Technological Change*, Harmondsworth: Pelican, pp. 164–181.

Bush, V. (1980), *Science – the Endless Frontier. A Report to the President on a Program for Postwar Scientific Research*, New York: Arno Press (facsimile reprint of National Science Foundation Edition).

Dosi, G., Pavitt, K. and Soete, L. (1990), *The Economics of Technical Change and International Trade*, London: Pinter.

Ergas, H. (1987), 'The importance of technology policy', in P. Dasgupta and P. Stoneman (eds) *Economic Policy and Technological Performance*, Cambridge: CUP.

European Commission (1994), *The European Report on Science and Technology Indicators 1994.*

Fagerberg, J. (1988), 'International Competitiveness', *Economic Journal*, vol. 98, no. 391.

Fransman, M. (1990), *The Market and Beyond. Cooperation and Competition in Information Technology in the Japanese System*, Cambridge: CUP.

Freeman, C. (ed.) (1987), *Output Measurement in Science and Technology*, Amsterdam: North Holland.

Griliches, Z. (1986), *R&D, Patents and Productivity*, Chicago: University of Chicago Press.

Hagedoorn, J. (1991), 'Networks in research and production', *International Journal of Technology Management*, pp. 81–95.

Håkonsson, H. (1988), *Corporate Technological Behaviour: Co-operation and Networks*, London: Routledge.

Klein, S. and Rosenberg, N. (1986), 'An overview of innovation' in R. Landau and N. Rosenberg (eds) *The Positive Sum Strategy. Harnessing Technology for Economic Growth*, Washington: National Academy Press.

Langlois, R. and Nelson, R. (1988), *Microelectronics: An Industry in Transition*, London: Unwin Hyman.

Narin, F. (1988), 'Technology indicators based on patents and patent citations', in A.F.J. Van Raan (ed.) *Handbook of Quantitative Studies in Science and Technology*, Elsevier: Amsterdam.

Narin, F. and Noma, E. (1985), 'Is technology becoming science?', *Scientometrics*, 7, pp. 369–381.

Nelson, R. (1987), *Understanding Technological Change as an Evolutionary Process*, Elsevier: Amsterdam.

OECD (1988), *New Technologies in the 1990s: A Socio-Economic Strategy*, OECD: Paris.

OECD (1991), *Technology in a Changing World*, OECD: Paris.

OECD (1992), *Technology and the Economy: The Key Relationships*, OECD: Paris.

Pavitt, K. (1984), 'Sectoral patterns of technical change: towards a taxonomy and a theory', *Research Policy*, 13, pp. 343–373.

Poole, M.S. and Van de Ven, A.H. (1988), 'Toward a general theory of innovation processes', in Andrew H. Van de Ven (ed.) *Research on the Management of Innovation: The Minnesota Studies*, Minneapolis: University of Minnesota Press.

Von Hippel, E. (1989), *Sources of Innovation*, Oxford: OUP.

6

FROM COMMON SENSE TO SHORT-TERMISM

Reflections on R&D managers' perceptions

Istemi Demirag

In international comparisons, British manufacturing firms do not perform well in terms of R&D spending, patenting rates, market shares and product innovation. The results of the most recent studies and surveys provide statistical evidence for the poor state of British manufacturing firms (for example see Innovation Advisory Board 1990; House of Lords 1991; Patel and Pavitt 1992; Centre for Exploitation of Science and Technology 1991; and Demirag and Tonkin 1991 and 1992). It is often argued that this poor performance is mainly the result of 'short-term' pressures in the UK. Porter (1992) and Jacobs (1991) also provide some support for this prognosis in the US economy. So, what is meant by short-termism and what factors cause short-term pressures? Many authors writing on short-termism have defined the term differently. The most common definition of short-termism adopted by many authors is 'a propensity for short-term gains taken at the expense of longer term benefits'. Demirag and Tylecote (1992) define short-termism, at the level of the firm, as the application of a time rate of discount which *exceeds the firm's opportunity cost of capital*, and/or the foreshortening of the time horizon to exclude relatively distant revenues. This definition of short-termism is clearly distinct in principle, though perhaps similar in its practical effects, from a shortage or high price of capital such as might be produced generally by tight monetary policy or specifically by negative cash flows.

Possible causes of short-termism have been debated widely in the finance and accounting literature (see Demirag and Tylecote 1992; Tylecote and Demirag 1992; and Demirag, Tylecote and Morris 1994). Capital markets are often accused of putting inappropriate short-term pressures on management. Hostile take-overs also lead to short-term pressures by threatening to change management policy and ultimately to the management's dismissal (Froot, Perold, Andre and Stein, 1993; Jenkinson and Mayer 1993). For example Frank and

Mayer (1990) found that the combination of take-overs and institutional investor intervention has created a high level of recorded executive dismissals in the UK. The pressures put by capital markets, as Arnold and Moizer (1984) and Cosh, Hughes and Singh (1990) found, also result in short-term financial evaluation of institutional fund managers. For example, they found that merchant banks and stockbrokers, carrying out investment for pension fund clients and other private clients, were assessed more frequently and professionally than before. The conclusion of these studies indicates that institutional investors have become more short-term oriented and their success is judged over a short period like three years or even shorter. The use of short-term performance measures such as quarterly figures and frequent changes of clients appears to have put pressures on fund managers to look for short-term performance. Those who argue in favour of the capital markets (for example see Marsh 1990; National Association of Pension Funds 1990; National Economic Development Council 1991; Coopers and Lybrand/Mori 1991; and Ball 1991) accuse management either of generating the short-term pressure itself, or not supplying the capital market with the information it requires to exert appropriate pressures.

The above studies and some other recent work on short-termism (for example see Confederation of British Industry 1987; Williams 1991; Carr 1990; and Carr, Tomkins and Bayliss 1994) have tended to focus on certain aspects of this phenomenon. They have argued either in favour of capital markets or management while generally acknowledging the importance of managerial perceptions of short-term pressures from capital markets; none of these studies, however, have considered this issue as a possible cause of short-termism. The debate as to whether or not British managers actually *perceive* short-term pressures from the capital markets and whether this in turn results in short-term behaviour in firms has not been widely argued. In this chapter I will examine the Research and Development managers' perceptions of short-termism in UK companies. R&D managers' perception of short-termism is an important issue because if managers perceive short-term pressures then it is reasonable to assume that their organizational structure, performance evaluation and control of R&D activities may be influenced by these perceptions.

It would seem from the above discussion that factors causing short-term pressures may be examined under two main headings: capital markets and management control systems. The following discussion will review the literature on causes of short-termism.

THE INFLUENCE OF CAPITAL MARKETS ON SHORT-TERMISM

The large majority of UK institutional shareholders, 'The City', own the majority of shares in UK public companies and there is some evidence to suggest that their percentage of ownership has been increasing in recent years. It is argued that these shareholders are only 'concerned' with the short term. Studies by Arnold and Moizer (1984) and Day (1986), indicate that UK investment analysts view published financial information such as earnings and dividends with significant importance thus suggesting short-term behaviour in their investment appraisals. Fund managers' objectives are short-term because, it is alleged they operate under intense short-term pressures, due to the fact that their portfolio performance is measured on a quarterly basis. If they do badly they may lose their jobs, as is evidenced by the fact that they (at least the *external* fund managers) frequently do. However, Marsh (1990) argues that although performance measurers collect their data on a quarterly cycle, the published information showing their comparative performance figures are for one year or longer periods. However, a recent study of the performance evaluation of fund managers by Ashton *et al.* (1991) shows that in all the cases the fund was valued at least four times per annum and the fund managers were evaluated on a slightly longer time scale. Moreover they found that the main reward fund managers seemed to receive from their work was the feeling of satisfaction at having performed better than the average on their quarterly short-term evaluations.

It is also reasonable to argue that pressures of this kind are in principle entirely compatible with a willingness to ignore short-term cash flows, profits, and dividends in favour of long-term prospects: a fund manager who consistently recognized such prospects and invested accordingly, shortly before others did, would 'perform' extremely well. If short-term performance was all that counted then companies and sectors would all have more or less the same price/earnings ratios, which is of course very far from the truth. There is no reason to think that, where evidence exists of a company's long-term prospects, it will not be given appropriate consideration: in other words, anticipated future profits, discounted at the ruling rate, will be valued on an equal basis with current profits. There is no evidence of short-termism in the objectives of fund managers. There is, on the other hand, no evidence either of *long-termism*, i.e. more attention to (distant) future profits than economic rationality would dictate, and since there is some reason to believe that those in control of Japanese companies do exhibit such objectives to some extent (Kester 1990) we might infer relative short-termism in the UK by comparison with Japan at least. A recent study by Pike,

Meerjanssen and Chadwick (1993) investigated the relative short-term attitudes of UK and German investors. The study found that there has been a change in the importance attached to different types of information by analysts in the last ten years. German analysts placed 'slightly more importance on new non-financial information, particularly of a research and development or product quality nature, than UK analysts'. The study, however, rejected the conclusion that UK analysts place more emphasis on short-term goals. Although German analysts appeared to be more interested in long-term goals, the study did not find any significant evidence to support the claims that UK capital markets behave in a short-term manner. However, I shall later argue that the relationship between shareholders and management is more important to the short-termism debate than the objectives of the shareholders.

There is also a significant difference in how companies are financed in Germany and Britain. Most German companies prefer to finance their operations from bank borrowings. In contrast, British companies prefer equity finance from capital markets. One of the reasons for this difference is that banks in the UK, although financially profitable, are neither interested in nor have the in-house ability to understand technology and long-term perspectives of companies they lend money to. Furthermore, as Hutton (1995, p. 149) argues, British banks themselves have to borrow large amounts of cash in the short-term money markets that they are reluctant to lend at long-term fixed interest rates. There is some international evidence provided by the Cranfield European Enterprise Centre (1994) which indicates that from 1992, 58 per cent of all lending to British small and medium-sized companies was in the form of overdrafts, compared with 14 per cent for Germany, 31 per cent for France and 35 per cent for Italy. UK companies also obtained all of their debt capital at variable interest rates. The overall effect of this is that the average cost of finance British companies have to pay to finance their operations is higher than their German counterparts (for example see Coopers and Lybrand 1993). Over the period 1983–1991 the overall cost of capital in Japan was 14.7 per cent, in the USA 15.1 per cent and in Germany 15.7 per cent, but in Britain it was 19.9 per cent (Coopers and Lybrand 1993). One of the reasons for this high cost of capital in the UK is because British companies have to raise their equity capital earlier than debt capital which takes shorter time to arrange through banks. Given the significant influence of the cost of capital on the investment appraisal techniques, it would seem reasonable to suggest that the way companies are financed may influence their level of investment and subsequent financial performance.

The alternative to debt finance is to raise equity capital in the stock market. The problem here is the possibility that shareholders may put short-term pressures on management. To the extent that shareholders lack or do not understand information relevant to the longer-term performance of companies – e.g. on technological progress 'in the pipeline' – they will respond excessively to current profit, dividend announcements, earnings per share, and similar easily available financial data based on historical performance or other short-term performance measures. It is therefore argued that this short-term emphasis by analysts and fund managers will create a corresponding short-term bias in stock prices. One key issue here is the effect of variations in dividends. Other things being equal, an increase in the dividend should reduce the expected return on a company's shares. Anything less than a one-for-one reduction in share price for an increase in dividend would constitute short-termism on the shareholders' part and impose short-term pressures on managers. Litzenberger and Ramaswamy (1982) and Poterba and Summers (1984) claim to find from the econometric evidence that raising dividends does reduce the expected return on a company's shares; Miller and Scholes (1982) and Nickell and Wadhwani (1987) argue that it does not. The traditional view within finance theory is that high dividend payouts should be irrelevant to investment. Companies that have attractive investment projects but not sufficient internal funds to finance these projects should be able to raise suitable external finance, either by borrowing or by issuing new shares from the capital markets. Given the expected return on investment, the current level of profits and dividend payments should not influence investment levels. However, empirical evidence provided by the Confederation of British Industry trends survey consistently indicates that a shortage of internal funds is one of the main factors limiting investment levels in Britain, indicating that external finance costs more than internally generated funds, as supported by the survey results of the Cranfield European Enterprise Centre (1994). The recent increases in company profitability in real terms did not seem to have increased investment levels. Yet, it did reduce the availability of internal funds.

Some defenders of investment analysts and fund managers argue, however, that dividend announcements, like earnings, convey significant information about the future. Management decisions on the level of the current year's dividend take into account judgements about future profitability and cash flows; the dividend has to be consistent with this, and with sustaining a steady growth rate of future dividends. Thus dividend announcements are an important signal of the management's knowledge and judgement about the longer term future of the companies they manage. Given this downward inflexibility of dividend payments, the availability of internal finance will be further reduced by the decline in company profitability in a recession.

It is generally accepted that the market requires a steady growth rate of future dividends, and if this is not achieved share prices may decline as the market punishes those who do not provide it. The British tax system also gives a big tax incentive in favour of paying out dividends rather than retaining profits; the relatively high level of dividend payments by UK companies may be one of the reasons for the low levels of investment. Bond and Meghir (1994) argue that this is because the tax credits associated with dividends make dividend income more attractive than capital gains for tax exempt institutional shareholders, including pension funds. Furthermore, if the companies establish that their share price responds positively to the dividends they announce, then the firm may be encouraged to raise/hold its dividend when it really should be reducing it.

It is also suggested that tax incentives may encourage spending on R&D (for example see Thomas 1995). However, a survey carried out by the Inland Revenue and HM Treasury (1987) found that tax incentives were not efficient because they did not increase industrial R&D expenditure by as much as the tax revenues forgone by the Government; companies' cash flow and post-tax profits did improve as a result though. But a study carried out by Hall (1992) challenged the results of the survey. Moreover, a report published by The Advisory Council On Science and Technology (ACOST) (1994) acknowledged that tax subsidies for R&D were difficult to target and that their effects were difficult to assess. The report by ACOST considered changing the rate of tax imposed on distributed profits in the form of dividends to institutional shareholders thus encouraging firms to retain profits within their business for investment purposes. However, the report concluded that the capital markets have much greater influence than the structure of the tax systems over the level of profits.

It is claimed that the 'visibility' of desired investment is yet another important factor for determining the level of short-term performance pressures put on firms by capital markets. Certain inputs to the process of innovation are highly visible – in particular fixed investment appears in the balance sheet and need not be deducted from profits. Likewise some types of research and development costs may be capitalized and easily noticed by capital markets. A variety of approaches to the treatment of research and development is possible. Companies may write off such expenditures immediately against earnings as it is impossible to assess the future economic benefits of such expenditures with a reasonable degree of certainty. Any attempt to match expenditure and benefits would also be an arbitrary process as there could be no supportable basis on which to carry it out. Others prefer to capitalize and amortize on the grounds that such expenditures are incurred with the expectation of producing future economic benefits and that the accrual accounting concept therefore should be applied. The opponents of this method argue that the future economic benefits of research and development expenditures are too uncertain to warrant 'recognition' as assets and that a 'prudent' approach should be adopted. In the UK all research costs must be written off immediately but development costs may be capitalized in certain specified circumstances and amortized to match the future revenues generated by the asset. In practice, however, most UK companies write off immediately both research and development.

In general, as in the case of research and development, training and marketing costs are also incurred in a decentralized and fragmentary fashion, and may not easily be distinguished from the results of sheer inefficiency in the process of production and distribution. The inputs in the pharmaceutical industry, however, tend to be more centralized than in the other industries. These, and other factors, notably the degree of centralization of the process, greatly affect its visibility.

Where the overwhelming bulk of inputs is fixed investment and/or R&D, and they are deployed in a relatively centralized manner, the process of innovation has high visibility, and 'thin' information flows may be sufficient. Where in addition the innovation is lumpy and risky, the stock exchange-based system may come into its own, since it is of its nature relatively tolerant of risk. It follows that stock exchange-based systems like that of the UK are likely to engender external short-term pressures from capital markets in industries where the visibility of the process of innovation is low.

The significance of the visibility of investment in generating short-term pressures will be determined to a large extent by the efficiency of the financial markets. An efficient market hypothesis suggests that a company's share price, at any moment in time, will reflect all the relevant information which is available on its future prospects. The efficiency of the UK stock market in general has been confirmed by some recent work such as that of O'Hanlon *et al.* (1992). In the case of the short-termism debate, in addition to the visibility of desired investment as discussed earlier, the 'market' will also have to understand and interpret the accounting regulations relating to R&D and training expenditure. Investment in tangible assets does not reduce current profit as it is capitalized in the balance sheet. But for intangible assets, such as R&D, accounting regulations limit the amount which can be capitalized. Gray (1986), for example, found that R&D information was considered to be important by investment analysts for the 'high-tech' sector. The analysts wanted to know how much companies spent on R&D and tended to discriminate against those spending below the 'industry norm', and they preferred R&D to be written off against profit immediately as well. Goodacre *et al.* (1990) and Goodacre (1991) also provide further evidence on the efficiency of the market in interpreting the R&D expenditure by investor analysts. They investigated whether investment analysts discriminated against R&D investment and also whether the method of accounting for R&D was likely to have any impact on the valuation of companies by analysts. They provided a number of investment analysts with hypothetical company accounts using two different methods of reporting R&D. Their findings suggest that analysts were able to 'see through' the essentially cosmetic difference between the two reporting methods and reacted to the underlying economic reality rather than the reported earnings. Moreover, the analysts did not exhibit data fixation and appeared to place value on what they perceived to be an appropriate level of R&D expenditure. As in Gray's (1986) findings they found that the company which spent less on R&D, investing in plant and equipment instead, was valued significantly less highly than the company investing in R&D at an industry-average level. These results tend to support the view that short-termism in the market does not seem to extend to analysts' view on R&D. Goodacre *et al.* thus conclude their results do not support the view that the market discriminates against long-term (R&D) investment, at least not up to a level which is viewed as appropriate (the industry norm). Research in the USA also provides similar findings. The Securities and Exchange Commission Office of Economic Analysis (1985) found, for example, that the US stock market responded to announcements that firms were embarking on R&D projects by *raising* their share prices. Again in the USA, Chaney and Devinney (1992) found a similar response to announcements of new product innovations.

There are different levels of market efficiency. For example, market efficiency is sometimes referred to as the markets' ability to incorporate all new information; efficiency in the information arbitrage sense (Tobin 1984). However, those who support the efficiency of markets do not necessarily make a claim for the 'technical quality' of the information. In this context, the market efficiency claimed is purely based on its technical quality: it is in the use of the information available. It remains possible that information required for a correct valuation of future profits is not being gathered in the fundamental valuation sense. Empirical studies by Shiller (1981), Modigliani and Cohen (1979), Poterba and Summers (1988), Summers (1986), and Nickell and Wadhwani (1987) have all shown the myopia of stock market prices by short-term considerations. Moreover it is not enough that such information be available to a minority. As Schleifer and Vishny (1990) have shown, arbitrage based on superior information about long-term potential will be much less lucrative than that based on information today which the rest will have tomorrow. The information required to assess the future profitability and innovation success of a company is a great deal more complex and difficult to obtain than the mere level of R&D expenditure. To be a successful innovator and also to be profitable you need to be good at market research, training, the purchase of capital equipment, coping with teething troubles in the early stages of manufacture, building up distribution channels, and pricing policies appropriate to build market share. However, most of these activities which are closely associated with being a successful innovator cannot be capitalized and cannot be assessed by analysts in the way they treat R&D. There is some evidence to suggest that these activities are widely believed to be underfunded in the UK in order to improve short-term profitability. (On training, for example, see Mayhew 1991; on marketing, see Doyle 1987.) If the evidence provided from these sources is correct then it will have two consequences: for a given rate of spending on R&D, firstly, it will reduce the return to be expected from R&D for product innovation and therefore depress R&D spending, secondly, it will depress the rate of successful product innovation.

It is also not reasonable to expect capital markets to have all the relevant information about companies' prospects. Moody (1989) argues that investment analysts and fund managers often lack the knowledge and technological expertise required to evaluate 'technology in the pipeline'. In their study only 8 out of 25 electronics analysts had a relevant science qualification, despite that industry's research intensity. On the other hand chemical and pharmaceutical sectors were exceptionally fortunate: Moody found that 9 out of 11 chemicals and 16 out of 18 pharmaceutical analysts were relevant science graduates. It is also worth mentioning here the rules against insider dealing. These rules in general inhibit companies giving 'price-sensitive' information to only one shareholder. Moreover, the fear of this valuable information passing on to competitors can also inhibit companies from giving this information to their anlaysts.

There are many reasons why management will be sensitive to its company's share price. Among others, the extent of management's concern over the market value of the share price will be determined mainly by a) how far it is afraid of a contested take-over bid, b) whether it wishes to raise new equity capital – which may be for organic growth or for acquisitions, and c) where share prices form part of their reward. Here we shall focus on the first reason, the second reason is straightforward and requires little discussion and the last reason will be examined in the next section.

It is often claimed that British shareholders are inclined to 'Exit' rather than 'Voice': shareholders who are not satisfied with companies' performance and/or policies are likely to sell their holdings in those companies rather than work with them and seek to change them by putting pressures on the board of directors and eventually voting against them. For example, the Innovation Advisory Board (1990) argues that the institutions which own shares in British companies are too ready to 'sell out' either in the market, or by accepting a take-over bid, in order to make a quick short-term profit; there is little loyalty to companies among the institutions. They suggest that one of the main reasons for this lack of loyalty is that share holding by pension funds and insurance companies is highly fragmented. These small fragmented ownerships in companies may hinder their efforts to work with the management of these companies.

However, the 'Exit' behaviour, so often shown by the institutional shareholders, may have some benefits to the economy as it facilitates take-overs. The take-over process and the market for corporate control ensure that existing assets in an economy are most profitably employed. Any management which is not efficiently using its resources should be subject to a threat of a take-over from the more efficient companies who can manage those resources better. Moreover, the combined resources of two separate profit maximizing companies may lead to better results after their amalgamation than before. However, empirical evidence indicates (see for example Cosh, Hughes and Singh 1990) that in general only the unprofitable companies are taken over; the greater the profitability or stock market valuation of a company, less is the chance of its being taken over by a hostile bidder. There is also some evidence to indicate that the size of a company also affects its chances of acquisition (see, for example, Singh 1975; Hughes 1989).

Indeed, evidence cited by Greer (1986) and Singh (1971) shows that making an acquisition to increase size might itself become a tactic to avoid take-over. It would appear that some UK companies may be using acquisitions and short-term profit maximization as a means of protecting themselves from hostile take-over threats.

MANAGEMENT CONTROL AND REWARD SYSTEMS

Internal management control systems, such as the types of financial measures used for performance evaluations, non-financial measures, communication channels between the top and lower management and the type of remuneration used for managers will also determine the extent of short-term pressures. For example, when only financial measures of performance are used, and when management pay is highly geared to such measures, we would expect strong short-term pressures. Indeed there is some evidence from the UK company practice that management incentives based on Earning per Share and share option schemes are widely used as a means of motivating and rewarding corporate performance which increases management sensitivity to reported earnings and share prices. Healy (1985) points out that bonus schemes create incentives for managers to select accounting rules to maximize the value of their bonus awards. His findings suggest that 1) accrual policies of managers are related to income-reporting incentives of their bonus contracts and 2) changes in accounting procedures by managers are associated with adoption or modification of their bonus plan. Brickley, Bhagat and Lease (1985) examined the impact on shareholder wealth of a variety of long-range compensation plans. These plans differed from short-term bonus plans in that the compensation was designed to be a function of performance over a longer period of time (normally several years). In the case of bonus schemes management is generally rewarded for good performance in a given year. The results indicated that the long-range bonus plans (such as stock options or stock appreciation rights) increased shareholder wealth. Empirical evidence from the US studies carried out by Tehranian and Waegelein (1985), Brickley *et al.* (1985) and Kumar and Sopariwala (1992) have all found that the US financial market has favourably reacted to the announcement of many executive incentive schemes. While Brickley *et al.* (1985) admit that the benefits of these incentive schemes to shareholders could be derived by the sharing of tax benefits with managers in tax-motivated plans, the findings nevertheless support the notion that different types of plans may be appropriate in different situations. For example Ball (1991) also suggests that profit-related bonuses and share option schemes are responsible for short-term behaviour in the UK.

Marsh (1990) points out that short-term pressures are generated within the firm, and they do not arise as a result of market inefficiency. He argues (pp. 35–41) that performance-related payments systems for managers tend to reward them for short-term profitability rather than contribution to long-term performance. High mobility within and between firms compounds the effect. However, Cosh and Hughes (1987) suggest that UK executive remuneration is less sensitive to performance than in the USA, although this difference between the two countries has been waning in recent years.

It is interesting also to relate such 'internal' performance pressures to external pressures. 'Principal-agent' theory (Thompson 1988) would see performance-related pay as a means for shareholders ('principals') to motivate management ('agents'). This may seem a little unrealistic in the British context where top managers are not normally under *direct* shareholder control. However, the increasing use of performance-related pay can be seen as a way for managers to reassure shareholders that they are binding themselves to act in their interest. To the extent that the performance-related element is short-term – as contrasted to very long-dated stock options – this suggests that the top managers concerned perceive shareholders as short-termist. The share option scheme appears to be more common among large public quoted companies than smaller ones. For example Harcourt (1987) found that share option schemes in the UK related to company size; 97 per cent of the companies with sales exceeding £1 billion operated executive share option schemes. Smith and Watts (1982) quote similar figures for the US companies. In most cases these option schemes adopt a static exercise price based on the share price when the option is granted, and when expectations are downgraded or pessimism affects share prices, option can become worthless even though management might be performing well in difficult circumstances. Conversely, when markets boom, under-performing management can still reap rewards, despite their poor performance.

Goold and Campbell (1987) argue that short-term pressures are likely to arise within firms subject to their 'financial control' style of control, as distinct from their 'strategic control' and 'strategic planning' categories. In financially controlled companies internal short-term pressures are likely to be associated with 'sectionalism', an unwillingness of the managers of one profit centre to take account of costs or benefits affecting other profit centres in the firm. This is likely to be quite as damaging to innovation as short-termism itself. Other self-imposed short-term pressures relate to relationships between top management and sub-units within firms. Here there is no doubt that British management is as much affected as US. Barton *et al.* (1989) found that over 70 per cent of senior divisional managers in large UK firms believed that their division's current profitability level was a very important determinant of the capital budget they were allocated by Head Office; and the measure used was the crude one of return on investment (ROI). The problems of HQ–divisional relationships go deeper – and are multiplied when the divisions themselves have sub-units and sub-sub-units. Potentially HQ is as ignorant of the rest of the company as shareholders are about the firm as a whole. Such ignorance is once again most likely to occur in firms which are highly diversified and financially controlled (Goold and Campbell 1987).

Companies which are financially controlled may evaluate and reward divisional managers with financial accounting measures which engender short-term pressures. They may also impose constraints which have a similar effect. One constraint is the criterion for evaluating investment proposals. Two-thirds of Barton *et al.*'s firms used *payback* methods of evaluating investment proposals which suggests an increase in this deplorably short-termist practice since the survey by Rockley (1973). Where companies used the more rational DCF methods, discount rates at levels above those implied by capital markets were often used (Myers 1984). There is some anecdotal evidence of UK companies using nominal interest rates to discount real cash flows (Demirag and Tylecote 1992). On the other hand, Japanese companies do not use payback, and where they use a discount rate it tends to be the interest rate – below the implicit discount rate (Abegglen and Stalk 1985; Hodder 1986; Odagiri 1989; Demirag 1995). Demirag (1995) found that Japanese companies operating in the UK emphasized corporate growth as the major objective in investment decisions. But a recent study by Coates, Davis and Stacey (1994) found little evidence of a difference between UK and German multinationals as to their preferred objectives and performance measures or incentive schemes. Companies in both countries appeared to use measures of performance or pay which tend to improve short-term results.

Relationships within firms are closely related to their manner of growth. Firms which have grown mainly by acquisition are likely to be relatively diverse in terms of product and location and bound to be diverse (initially) in culture and managerial style. This must encourage the 'financial control style' of central management and helps to explain why Japan, which has very little growth by acquisition, has very little 'financial control' (Odagiri 1988). It has been found for the USA that firm diversification has negative effects on R&D intensity (Baysinger and Hoskisson 1989; Hoskisson and Hitt 1988). However, Hitt *et al.* (1991) have found that diversification *per se* appears to have little effect: it is acquisition which is really at fault in reducing R&D intensity. Diversifying acquisitions, on the other hand, appear to reduce patent intensity (patents granted divided by sales), taken as a measure of the output of R&D.

It may well be possible to explain variations in the stock market–firm relationship in terms of variations in diversification, means of growth and internal relationships. Thus, Hoskisson and Hitt (1988) in a study of 124 major US firms found that those which were relatively diversified and financially controlled not only spent less on R&D than the rest but got no appreciation from the stock market for what they did spend; while the rest – 'single and dominant business firms' – found that their R&D investment evaluated positively. This raises the possibility that the stock market rightly judged diversified firms' R&D as likely to yield a poor return, and/or that their top management was unable, through its own ignorance, to explain the real merits of what its subordinates were doing. There is an interesting parallel to these results in Sciteb (1991), which divided British higher-technology firms into 'chemistry-based' and 'physics-based', the former including pharmaceuticals, chemicals, glass and steel, the latter aerospace, electronics and other engineering. Though the sample size was too small for high statistical significance, Sciteb found that 'chemistry-based' firms' R&D spending was positively correlated with stock market valuation, 'physics-based' firms' not. It would seem that the chemistry-based firms are much more inclined to centralize their research (and to a lesser extent their development). This makes two differences, noted also by Hoskisson and Hitt. Firstly, centralized R&D functions are almost always cost centres rather than (part of) profit centres within the firm. As such they are relatively exempt from short-term pressures. Secondly, greater centralization reflects and facilitates the search for synergies among divisions, which is of course easier where diversification is less. The UK stock market may thus have considerable justification for its neglect of 'physics-based' firms' R&D; and we now find it rather easier to understand the difference between the relatively qualified chemicals and pharmaceutical analysts on the one hand, and the less qualified electronics analysts, on the other.

This analysis also reflects well on the national characteristics of individual countries. The more innovative and successful Japanese and German economies are in general characterized by less acquisition (and to a smaller extent less diversification). The survey carried out by the PA Consulting Group (1989) found that responsibility for R&D strategy tended to be at relatively low levels in British firms: in only 21 per cent did it lie with a main board director (57 per cent in Japan), and in 22 per cent with middle management (Japan 1 per cent). Moreover, as the McKinsey Report (1988) pointed out, the still-successful US electronics industry is notably more 'focused' and characterized by organic growth than most of what then remained of the UK electronics industry: contrast IBM, Apple, Texas Instruments, Motorola, etc. with (as of 1988) GEC, Plessey, Ferranti, etc. – let alone the situation after recent take-overs. The UK manufacturing industry with the highest R&D intensity, and most successful in terms of innovative output, balance of payments, profitability and price-earnings ratio is pharmaceuticals – led by Glaxo. UK pharmaceuticals in general, and Glaxo in particular, is characterized over the last 20 years by low diversification, organic growth, and centralized R&D.

So far, I have synthesized the available literature on possible causes of short-termism. This literature suggests that the behaviour of capital markets and the internal management control systems of firms may contribute to short-termism. The main reason behind the capital market influence is that institutional investors prefer short-term gains to longer term because they operate under intense short-term pressures, due to the fact that their portfolio performance is measured on a short-term basis. It has also been argued that the efficiency of the markets and the communication between the institutional shareholders and managers play an important role in the short-term behaviour of firms. Management control systems which may also contribute to short-term behaviour in organizations included divisionalization of the firm, strategy for long-term growth, R&D performance measures and control systems.

While all these factors may contribute to short-termism in firms, perceptions of managers are probably the most important single factor determining short-term pressures. Demirag (1996) found that where UK Finance Directors perceived capital markets as short-termist, these short-term perceptions contributed to short-term behaviour in their companies. The remainder of this chapter will therefore report the results of a questionnaire study undertaken to determine Research and Development managers' perceptions of UK capital markets' behaviour. Moreover, the study will identify a number of internal organizational characteristics, based on the literature review in the chapter, which may have an association with these perceptions.

RESEARCH METHODS

A questionnaire was used to collect the data from R&D directors/managers of UK companies. The R&D scoreboard prepared by Demirag and Tonkin in June 1992 was used as the population for the survey. The scoreboard included 331 listed companies in the London Stock Exchange which disclosed their R&D expenditure in their annual reports published up to and including 31 May 1992.

The questionnaires were sent to the R&D directors and in cases where the post of R&D director did not exist, the most senior manager responsible for the R&D activity was contacted. In order to find out the names of the R&D directors, each company was contacted on the telephone (over a period of two weeks) to determine the names and addresses of the R&D directors. Where there was more than one director or manager responsible for R&D activities within the same firm, the largest division's (based on turnover and R&D activity) R&D director or manager was contacted. A pre-paid envelope with the return address was included with the questionnaire together with a letter indicating the purpose of the questionnaire, assuring the confidentiality of the information provided by the respondents to the author. The questionnaire was pilot tested with 15 R&D directors and interviews were held with six of them. As a result of the pilot testing several questions were revised before sending them out to the sample population.

Of the 331 questionnaires sent to the R&D directors/managers, there were 135 responses giving a response rate of 40.8 per cent. Of these 135 responses, 19 (5.7 per cent) were negative. The remaining 116 responses were positive, giving a positive response rate of 35 per cent of all questionnaires sent.

The main objective of the questionnaire was to determine the extent of short-term pressures perceived by R&D directors/managers from capital markets. In addition I wanted to find out how their R&D activities were organized. Respondents were asked to indicate their perceptions of short-termism by answering five-point Likert scales (1 = Disagree strongly and 5 = Agree strongly). In order to supplement the data collected through the questionnaire, semi-structured interviews with the R&D directors in thirteen of the companies were also carried out.

Statistical analysis was used to check for any possible non-response bias in the responses using size of R&D expenditure and industry groups. I did not find any significant differences between the respondents and non-respondents.

THE FINDINGS OF THE STUDY

Perceptions of R&D managers were determined using four key questions. The first question attempted to determine whether it was difficult to provide profit figures which satisfy shareholders whilst funding R&D projects which were right for the business. The results indicated that 42.2 per cent of the firms either agreed or strongly agreed with this statement. 18.1 per cent indicated that they were neutral. The rest of the respondents, 39.7 per cent, either disagreed or disagreed strongly with this statement. The mean response rate to this question was 2.991, indicating that capital markets may be partly to blame for the inadequate financing of R&D projects.

The second question was used to determine managers' perception related to short-term profit maximization and cancellation of long-term projects. 47.4 per cent of the respondents agreed that they frequently experience pressures for short-term profit maximization from their owners and therefore sometimes cancel projects which ought to be undertaken in the long-term interests of the company. The mean response rate of 3.121 to this question seems to indicate that the respondents perceive short-term pressures from capital markets.

The third question was asked in order to explore the extent of institutional shareholders' ability to understand the technology used in the R&D projects of their firms. A majority of the respondents disagreed that analysts and major shareholders are able to make decisions based upon adequate technically informed analysis of the quality and value of R&D undertaken. The mean response was 2.530 with 53.1 per cent disagreeing. The analysts' ignorance and lack of understanding of the technical characteristics of R&D projects, as perceived by the respondents, may well have contributed to short-term pressures.

The fourth question was used to determine whether institutional investors, analysts and major shareholders often exhibit a strong bias against high-risk long-term research in favour of lower-risk short-term product development. A significant majority (53.5 per cent) of the R&D directors perceived that this was the case. The mean was 3.578 indicating positive agreement on short-term pressures from the capital markets (see Table 6.1).

There were also additional questions relating to the R&D managers' perception of short-termism among institutional shareholders. The following additional questions were used to determine this. Only a small minority of the companies (26.1 per cent) believed that their companies were a possible candidate for take-over. However, a significant majority of the companies (64.3 per cent) disagreed with the statement that their company paid little attention to the City opinion. The mean response of 2.304 indicates that managers on the whole can not ignore the City opinion. Given that they perceive short-term pressures from capital markets it is not surprising that these pressures may engender short-term behaviour within the firms.

There was definite agreement that shareholders today are better informed than they were ten years ago. Only 11.2 per cent disagreed with this statement while 50.9 per cent agreed. The mean of 3.517 illustrates the positive agreement. Similarly, there was strong agreement that shareholders today demand more information than they did ten years ago. 55.7 per cent agreed with this, while only 8.7 per cent disagreed. Again a high mean of 3.591 illustrates the point.

Although it is difficult to draw firm conclusions from these responses, there nevertheless appears to be an indication that the majority of the UK R&D directors/managers regard capital markets as being biased towards short-termism.

Other questions were asked to determine some of the industry characteristics of the firms. Of those questioned, 40.3 per cent indicated that their companies operate in a mature industry in which the emphasis is on production costs rather than product innovation. However, 44.2 per cent of the firms did not think that, relative to their main competitors, they lean towards competition on cost rather than competition on innovation. A significant majority of the firms (74.5 per cent) undertook research which was more market-driven than science-driven. For 36 per cent of the firms this was also true in relation to their major competitors. Half of the firms (42.1 per cent) agreed that innovation through organic growth was more effective than innovation through acquisition. Almost half of the R&D directors perceived that R&D had to be cut back in their firms during a recession. For a majority of these firms, these attitudes and this behaviour indicate short-term characteristics.

While a significant minority of the firms (46.5 per cent) indicated that partnerships with customers in R&D were important to competitive success in their industry, 31.6 per cent of the respondents said that this applied little to them. A similar number of companies indicated that partnerships with suppliers in R&D were not important to competitive success in their industry. In contrast, empirical evidence available on companies operating in Japan and Scandinavia indicates that the collaboration between manufacturers and customers has been much more common in these countries (for example see Clark 1979, p. 73; Sasaki 1981; and Whitehill 1991, p. 95).

Table 6.1 Pressures from capital markets

Capital market pressures	*Frequency*						
Please give your opinions of the following statements:	*Disagree strongly* *1*	*Disagree* *2*	*Neutral* *3*	*Agree* *4*	*Agree strongly* *5*	*Total*	*Mean*
1 It is difficult to provide profit figures which satisfy shareholders whilst funding R&D projects which are right for the business.	14 12.1%	32 27.6%	21 18.1%	39 33.6%	10 8.6%	116 100.0%	2.991
2 We frequently experience pressures for short-term profit maximization from our owners and therefore sometimes cancel projects which ought to be undertaken in the long-term interest of the company.	21 18.1%	17 14.7%	23 19.8%	37 31.9%	18 15.5%	116 100.0%	3.121
3 Analysts and major shareholders are able to make decisions based upon adequate technically informed analysis of the quality and value of R&D undertaken.	27 23.5%	34 29.6%	26 22.6%	22 19.1%	6 5.2%	115 100.0%	2.530
4 Analysts and major shareholders often exhibit a strong bias against high-risk long-term research in favour of lower-risk short-term product development.	3 2.6%	13 11.2%	38 32.8%	38 32.8%	24 20.7%	116 100.0%	3.578

5 My company is perceived as being a possible candidate for take-over and this exacerbates the problem of pressures to deliver short-term profits at the expense of long-term R&D.	33 28.7%	24 20.9%	28 24.3%	22 19.1%	8 7.0%	115 100.0%	2.548
6 My company pays little regard to City opinion as we generate sufficient cash to finance all our requirements and we do not feel vulnerable to take-over.	32 27.8%	42 36.5%	21 18.3%	14 12.2%	6 5.2%	115 100.0%	2.304
7 Shareholders today are better informed than they were ten years ago.	5 4.3%	8 6.9%	44 37.9%	40 34.5%	19 16.4%	116 100.0%	3.517
8 Shareholders today demand more information than they did ten years ago.	4 3.5%	6 5.2%	41 35.7%	46 40.0%	18 15.7%	115 100.0%	3.591

The companies were asked to consider the most important sources for the development of new products. In-house research was rated very important by a significant majority of the firms (91.1 per cent). Joint ventures were rated as the second most important, followed by acquisitions and licensing. Other important sources for the new products included collaborations and alliances with other organizations, and joint research work with universities.

I also wanted to find out about the companies' strategies and structures for R&D activities. Nearly half (46.5 per cent) of the managers did not agree that it was often necessary to sacrifice potential 'synergy' between divisions in order to provide the motivation and improved inter-functional co-ordination that goes with devolved strategic responsibility. There was also some disagreement (69.0 per cent) that it was sometimes difficult to get central initiatives under way in a decentralized structure. Yet, most managers (53.3 per cent) agreed that R&D in their companies needed to be more centralized. Interestingly, a majority of the managers (74 per cent) disagreed that if strategic planning of R&D was reduced to purely financial equations then it failed. Most R&D managers (58.5 per cent) did not think that it was necessary to adopt structures which protect long-term research against the pressures of shorter term applied research and product development. A majority of the managers indicated that top management participated in the R&D budget-setting process and in the strategic planning of R&D (68.9 per cent and 60.9 per cent respectively).

A significant majority of the respondents (86.2 per cent) indicated that their organization had adopted a multi-divisional form. Almost half of the firms had a central R&D laboratory which worked for the group as a whole. Just over half of these respondents with centralized R&D laboratories indicated that more than 50 per cent of their work was contracted directly by the divisions. Forty-seven per cent of the respondents with centralized R&D laboratories operated a fund paid for centrally or by levy on divisions which allocated to speculative R&D.

Finally I wanted to know how the firms in the sample evaluated and controlled their R&D activities. Factors which determined the size of the R&D budgets included (in order of importance) company objectives for growth and market share, company-wide cash limits, detailed costing/evaluation of projects in hand, last year's profit, activities of competitors, and last year's R&D budgets. Other factors mentioned as determinants of the size of the R&D budget included ability of the company successfully to implement research and development projects, predicted sales and profits.

R&D managers were asked to assess the importance attached to several objectives in evaluating R&D projects. The results indicated that payback on R&D projects was of importance to 73.3 per cent, with a mean of 4.00. The second most important criteria was increased market share (77.6 per cent and a mean of 3.750) closely followed by a project's suitability to existing activities of the firm. Added-value, return-on-capital investment, originality, creativity and innovation, and discounted cash flows were also other important objectives in evaluating R&D projects (see Table 6.2). In addition, 69.8 per cent of the R&D managers found budget targets important for R&D projects.

SUMMARY AND CONCLUSIONS

The findings of this study seem to suggest that R&D directors in the UK perceive short-term pressures from capital markets. The extent of these perceived short-term pressures vary significantly according to the types of questions asked. According to the R&D directors in the survey it would appear that investment analysts and institutional shareholders do not easily understand and do not have sufficient information relevant to the long-term performance of companies. They also respond excessively to short-term financial measures.

The evidence for (perceived) short-term pressures from the capital market can be seen from the following responses: a majority (53.5 per cent) of R&D directors perceived strong bias against long-term research in favour of product development amongst analysts and shareholders; analysts and shareholders did not generally make informed analyses of the quality and value of R&D projects; 47.4 per cent of the R&D directors frequently experienced pressures for short-term profit maximization from capital markets and R&D managers found it difficult to provide profit figures which satisfied shareholders whilst funding R&D projects which were right for the business. If top managers perceive this short-termist behaviour from capital markets, then they may react to these pressures and may try to please them by taking a short-term perspective such as putting excessive reliance on financial controls.

The findings of this study contradict the results of a recent study by Marston and Craven (1994) who found that UK company directors did not believe that short-termism exists among institutional analysts and fund managers in the UK. However, the perceptions gathered in their study were obtained from financial managers who may have a different view of the capital markets than Research and Development managers.

The lack of strategy for long-term investment and R&D, poor communication between institutional investors and managers and decentralized structure in Research and Development may also have contributed to these perceptions. If companies do not have a clear long-term strategy for their R&D it is not possible to expect institutional shareholders to understand and support their strategy for long-term R&D investment and innovation. Top management should also have a

Table 6.2 Evaluation of R&D projects

Control mechanisms	*Frequency*						
How much importance does your company attach to each of the following criteria in evaluating R&D projects:	*Of no importance* *1*	*2*	*3*	*4*	*Crucial* *5*	*Total*	*Mean*
1 Payback	1	9	21	42	43	116	4.009
	0.9%	7.8%	18.1%	36.2%	37.1%	100.0%	
2 Return-on-capital investment	4	14	20	47	31	116	3.750
	3.4%	12.1%	17.2%	40.5%	26.7%	100.0%	
3 Added-value	2	10	21	60	22	115	3.783
	1.7%	8.7%	18.3%	52.2%	19.1%	100.0%	
4 Fit to existing activities	0	6	26	60	23	115	3.870
	0.0%	5.2%	22.6%	52.2%	20.0%	100.0%	
5 Originality, creativity and innovation	7	38	24	34	13	116	3.069
	6.0%	32.8%	20.7%	29.3%	11.2%	100.0%	
6 Increased market share	1	6	19	52	38	116	4.034
	0.9%	5.2%	16.4%	44.8%	32.8%	100.0%	
7 Discounted cash flows	9	29	40	25	9	112	2.964
	8.0%	25.9%	35.7%	22.3%	8.0%	100.0%	
8 Other	1	1	0	4	2	8	3.625
	12.5%	12.5%	0.0%	50.0%	25.0%	100.0%	

good understanding of what projects are currently being developed and researched and how they may contribute to the firm's long-term profitability. Once this is achieved they will be able to present their firm's performance persuasively to their shareholders. They will have to accept the 'downside' of this improved communication and understanding: if the firm is not performing well, improvements in communications will ensure that shareholders know about the firm's poor performance. However, the better the shareholders understand the activities of the firms in which they have substantial share holdings, the more carefully the managers of those firms will evaluate their companies' performance. Accordingly firms most affected by short-term pressures need to control their financial performance and also need to be much more sceptical about the case for acquisitions in future. They may also need to ensure co-ordination between their existing divisions and establish a much closer central co-ordination of innovative activity – even where a centralized *structure* for R&D is unsuitable. There is some evidence to suggest that in a divisionalized organization top managers can improve their understanding of R&D activities by having their R&D function centralized. It is not surprising that 53.9 per cent of the managers in the study believed that R&D should be more centralized in their organizations.

Performance evaluation and control systems for R&D activities may also have contributed to the managers' perceptions of the short-term pressures from capital markets. The existing system of performance evaluation and performance-based remuneration should be broadened by the use of 'leading indicators' like market share, new products in the pipeline, customer satisfaction and quality improvements. Profitability as a measure of performance and rewards closely associated with profit-related bonuses may also generate internal short-term pressures among the top management. These measures should be supplemented with performance indicators which measure long-term market share, employment stability and long-term profits which are in accordance with the firm's strategic plans. The findings of this study show that in evaluating R&D projects there is evidence of attaching importance to short-term financial measures. Payback is considered to be important by 73.3 per cent of the managers and return on capital investment by 67.2 per cent. Interestingly, market share is also considered to be important by 77.6 per cent.

It can be argued that the more short-term pressures are perceived by the company managers, the higher will the incidence of short-termism be, as managers are likely to act in accordance with their perceptions. In other words, managers to a certain extent will internalize the *external* short-term pressures upon them. However, shareholders also have responsibility, and power, and it is not possible to suggest that short-termism can be eliminated without the institutional shareholders' willingness to take a closer interest in the affairs of the companies they own.

This would help to change managers' perceptions of capital markets by providing *direct* pressure on company boards which will lead to improvements in performance, including innovation. Moreover, it would lead to a more accurate stock market valuation of companies, and particularly of their 'technology in the pipeline'. This will encourage more spending for innovation, and it will also discourage take-overs which rely on a predator knowing about value which the market does not know. In this connection, Ormerod (1989) has also proposed the creation of a 'golden share' in public companies which would rest with the Secretary of State. Control of the company cannot be affected in this scheme without the consent of the golden shareholder. It is clear that the existence of such a share could act as a deterrent to hostile take-overs. Moreover, as Ormerod argues, in the event of a take-over, the golden shareholder could exercise the powers of the share by requesting the acquirer to undertake certain investments in areas such as technology and machinery, R&D, and training. The only drawback with this scheme is that it would require extensive intervention by the Secretary of State in almost every take-over situation on the stock market.

Governments also have a responsibility to facilitate the *rapprochement* of management and owners by (a) obliging more information to be disclosed by companies, and (b) changing the structure of 'corporate governance'. This gives non-executive directors much greater power than they will normally have under present UK arrangements, and much more information with which to help them exercise it. The Committee on the Financial Aspects of Corporate Governance (Cadbury 1992) has recognized the potential conflicts of interest which could arise where non-executive directors are actively participating in board decision-making and also acting as controllers of the board. In its recommendation the Committee wanted to separate the offices of the chairman and chief executive to prevent excessive concentration of power in boardrooms and sought to promote the power and influence of non-executive directors.

Audit committees selected from non-executive directors could also help to monitor the behaviour of executive directors. The report also recognizes the conflict of interest between auditors who are appointed by managers and are responsible for the interest of the shareholders. It would therefore be more appropriate to let the audit committees advise companies on the appointment of their auditors and discuss any problems arising during the course of the audit. Dimsdale (1994, p. 46) argues recommendations made by the Committee on the Financial Aspects of Corporate Governance do not go far enough and suggests that it will be relatively easy for companies to claim compliance without the provision of an adequate system for evaluating and monitoring the implementation of the report's recommendations.

REFERENCES

Advisory Council on Science and Technology (1994) *Innovation and the Tax System*, HMSO, London.

Abegglen, J.C. and Stalk, G. (1985) *Kaisha, The Japanese Corporation*, Basic Books, New York.

Allen, D. (1988) *Long Term Financial Health – A Structure for Strategic Financial Management*, Chartered Institute of Management Accountants, London.

Arnold, J. and Moizer, P. (1984) 'A Survey of the Methods used by UK Investment Analysts to Appraise Investments in Ordinary Shares', *Accounting and Business Research*, Summer, pp. 195–207.

Ashton, D., Crossland, M. and Moizer, P. (1991) 'The Performance Evaluation of Fund Managers', paper presented at the British Accounting Association Annual Conference, University of Salford, April.

Ball, J. (1991) 'Short Termism – Myth or Reality?', *National Westminster Bank Quarterly Review*, August, pp. 20–30.

Barton, H., Brown, D., Cound, J. and Willey, K. (1989) 'Decision Processes for Strategic Capital Investment Within UK-Based Diversified Industry', MBA Project Report, London Business School, May.

Batstone, E.V. (1986) 'Labour and Productivity', *Oxford Review of Economic Policy*, vol. 2, no. 3, pp. 32–43.

Baysinger, B. and Hoskisson, R.E. (1989) 'Diversification Strategy and R&D Intensity in Multi-product Firms', *Academy of Management Journal*, no. 32, pp. 310–332.

Bond, S. and Meghir, C. (1994) 'High on Dividends, Low on Investment', *Financial Times*, 20 May.

Brickley, A., Bhagat, S. and Lease, R.C. (1985) 'The Impact of Long-range Managerial Compensation Plans on Shareholder Wealth', *Journal of Accounting and Economics*, vol. 7, pp. 151–174.

Bromwich, M. and Bhimani, A. (1989) *Management Accounting: Evolution Not Revolution*, Research Studies, Chartered Institute of Management Accountants, London.

Cadbury, A. (1992) *Report of the Committee on the Financial Aspects of Corporate Governance*, Gee and Co. Ltd, London.

Carr, C.H. (1990) *Britain's Competitiveness: The Management of the Vehicle Components Industry*, Routledge, London.

Carr, C.H., Tomkins, C. and Bayliss, B. (1994) *Strategic Investment Decisions*, Avebury, Aldershot.

Centre for Exploitation of Science and Technology (1991) *Attitudes to Innovation in Germany and Britain: A Comparison*, June, CEST, London.

Chaney, P.K. and Devinney, T.M. (1992) 'New Product Innovations and Stock Price Performance', *Journal of Business Finance and Accounting*, vol. 19, no. 5, September, pp. 677–695.

Charkham, J. (1989a) 'Corporate Governance and the Market for Control Companies', Bank of England Panel paper, no. 25, March.

Charkham, J. (1989b) 'Corporate Governance and the Market for Companies: Aspects of the Shareholder's Role', Bank of England Discussion Paper, no. 44, November.

Clark, R. (1979) *The Japanese Company*, Yale University Press, New Haven.

Clements, A. (1991) 'Why Perceptions and Reality do not Tally', *Financial Times*, 22 July, p. 9.

Coates, J., Davis, E.W. and Stacey, R.J. (1994) 'Managerial Short-Termism in

Multi-National Companies: The Role of a Distributed Corporate Performance Measurement System', paper presented to 17th Annual Congress of the European Accounting Association, Venice, April, pp. 1–19.

Confederation of British Industry (1987) *Investing for Britain's Future: Report of the City/Industry Task Force*, London.

Coopers and Lybrand/Mori (1991) *Shareholder Value Analysis Survey*, Coopers and Lybrand Deloitte Ltd, London.

Coopers and Lybrand (1993) *Final Report for Study on International Differences in the Cost of Capital for the European Commission*, London, April.

Cosh, A.D. and Hughes, A. (1987) 'The Anatomy of Corporate Control: Directors, Shareholders and Executive Remuneration in Giant US and UK Corporations', *Cambridge Journal of Economics*, vol. 11, pp. 401–422.

Cosh, A.D., Hughes, A. and Singh, A. (1990) 'Takeovers, Short-termism and Finance – Industry Relations in the UK Economy', paper presented at an IPPR seminar on Takeovers: A Study of Short-Termism? London, 22 May.

Cranfield European Enterprise Centre (1994), quoted in Davis, E.P. 'Whither Corporate-Banking Relations?' in K. Hughes (ed.) *The Future of UK Competitiveness and the Role of Industrial Policy*, PSI, London.

Day, J.F.S. (1986) 'The Use of Annual Reports by UK Investment Analysts', *Accounting and Business Research*, Autumn, pp. 295–307.

Demirag, I.S. (1996) 'Management Control Systems of Japanese Companies Operating in the United Kingdom', in A. Berry, J. Broadbent and D. Otley (eds) *Management Control*, Macmillan, London, pp. 203–220.

Demirag, I.S. (1996) 'The Impact of Managers' Short-Term Perceptions on Technology Management and Research and Development in UK Companies', vol. 8, no. I, *Technology Analysis and Strategic Management*, pp. 21–32.

Demirag, I.S. and Tonkin, D. (1991) 'The UK Research and Development Scoreboard', *The Independent*, 10 June, pp. 20–21.

Demirag, I.S. and Tonkin, D. (1992) 'The UK Research and Development Scoreboard', *The Independent*, 9 June, pp. 18–19.

Demirag, I.S. and Tylecote, A. (1992) 'The Effects of Organisational Culture, Structure and Market Expectations on Technological Innovation: A Hypothesis', *British Journal of Management*, vol. 3, no. 1, pp. 7–20.

Demirag, I.S., Tylecote, A. and Morris, B. (1994) 'Accounting for Financial and Managerial Causes of Short-term Pressures in British Corporations', *Journal of Business Finance and Accounting*, vol. 21, no. 8, December, pp. 1195–1213.

Dimsdale, N.H. (1994) 'A Postscript on the Draft of the Cadbury Committee', in N. Dimsdale and M. Prevezer *Capital Markets and Corporate Governance*, Oxford University Press, Oxford.

Doyle, P. (1987) 'Marketing and the British Chief Executive', *Journal of Marketing Management*, Winter, pp. 121–32.

Frank, J. and Mayer, C. (1990) 'Corporate Ownership and Corporate Control: A Study of France, Germany, and the UK', *Economic Policy*, pp. 191–231.

Froot, K., Perold, A., Andre, F. and Stein, J.C. (1993) 'Shareholder Trading Practices and Corporate Investment Horizons', *Journal of Applied Corporate Finance*, vol. 5, no. 2, Summer, pp. 42–52.

Goodacre, A. (1991) 'R&D Expenditure and the Analysts' View', *Accountancy*, April, pp. 78–79.

Goodacre, A., Pratt, K.C., Thomas, R.E., Ball, R. and MacGrath, J. (1990) 'Perceptions of Accounting Disclosure of R&D Expenditure: An Experimental Study', unpublished paper, presented at the British Accounting Association, University of Salford, April.

Goold, M.C. and Campbell, A. (1987) *Strategies and Styles: The Role of the Centre in Managing Diversified Corporations*, Basil Blackwell, Oxford and New York.

Gray, R. (1986) *Accounting for R&D*, The Institute of Chartered Accountants in England and Wales, London.

Greer, D.F. (1986) 'Acquiring in Order to Avoid Acquisition', *The Anti-Trust Bulletin*, Spring.

Hall, B. (1992) 'R&D Tax Policy During the Eighties: Success or Failure?', *R&D Tax Policy*, November.

Harcourt, T.V. (1987) *Charterhouse Top Management Remuneration United Kingdom 1987–1988*, Monks Publication, London.

Healy, P.M. (1985) 'The Effects of Bonus Schemes on Accounting Decisions', *Journal of Accounting and Economics*, pp. 85–107.

Hitt, M.A., Hoskisson, R.E., Ireland, R.D. and Harrison, J.S. (1991) 'Effects of Acquisitions on R&D Inputs and Outputs', *Academy of Management Journal*, vol. 34, no. 3, pp. 693–703.

Hodder, J.E. (1986) 'Evaluation of Manufacturing Investments: A Comparison of U.S. and Japanese Practices', *Financial Management*, Spring, pp. 17–24.

Hoskisson, R.E. and Hitt, M.A. (1988) 'Strategic Control Systems and Relative R&D Investment in Large Multiproduct Firms', *Strategic Management Journal*, vol. 9, pp. 605–621.

House of Lords (1991) 'Innovation in Manufacturing Industry', Select Committee on Science and Technology, vol. 1, Report, HL Paper 18–1, HMSO, London.

Hughes, A. (1989) 'The Impact of Merger: A Survey of Empirical Evidence for the U.K.', in J. Fairburn and J.A. Kay (eds) *Merger and Merger Policy*, Oxford University Press, Oxford.

Hutton, W. (1995) *The State We're In*, Jonathan Cape, London.

Inland Revenue/HM Treasury (1987) *Fiscal Incentives For R&D Spending: An International Survey*, HMSO, London.

Innovation Advisory Board (1990) *Innovation: City Attitudes and Practices*, Department of Trade and Industry, London.

Jacobs, M.T. (1991) *Short-term America: The Causes and Cures of Our Business Myopia*, Harvard Business School Press, Boston, Mass.

Jenkinson, T. and Mayer, C. (1993) *Hostile Takeovers*, McGraw-Hill, London.

Kester, W.C. (1990) *Japanese Takeovers*, Harvard Business School Press, New York.

Kumar, R. and Sopariwala, P.R. (1992) 'The Effect of Adoption of Long-Term Performance Plans on Stock Prices and Accounting Numbers', *Journal of Financial and Quantitative Analysis*, vol. 27, pp. 561–580.

Litzenberger, R.H. and Ramaswamy, K. (1982) 'The Effects of Dividends on Common Stock Prices: Tax Effects or Information Effects', *Journal of Finance*, no. 37, pp. 429–443.

McKinsey and Company Inc. (1988) *Performance and Competitive Success: Strengthening Competitiveness in UK Electronics: A Report Prepared for the NEDC Electronics Industry Sector Group*, National Economic Development Office, London.

Marsh, P. (1990) *Short-termism on Trial*, Institutional Fund Managers Association, London.

Marston, C.L. and Craven, B.M. (1994) 'An Empirical Study of Corporate Perceptions of Short-termism in Large UK Corporations', paper presented to 17th Annual Congress of the European Accounting Association, Venice, April, pp. 1–19.

Mayhew, K. (1991) 'Training – the Problem for Employers', *Employment Institute Economic Report*, vol. 5, no. 10, March/April.

Miller, M.H. and Modigliani, F. (1961) 'Dividend Policy, Growth and the Valuation of Shares', *Journal of Business*, vol. 34, pp. 411–433.

Miller, M.H. and Scholes, M.S. (1982) 'Dividends and Taxes: Some Empirical Evidence', *Journal of Political Economy*, vol. 90, no. 6, pp. 1118–1141.

Modigliani, F. and Cohen, R. (1979) 'Inflation, Rational Valuation and the Market', *Financial Analyst Journal*, March–April, pp. 24–44.

Modigliani, F. and Miller, M.H. (1963) 'Corporate Income Taxes and the Cost of Capital: A Correction', *American Economic Review*, vol. 53, pp. 433–443.

Moody, J. (1989) *How the City Appraises Technology Investments*, Scientific Resources Ltd, Cambridge.

Myers, S.C. (1984) 'Finance Theory and Financial Strategy', *Interfaces*, vol. 14, pp. 126–137.

National Association of Pension Funds (1990) *Creative Tension?*, NAPF, London.

National Economic Development Council (1991) 'Partners for the Long Term: Lessons from the Success of Germany and Japan', Joint Memorandum by the Chairman of the NEDC's Sector Groups and Working Parties, 19 June, NEDO.

Nickell, S.J. and Wadhwani, S.B. (1987) 'Myopia, the "Dividend Puzzle", and Share Prices', Centre for Labour Economics, Discussion Paper No. 272, London School of Economics and Political Science.

Odagiri, H. (1988) 'Japanese Management: An "Economic" View', Working Paper 60, Centre for Business Strategy, London Business School.

Odagiri, H. (1989) 'Industrial Innovation in Japan: A View on Policy and Management', Working Paper 70, Centre for Business Strategy, London Business School.

O'Hanlon, J., Poon, S. and Yaansah, R.A. (1992) 'Market Recognition of Differences in Earnings Persistence: UK Evidence', *Journal of Business Finance and Accounting*, vol. 19, no. 4, June, pp. 625–639.

Ormerod, P. (1989) 'Takeovers and Short-termism: Some Policy Options', unpublished paper presented at an IPPR seminar on Contested Takeovers and Long-term Industrial Policy, 11 May, London.

PA Consulting Group (1989) *Attitudes to R&D and the Application of Technology*, P.A. Consulting Group, Cambridge.

Patel, P. and Pavitt, K. (1992) 'Europe's technological performance', Ch. 3 in C. Freeman, M. Sharp, and W. Walker (eds) *Technology and the Future of Europe*, Pinter, London.

Pike, R., Meerjanssen, J. and Chadwick, L. (1993) 'The Appraisal of Ordinary Shares by Investment Analysts in the UK and Germany', *Accounting and Business Research*, vol. 23, no. 92, pp. 489–499.

Porter, M. (1992) *Capital Choices: Changing the Way America Invests in Industry*, Boston, Council on Competitiveness, Harvard Business School.

Poterba, J.M. and Summers, L.H. (1984) 'New Evidence that Taxes Affect the Valuation of Dividends', *Journal of Finance*, vol. 34, no. 5, pp. 1397–1141.

Poterba, J.M. and Summers, L.H. (1988) 'Mean Reversion in Stock Prices: Evidence and Implications', *Journal of Financial Economics*, vol. 22, pp. 27–59.

Rockley, L.E. (1973) *Investment for Profitability*, Business Books, London.

Sasaki, N. (1981) *Management and Industrial Structure in Japan*, Pergamon Press, Oxford.

Schleifer, A. and Vishny, R. (1990) 'Equilibrium Short Horizons of Investors and Firms', *American Economic Association Papers and Proceedings*, vol. 80, no. 2, May, pp. 148–153.

Sciteb (1991) *R&D Short-termism? Enhancing the Performance of the UK Team*, Orbic, Faversham.

Securities and Exchange Commission Office of Economic Analysis (1985) *Institutional Ownership, Tender Offers, and Long-term Investments*, 19 April.

Shiller, R.J. (1981) 'Do Stock Prices Move too Much to be Justified by Subsequent Changes in Dividends?', *American Economic Review*, vol. 71, pp. 421–436.

Singh, A. (1971) *Takeovers: Their Relevance to the Stock Market and the Theory of the Firm*, Cambridge University Press, Cambridge.

Singh, A. (1975) 'Takeovers, Economic Natural Selection and the Theory of the Firm: Evidence from the Post-war U.K. Experience', *Economic Journal, September.*

Smith, C.W. and Watts, R.L. (1982) 'Incentive and Tax Effects of Executive Compensation Plans', *Australian Journal of Management*, pp. 139–157.

Summers, L.H. (1986) 'Does Stock Market Rationality reflect Fundamental Values?', *Journal of Finance*, vol. 41, July, pp. 591–601.

Tehranian, H. and Waegelein, J. (1985) 'Market Reaction to Short-Term Executive Compensation Plan Adoptions', *Journal of Accounting and Economics*, vol. 7, pp. 131–144.

Thomas, R. (1995) 'R&D Tax Breaks Must be Part of Long-term Strategy', *The Guardian*, 29 May, p. 15.

Thompson, S. (1988) 'Agency Costs of Internal Organisation', Ch. 4 in S. Thompson and M. Wright (eds) *Internal Organisation, Efficiency and Profit*, Philip Allan, Oxford.

Tobin, J. (1984) 'On the Efficiency of the Financial System', *Lloyds Bank Review*, July, pp. 1–15.

Tylecote, A. and Demirag, I.S. (1992) 'Short-termism: Culture and Structures as Factors in Technological Innovation', in R. Coombs, V. Walsh and P. Saviotti (eds) *Technological Change and Company Strategies*, Academic Press, London.

Whitehill, A.M. (1991) *Japanese Management*, Routledge, London.

Williams, P. (1991) 'Time and the City: Short Termism in the UK, Myth or Reality?', *National Westminster Bank Quarterly Review*, August, pp. 31–38.

7

HIGH TECHNOLOGY EMPLOYMENT AND THE ACHIEVEMENT OF R&D SPILLOVERS

Zoltan Acs, Felix Fitzroy and Ian Smith

The geographical concentration of high technology firms, such as California's famous Silicon Valley or Boston's Route 128, is of significant interest to policy-makers and economists alike. For as well as favourable effects on international competitiveness, such clusters generate considerable regional benefits in terms of jobs and economic growth. An explanation of the spatial distribution of high technology activities is therefore important for both regional and industrial policy.

Traditionally, transportation costs and proximity to raw material, fuel or labour inputs have been cited as major factors in the agglomerative process. Recent studies, however, have considered the role of geographically-bounded knowledge spillovers from universities and federal laboratories in the location decision of firms. Informal accounts indicate that there is a close association between high technology clusters and major research universities in the USA (Acs, 1993). Frequently cited examples include the links between Stanford University and Silicon Valley and between MIT and Route 128. Comparable local concentrations of R&D have not yet emerged in Europe except in the form of a few fledgling research parks such as Cambridge, England (Lumme *et al.*, 1993). Formal tests conducted by Jaffee (1989) provide econometric evidence for the real effects of academic research in terms of its spillover to corporate patenting activity. In addition, a further paper by Jaffee, Trajtenberg, and Henderson (1993) demonstrates the significant degree of localization of these knowledge externalities with respect to patent citations. However, spillovers from university research to commercial innovation are not the only effects of relevance to theory and policy. The ultimate economic interest lies chiefly in the product markets and jobs that are generated by R&D. The aim of this chapter is to test for the existence of such spillovers from university R&D to local high technology employment. This is a question of considerable policy importance (*Business Week*, 1994), which has been discussed systematically to date only by Beeson and Montgomery (1993) who, in contrast to our results, find no statistically significant effect of university R&D expenditures on high technology employment shares.

This chapter is organized into five sections. The first provides an informal outline of the theoretical background. The second section offers a preliminary analysis of the data. We use unique annual data for six high technology sectors in thirty-seven American Standard Metropolitan Statistical Areas (SMSA) for the period from 1988 to 1991 to explain the relationship between university R&D expenditure and employment. Jaffee (1989) used American states as his (much larger) geographical unit of analysis. This can have drawbacks in those cases where state borders cut through important economic areas or where states contain several large cities. Our use of SMSA data should clearly be able to subject the theoretical argument for spillovers based on spatial proximity to a much more precise test. The model is specified in section three and, in the fourth section, the econometric results are reported and discussed. A final section concludes the paper.

THEORETICAL BACKGROUND

There are two related hypotheses explaining the development of high technology clusters in the vicinity of major university R&D activity.

Research spillovers

The first explanation argues that university research is a source of significant innovation-generating knowledge which diffuses initially through informal discussions and personal contacts to adjacent firms. Since both basic and applied university research may benefit private enterprise in various ways it induces firms to locate nearby. Lund (1986), in a survey of industrial R&D managers, confirms the proximity of university R&D as a factor in the location decision due to the initial spillover from neighbouring university research to commercial innovation. Of course, as research results are used and disseminated, the learning advantage created by close geographic proximity between local high technology activity and the university would fade, but these learning lags may be long. Information flows locally, therefore, through a variety of channels more easily and efficiently than over greater distances in spite of all the advances in communication technology.

There is a growing body of empirical evidence which supports this hypothesis, particularly in the USA. Spillovers from university R&D

to patent activity in the same state have already been identified econometrically by Jaffee (1989). Acs, Audretsch and Feldman (1992, 1994) reinforce this result with a more direct measure of economically useful knowledge production, namely the number of innovations recorded in 1982 by the US Small Business Administration from the leading technology, engineering and trade journals. Likewise, Nelson (1986), using surveys of research managers, finds university research to be a key source of innovation in some industries, especially those related to the biological sciences where he finds some degree of corporate funding of university projects. University research spillovers may be a factor which explains how small, and often new, firms are able to generate innovations while frequently undertaking negligible amounts of R&D themselves.[1] There is econometric evidence for this result based on data from both the USA (Acs, Audretsch and Feldman, 1994) and Italy (Audretsch and Vivarelli, 1994).

Despite the many presumed advantages of geographical proximity for receiving spillovers, the precise mechanisms by which knowledge is transferred are not well understood. Information flows are usually attributed to the use of university faculty as technical consultants and post-graduate students as research assistants, the use of university facilities, informal communication between individuals at trade shows, industry conferences, seminars, talks and social activities, or joint participation in commercial ventures by university and corporate scientists through contracted research projects. Such joint participation has grown in importance since the late 1970s as the universities have established formal Offices of Technology Transfer (or Licensing) to foster interaction with industry and the commercialization of research results. This partly reflects pressure applied by US government agencies to universities, for economic growth reasons, to hasten technology transfer from their laboratories to the private sector (Parker and Zilberman, 1993). Federal Acts passed in the early 1980s also promote knowledge spillovers. The Stevenson-Wydler Technology Innovation Act of 1980, for example, encourages co-operative research and technology transfer and the 1981 Economic Recovery Tax Act gives tax discounts to firms that provide research equipment to universities. Several universities have created industry consortia to assist the funding of research. Firms pay membership fees to join these consortia and in return benefit both from access to the research output and from voice in determining the research agenda. Such channels would be expected to flourish given that universities as public institutions do not face the same incentives as private corporations to keep research results secret. In both the San Francisco Bay and Boston areas, for example, the introduction and growth of the biotechnology industry is a direct result of university R&D spillovers. Presumably, the chief benefits of geographical proximity to the spillover source consist in a reduction in both the transactions costs of knowledge transfer and in the costs of commercial research and product development. As a caveat, it ought to be noted that we do not argue that proximity is a necessary condition for spillovers to occur, only that it offers advantages in capturing them.

The labour market

The second university-based explanation of clustering highlights the provision of a pool of trained and highly qualified science and engineering graduates. The high level of human capital embodied in their general and specific skills is a further mechanism by which knowledge is transmitted. To the extent that they do not migrate, such graduates may provide a supply of labour to local firms or else a supply of entrepreneurs for new start-ups in the high technology sector (Link and Rees, 1990). Some evidence for this latter link is provided by Bania, Eberts and Fogarty (1987, 1993) who, using cross-section data, find a significant effect of university research expenditure on new firm start-ups. University scientists themselves, of course, may provide the entrepreneurial input, working part-time as directors of their own start-up companies, or even leaving academia to take a position in a high technology firm. Parker and Zilberman (1993: 97) report, for example, that MIT has incubated about forty biotechnology firms since the late 1980s. Lumme *et al.* (1993) in their study of academic entrepreneurship in Cambridge (England) identified sixty-two high technology companies whose business idea was based on the exploitation of knowledge developed or acquired in either a university or a research institute. However, even if university research is either negligible or irrelevant to industry, university training of new industrial scientists alone may be sufficient to generate local labour market spillovers. Nelson (1986: 187), for example, notes that industrial interest in academic departments of physics is confined mainly to their output of potential industrial scientists rather than to their research results.

PRELIMINARY DATA ANALYSIS

The first step[2] is to identify the high technology sectors. We proceeded by selecting those with a relatively high ratio of R&D to industry sales. Thirty-two three-digit Standard Industrial Classification (SIC) industries were identified in this way, and then grouped into the six sectors detailed in Figure 7.1: Biotechnology and Biomedical; Information Technology

Biotechnology and Biomedical

Medicinals and botanicals (283)
Medical instruments and supplies (384)
Ophthalmic goods (385)

Defence and Aerospace

Ordnance and accessories (348)
Aircraft and parts (372)
Guided missiles and space (376)
Search and navigation equipment (381)

Information Technology and Services

Computer and office equipment (357)
Electronic distribution equipment (361)
Audio and video equipment (365)
Communications equipment (366)
Electronic components and accessories (367)
Communication services (489)
Computer and data processing services (737)

Energy and Chemicals

Crude petroleum and natural gas (131)
Industrial inorganic chemicals (281)
Plastic materials and synthetics (282)
Industrial organic chemicals (286)
Miscellaneous chemical products (289)
Petroleum refining (291)

High Technology Machinery and Instruments

Engines and turbines (351)
Construction and related machinery (353)
General industrial machinery (356)
Electrical industrial apparatus (362)
Household appliances (363)
Electric lighting and wiring (364)
Miscellaneous electrical equipment and suppliers (369)
Measuring and controlling devices (382)
Photographic equipment and supplies (386)

High Technology Research

Research, development and testing services (873)

Figure 7.1 Industry groupings
Source: Office of Management and Budget, *Standard Industrial Classification Manual, 1987*, Washington DC, 1988

and Services; High Technology Machinery and Instruments; Defence and Aerospace; Energy and Chemicals; and High Technology Research.

Next we selected the twenty-two most important SMSAs (cities) for these industries, most of which also have major university R&D activity. For comparison and sample variation we also include fifteen additional SMSAs with only minor university research.

The relationship between university R&D and high technology employment can be analysed in a preliminary fashion using scatter diagrams. Figure 7.2 plots aggregate high technology employment in 1989 against university research expenditure in 1985 for all thirty-seven SMSAs. Both variables display great variation across metropolitan areas though there is a clear positive association between them. The simple correlation coefficient is 0.60. University research expenditure and high technology employment are both high in the major cities of Los Angeles, Boston, New York and Baltimore. Since size of city may be a factor

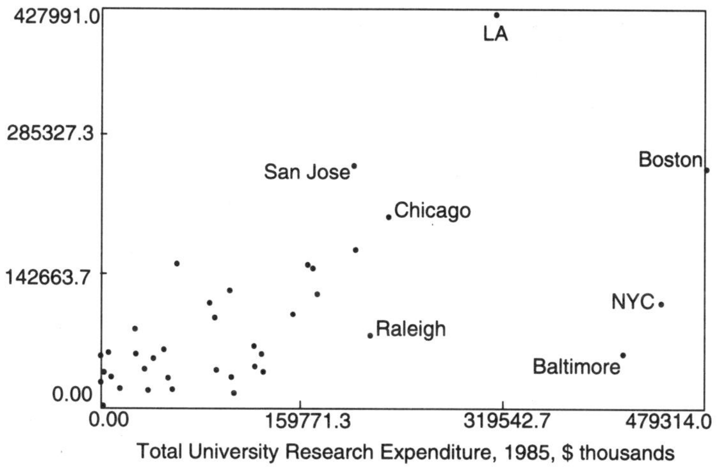

Figure 7.2 Plot of aggregate high technology employment, 1989 and university research expenditure, 1985

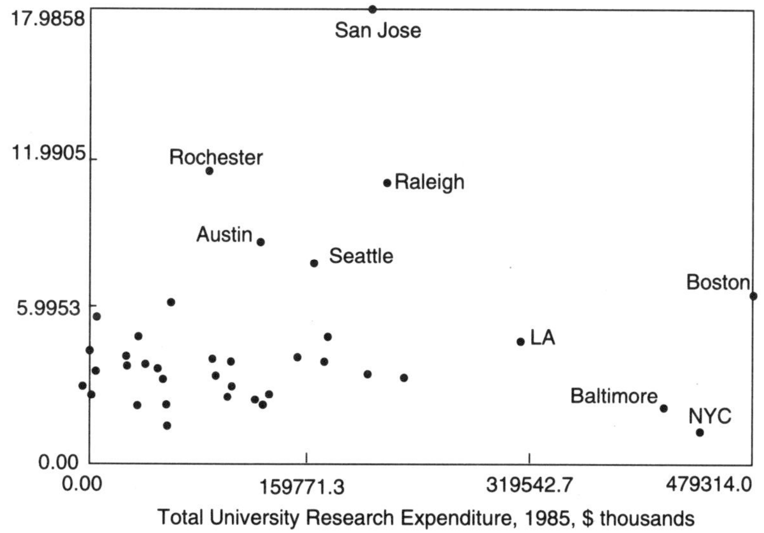

Figure 7.3 Plot of the high technology employment–population ratio, 1989 and university research expenditure, 1985

inducing a spurious correlation, Figure 7.3 plots high technology employment as a proportion of the SMSA population in 1989 against research expenditure. The simple correlation drops markedly to 0.15. Controlling for city size, our major SMSAs now generate few jobs

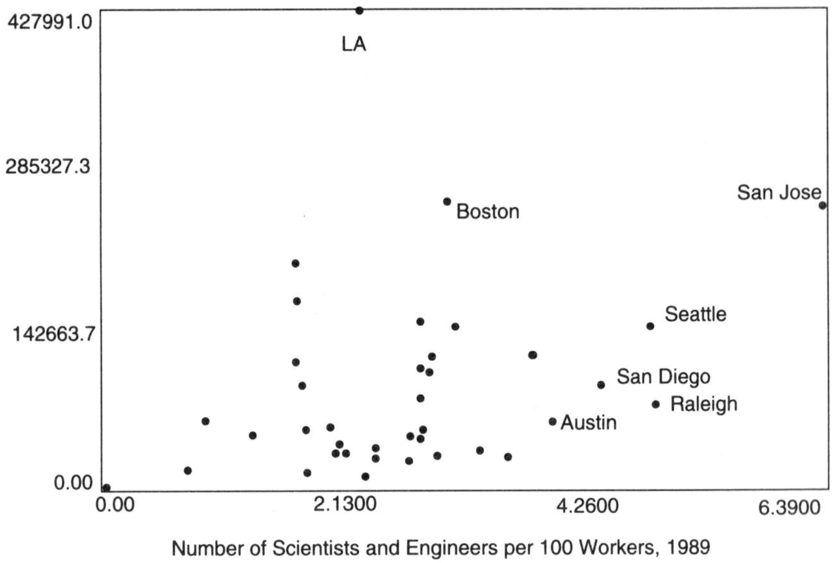

Figure 7.4 Plot of aggregate high technology employment and the number of scientists and engineers per 100 workers, 1989

relative to their university research expenditure. Rather it is San Jose, Raleigh-Durham, Seattle, Austin and Rochester which emerge as benefiting most from university research spillovers.

Figure 7.4 plots a scatter diagram of high technology employment against the number of scientists and engineers per 100 workers by SMSA. The motivation is that the supply of university science graduates with good general and specific skills influences the location of a high technology cluster. We do not have data on the SMSA science graduating students so use instead the human capital variable specified above. The proportion of scientists and engineers in the workforce is a slightly problematic proxy for local university training since it may reflect the outcome of prior location decisions, rather than the inducement to cluster *per se.* Empirically the association with high technology employment is not that strong. The simple correlation coefficient is 0.26. Significantly, Austin, San Jose, Seattle and Raleigh not only have a high proportion of the population in high technology employment but also a high share of engineers and scientists. In contrast, the large number of employees in Los Angeles appear to be concentrated in low skilled occupations. To control for the variation in shares we next consider the *share* of high technology employment in the population. In the whole sample, the correlation with the proportion of engineers and scientists is much stronger at 0.73. These data are plotted in Figure 7.5.

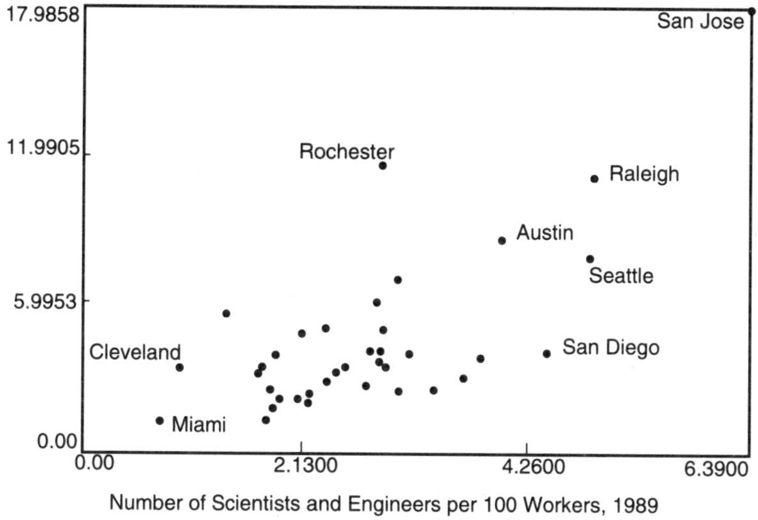

Figure 7.5 Plot of employment ratio against the proportion of scientists and engineers in each MSA, 1989

MODEL SPECIFICATION

Our data set does not contain all the variables that would be required for a conventional estimation of an employment equation. In particular, a proxy for product demand faced by high technology firms, such as sales, is not available for individual SMSAs. Our specification for the employment equation is written down in natural logarithms as:

$$EMP_{mit} = a_0 + a_1 W_{mit} + a_2 RD_{mi} + a_3 HK_m + a_4 INNOV_m + aX + u_{mit} \quad (1)$$

where 'm' indexes SMSA, 'i' indexes industry, and 't' indexes time: m = 1, . . . , 37; i = 1, . . . , 6; and t = 1988, . . . , 1991. EMP_{mit} refers to high technology employment and W_{mit} is the corresponding annual real wage per employee, defined as nominal wages deflated by the appropriate industry producer price index. Since the panel includes only four years of annual data, cross-sectional variability dominates. Experiments with a lagged dependent variable produced a coefficient close to unity and impaired the explanatory power of most other variables, suggesting a relative lack of time series variation in the employment data. For this reason, attempts to estimate equations specified in terms of employment growth rates proved fruitless.

For reasons of data availability, RD_{mi}, university R&D, is specified for only a single year, 1985. Given the time period of our data set, it seems reasonable that the use of R&D inputs dated in 1985 provides an

Table 7.1 Correspondence of university departments and industries

Industry	*University departments*
Biotechnology and Biomedical	Life Sciences
Information Technology and Services	Maths and Computer Sciences
High Technology Machinery and Instruments	Environmental Sciences and Engineering
Defence and Aerospace	Engineering and Physical Sciences
Energy and Chemicals	Physical Sciences
High Technology Research	All Hard Sciences

appropriate lag for the knowledge externality to be transmitted into commercial products and employment. Edwards and Gordon (1984), for example, found that innovations made in 1982 resulted from inventions made on average 4.2 years earlier. The R&D data include industry funded university research, a component which rarely exceeds 10 per cent of the total and is usually considerably less. Notice that RD_{mi} varies by both SMSA and industry. Total university R&D spending in each city is disaggregated by broad science department and allocated to each of the six industries. This is appropriate given substantial differences in the commercial applicability of university research across academic departments. Thus employment data by industry sector are linked to the relevant component of university research expenditure. The assignment of university department to industrial sector is listed in Table 7.1. This is close to Jaffee (1989) but it is doubtless not the only plausible allocation.

The number of scientists and engineers of each SMSA represents the potential human capital, or quality of the labour force, available for employers, HK_m. Its limitations as a proxy for university labour market spillovers were discussed earlier. Data are only available for a single year, 1989. $INNOV_m$ is a simple count of the number of innovations by SMSA in 1982, the year for which this variable has been collected. It attempts to control for the effect of pre-existing commercial innovation, that leads to product development and marketing with substantial time lags, on subsequent employment levels. Finally X represents a vector of industry, region and time dummies. These control for effects specific to each which may not have been captured by the continuous variables.

Table 7.2 presents the main summary statistics by variable for the thirty-seven SMSAs in aggregate.

RESULTS

Table 7.3 reports the OLS estimates of the employment equation estimated in natural logarithms over the four-year period 1988 to 1991 using 888 observations (4 years, 6 sectors, 37 cities). The coeffi-

Table 7.2 Summary statistics by variable

Variable	*Maximum*	*Minimum*	*Mean*	*Standard deviation*	*Coefficient of variation*
EMP_{mit}	219500	67	15537	24713	1.59
W_{mit}	60114	7822	30920	7564	0.24
RD_{mi}	479314	0	55568	77377	1.39
HK_m	57075	1152	10587	11655	1.10
$INNOV_m$	384	4	54.76	76.58	1.40

Table 7.3 OLS employment equation estimates with industry, region and time fixed effects

Regressor	*Estimate*	*t-ratio*
constant	−19.02	−8.01
W_{mit}	2.56	10.89
RD_{mi}	0.04	3.95
HK_m	0.11	2.35
$INNOV_m$	0.33	8.18
1988	0.14	1.59
1989	0.16	1.78
1990	0.12	1.35
Biology & Biomedical	−1.02	−8.97
Defence & Aerospace	−0.93	−7.27
High Tech Machinery	−0.21	−2.33
Energy and Chemicals	−2.13	−19.35
High Tech Research	−1.07	−9.85
North East	−0.39	−3.89
Mid West	−0.17	−1.80
South West	−0.51	−4.76
North West	−0.12	−0.98
$\bar{R}^2$	0.56	
$\hat{\sigma}$	0.913	
n	888	
$\chi^2_H(1)$	10.25	

Notes: (i) t-statistics are calculated using White standard errors; (ii) all variables are in natural logarithms; (iii) $\bar{R}^2$ is the adjusted multiple correlation coefficient, $\hat{\sigma}$ is the standard error of the regression, and n is the sample size; (iv) $\chi^2_H(1)$ is a diagnostic statistic distributed approximately as a chi-squared variable (with degrees of freedom in parentheses) testing for heteroscedasticity. For details, see Pesaran and Pesaran (1989).

cients should therefore be interpreted as elasticities. Statistically the equation is satisfactory, with a reasonable goodness of fit. All the coefficients of the continuous variables have the expected signs and are statistically significant at conventional levels. Given that the equation fails a Breusch–Pagan heteroscedasticity test (the chi-squared statistic has a value of 10.25 which is greater than the 5 per cent critical value of 3.84, so we reject the null hypothesis of homoscedasticity), the t-statistics are calculated using standard errors based on White's (1980) heteroscedasticity consistent covariance matrix. These standard errors do not differ greatly, however, from those obtained by OLS.

The central result is a positive and statistically significant coefficient on the R&D variable in the employment equation. Although the magnitude of the employment elasticity is small (0.04), this is evidence of a direct spillover of university research on to high technology employment.[3]

A further result is that real wages and employment are *positively* related *ceteris paribus*. This is counter to our theoretical priors based on the perfectly competitive model. Dropping the wage variable did not markedly affect the signs and significance of the remaining regressors so this outcome does not vitiate our spillover story. To take account of the simultaneity between wages and employment, the equation was re-estimated replacing the current real wage with its first lag. However, this did not produce any major differences in the results. Elsewhere (Acs, FitzRoy and Smith, 1994) we estimate a simultaneous model by two stage least squares and again find that the coefficients are robust with respect to estimation technique.

At first blush, the wage result is quite surprising. However, it is quite consistent with two important features of high technology industries. Firstly, output markets with continual product innovation and imperfect information are far from the traditional model of perfect competition. It follows that some proxy for product demand should be included in the employment equation but such a variable was not available. Thus we are estimating a reduced form rather than a true structural demand model. Secondly, specialized skills are often required in high technology sectors. Locational advantages that attract high technology firms may also generate shortages of skilled workers that lead to higher wages. Other wages typically follow to maintain differentials. The positive correlation between high technology employment and wages thus probably reflects the crucial shortages and imperfect mobility of skilled labour that has been the subject of much policy discussion and concern. Equally plausibly, and without relying on market imperfections, it may simply be the demand for products produced by the most skilled and highest paid workers that has grown most rapidly.

The university based labour market spillover story also has some support. The number of engineers and scientists in a city, the human capital variable in the employment equation, is statistically significant at conventional levels. Our technical innovation variable is likewise well determined. With respect to the fixed effects, their joint significance cannot be rejected by an F-test. Taking the fixed effect groups separately, only the time dummies fail a variable deletion test. The categories excluded to avoid the dummy variable trap are 1991, Information and Technology Services and the South East.

CONCLUSIONS

Previous empirical work on university R&D spillovers has focused on their relationship with innovation and patent counts at the level of individual US states. With new data for thirty-seven American Standard Metropolitan Statistical Areas including the main university R&D centres we have found a statistically significant and robust spillover to employment, after controlling for regional, industry and time fixed effects. This confirms the popular view of high technology clusters and provides the first quantitative evidence that academic research has a positive local high technology employment effect at the city level. A further result is that innovation was also strongly related to high technology industry employment after a long time lag, again a plausible but hitherto untested proposition. Wages in high technology sectors are strongly positively correlated with employment, supporting survey evidence that suggests serious shortages or bottlenecks of key skilled personnel, even while controlling for the average quality of the labour force.

These results, showing very localized spillovers from university R&D to employment, are clearly of relevance for regional policy. They provide support for the importance of high technology clusters in the USA and possible lessons for Europe and Japan where such clusters are much less well-developed and where there is no evidence of the localization of knowledge spillovers, at least in the semiconductor industry (Almeida and Kogut, 1994). In spite of dramatic declines in the costs of information transmission, local spillovers underline the importance of personal contacts and face-to-face communication in transferring scientific progress into jobs and products. Clearly more research is required on the nature of the transmission process, as well as on the skill composition of high technology employment and the relationship of training and skills to wages and employment in local labour markets. Another significant unexplored issue is the role of rent sharing in an industry where human capital is particularly important. Our short panel precluded any dynamic analysis but longer time series could throw light on the determinants of high technology employment growth that have generated the distribution and composition of existing clusters. Our results at least suggest a plausible role for university R&D and human capital in the form of the number of scientists and engineers, though elucidating the role of blue collar and other skills requires more disaggregated data.

The second and initially somewhat surprising result is the strong positive correlation between wages and employment in high technology industries. Our view is that the positive partial correlation in the employment equation arises mainly from the lack of a demand or sales variable.

The equation therefore essentially captures a labour supply relationship. For example, if the demand for products produced by the most highly skilled, and paid, labour grows fastest due to innovation, government procurement or whatever, employment and real wages would be positively related in a regression which did not control for demand effects. Another example would be shortages of some kinds of skills, so that these wages rise with demand for their products or services to include a scarcity rent. Wages may also include a rent-sharing component to complement the widespread use of explicit profit-sharing schemes in high technology sectors. These explanations are of course not mutually exclusive but are difficult to test without more extensive micro data. Both of these examples underline the point that since high technology employment is quite heterogeneous, it is obviously rather crude to estimate the demand for a single, homogeneous category of labour. The positive wage–employment correlation in our sample thus poses no fundamental puzzle but merely underlines the limitations of the data in terms of omitted variables and disaggregation.

Naturally, university knowledge spillovers are not the only reason for high technology clusters. Other forces for localization are quite strong. They would include the development of specialized intermediate goods industries, economies of scale and scope, and network externalities. With respect to the latter, innovations by different producers may be complementary, yielding related new products or processes when combined. On these questions too, further research is called for.

ACKNOWLEDGEMENTS

The authors would like to thank participants for valuable comments received during seminars given at the University of St Andrews, the R&D Decisions Conference at the University of Keele, the ESRC conference on R&D, Technology and Policy at the London Business School, the forty-first North American Meetings of the International Regional Science Association in Ontario, Canada, and the Evolutionary Economics of Technological Change Conference in Strasbourg, France.

NOTES

1 It should be noted that R&D is not a good measure of small firm inputs into knowledge production since such inputs often arise informally without the support of an R&D laboratory.
2 See Acs (1993) for a detailed description.
3 In a more technical paper (Acs, FitzRoy and Smith, 1994) we estimate the employment equation with finer state, instead of regional, fixed effects, yielding very similar results. Indeed the employment elasticity with respect to R&D was larger in this model.

REFERENCES

Acs, Z.J. (1993) 'US High Technology Clusters', Department of Economics, University of St Andrews, Discussion Paper No. 9315.

Acs, Z.J., Audretsch, D.B. and Feldman, M. (1992) 'Real Effects of Academic Research: Comment', *American Economic Review*, 82, 1: 363–367.

Acs, Z.J., Audretsch, D.B. and Feldman, M. (1994) 'R&D Spillovers and Recipient Firm Size', *Review of Economics and Statistics*, 76, 2: 336–340.

Acs, Z.J., FitzRoy, F.R. and Smith, I. (1994) 'High Technology Employment, Wages and University R&D Spillovers: Evidence from US Cities', mimeo, Department of Economics, University of St Andrews.

Almeida, P. and Kogut, B. (1994) 'Technology and Geography: The Localization of Knowledge and the Mobility of Patent Holders', Department of Management, Wharton School, University of Pennsylvania.

Audretsch, D.B. and Feldman, M. (1994) 'Knowledge Spillovers and the Geography of Innovation and Production', Centre for Economic Policy Research Discussion Paper, No. 953.

Audretsch, D.B. and Vivarelli, M. (1994) 'Small Firms and R&D Spillovers: Evidence from Italy', Centre for Economic Policy Research Discussion Paper, No. 927.

Bania, N., Eberts, R., and Fogarty, M. (1987) 'The Role of Technical Capital in Regional Growth', presented at the Western Economic Association Meetings.

Bania, N., Eberts, R. and Fogarty, M. (1993) 'Universities and the Start-Up of New Companies: Can we Generalize from Route 128 and Silicon Valley?', *Review of Economics and Statistics*, 75: 761–766.

Beeson, P. and Montgomery, E. (1993) 'The Effects of Colleges and Universities on Local Labour Markets', *Review of Economics and Statistics*, 75: 753–761.

Business Week (1994) 'Why are we so afraid of Growth?' Cover Story, 62–72, 16 May.

Edwards, K.L. and Gordon, T.J. (1984) 'Characterization of Innovations Introduced in the US Market in 1982', The Futures Group.

Jaffee, A.B. (1989) 'Real Effects of Academic Research', *American Economic Review*, 79, 5: 957–970.

Jaffee, A.B., Trajtenberg, M. and Henderson, R. (1993) 'Geographic Localization of Knowledge Spillovers as Evidenced by Patent Citations', *Quarterly Journal of Economics*, 108: 577–598.

Krugman, P. (1991) 'Increasing Returns and Economic Geography', *Journal of Political Economy*, 99, 3: 483–499.

Link, A.N. and Rees, J. (1990) 'Firm Size, University Based Research, and the Returns to R&D', *Small Business Economics*, 2: 25–31.

Lumme, A., Kauranen, L., Autio, E. and Kaila, M.M. (1993) 'New Technology Based Companies in Cambridge in an International Perspective', Working Paper No. 35, Small Business Research Centre, University of Cambridge.

Lund, L. (1986) 'Locating Corporate R&D Facilities', Conference Board Report No. 892, Conference Board, New York.

Nelson, R.R. (1986) 'Institutions Supporting Technical Advance in Industry', *American Economic Review, Papers and Proceedings*, 76, 2: 186–189.

Parker, D.D. and Zilberman, D. (1993) 'University Technology Transfers: Impacts on Local and U.S. Economies', *Contemporary Policy Issues*, XI, 2: 87–99.

Pesaran, M.H. and Pesaran, B. (1989) *Microfit: An Interactive Econometric Software Package*, Oxford: Oxford University Press.

White, H. (1980) 'A Heteroskedasticity-Consistent Covariance Matrix Estimator and a Direct Test for Heteroskedasticity', *Econometrica* 48: 817–838.

Data appendix sources

University R&D Expenditure: National Science Foundation, Academic Science and Engineering R&D Expenditures, Fiscal Year 1989, Washington DC. Grouped by metropolitan areas using the State and Metropolitan Area Databook, 1986.

Employment, Wages, Human Capital: US Department of Labor, Bureau of Labor Statistics, Employment and Earnings, May 1989, 1990, 1991, 1992.

Innovations: U.S. Small Business Administration, Innovation Database.

8

PERFORMANCE IMPLICATIONS OF PATENT FAMILY SIZE

Gavin Reid and Colin Roberts

1 INTRODUCTION

Patent families are created as firms take steps to secure intellectual property over a variety of regimes. They provide a measure of patenting activity which emphasizes scope rather than duration. Here, the idea is used to construct a patent activity variable for firms in the UK scientific instruments industry over the period 1981–90. This variable is considered along with size and financial variables for the same firms over the period 1983–90. The database so created is an unbalanced panel for 92 firms in this patent-intensive industry.[1] As all the significant firms in the industry are included, a fixed effects, rather than random effects, model is used for estimation on this database.[2] The core of the empirical analysis in this chapter is a set of estimates which seek the principal determinants of patenting activity in size and financial variables.

As a preliminary to this analysis, the theoretical and conceptual background for the patent scope variable is developed, followed by a presentation of the empirical background to the estimates. The next section considers one-way and two-way fixed effects regression estimates of the determinants of patenting activity within the UK scientific instruments industry. The chapter concludes by exploring the roles of ownership, and of spillover effects.

2 MEASURING APPROPRIABILITY BY PATENT SCOPE

The theoretical focus in this chapter is on appropriability. Firms in the scientific instruments industry are patenting to prevent the fruits of their innovative labours becoming common knowledge. This is tolerated by society because it is feared that an inability to establish a property right over knowledge will diminish the incentive of such firms to innovate. The dynamic gains from innovation are put ahead of the potential static gains from allocative efficiency, which would say that knowledge, once created, should be available at marginal cost – which would be close to zero.

The standard theoretical preoccupation through the 1970s and 1980s has been with patent length, following the seminal paper of Nordhaus (1969) and its popularization by Scherer (1972). Suppose an initially competitive market has within it a firm which creates a new technology, giving it a clear marginal cost advantage over other firms in the industry. The state permits this firm to hold an exclusive right of production in the industry for T years (i.e. awards a patent right). For time periods T + 1, T + 2, . . . this right relapses, all firms in the industry get free access to the technology, and all produce competitively using the new, lower marginal cost technology. The innovating firm may choose to exercise its monopoly right under the patent if the marginal cost reduction achieved by the innovation has been very great, or if not, may choose to license the innovation to rivals at a fee just less than the marginal cost reduction achieved. From the viewpoint of society, taking the maximization of net social welfare as the relevant criterion, the optimal patent length set by the state would make the marginal loss in consumers' surplus whilst the patent was in force equal to the marginal gain in producer's surplus over the same period, plus the marginal gain in consumers' surplus after this period. This simple picture, which provides no explanation of the innovation process itself, can be complemented with the work of Loury (1979) and Reinganum (1983) which models this process as a non-cooperative oligopoly in which each firm chooses its research intensity to maximize its value, taking its rivals' research intensities as given. It can be shown that it is socially optimal to grant a permanent patent monopoly (i.e. net social welfare is monotonically increasing in patent length).

In the 1990s, theoretical interest has shifted away from patent length to patent breadth or width. In the analysis of Klemperer (1990), width is interpreted in terms of the technological coverage of the patent. For example, if the original innovating firm invented a new optical reading device, how similar a device could a rival produce without infringing a patent right?[3] Thus width is being interpreted in terms of a region of differentiated product space. In Gilbert and Shapiro (1990: 106) the interpretation of breadth is far less specific, and is simply identified with 'the flow rate of profit available to the patentee while the patent is in force'. Thus breadth is interpreted in terms of the scope for exploiting the market power which the patent monopoly confers on the innovator while the patent is in force.

Our own approach also appeals to patent breadth or width, but is as much empirically as theoretically inspired. It admits the force of the argument of Schankerman and Pakes (1986) to the effect that the willingness to exploit the right to monopoly production implied by a grant of patent is an important indicator of the value of the intellectual property it aims to protect. In their case, renewal of the patent right, which involves the payment of a fee on a rising annual basis, is the chosen indicator. In our case, extension of the scope of the patent protection, across various regimes, is chosen as the indicator of the value of the intellectual property.

Generally, the greater the internationality of the patent protection sought, the greater the cost incurred to establish the property right (*cf.* Reid, Siler and Smith (1994)). Our measure of width or breadth, which may be called scope, is the size of *patent family*.[4] The starting point for a patent family is the filing for a patent in a specific domestic regime, which establishes a priority date. This priority date effectively identifies or dates the claim to a unique inventive step in all further attempts to secure the underlying intellectual property right across various patent regimes. Neither the Klemperer (1990) nor Gilbert and Shapiro (1990) notions of breadth have sufficiently precise economic definitions to make their method of measurement apparent.[5]

By contrast, our approach, that of *scope*, is very precisely defined, and has the additional merit of being readily related to a search procedure which is commonplace amongst practising Patent Officers.[6] As contrasted with the approach of Schankerman and Pakes (1986) which emphasizes renewals, we feel that our emphasis on scope is more important, for two reasons. Firstly, renewal up to the full permissible term of a patent is uncommon, suggesting that typically the implied value of the intellectual property is harvested, or dissipated, early in the potential patent life (see Schott (1978)). Secondly, given this, the fruits of intellectual property are best exploited early in as many potentially profitable market areas as possible, given the rapid pace of diffusion in high technology industries (see Mansfield (1981, 1985)).

From the viewpoint of a particular firm, as distinct from the viewpoint of society, patent protection will only be sought in the *i*th regime if it generates a positive net present value ($V_i > 0$), net of production and patenting costs. If π_i is the profit rate while a patent is in force, over the time period τ_i^0 to τ_i' and $\bar{\pi}_i$ is the profit rate after the lapse of protection, assuming a return to competitive conditions, V_i may be written:

$$V_i = \int_{\tau_i^0}^{\tau_i'} \pi_i(t) e^{-rt} dt + \int_{\tau_i'}^{\infty} \bar{\pi}_i(t) e^{-rt} dt > 0$$

Different regimes are typically exploited at different times, often proceeding from the domestic to the continental and then to the world. The total net present value generated in the various available value creating regimes is ΣV_i which is increasing in the V_i. The V_i are hard to measure directly, but an index of their value is given by the amount of patenting activity which takes place within each regime. This itself is measured by counts of stages (e.g. filing, grant) in what may be called (*cf.* Reid, Siler and Smith (1994)) *the patenting process*. We denote by S_{ct}^{ij} the *i*th stage of the patenting process for the *j*th patent family of company *c* at time period *t*. This is a count variable.

In an earlier cross-section study (Reid, Siler and Smith (1996)) an aggregate count variable was constructed for the decade by summing over stages, patent families and time, giving a new count variable (κ_c) indexed only by the company. Thus $\kappa_c = \sum_i \sum_j \sum_t S_{ct}^{ij}$. Then κ_c was related to various other company characteristics, including measures of size and liquidity. In the present study, we work with a panel (rather than cross-section) database, creating a new count variable $\kappa_{ct} = \sum_i \sum_j S_{ct}^{ij}$ which measures the total patenting activity of firm *c* at time period *t*, across all patent families it has created, over all regimes in which it is active. Throughout the rest of this paper, this variable will be called *Tcount*.[7]

3 EMPIRICAL BACKGROUND

In Table 8.1 the principal characteristics of the patenting and non-patenting firms are displayed. Regarding size variables, the patent-active firms are at least three times bigger on average than the patent-inactive firms. This is true of real sales, employees and especially real assets. Real net profit before tax is very much greater on average for the patent-active firms compared to the patent-inactive. We would of course expect the aforementioned size difference to be reflected in a profits difference between these two groups, but there is more to it than simply this. If the ratio of real net profit before tax is taken to real sales, the figures are 8.39 per cent for the patent-active firms and 3.29 per cent for the patent-inactive firms, the former being two and a half times the latter. These figures are probably each underestimates of the price–cost margin, and therefore of the required competitive rental on assets employed expressed as a ratio to sales. Though comparisons using accounting data are fraught with measurement problems, there is at least the suggestion that the price–cost margin measure of profitability indicates a performance advantage of the patent-active over the patent-inactive firms.

Putting aside the average figures for return on capital and return on shareholders' funds for patent-inactive firms (caused by very high sample variation) other indicators of profitability, return on assets and profit margins (trading, operating and pre-tax) all point to a performance advantage of the patent-active firms. However, these differences are not great, and in individual cases may not even be statistically significant.[8] What clinches the weight of evidence in favour of a small performance advantage of the patent-active firms is the preponderance of financial indicators that favour that view rather than the reverse. The

Table 8.1 Size, capital structure and financial performance for patent-active and patent-inactive firms in the UK scientific instruments industry

Variable	*Firm type* *Patent-active firms (1 to 35)*	*Patent-inactive firms (36 to 92)*
Real sales	19073	6086
	(26180)	(9131)
Employees	774	203
	(1077)	(289)
Real assets	16836	4268
	(24621)	(6260)
Real net profit before tax	1601	200
	(2937)	(919)
Return on capital[3]	17.4	66.6
	(77.1)	(1083)
Return on assets	5.98	5.56
	(12.55)	(16.27)
Return on shareholders' funds[4]	10.14	-69.25
	(183.3)	(1114.2)
Trading profit margin	9.29	6.78
	(10.02)	(8.77)
Operating profit margin	6.44	4.66
	(10.00)	(9.02)
Pre-tax profit margin	5.25	4.06
	(10.56)	(10.89)
Gearing ratio	0.40	0.38
	(0.20)	(0.20)
Liquidity ratio	1.82	1.80
	(0.79)	(0.91)
Export to sales ratio	42.05	37.73
	(22.35)	(23.81)

Source: *ICC Business Ratio Report* on Scientific Instrument Manufacturers (various issues)

Notes: 1 Entries are mean values with standard deviations in brackets, for period 1983–90.

2 For real variables, the deflator used was the domestic output producer price index for the instrument engineering sector (SIC 37) with 1980 = 100 as the base. Source: *UK Business Statistics*.

3 This return is highly variable, with a range of (−141.9, 929.2) for patent-active and (−2222, 20.40×10^3) for patent-inactive firms.

4 Also a highly variable return, with a range of (−2369, 733.3) for patent-active, and (−2754, 20.41×10^3) for patent-inactive firms.

5 Full definitions of variables are given in the Appendix.

matter that remains to be answered is whether financial performance in itself, however measured, provides a good predictor of patenting activity.

Gearing, liquidity and export intensity ratios are rather similar between the patent-active and patent-inactive firms. In the case of the gearing ratio it may be that accounting conventions within the industry tend to maintain a value of around 0.4 for this ratio, with a small standard deviation.[9] Any departure from this might therefore be of particular importance in an explanatory sense.

Moving on from these descriptive statistics, we propose to develop below an inferential approach to explaining patenting activity, as measured by the *Tcount* variable. Our initial focus of interest is on the size/innovation relation which has been so widely explored in the literature. This is the first of the so-called Schumpeterian hypotheses,[10] this one being that larger firms have advantages over smaller firms in the innovations process. Reasons for this are several: scale and scope economies, risk spreading, complementarities, cost spreading, fund generation, and so on. As against this, disadvantages of scale could include managerial diseconomies, perverse incentives, and bureaucratic stultification. The increased interest in small firms in the last ten years has led to a recognition of some of their advantages, as against large firms, in the innovations process. These include flexibility, the tight alignment of incentives, affiliative benefits, and the capacity for rapid growth.

Previous work[11] has suggested a non-linear (indeed concave from below) relationship between patent activity, using the count variable κ_c as the appropriate measure, and size, using sales, assets or employment as the size measure. Indeed, for the years 1986 and 1987, within the UK scientific instruments industry, it is possible to derive a patent activity maximizing firm, so great is the concavity of this relationship. During these years it defines a firm size which is close to that of Cambridge Instruments, which was ranked only seventh in size by employment. In terms of performance it was one of the most outstanding firms in the industry in the 1980s. That study used only cross-section methods. With the much larger panel dataset that we are reporting upon here, a more ambitious look at non-linearity in the size/innvoation relationship becomes possible. Two well-known studies, Scherer (1965), and Scherer and Ross (1990), explored the use of quadratic and cubic (i.e. second and third order polynomial) relationships, and the possibility of such forms of non-linearity has been explored intensively up to the present time (e.g. Pavitt, Robson and Townsend (1987); Roberts and Siler (1994)). There seems to be widespread agreement about the non-linearity of the relationships. If the most general hypothesis is adopted, then the evidence of Scherer suggests a positive coefficient on the linear term, a negative coefficient on the quadratic, and a positive coefficient on the cubic. There is some doubt about the statistical significance of the cubic term. Overall, this suggests a general tendency amongst firms to diminishing returns of innovation with respect to firm size, apart from the very largest firms. This is a hypothesis that we test below.

Whilst the 1960s saw a considerable interest in the relationship between innovation and market concentration, by the 1980s there had been a loss of confidence in the robustness of early findings of a positive relationship. Some found a negative relationship, and an inverted-U relationship also found strong support. Industry level variables (e.g. technology, durability) seem to be more important in explaining variations in innovation, and the concentration variable seems to behave in the expected way (albeit with little statistical leverage) only when considered in conjunction with such industry level variables (e.g. in low opportunity industries in the study of Lunn and Martin (1986), where the sample is dichotomised into low and high opportunity technology classes). Currently, a shift of interest has come about, attributing innovation to three classes of factors (demand, opportunity and appropriability) as in, for example, Cohen *et al.* (1987). However, severe conceptual problems remain in relating this approach to a coherent body of theory, and empirical difficulties of data acquisition and the proper operational definition of variables are acute. We have therefore rejected the market structure approach as too fragile, and rejected the industry characteristics approach as too problematical.

By contrast, financial variables are well defined, according to widely agreed conventions, and can be related to a coherent body of theory. Because the firm's accounting rate of return can be directly related to cash flow (minus depreciation),[12] and because cash flow has the additional appealing interpretation of internal financial capability it has been used as a potential explanation of innovative activity. Whilst the common finding[13] has been of a positive cash flow/innovation relationship, discussion of its interpretation has been equivocal. Causality and time lags are important here, and studies have not satisfactorily answered questions about cash flow as a signal of future profitability of innovative activity, or as a mere consequence of past profitable innovative activity.

However, there are many other important aspects of financial structure (e.g. returns, margins, gearing) which have been widely neglected in the literature, and which we would aim to consider in conjunction with the more familiar size variables. The range of financial variables under consideration is already apparent from Table 8.1, and we have chosen to look at these as co-determinants of innovative activity, rather than the more conventional market structure variables, or the more controversial demand, opportunity and appropriability variables.

4 FIXED EFFECTS MODELS OF PATENTING ACTIVITY

The dependent variable to be explained is the *Tcount* variable. As section 2 indicated, it is derived from patent families, and motivated by the notion of patent scope. The independent variables are polynomial terms in size, and various financial characteristics. In addition, fixed firm-level effects are considered, because even though the art of discovering and explaining these underlying effects is underdeveloped, they do seem to be statistically important. Furthermore, a useful test of the robustness of the specification of our chosen size and financial variables model is to discover whether fixed effects, once introduced, act as dominating variables (as they do, with undesirable consequences, for example, in innovation/concentration equations) (see Cohen and Levin (1989)). In a robust model, the size and financial variables should remain significant even when fixed effects are considered. As a matter of refinement, one-way and two-way fixed effects models are used, the former assigning dummy variables to firms and the latter to both firms and time periods (see notes to Table 8.2). The full database has, in principle, 920 observations on 24 variables (i.e. over 22,000 data points) but missing or incomplete data reduce this number of observations considerably in running any given model. Technically, the database is an unbalanced panel. Fortunately, the typical number of observations available still runs to several hundreds for any model estimated.

The first column of Table 8.2 reports upon the one-way fixed effects model. In this case, an unconditional analysis of variance on *Tcount* (or equivalently a regression of *Tcount* on a constant and the set of firm dummy variables) is rejected in favour of the model reported in column 1 of Table 8.2 with size, financial *and* firm dummy variables, the relevant statistic being $F(8, 382) = 11.800$. A classical regression model, using just the size and financial variables, estimated by ordinary least squares on the full set of (pooled) observations is also rejected, with a test statistic of $F(84, 382) = 12.542$. Both these test values are highly statistically significant, and have probability values close to zero. Firm dummy variables, which number over eighty, are not reported for lack of space.

Turning to the size and financial variables, the coefficients of the linear and quadratic terms on size (measured by employees) are positive and negative, respectively, and highly statistically significant. This result is in agreement with both related and independent work[14] and suggests diminishing returns to patent directed R&D. Put more precisely for the case at hand, it shows that whilst firms in the UK scientific instruments industry generally become more patent-active as they get larger (creating, for example, more and larger patent families), for a proportional increase in size there is a less than proportional increase in patenting activity. If the concavity implied by the negative coefficient on the quadratic term is sufficiently great, decreasing returns for patent directed R&D may set in, and a patent activity maximizing firm size can be determined. In this case it exists, and is determined[15] at an employment size of 1,503. This is over twice the average size of the industry, but well short of maximum employment size, which is 4,444. In this narrow sense, an 'optimal' patenting size is determined. It is a size which is close to that of a firm like Cambridge Instruments, which was also identified as

Table 8.2 One-way and two-way fixed effects models

Independent variables	*Model (t-values in brackets)* One-way (1)	Two-way (2)
Employees	0.0230	0.0229
	(5.071)	(5.037)
Employees^2	-0.7861×10^{-5}	-0.7836×10^{-5}
	(−3.327)	(−3.311)
Employees^3	0.7661×10^{-9}	0.7648×10^{-9}
	(1.942)	(1.945)
Real net profit before tax	0.7912×10^{-3}	0.7731×10^{-3}
	(4.978)	(4.831)
Return on capital	0.00177	0.00226
	(.0599)	(0.754)
Trading profit margin	−0.0928	−0.0862
	(−2.799)	(−2.557)
Gearing	4.1074	4.0279
	(2.633)	(2.568)
Liquidity	0.35194	0.2968
	(0.953)	(0.798)
Constant	N/A	−6.0805
		(−4.769)
Diagnostics		
$t_{.025}(120) = 1.980$;	$\bar{R}^2 = 0.7477$	$\bar{R}^2 = 0.7448$
$F_{.001}(40,120) = 2.11$;	$F(92,382) = 16.27$	$F(100,374) = 14.3$
$F(\infty,\infty) = 1$		

Notes: 1 Model (1) is the one-way fixed effects model:

$$y_{it} = \alpha_i + \beta' \mathbf{x}_{it} + \varepsilon_{it}$$

where $i = 1, \ldots n$; $t = 1, \ldots T_i$ are the numbers of firms and time periods, respectively.
y_{it} is the patent count measure and $\mathbf{x}_{it}$ is a vector of explanatory variables; ε_{it} has zero mean and constant variance.

2 Model (2) is the two-way fixed effects model:

$$y_{it} = \alpha_0 + \alpha_i + \gamma_t + \beta' \mathbf{x}_{it} + \varepsilon_{it}$$

with the restriction imposed of $\Sigma\alpha_i = \Sigma\,\gamma_t = 0$

optimal, in this sense, in an earlier cross-section study (see Reid, Smith and Siler (1996)). The cubic term just fails to have a coefficient which is significantly different from zero, on a two-tailed test at the 5 per cent level (its probability value being 5.3 per cent). Its marginal significance is consistent with the original finding of Scherer's (1965) classical study and has most recently been confirmed in the work of Roberts and Siler (1994) on patent activity in the Scottish engineering industry. Also of note is the very small magnitude of the coefficient on the cubic term. Writers like Schmalensee (1989) would argue that, in contexts like this, magnitudes are just as important as significance. This would suggest dropping the cubic term from the model.

If this coefficient on the new cubic term were larger and slightly more significant, the argument on the innovative/size relationship would need to be modified. Calling the coefficients of the linear, quadratic and cubic terms b, c, and d respectively, then if $c < 0$ and $d > 0$, which are the restrictions suggested by the estimates, then *Tcount* is convex in the size variable *Employees* if *Employees* $> -c/3d$ and concave if the inequality is reversed. Direct calculation from the estimated coefficients shows that the switch-over point in this case occurs at an employment size of 3,420. For lower levels of employment, firms experience diminishing returns for patent directed R&D, and for higher levels increasing returns. The mean employee size in the sample is 774, and the previously suggested 'optimal' (i.e. patent activity maximizing) size is 1,503 so the employment size of 3,420 required before increasing returns are apparent is very large in relation to even leading firms in the industry. Indeed, it is nearly two and a half standard deviations above the mean employment size. Only firms like United Scientific, Marconi and ABB Kent have as many employees as this. On balance, we are inclined to accept the strict canons of statistical inference and reject the cubic term. However, we recognize that an element of judgement of evidence is involved here, and have provided therefore a reasonably full discussion, on the basis of which the reader can make his or her own judgement.

Turning now to the financial variables, real net profit before tax, the trading profit margin and gearing all have highly statistically significant coefficients, with probability values of almost zero, 2 per cent and $2\frac{1}{2}$ per cent respectively. The interpretation suggested by these results is that whilst profits encourage higher patenting activity, the more patent-active firms are willing to trim profit margins and to increase total liabilities relative to shareholders' funds in order to sustain innovative output. Neither return on capital nor liquidity have coefficients which are significantly different from zero. These are two very widely used financial performance ratios and their lack of significance warrants further discussion.

Return on capital is defined as pre-tax profit divided by capital employed. It is a variable with a very high standard deviation, and this makes it difficult to reject the null hypothesis of no difference between the mean returns on capital, as between the patent-active and patent-inactive firms. A 95 per cent confidence interval for this difference is 22 ± 294 which is a very wide interval about zero. In effect, the data cannot tell us that there is a performance difference in terms of rate of return on capital, as between the patent-active and patent-inactive firms. This immediately poses the question as to how the patent-inactive firms do no worse than patent-active firms, and a possible answer, explored below, is that they enjoy positive spillover benefits from the patent-active firms. Cohen and Levin (1989) report from conversations with R&D managers that even simply knowing what technical problems rivals were addressing (which a patent filing, for example, certainly reveals) was in itself very useful trade intelligence, let alone knowing detailed technical specifications. Rivals which did not specialize in patent-intensive R&D might as an alternative specialize in developing so-called 'absorptive capability' which enables them to free-ride on others' innovative efforts. In this way, free-riding firms avoid marketplace disadvantage and on average no discernible difference in rate of return on capital arises. This issue is explored further in section 6 below.

Liquidity is a variable which behaves in a quite different way, statistically speaking, from return on capital. Here it is defined as current assets divided by current liabilities. The coefficient of variation (i.e. 'signal to noise ratio') is 2.30 and 1.97 for the liquidity variable in the case of patent-active and patent-inactive firms. For the return on capital, by contrast, it is much lower, at 0.225 and 0.615 respectively. Nevertheless, a 95 per cent confidence interval for the difference between mean liquidity in the patent-active and patent-inactive groups of firms is 0.02 ± 0.3673 which fails to reject the null hypothesis of equal means. In the return on capital case we have a 'noisy' variable which prevents us from distinguishing means; whereas in the liquidity case we have a high precision variable, but probably conventionality in its expected value (as in the case of the gearing ratio). The liquidity ratio we use is related to, but is not identical with, the cash flow variable that previous studies (e.g. Elliot (1971); Branch (1974)) have examined thoroughly, but without reaching conclusive results. The expectation is, if liquidity measures financial capability, that fund availability creates a pool of financial resources that are not necessarily immediately committed to operational uses, but can be diverted into patent-directed R&D. In the case of UK scientific instruments this expectation is denied, adding yet greater weight of evidence against cash flow or liquidity arguments for innovation.

Considering equation (1) of Table 8.2 overall, it conveys a great deal about the industry both positively and negatively. It facilitates detailed discussion of the size/innovation relationship, and finely discriminates between various financial variables, all of which one might feel *a priori* have a bearing on innovation. Liquidity and return on capital appear to have no bearing on innovation, whereas the effects of net profit, the profit margin and gearing are highly significant. Concerning the latter findings, what is perhaps most noteworthy are the profit margin and gearing results. Firms are manifestly willing to squeeze margins in their quest for innovative products, presumably to assist in market growth. They are, further, willing to let gearing rise (with the attendant increase in risk exposure) to attain the same goal. In short, innovation seems to be achieved partly at the cost of a deterioration in financial performance. Finally, the statistical performance of this equation overall is good. The adjusted R^2 is high for models of this sort, with about three-quarters of the variation in *Tcount* being explained by the size, financial and dummy variables. The F statistic of 16.27 is highly statistically significant and has a probability value of close to zero.

For comparative purposes, the two-way fixed effects model is also reported in column 2 of Table 8.2. Qualitative results on the size and financial variables are unaffected by the introduction of time dummy variables. Thus the linear and quadratic size variables' coefficients remain positive and negative respectively, and highly significant, whilst the coefficient on the cubic term is small in absolute value, positive, and marginally significant. Of the financial variables, net profit and gearing have coefficients which remain positive and the trading profit margin's coefficient remains negative, all being significant. The coefficients on liquidity and return on capital remain insignificant. Again, about 75 per cent of variation in *Tcount* is explained and the F statistic for overall fit is highly significant. In this two-way fixed effects model, a constant term appears and is significant. For reasons of lack of space, the 90 or so dummy variable coefficients are not reported. On a likelihood ratio test of the model in column 2 against the model in column 1 we get a test statistic of $\chi^2(8) = 5.858$ which is less than the 5 per cent and 1 per cent critical values of the χ^2 distribution with 8 d.f., these being 15.5 and 20.1 respectively. One therefore cannot reject the model of column 1 in favour of the model of column 2. The main value of the rejected model is that it provides a robustness test of the results of the economic variables in the accepted model (column 1, Table 8.2). Signs, magnitudes and significance of coefficients are well preserved in the alternative model, thereby adding to our confidence in the accepted model.

5 OWNERSHIP AND PATENTING ACTIVITY

A variable of potential interest that was not mentioned in the previous section is ownership. In previous work (Roberts and Siler (1994)) it was found that ownership had some influence on patenting activity[16] in the Scottish engineering industry over a similar time period. For example, being a US subsidiary rather than a UK subsidiary had a negative effect on patent activity and one which was significant. However, these results were not robust under all alternative model specifications, though they are suggestive of an effect which advocates of an organizational theory of the firm might expect to be important.

The incentive and monitoring systems which are embodied in organizational structure can have a major effect on innovation. Successful organizational forms, in an innovative sense, will use devices to identify and reward creative personnel. Such rewards may not arise naturally, because in situations of 'small numbers competition' within organizations, uncreative staff are motivated to create devices for free-riding upon, or creaming off the rewards attributable to, creative staff. Levin *et al.* (1987) have found that patenting activity itself is part of the method for monitoring the performance of R&D employees by progressive firms, quite apart from its role of protecting intellectual property. It is possible that the use of this device varies by country of ownership, in the same way as some countries favour the multi-divisional (M-form) organization over the unitary form (U-form) (e.g. the USA) or the reverse (e.g. Germany). We have no clear priors on this, but potential effects of this sort are worthy of investigation. For example, they can point to areas where comparative case studies of organizational forms may be illuminating.

The most obvious comparison to be made is illustrated in Figure 8.1. This displays two histograms: for the ownership patterns of patent-active, and patent-inactive firms. The histograms were constructed using raw frequencies, and in Table 8.3 these are standardized in percentages terms to assist in comparisons of the histograms by the reference to the heights of each bar for a certain ownership category. The modal ownership type is Independent (= 1) for patent-active firms, and UK subsidiary (= 2) for patent-inactive firms. The US subsidiary category is almost as important amongst patent-inactive firms as the Independent category. Both the US and European subsidiary categories are more important for patent-inactive compared to patent-active firms. In short, there appears to be a greater heterogeneity of ownership pattern with the patent-inactive firms.

Turning now to Table 8.3 gives a more precise quantitative picture. Two major differences are apparent. The Independent status of ownership has almost exactly twice the proportional representation amongst patent-active, as compared to patent-inactive firms (47 per cent compared to 24 per cent). The European subsidiary is much more important amongst patent-inactive, as compared to patent-active firms (17 per cent compared to 4 per cent). The data in this table use all the ownership observations for the period 1983 to 1990, which amount to 616 in all, when account is taken of missing values. Going back to the raw data from which the histograms were constructed, one has a cross-tabulation of ownership and patent activity.[17] This can be used as a contingency table to test the null hypothesis of no dependence of patent activity on ownership. The χ^2 test of independence in this case produces a test statistic of $\chi^2(4) = 49.5398$ which has a probability value of close to zero. In other words, patent activity does seem to depend on ownership.

Whilst this is clearly established, it is much more difficult to establish what effect each ownership category has, or even what effect the

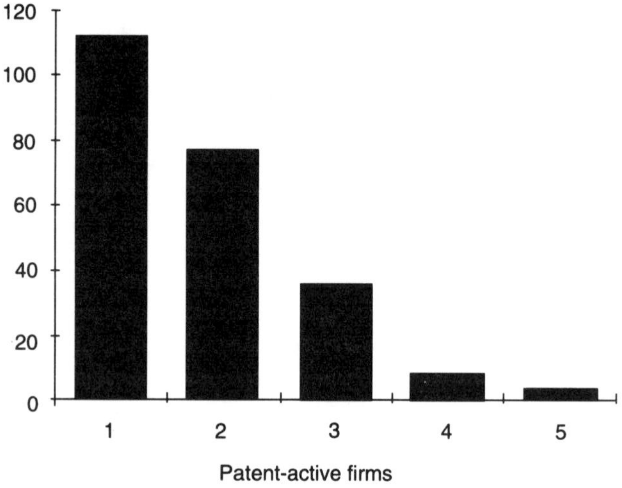

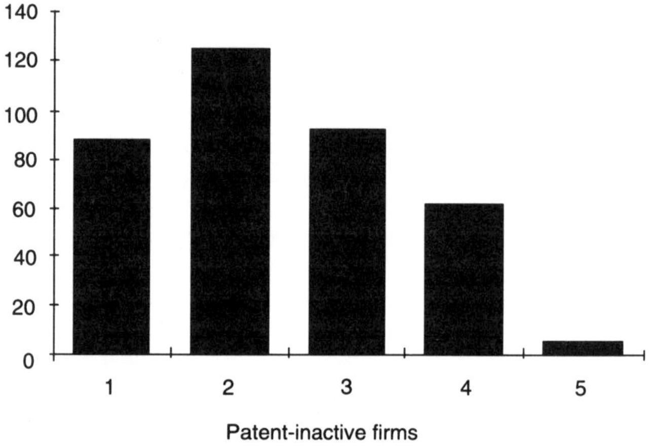

Figure 8.1 Histograms of ownership for patent-active and patent-inactive firms
Notes: 1 Data sources are as in Table 8.3
2 1 = independent, 2 = UK owned, 3 = US owned, 4 = European owned, 5 = Other
3 Vertical axis gives raw frequency in each case

heterogeneity of ownership has (e.g. by degree of internationality). We proceeded in two ways. Firstly, a categorical variable was created, using the same integer values for ownership as were used on the horizontal axis of the histograms. In other words, this variable generally rose the greater the internationality of the subsidiarity to which the firm was subject. This variable was generally insignificant in a variety of specifications of the

Table 8.3 Ownership pattern in the UK scientific instruments industry (1983–90)

Ownership	*Patent-active firms (1 to 35)*	*Patent-active firms (36 to 92)*
Independent	47	24
UK owned	32	34
US owned	16	25
European owned	4	17
Other	1	1

Notes: 1 Small rounding errors in percentages.
2 Ownership as specified in various issues of the *ICC Business Ratio Report* on Scientific Instrument Manufacturers.
3 Frequencies are based on all ownership observations for 1983–90.

Tcount regression. Secondly, four dummy variables were created, to try to judge the individual effects of specific ownership types on the *Tcount* variable. Under a variety of specifications of the *Tcount* regressions these dummy variables also proved to be insignificant.

We conclude that whilst ownership does clearly have some bearing on patenting activity in the scientific instruments industry, the nature of its impact is somewhat elusive, and is in any case of second-order of importance compared to those other explanatory variables like size and profitability, which were generally included with the categorical and dummy variables versions of ownership measures.

6 SPILLOVERS AND FREE-RIDING

It is apparent from section 4 above that patenting activity is not as closely associated with favourable financial performance as might be expected if appropriability of intellectual property is secure in the scientific instruments industry. From the work of Mansfield (1981, 1985) it is known, firstly, that most successful patents are rapidly imitated (within four years) and, secondly, that rivals rapidly gain knowledge about products or processes (within a year) and about R&D expenditure (within one and a half years). The work of Levin (1988) suggests that in R&D-intensive industries patents are generally thought to be less important for extracting value from intellectual property than trade secrecy, lead time, moving down the learning curve and sales or service effort. If these arguments are of relevance to scientific instruments, and we believe they are, then consideration has to be given to externalities that occur when new intellectual property is created. A well known approach, due initially to Spence (1984) is to say that if a firm spends a certain amount on R&D, then its stock of knowledge is equal to this plus a spillover term which is the product of the total spending by other firms on R&D and an appropriability parameter.

An empirical implementation of this idea has recently been undertaken by Henriques (1994). For two US industries (drugs, toiletries) she estimates a model in which R&D expenditure depends upon sales and a lagged spillover term. The latter is defined as total R&D expenditure in the sample, less a specific firm's own R&D expenditure. If free-riding occurs, the spillover term will have a negative coefficient, as the greater the R&D undertaken by rivals in the previous period, the lower the R&D undertaken by a specific firm in the current period. If this coefficient is positive, on the other hand, this implies that the firm is trying to keep up with rivals.

We do not use data on R&D expenditure, because of reporting problems, and therefore the unreliability of data.[18] However, a similar argument to Henriques' can be advanced using our count variable, *Tcount*, instead of R&D expenditure. In this new variant we regress *Tcount* for a specific firm in a specific year on real sales (*Rsales*) that year, and the sum of *Tcount* for all other firms in the preceding years ($Spill_{-1}$).

Our findings are as below. Using OLS estimation we get

$$\underset{}{Tcount} = \underset{(3.005)}{2.9050} + \underset{(8.956)}{0.12027.10^{-3}}\, Rsales - \underset{(-2.839)}{0.01943}\, Spill_{-1}$$

$$F(2,570) = 45.14 \qquad \bar{R}^2 = 0.13$$

The coefficient of the lagged spillover variable is negative, suggesting positive spillover benefits being conferred on patent-inactive firms by patent-active firms. Put alternatively, the former firms are free-riding on the innovativeness of the latter firms. The probability value of the t-statistic on the spillover coefficient is less than .005, which implies high significance.[19]

The evidence is not overwhelming but is at least suggestive of free-riding of patent-inactive firms on patent-active rivals' advances in technology within the scientific instruments industry. This goes some way to explaining the surprisingly small performance advantage enjoyed by patent-active firms.

7 CONCLUSION

This chapter has aimed to provide an account of what determines the scope of patenting, as measured by the size of patent families. Members of such families are stages in the patenting process over all known patent regimes. The most patent-intensive industry in the UK, scientific instruments, is chosen for estimation purposes, on a panel of 92 firms (1983–90). A robust model is reported upon, which explains patenting in the above sense very well. Principal determinants are size, net profit, the profit margin, gearing and firm-level fixed effects. The size variable suggests diminishing returns to patent-directed R&D, and the existence of an optimal firm size which is well below the maximum size in the industry. The financial variables suggest that patenting activity increases with profit, but that margins may be squeezed and gearing increased to foster such innovation. Thus some sacrifice of short-term financial performance is accepted to advance innovation. Ownership plays some role, but its effects are difficult to display in this model. Performance differences between patent-active and patent-inactive firms are shown not to be great, suggesting possibilities of positive spillovers and therefore an incentive for free-riding. Such effects are identified, and found to be statistically significant: relatively patent-inactive firms enjoy positive patent spillover effects.

APPENDIX: DEFINITIONS OF VARIABLES (THESE RELATE MAINLY TO TABLE 8.2)

Assets: Sum of stocks, trade debtors and other current assets

Net profit before tax: Net profit on ordinary activities before taxation

Return on capital: Pre-tax profit/capital employed

Return on assets: Pre-tax profit/total assets

Return on shareholders' funds: Pre-tax profit/shareholder's funds

Trading profit margin: Operating profit plus depreciation/sales

Operating profit margin: Pre-tax profit plus interest less non-trading income/sales

Pre-tax profit margin: Pre-tax profit/sales

Gearing: Total liabilities/shareholders' funds

Liquidity: Current assets/current liabilities (i.e. 'current ratio')

Export ratio: Export/sales

Source: *ICC Business Ratio Report* (1989)

NOTES

This research has been funded by a grant from the Nuffield Foundation, without which the work reported upon would have been impossible. The authors gratefully acknowledge the advice and assistance of our co-workers, Dr Pamela Siler, Department of Economics and Law, University of Abertay Dundee, and Miss Julia Smith, CRIEFF, Department of Economics, University of St Andrews. Errors of omission or commission that may remain are the authors' own responsibility.

1 See Silberston (1987) where it is shown that this industry has particularly high patent intensity, as measured by the ratio of patent count for the industry to proportion of GDP attributable to the industry.

2 For a discussion of this point, see Greene (1993: 469). The essential point is that if the sample includes all the units for which the model is relevant, a fixed effects model is indicated, whereas if the sample were drawn from a larger population, a random effects model is indicated.

3 Suppose, for example, the rival device were physically the same, but the lenses used had differing refractive properties. Is the patent wide enough to protect the original innovation against this rival device?

4 See Reid, Siler and Smith (1994).

5 Further, in both cases, the authors urge against use of their analyses for policy purposes.

6 We owe this point to Ms Alison Coleman of the Patent Office.

7 An alternative count measure was also used. This allocated counts to companies according to the date at which a patent family was started (i.e. the priority date). This is therefore a type of prospective value index. It proved less satisfactory a measure of patenting activity than the *Tcount* variable.

8 For a detailed analysis of this point, see Reid, Siler and Smith (1996).

9 We are indebted to Mr Nicholas Terry, University of Edinburgh, for this point.

10 The other, or second, Schumpeterian hypothesis is that market structure, especially the presence of market concentration, is an important determinant of innovation.

11 Reid, Siler and Smith (1996).

12 See, for example, Schmalensee (1989: 963).

13 See Link (1981) and Armour and Teece (1981).

14 The related work is Reid, Siler and Smith (1996) and the independent work is Roberts and Siler (1994). A standard reference, confirming this sort of result is Scherer and Ross (1990).

15 Fixing other variables constant (say at their mean values), the optimal size is given as the negative of half the ratio of the linear to the quadratic coefficient.

16 Measured here without reference to patent families, but simply by looking at the patent count in each year for each firm.

17

	Patent-active	*Patent-inactive*	*Total*
Independent	113	88	201
UK subsidiary	78	126	204
US subsidiary	38	93	131
European subsidiary	10	62	72
Other	3	5	8
Total	242	374	616

This is the contingency table referred to in the text.

18 Most of the data predate the accounting protocol of SSAP 13 which now requires the reporting of R&D expenditure on a consistent basis.

19 A similar relationship holds if this equation is run using just the thirty-five patent-active firms. OLS estimation gives:

$$\underset{}{\mathit{Tcount}} = \underset{(3.257)}{7.6134} + \underset{(4.585)}{0.10975.10^{-3}}\ (\mathit{Rsales}) - \underset{(-2.530)}{0.041917}\ \mathit{Spill}_{-1}$$

$$F(2,223) = 14.53 \qquad \bar{R}^2 = 0.10$$

Whilst this does not improve the overall fit, which we would expect anyway, given the smaller sample size, it does suggest that even amongst the patent-active firms, the *more* patent-active firms confer positive spillover benefits on the *less* patent-active firms. The t-statistic for the coefficient of the spillover variable has a probability value of 0.012, which would conventionally be regarded as highly significant. Its negative sign and high significance indicate positive externalities are enjoyed by relatively patent-inactive firms, whereas the estimate in the test suggests this holds for absolutely patent-inactive firms.

REFERENCES

Armour, H.O. and Teece, D.J. (1981) 'Vertical integration and technical innovation', *Review of Economics and Statistics* 62: 470–474.

Branch, B. (1974) 'Research and development activity and profitability: a distributed lag analysis', *Journal of Political Economy* 82: 999–1011.

Cohen, W.M. and Levin, R.C. (1989) 'Empirical studies of innovation and market structure', in R. Schmalensee and R.D. Willig (eds) *Handbook of Industrial Organization* (Volume II), Chapter 18, Amsterdam: Elsevier, 1059–1107.

Cohen, W.M., Levin, R.C. and Mowery, D.C. (1987) 'Firm size and R&D intensity: a re-examination', *Journal of Industrial Economics* 35: 543–563.

Elliot, J.W. (1971) 'Funds flow versus expectational theories of research and development expenditures in the firm', *Southern Economic Journal* 37: 409–422.

Gilbert, R. and Shapiro, C. (1990) 'Optimal patent length and breadth', *Rand Journal of Economics* 21: 106–112.

Greene, W.H. (1993) *Econometric Analysis* (2nd edn), New York: Macmillan.

Henriques, I. (1994) 'Do firms free-ride on rivals' R&D expenditure? An empirical analysis', *Applied Economics* 26: 551–561.

Klemperer, P. (1990) 'How broad should the scope of patent protection be?', *Rand Journal of Economics* 21: 113–130.

Levin, R.C. (1988) 'Appropriability, R&D spending and technological performance', *American Economic Review Papers and Proceedings* 78: 424–428.

Levin, R.C., Klevorick, A.K., Nelson, R.R. and Winters, S.G. (1987) 'Appropriating the returns from industrial R&D', *Brookings Papers on Economic Activity*: 783–820.

Link, A.N. (1981) *Research and Development in US Manufacturing*, New York: Praeger.

Loury, G.C. (1979) 'Market structure and innovation', *Quarterly Journal of Economics* 93: 395–410.

Lunn, J. and Martin, S. (1986) 'Market structure, firm structure, and research and development', *Quarterly Review of Economics and Business* 26: 31–44.

Mansfield, E. (1981) 'Composition of R&D expenditures: relationships to size, concentration and innovation output', *Review of Economics and Statistics* 62: 610–614.

Mansfield, E. (1985) 'How rapidly does new industrial technology leak out?', *Journal of Industrial Economics* 34: 217–223.

Nordhaus, W.D. (1969) *Invention, Growth and Welfare*, Cambridge, Mass.: MIT Press.

Pavitt, K., Robson, M. and Townsend, J. (1987) 'The size distribution of innovating firms in the UK: 1945–1983', *Journal of Industrial Economics* 35: 297–316.

Reid, G.C., Siler, P.A. and Smith, J.A. (1994) 'Intellectual property and patent quality', Discussion Paper, Department of Economics and Law, Dundee Institute of Technology (now University of Abertay Dundee).

Reid, G.C., Siler, P.A. and Smith, J.A. (1996) 'Quality of patenting in the UK scientific instruments industry' in A. Webster and K. Packer (eds) *Innovation and the Intellectual Property System*, Dordrecht: Kluwer: 23–46.

Reinganum, J.F. (1983) 'Uncertain innovation and the persistence of monopoly', *American Economic Review* 73: 741–748.

Roberts, C.J. and Siler, P.A. (1994) 'International patenting activity in the Scottish engineering sector', Discussion Paper, Department of Economics and Law, University of Abertay Dundee.

Schankerman, M. and Pakes, A. (1986) 'Estimates of the value of patent rights in European countries during the post-1950 period', *Economic Journal* 96: 1052–1076.

Scherer, F.M. (1965) 'Firm size, market structure, opportunity and the output of patented inventions', *American Economic Review* 55: 1097–1125.

Scherer, F.M. (1972) 'Nordhaus' theory of the optimal patent life: a geometric reinterpretation', *American Economic Review* 62: 422–427.

Scherer, F.M. and Ross, D. (1990) *Industrial Market Structure and Economic Performance* (3rd edn), Boston: Houghton Mifflin.

Schmalensee, R. (1989) 'Inter-industry studies of structure and performance', in R. Schmalensee and R.D. Willig (eds) *Handbook of Industrial Organization* (Volume II), Chapter 16, Amsterdam: Elsevier, 951–1009.

Schott, K. (1978) 'The relations between industrial research and development and factor demands', *Economic Journal* 88: 85–106.

Silberston, A. (1987) *The Economic Importance of Patents*, London: The Common Law Institute of Intellectual Property.

Spence, A.M. (1984) 'Cost reduction, competition and industrial performance', *Econometrica* 52: 101–121.

9

CONFLICTS OF INTEREST IN R&D COLLABORATION

Negotiating the function–performance link

Nikos Kastrinos

It is common knowledge that R&D co-operation has been on the increase in recent years together with theoretical and empirical arguments as to its value and public policies actively promoting it. Co-operation between producers and users is perhaps only part of the relevant scholarly and policy domains, but it is certainly a central one. In the policy domain, such co-operation is often linked to the promotion of diffusion of new technologies in manufacturing industries. In scholarly quarters, such co-operation is seen as taking place under ideal conditions (Lundvall 1988; Georghiou *et al.* 1990), where the behaviour of the partners is either self-regulated by trust or fear of acquisition, or regulated by carefully drafted consortium agreements. In practice, R&D co-operation between producers and users has benefits as well as pitfalls. For example, authors have expressed concern over the possibilities for technological leakages, differences in the level of commitment between individual partners, and the potential for competition after the project has finished (Nueno and Ostervald 1988; Buisseret 1993). The potential for competition is seen in terms of the co-operating firms producing the same products or close substitutes after the project. This chapter aims to illuminate another aspect of competitive behaviour between partners during the R&D projects, the terms of which are set by analysis of the links between technology and competitive advantage.

Of particular concern are the incentives of users to participate in R&D consortia. In the literature these are linked to the novelty or complexity of the technology in question. The more novel or complex the technology in use, the more time is needed for a user to master and exploit it (Lundvall 1988; Von Hippel 1988). Accordingly, sophisticated users would be appropriate for collaboration at early stages of development while lay users would be appropriate for market testing at late stages of development (Buisseret 1993).

The assumption is, of course, that users would be willing to collaborate because the use of the innovation would provide them with competitive advantage. However, novelty and complexity are relative terms, and their links to competitive advantage for user firms is not very clear. The most complex technologies are not always the most beneficial for users, and thus climbing up a learning curve is not synonymous to acquiring competitive advantage (see Clark 1989; Warner 1989). It is argued here that the use of new complex technologies are more suitable for some firms than others, simply because of risk and sunk costs considerations. The implications of this for R&D co-operation between producers and users constitute the main part of this chapter.

The central argument is that there is a conflict of interests between producers and users as regards the technological configuration of the envisaged innovations. This is because technological configurations are important for the diffusion of innovations. In principle, producers aim at maximizing diffusion amongst users in order to appropriate the innovation benefit, while users aim at minimizing it so that benefits are not available to their competitors. Thus, the shape of the envisaged innovations, the link between their function (what they do) and their performance (how well they do it), can be seen as the outcome of a negotiation between their producers and users. To the extent that collaborative R&D ventures between producers and users constitute a social context of innovative activity, the conflict of interests between them characterizes that context.

This is a particularly important consideration for public collaborative R&D programmes. These, by abiding to the principle of additionality, provide the parties negotiating the links between function and performance with additional room to manoeuvre. Observations of collaborative projects under such programmes, which provide the empirical basis of this chapter, provide insights into these negotiations and the mechanisms through which project management structure is linked to project success (Barker 1996; Haeusler *et al.* 1994). The conclusions draw lessons for the involvement of users in collaborative R&D projects, as well as issues for further investigation.

TECHNOLOGY AND COMPETITIVE ADVANTAGE: IMPLICATIONS FOR COLLABORATIVE BEHAVIOUR

In analysing the relations between technology and competitive advantage Ford (1988) distinguishes between basic, distinctive, and external technologies. Basic technologies are those which are necessary for a business. They play a central role in defining the business and are by definition shared by all firms in the business. Distinctive technologies are those that differentiate a firm from others within the same business. Distinctive technologies play an important role in competitive advantage. External technologies are those supplied by other companies either embedded in artifacts such as components and equipment, or in other media, such as blue-prints or even people.

Using these categories, competition can be seen as a battle between firms to transform, through innovation, their distinctive technologies into basic while keeping control over their diffusion. Indeed, the links between the competitive significance of technologies and their diffusion are depicted by the industry life-cycle model (Abernathy and Utterback 1978). At the early stages of the life-cycle, basic technologies have not yet developed as business is in a state of flux. Groups of firms may share some competencies, but not all firms in the industry share them to the extent that they could be characterized as basic. The objective of competition between firms is to define the business according to their distinctive technologies. At the second stage of industry growth, these technologies become basic, as all successful firms must share them. However, control over the technology and its diffusion is still essential for blocking new entrants. At the later stage of maturity economies of scale provide the firms that have grown with the market with adequate barriers to entry. The same technologies which were distinctive to start with, can now be externalized as their importance in competitive advantage fades away. The firm specific elements that provide competitive advantage shift according to the development of competitive rivalry in time (Utterback and Suarez 1993).

However, a firm's technologies do not exist in isolation from one another. They interface with each other within the firm, and are embedded in its structure. At the early stages of the life-cycle firms tend to be small and flexible. They sacrifice efficiency in production for effectiveness in innovation. According to Burns and Stalker (1961) in order to be effective in innovation a firm has to have a fluid 'organic' structure. This implies that, within it, functions are performed on an ad hoc basis, as relevant needs emerge. At the later stages of the life-cycle, on the contrary, flexibility in innovation is sacrificed for efficiency in production. Firms grow large, production-intensive and bureaucratic, and in the terms of Burns and Stalker (1961), mechanistic.

The life-cycle model embodies the fundamental trade-off between efficiency in production and effectiveness in innovation, which also underlies the distinction between organic and mechanistic organizations. Organic organizations 'live' by embodying new knowledge into their outputs. Their effectiveness in innovation makes up for their inefficiencies in production. At the other end of the spectrum, mechanistic organizations 'live' by organizing efficiently the transformation of inputs into outputs. Their efficiency is rooted in standardization. Mechanistic organizations are characterized by standard functions performed mainly by machines operated in standard ways by their personnel.

These considerations give rise to two important points. Firstly, the more mechanistic an organization the more difficult it is to adopt innovations. This is because the concomitant reorganizations have to take place within the framework of standardized technical and organizational interfaces. The wider the functional span of the innovation the more reorganization is required. Thus, the costs of adopting an innovation and adapting it to the organization or vice versa rise with the mechanistic qualities of an organization. Secondly, for a firm to acquire competitive advantages through the use of an innovation, not only must its adaptation costs be overshadowed by its productivity benefits, but also its ratio of productivity benefits to adaptation costs must be higher than that of its competitors.

Thus, the argument follows that in collaborative technological developments users would tend to build into the technological function user-specific aspects, which would increase adaptation costs for their competitors. However, the more mechanistic the user firm is, and the more mature the industry it operates in, the less firm-specific are the technologies it employs. Accordingly, firms in mature industries would tend to find it difficult to build firm-specific elements in new technologies they develop for production or use. While producers would also want to build their firm-specific technologies into the innovation to deter imitation, they have an obvious interest in developing innovations that perform generic, widely applicable functions to achieve volume sales.

Some suppliers of new technologies are firms that produce fairly standardized outputs, such as in fact most equipment suppliers. The new elements which they introduce to differentiate their products from those of their competitors are limited to peripheral roles, and do not involve radically new technical and organizational interfaces. Other suppliers are specialized. They exploit a core technological capability by producing customized designs. Each design is typically new, based on some generic function linked to technological competencies distinctive to the firm. Such firms would have an incentive not to build user-specific elements within their R&D projects. Customization is part of their production activities.[1]

THE FUNCTION–PERFORMANCE LINK IN COLLABORATIVE R&D PROJECTS

Behind every innovation lies the identification of a need to be fulfilled by a new good, which will perform a particular function and will be characterized by certain technical and organizational interfaces. The initial concept is based on function: what will the innovation do. The first step is to establish the feasibility of performing the function with the means at hand. The need for collaboration emerges when the means at hand are deemed inadequate for this purpose.[2] This situation gives rise to a search for suitable partners, who have to be technically competent and trustworthy (Georghiou and Barker 1993; Jorde and Teece 1989) and a process of designing an R&D project.

This is because opportunistic behaviour within the consortium has to be restricted, especially between partners who, as the previous analysis indicated, often have conflicting interests as to the shape of the innovation. Thus, the process of starting a collaborative venture can be seen as a negotiation process, through which a balance between the interests of the partners is sought. This negotiation concerns three aspects of a collaborative R&D project: the property rights over knowledge that is generated by the project (Georghiou and Barker 1993; Georghiou and Metcalfe 1990; Jacquemin 1987); the division of labour within the project; and the leadership of the project.

The arrangement of the standard contract used in EC R&D programmes as regards intellectual property rights, is that each partner has the right to exploit the knowledge which is relevant to its activities, while it cannot prevent any other partner from exploiting knowledge generated within the project. Users are often granted special privileges such as exclusive use of the outcomes for a limited period, e.g. two years, and free service and maintenance by the producers, again for a limited period. This can be a beneficial arrangement when the outcome of the project is immediately usable with minimal adaptation costs. However, if the project is not successful, then the producer has moved closer to developing a functional system for which it has acquired the specifications. The user, though, has little to use, other than the experience of the difficulties and frustrations involved in such projects.

The division of labour within the project is important in two respects. Firstly, it is crucial for the level of access partners have to particular pieces of knowledge generated by the project. While project reports may be available to all, it is difficult to implement a technology on the basis of a project report. In the words of an engineer interviewed (Kastrinos 1994), such reports provide 'a good enough guide of roughly what to do, and what sort of errors we can avoid'. Command over tacit aspects of knowledge is essential for technology implementation, and these aspects can be learned only by participating in the actual work.

Secondly, the division of labour within a project reflects the modular structure of the envisaged innovation (see Henderson and Clark 1990). Collaborative R&D projects typically evolve around a 'research prototype'. This is a demonstrator that either performs the function, or it can be proven that it does, and it incorporates functional (as well as physical if it is a good) modules. Because of the importance of the ways in which technological characteristics are linked to the interests of the individual partners, the performance characteristics of the research prototype are improved in a modular fashion, in order not to disturb the, implicitly or explicitly, agreed balance of interests.

Performance criteria stem from perceived user needs. To the extent to which the function is already performed by potential users, or there is a good chance that it will be performed, then performance criteria are relatively easy to establish. Adaptation costs are taken into account by specifying the ways in which the system would interface with its user environment at the outset. Modular improvements leading to improved performance take place within the framework of established interfaces. A trade-off between function and performance emerges when the 'research prototype' does not take into account all aspects of the user environment, that is when adaptation costs are not included in the determination of performance criteria.

Case A

The project was initiated by a firm producing equipment for the textiles industry. The firm had greatly automated design and production functions, and it envisaged an innovation that would provide for further integration between the two. As it needed further expertise, it approached a national research organization as a potential partner. Together they decided that the idea was worth pursuing and tried to get funding from national programmes. As this proved difficult, the research organization proposed EC programmes and the firm accepted. The research organization, which at this stage acquired the leading role in the project, found similar partners in another country, and developed a proposal for the EC with itself in the co-ordinating role. The Commission insisted that in order to support the project two large software houses had to participate, 'in order to enhance the exploitability of the results'. This was accepted, and a simple consortium agreement was signed, through which in case of project success the users would have had free maintenance by the systems houses for two years.

The project was very successful. After its end the system was installed by the user firms and was very well evaluated. The only problem was that it was a little slow. This did not prevent the anticipated productivity gains from its use, but was seen as a nuisance for the engineers using the system. The engineers of the user-firm knew what to do to make the system faster, but they could not do it because they had to alter software the copyright for which belonged to one of the software houses. While they were trying to find a solution to this problem, the software house commercialized a similar system in which the problem had been dealt with. So, the user firm had to buy this new system as otherwise productivity gains in its competitors would overshadow its own. While the firm did not doubt the benefits of its participation in the project, in terms of better understanding of its operations and the issues involved in systems design, its managers were very frustrated by this development.

In collaborations between producers and users it is largely the technology of the producer that will be linked to the functions of the user. If the user implements some functional modules, these would tend to lie towards the external interfaces of the system rather than towards its internal structure. Considering the inherent initial uncertainty as to the structure and performance of the system, and the importance of the research prototype for performance, producers seem to have the upper hand in determining the function–performance link.

In case A, when the research organization undertook the leadership the targets of the project changed in an essential way. From being to develop a system that would satisfy the specific needs of the user firm, the objective became to develop 'such a system'. Furthermore, when the two large producers were placed into the project, the user firm did not realize that control over the specifications of the innovation slipped further away from its hands. The fact that the user was not the project leader was clearly important in that respect (see also Buisseret 1993).

While leadership by the user can be used for leverage over the solutions given to implementation problems, its power can be enhanced by building mechanisms for effective knowledge transfer within the collaboration. The most effective such mechanism is the collocation of the activities of the partners. And as it is these aspects that producers are most wary of; being afraid of a user innovator scenario (Von Hippel 1988), users often need to use the leverage of their complementary assets.

Case B

This project was initiated by a large textiles manufacturer looking to automate its quality control processes. While automated systems were already in the market the firm found their performance and reliability to be unacceptably low. It contacted a small firm that had experience in automating quality control processes in the steel industry and together they started designing a project involving also an equipment supplier. The textiles firm provided broad specifications for the performance of the envisaged system and became the leader of the project.

The collaboration was designed to involve as much work performed jointly as it seemed economically possible, considering that the management of the project was going to be scrutinized by the EC. The partners accepted this arrangement as they all lacked essential pieces of knowledge of the technologies and markets involved. What sealed their community of interest was an agreement to set up a joint venture to market the system. To that end the textiles firm stressed that its reputation would provide a great advantage in the marketing of the system.

The project ran into a great deal of technical problems and its functional specifications went under two sets of major changes, before it met relative success. This accounted for the minimum required performance being met. The system was only slightly cheaper and more reliable than its rivals. However, it was seen as a 'winner' as the partners built into it a number of attractive features for a wide variety of users. And the user of the consortium was going to benefit from the system's diffusion far more than from its use.

CONCLUSIONS

Appropriability considerations for producers and users of an envisaged innovation are crucial for R&D co-operation between them. Such considerations shape decisions as to the functions to be performed by the envisaged innovation, and the criteria by which its performance is to be determined. While there may be a natural community of interests between producers and users as regards the function of an innovation, there may also be a natural conflict of interests in relation to performance. In particular, such conflicts emerge when a research prototype does not take into account all aspects of the user environment which determines performance criteria. This may be because the users themselves are unable to formulate their specifications adequately. It may also be because these specifications involve elements which are regarded as user-specific by the producers. Finally, it may be because producer-specific technologies are inadequate to provide for such specifications.

This has important implications for the ways in which collaborative projects are designed and managed. Project design elements such as intellectual property rights agreements and the leadership of the collaborative R&D project may influence the emergence and outcome of such conflicts. However, the most important aspect of the management of such projects seems to lie with the mechanisms that ensure that a community of interests between the partners is sustained throughout the project including the exploitation of its results. Complementarity between the non-technological assets of partners can be instrumental here. Competitive positions between complementary activities of partners may undermine trust between partners and cause problems in the implementation of the project and the exploitation of its results (Buisseret 1993). Case A suggests that a user firm which does not use its complementary assets to guarantee the fulfilment of its goals through a collaborative R&D project may well become a losing partner when the project is over.

This is not contrary to the suggestion that R&D collaboration between producers and users is a positive sum game (Metcalfe 1992). However, it points out that the incentives of users to participate may be undermined by their inability to control the development of the technology. This hypothesis seems to provide a better explanation of users' participation than that of technological complexity. At the development stage, technological complexity may provide an incentive to the producers to pursue the involvement of users as real-life testbeds, but it may well provide a disincentive for the users to participate as it can be seen as a factor contributing to performance-related uncertainties.

Finally, this argument, which was generated by case study research, may be further empirically tested through the 'larger-user hypothesis'. This means that in mature industries, where basic technologies are largely of external origin, users would tend to collaborate with producers over which they have some kind of market-related leverage, such as being a large customer. Investigation of the larger-user hypothesis should not rest on the proportion of such collaborations, but should provide correlations with the users' perceptions of the extent to which they benefited from the projects. Needless to say, the function–performance link opens a wide agenda of empirical research on the conditions of participation of small firms as users in collaborative R&D projects.[3]

NOTES

The arguments presented in this chapter stem from the findings of a study funded by the European Commission, Directorate General for Science Research and Development (DG XII) SPEAR Programme. The contents of the chapter are the sole responsibility of the author and do not necessarily reflect the position of the European Commission, the financial support of which is gratefully acknowledged. The author wishes to thank his colleagues at PREST and Professor Stuart Macdonald, for their comments on earlier drafts.

1 This creates a lot of confusion in studying firms' R&D performance. Firms whose production activities are standardized often call customization R&D, while firms producing custom-made goods often maintain that they perform no R&D.

2 Collaboration often emerges for other reasons, such as risk sharing (see Kastrinos 1994). However, lack of suitable expertise is the main reason users would initiate collaboration with producers (see Von Hippel 1988).

3 It must be noted, here, that the argument refers to R&D co-operation rather than contract research, in which 'one partner, usually a large company, contracts another company, frequently a small one, to perform particular research projects' (Hagedoorn 1990, p. 25). The two should not be confused, as the customer–contractor relationship provides the user with very high levels of control over the project performed by the producer. It is another interesting empirical issue as to whether user firms see the two as different.

REFERENCES

Abernathy, W.J. and Utterback, J.M. (1978) 'Patterns of Innovation in Technology', *Technology Review* 80: 40–47.

Barker, K. (1996) *The Management of Collaboration in European Community R&D Programmes*. Report to the Commission of the European Communities, EUR 16169 EN.

Buisseret, T. (1993) 'The Role of Users in Collaborative IT Research: Experience from the UK's Information Engineering Advanced Technology Programme (IEATP)', *Science and Public Policy* 20, 5: 323–332.

Burns, T. and Stalker, G.M. (1961) *The Management of Innovation*, London: Tavistock.

Clark, K. (1989) 'What Strategy Can Do for Technology', *Harvard Business Review*, 67, 6: 94–98.

Ford, D. (1988) 'Develop Your Technology Strategy', *Long Range Planning* 21, 3: 85–95.

Freeman, C. (1982) *The Economics of Industrial Innovation*, 2nd edn, London: Frances Pinter.

Georghiou, L. and Barker, K. (1993) 'Management of International Collaboration', in P. Swann (ed.) *New Technologies and the Firm*, London: Routledge.

Georghiou, L. and Metcalfe, J.S. (1990) 'To Have and to Hold: Research Administration and Intellectual Property Rights', in J. de la Mothe and L. Ducharme (eds). *Science and Technology under Free Trade*, London: Routledge.

Haeusler, J., Hohn, H-W. and Luetz, S. (1994) 'Contingencies of Innovative Networks: A Case Study of Successful Interfirm R&D Collaboration', *Research Policy* 23, 1: 47–66.

Hagedoorn, J. (1990) 'Organizational Modes of Inter-firm Cooperation and Technology Transfer', *Technovation* 10, 1: 17–30.

Henderson, R.M. and Clark, K. (1990) 'Architectural Innovation: The Reconfiguration of Existing Product Technologies and the Failure of Established Firms', *Administrative Science Quarterly* 35, March: 9–30.

Jacquemin, A. (1987) 'Comportements collusifs et accords en recherche-developement', *Revue d'Economie Politique* 1, 1: 1–23.

Jorde, T.M. and Teece, D.J. (1989) 'Competition and Cooperation: Striking the Right Balance', Business and Public Policy Working Paper 39, Centre for Research in Management, Berkeley Business School.

Kastrinos, N. (1994) *The EC Framework Programme and the Technology Strategies of European Firms*, EUR 15784 EN, Brussels: Commission of the European Communities.

Lundvall, B.A. (1988) 'Innovation as an Interactive Process: From User–Producer Interaction to the National System of Innovation', in G. Dosi, C. Freeman, R. Nelson, G. Silveberg and L. Soete (eds) *Technical Change and Economic Theory*, London and New York: Pinter Publishers.

Metcalfe, J.S. (1992) 'Competition and Collaboration in the Innovation Process', in M. Bowen and M. Ricketts (eds) *Stimulating Innovation in Industry: The Challenge for the United Kingdom*, London: Kogan Page.

Nueno, P. and Ostervald, J. (1988) 'Managing Technology Alliances', *Long Range Planning* 21, 3: 11–17.

Utterback, J.M. and Suarez, F.F. (1993) 'Innovation, Competition, and Industry Structure', *Research Policy* 22: 1–21.

Von Hippel, E. (1988) *The Sources of Innovation*, New York and Oxford: Oxford University Press.

Warner, T.N. (1989) 'Information Technology as a Competitive Burden', in T. Forester (ed.) *Computers in the Human Context: Information Technology, Productivity and People*, Oxford: Basil Blackwell.

Part III

DISCLOSURE AND THE MARKET

10

R&D DISCLOSURE

Theory and practice

Alice Belcher

This chapter examines the theoretical issues concerning the disclosure of R&D information and the disclosure practices of UK companies. Regulatory history and political power struggles were important in the development of disclosure practice in the UK and it is in this setting that the theory and practice are investigated. The main theoretical considerations in the disclosure of R&D information concern the opposing forces which would encourage or discourage disclosure and the related issue of whether regulatory intervention is necessary. In so far as disclosure helps the capital market to value the company it should be encouraged. However, R&D information has the special characteristic of commercial sensitivity. In so far as disclosure benefits competitors, it should produce the correct amount of voluntary disclosure except where a) there are benefits from disclosure which do not accrue to individual companies, or b) the benefits from disclosure are not properly recognized by managers (for example if managers believe the market to suffer from short-termism which does not in fact exist).

Regulation of R&D disclosures in the UK is found in the Statement of Standard Accounting Practice 13 Accounting for Research and Development (SSAP 13) and in schedule 7 paragraph 6 (c) of the Companies Act 1985. The statutory requirement is for qualitative information only. The original version of SSAP 13 required no significant disclosures to be made. Revision of the Standard in 1989 made disclosure of R&D expenditure mandatory. Disclosure practice over the period of development of the revised version of the Standard is, therefore, of interest and the results of a survey of R&D reporting in UK company accounts are reported in this chapter. The chapter covers R&D disclosure theory and practice. Theory is based on models from information economics and appears in the next section. R&D disclosure practice is presented as a product of the UK's regulatory framework and so appears in two parts: disclosure requirements as a matter of regulatory history; and R&D disclosures made by UK companies as revealed in a survey of UK company accounts.

R&D DISCLOSURE THEORY

In this section the theoretical influences on directors' R&D disclosure decisions are set out. Some influences on the disclosure of R&D expenditure are general influences which could operate in the decision to disclose any accounting variable. A second group of influences are peculiar to R&D expenditure and a third group arise from changes in the political environment. Early models of disclosure showed that, if verifiable disclosure is costless, informed parties will voluntarily disclose all their information because failure to do so induces uninformed parties to believe that the withheld information is unfavourable (see Grossman, 1981; Milgrom, 1981 and Grossman and Hart, 1983). Before the revision of SSAP 13 companies could disclose R&D expenditure voluntarily and some did so, but many withheld this information. Theoretical models which allowed for and explained less-than-full disclosure were clearly needed. Later models explored the implications of relaxing one or more of the assumptions necessary for the full disclosure result. Two types of models can be distinguished: those where the value maximization assumption is retained and those where managerial motives which do not necessarily imply value maximization are allowed to come into play.

Managerial motives

The models involving managerial motives usually focus on managers' contracts, in particular contracts which link compensation to reported earnings. The issue is often one of designing a management compensation contract which is optimal in that by maximizing their own compensation managers will also maximize shareholder wealth. For instance, Verrecchia (1986) shows how it can be optimal for the principals (shareholders) to allow the agents (management) to choose between reporting alternatives even when that choice is unobservable. Managerial motives concerning R&D may be linked to remuneration. If remuneration is linked to reported earnings managers may want to choose reporting alternatives which increase current earnings, for instance the capitalization of R&D expenditure. It is the choice of accounting policy rather than disclosure which is likely to be influenced by the way management contracts are written. If opportunities exist for managers to pursue their own motives at the expense of shareholders then the disclosure of R&D expenditure is more likely to be influenced by the prestige it attracts. If R&D expenditure carries prestige for management, the reporting of R&D expenditure displays this prestigious activity. There are, however, arguments that suggest that the market will not allow managers to pursue their own goals at the expense of shareholders.

An efficient market should ensure that managers maximize the value of the company, in particular the market for corporate control (see Manne, 1965) should operate to remove inefficient managements and replace them with more efficient ones through the mechanism of take-overs.

Managerial beliefs

A characteristic of the early models of information disclosure is that the agents correctly interpret the signal being given by the principals. In relation to R&D this would mean correctly valuing the future cash flows arising from the R&D expenditure. Short-termism and its effect on R&D spending was thought to be a sufficiently large problem in the UK for the Department of Trade and Industry (DTI) to hold a conference in 1990 on 'Innovation and Short-Termism' and a spokesman for the DTI's Innovation Advisory Board said 'the first thing to go when companies are nervous about share price is often research'. A common view is that the UK capital market suffers from short-termism and R&D is viewed as an avoidable cost. Short-termism carries with it the implication that shareholders undervalue expected future returns relative to current earnings. If managers believe there is short-termism in the capital market they are likely to adjust their goals to be in line with what they believe the shareholders want. This will involve increasing current earnings and reducing expenditure on long-term projects. R&D will be particularly vulnerable because it is not only long term in nature but also very difficult to value. Myers and Majluf (1984) have provided a model which shows that investment can be discouraged where future prospects cannot be credibly communicated to shareholders. Short-termism could cause a reduction in spending on R&D. This may maximize the company's share price in what is an inefficient market and so prevent a take-over. However, short-termism implies the mis-pricing of shares. If secrecy is an option management may continue to spend on R&D but not report this expenditure, fearing an unfavourable reaction. This strategy implies that management believe that earnings (net of R&D expenditure) will satisfy the shareholders, but the news that there has been (unnecessary) spending on R&D will be viewed unfavourably. Whilst there is much anecdotal evidence of managers' beliefs in the short-term characteristics of the UK capital market, there is no simple way of testing the hypothesis that the belief in short-termism discourages disclosure of R&D expenditure.

Value-maximizing models

Disclosure models which move away from full disclosure whilst retaining the assumptions of an efficient market and value-maximizing managements will now be considered. The most obvious assumption to relax is that of costless disclosure. Verrecchia (1983) shows how the existence of disclosure-related costs offers an explanation of non-disclosure. Costs extend the range of interpretations of withheld information so the withholding of information cannot be interpreted unambiguously as bad news. Fishman and Hagerty (1989 and 1990) have considered two effects of costs. They begin with a model in which the costs of full disclosure are prohibitive so a disclosure choice must be made. Firstly, if the ordering of signals does not itself contain information, they show that disclosure will be randomized over items of good news (if any). Secondly, where there is a lexicographic ordering of signals items of good news will be disclosed in order of importance (Fishman and Hagerty, 1990). It is clear that disclosure of R&D expenditures is not costless. Accounting records must be kept in a particular form and collated and checked before figures can be reported. Full disclosure of all possible accounting numbers would be prohibitively expensive and to the extent that some disclosures are required whilst others are discretionary the ordering of disclosures is important. If the required disclosures have been made and there is room for some extra spending on disclosures there would at first seem to be no natural order of importance for such extra pieces of information. However, there may be a greater expectation of R&D expenditure being disclosed in certain industries. If the disclosure of R&D expenditure is an industry norm it could be part of a lexicographic ordering of disclosures as envisaged by Fishman and Hagerty. In another model (Fishman and Hagerty, 1989) greater expenditure on disclosure is associated with a more informative signal and companies have to compete for the attention of traders because the studying of disclosures is costly to the traders. The result of imposing these assumptions is that firms spend more on disclosure than is socially optimal.

Another typical assumption of the full disclosure models is that it is common knowledge that firms have private information. In the case of R&D expenditure non-disclosure could imply that there is no R&D expenditure or that it is not being disclosed. Darrough's (1993) is the first disclosure model which explicitly includes the possibility of the receivers of information being unsure whether non-disclosers have a signal that they choose to withhold or whether they do not have a signal to send. The result under this assumption is that disclosure occurs only when the signal is favourable. However, it is generally assumed in disclosure models that the management and the shareholders correctly interpret the information and, therefore, they can correctly classify news as good or bad. A problem with R&D expenditure is that this classification is far from clear-cut. As pointed out above the anecdotal evidence is that managers believe that R&D expenditure will generally be viewed as bad news but the actual amount reported may be an increase or decrease from the previous year and may be above or below the industry norm and these factors will also affect the good news/bad news classification. Verrecchia (1990) shows that when managers have better quality information they are more likely to disclose it. In the case of R&D expenditure managers are in possession of information which will potentially be viewed unfavourably and which is not easy to interpret. Information which is both unfavourable and of poor quality, in the sense that its implications for the value of the firm are not obvious, is less likely to be disclosed voluntarily than information which is favourable and of good quality, especially when shareholders cannot be certain that the unfavourable, poor quality information exists or not. These arguments explain non-disclosure of R&D but do not help to predict any voluntary disclosures of R&D.

A characteristic of R&D expenditure which has been included in only a few of the disclosure models to appear so far is that it is commercially sensitive information. If disclosure can benefit competitors this can be incorporated into a disclosure model in the same way as any other cost. Verrechia (1983) explicitly refers to costs as including any proprietary costs. The idea that the act of disclosure could have real, operational consequences appears in Dye (1986). This model distinguishes the effects of disclosing proprietary and non-proprietary information where proprietary information is defined as information whose disclosure reduces the present value of cash flows of the firm endowed with the information. R&D expenditure is proprietary information if competitors can benefit from its disclosure. The introduction of the notion of proprietary information means that 'there is a tension between the managers' incentives to disclose information that reveals their own and their firm's performance and the incentives to avoid the adverse [that is, unfavourable to the firm] reactions of parties external to the firm induced by those disclosures' (Dye, 1986: 353). In this model a value-maximizing manager has to trade off the potential damage inflicted by third parties against any positive effects of revealing information to shareholders. Real externalities arising from disclosures have been included in another paper by Dye (1990) that investigates the circumstances in which voluntary disclosures by firms would coincide with 'optimal' mandated disclosures. The disclosure of trade secrets is suggested as an example of information bestowing a real externality, yet in such cases the model allows no general statements to be made (Dye, 1990: 20).

In Darrough and Stoughton (1990) and Newman and Sansing (1993) the potential externality created by disclosure is the entry of a competitor. Darrough and Stoughton suggest that potential competition encourages voluntary disclosure through the threat of entry. The cost of a rival entering could be very large for a company engaged in R&D, but entry costs are also likely to be large, thus lowering the probability of entry if those costs are disclosed to potential entrants. The disclosure of R&D expenditures could be one way of signalling that entry costs are high, thus deterring entry. It is potential entrants, rather than existing competitors, who provide the threat in this setting. The pool of potential entrants and the probable effect of the entry of a rival or rivals are, however, difficult to measure. Newman and Sansing (1993) also model the entry of potential competitors and show that firms with very high entry costs will make more informative disclosures when the effect of entry is potentially large. However, Verrechia (1983) suggested that competition discourages disclosure. This is actual competition from rivals who have already entered rather than potential competitors threatening to enter. The costs of disclosing proprietary information to existing competitors have already been discussed. The additional reasoning by which more competition implies larger costs is that costs could increase with the number of rivals benefiting from the disclosure. The number of existing rivals may be easier to estimate than the number of potential entrants, but disclosures may not affect all rivals equally and companies in the same industry need not all be rivals.

The insights provided by the theoretical models of disclosure are (1) that in the simplest models full disclosure is predicted and therefore explanations are required for less-than-full disclosure; (2) that in the case of R&D explanations for non-disclosure can be provided by managerial motives if the market is not efficient and in value-maximizing models by preparation costs and proprietary costs; (3) that the quality of information in terms of helping to value future cash flows also influences disclosure; (4) that if managers believe the market to be subject to short-termism they will believe R&D expenditure to be unfavourable news to shareholders; and (5) that proprietary costs depend on the threat of entry by potential competitors and competition from existing rivals.

REGULATORY HISTORY OF R&D DISCLOSURE

Regulation of R&D reporting is found both in company law and in accounting standards. There is very little statutory regulation of R&D disclosure in the UK. Schedule 7 para 6 (c) Companies Act 1985 requires an indication to be given in the directors' report of the activities of the company in the field of R&D, if any. Also the Companies Act 1989 requires large companies to state whether or not their accounts comply with accounting standards one of which, SSAP 2, requires disclosure of accounting policies which includes any policy on accounting for R&D.

Accounting standards describe methods of accounting which are approved, in the main, by self-regulatory private sector bodies. In countries with strong legalistic traditions the contents of financial accounts are regulated by statute and there is little scope or need for self-regulation by accountancy bodies. This contrasts with the position in the UK, Australia, New Zealand, Canada, South Africa and the USA. Whittington (1989) pointed out that the system in the English-speaking world is associated with active stock markets where there is an emphasis on reporting relevant information to investors, whereas the continental European system is associated with economies where the stock market has a smaller part to play. 'Thus it can be hypothesised that private sector standard setting is associated with meeting shareholders' informational needs in an active capital market' (Whittington, 1989). The Statement of Standard Accounting Practice 13 (SSAP 13) provides most of the regulation of R&D reporting in the UK; in the USA the relevant accounting standard is FAS No. 2 Accounting for Research and Development Costs.

There are three major issues which an accounting standard on R&D can tackle: definition, accounting treatment and disclosure. The definition of research and development determines what items of expenditure come under these two heads. The main issue of accounting treatment (or measurement) in respect of R&D is whether such expenditure is best classified as an asset or an expense. As an asset it could appear on the balance sheet, thus carrying the expenditure forward; as an expense it should be written off as it is incurred. Varying degrees of disclosure may be required from no disclosure through to full disclosure on a project by project basis. In addition to the question of how much should be disclosed there is also the question of where the disclosure should be, in the accounts (audited) or in the directors' report (unaudited); audited information supposedly has more credibility than unaudited information.

Measurement and disclosure are not independent issues. It has been argued that if there is sufficient disclosure of both amounts and measurement techniques, users of accounts can adjust the information to fit the set of measurement techniques which they prefer. Measurement then becomes unimportant and there would be no need for standards requiring a particular accounting method. However, in the USA the SEC has taken the position that disclosure cannot be a substitute for acceptable measurement rules, hence financial statements even with optimal disclosure are 'presumed to be inaccurate and misleading' unless they comply with the authoritative rules of a standard setting body (see Horwitz and Kolodny, 1980: 41).

Table 10.1 shows the accounting treatment and disclosure requirements under FAS No 2 and the various versions of SSAP 13. EDs are exposure drafts which are issued as part of the standard setting process to allow comments to be received from interested parties. ED 14 followed FAS No. 2 closely. ED 17 moved to a position requiring far less disclosure and requiring deferral of some development expenditure. SSAP 13 introduced more flexibility by permitting deferral of

Table 10.1 Accounting treatment and disclosure: FAS No. 2 and SSAP 13

Date	*Document*	*Research*	*Development*	*Disclosure*
Oct. 1974	FAS No. 2	Write off immediately	Write off immediately	Full disclosure already required
Jan. 1975	ED 14	Write off immediately	Write off immediately	Amount written off
Apr. 1976	ED 17	Write off immediately	'Should' carry forward if specified criteria are met	Amount carried forward, balance and movement on deferred development account
Dec. 1977	SSAP 13	Write off immediately	'May' carry forward if specified criteria are met	Amount carried forward, balance and movement on deferred development account
June 1987	ED 41	Write off immediately	'May' carry forward if specified criteria are met	Total amount of R&D charged in the profit and loss account, analysed between current year's expenditure and amounts amortized from deferred expenditure. Balance and movement on deferred development account
Jan. 1989	SSAP 13 (revised)	Follows ED 41	Follows ED 41	Follows ED 41

development expenditure but not requiring it. The change proposed in ED 41 and implemented in the revised version of SSAP 13 requires full disclosure of total R&D expenditure. Before this change some companies were already disclosing this information voluntarily.

The UK standard-setting process involves seeking the views of researchers and interested parties. This makes the exercise of power or influence a real possibility, especially at the exposure draft stage. It can be seen from Table 10.1 that the requirements of SSAP 13 when it was issued in 1977 were significantly different from the first exposure draft. Hope and Gray investigated the way in which the Accounting Standards

Committee (ASC) was influenced in the setting of the original SSAP 13 and concluded that 'the ASC changed its position on the issues of accounting treatment and disclosure of R&D because of the wishes of industry – particularly the aerospace industry' (Hope and Gray, 1982: 551). The interest of the aerospace industry stemmed from its reliance on government contracts which award profit as a percentage of capital employed. If development expenditure must be written off immediately, capital employed and, therefore, profits must fall. Eight companies or their representative bodies commented adversely on the disclosure requirements of ED 14 ' – the unanimous view being that anything other than extensive disclosure of (e.g.) individual project expenditure and estimated success rates of projects, would be misleading to users of accounts' (Hope and Gray, 1982: 544). Two commentators indicated that the ED 14 proposals might inhibit their investment in R&D projects and one was specifically concerned that the disclosure proposals would benefit mainly competitors (MacArthur, 1988: 221). ED 17's minimal disclosure requirements caused only two adverse comments asking for fuller disclosure, these were from the professional accountants Arthur Young, McClellands Moore and from the Department of Industry.

I inspected comments submitted to the ASC on ED 41 using primary data held in the library of the ICAEW. Ten companies or their representative bodies commented on ED 41. Five companies either disagreed with the new disclosure requirements or agreed with certain reservations. Interestingly, in view of the response to ED 14 quoted above, some comments on ED 41 expressed a floodgates argument that the proposed increase in disclosure would lead to unacceptable, project by project disclosure in the future. The two major objections to ED 41 were that the additional information would either benefit competitors (Reckitt & Collman and Rover Group) or be of little value to users (BICC plc and Delta Group plc). One company appears to have changed its views, perhaps because the company had itself changed in the intervening time, perhaps because the company perceived benefits from expressing its own views to be in line with those of the government. Plessy commented adversely on the full disclosure requirements of ED 14, gave full support to the lesser requirements of ED 17, but supported 'the additional disclosure requirement as proposed in the draft [ED 41]'.

There are several points to be made about the analyses of comments outlined above. Firstly, in all cases the number of comments was very small. Secondly, the comments were, by definition, from interested parties. Finally, only those comments which were submitted formally and on-the-record could be analysed and there is reason to believe that informal comments may have as much influence as formal submissions; for instance Hope and Gray believed that in relation to the decision by the ASC to allow some deferral of expenditure in ED 17 it was 'most likely, the ASC took account of informal (possibly anecdotal) evidence from the electronics industry' (Hope and Gray, 1982: 552).

SSAP 13 was reviewed by an ASC working party and in 1984 Gray was commissioned to report on company experiences of the standard. This study involved a postal questionnaire sent to 320 companies which achieved only 44 responses, and 19 company interviews which resulted from approaches to 40 companies; the views of analysts and auditors were also sought. Gray's report (Gray, 1985) runs to 155 pages and covers the economics and accounting literature in the area as well as describing the empirical work undertaken. The study found that the absence of a requirement to disclose total R&D expenditure meant that most of the problems associated with accounting for R&D were obviated. These problems, especially problems concerning the definition of R&D, could be expected to surface on the revision of SSAP 13 requiring disclosure.

Pressure for SSAP 13 to be revised to require disclosure of R&D expenditure came from another source in 1986/87. The arguments concerning the importance of R&D activity to the economy had been brought to the attention of Parliament on more than one occasion and the House of Lords Select Committee on Science and Technology stated in its first report in 1986 that companies should be required to disclose R&D expenditure. This was an indication that if the accounting standard was not revised then a requirement for disclosure would appear in company law. The Accounting Standards Committee published ED 41 in June 1987 and this can be seen as a direct response to the possibility of legislation. Nixon (1991) describes the political urgency of the revision in some detail. It can be seen that pressure from companies which helped ED 14 evolve into the original SSAP 13 would be unlikely to have the same impact when ED 41 was published.

SURVEY OF UK ANNUAL REPORTS

Against the background of a strong initial resistance on the part of companies to any disclosure of R&D information and especially R&D expenditure figures, followed by the threat of legislation and the consequent revision of SSAP 13, a study of R&D disclosure practices was conducted. The sample of annual reports in the survey resulted from a postal request for companies to send copies of their accounts. The request was made to Britain's 1,000 largest firms ranked by sales of 1988/89 as reported in *Business 1000* issued as a supplement to *Business* magazine in November 1989. Large firms were targeted, firstly, in order to focus on companies covered by the new disclosure requirements of SSAP 13 (revised) and, secondly, because R&D activity is reputedly

Table 10.2 Disclosure categories

Category	*Description*	*Features*
A	Company performs no R&D.	Nothing reported
B	Company has policy of complete secrecy concerning R&D activity.	Nothing reported
C	Company gives some indication in the annual report that it performs R&D but does not fully comply with the law or SSAP 13.	Something reported (non-compliance)
D	Company performs R&D and fully complies with the disclosure requirements of the law and SSAP 13.	Full disclosure

concentrated in large firms. No attempt was made to select companies on the basis of industry as one of the aims of the survey was to see whether the SSAP 13 definition of R&D caused problems for companies in industries where R&D activity is not laboratory based. R&D reporting can be categorized as illustrated in Table 10.2.

It can be seen from Table 10.2 that it is impossible to distinguish reports in categories A and B. The first step in analysing the annual reports was to look for any indication of R&D activity, this separated reports in categories C and D from those in A and B which were discarded as giving no useful information. Four hundred and fifty-seven companies responded by sending at least one set of accounts from the period 1985 to 1990. The reports of 239 category A or B firms where nothing was reported concerning R&D were discarded. Of the remaining 218, 168 were the reports of public limited companies, 26 were of private limited companies, 9 were public sector organizations at the start of the period being studied and 15 were cases where the accounts offered were those of a foreign parent company and so subject to different reporting requirements. The results reported in Tables 10.3 to 10.7 below are for the accounts of the 168 plcs. A small random sample of company reports was used to test for possible response biases on the basis of the proportion in each category (A and B counting as a single category). It was concluded that response bias was not a problem in the survey sample. The questions addressed by the survey concerned whether R&D expenditure was disclosed, where such a disclosure was placed in the annual report, whether there was any pattern of voluntary disclosure according to industry, the level of compliance with R&D disclosure requirements, whether there was evidence of any interaction between accounting policy and disclosure and the qualitative nature of R&D disclosures.

Disclosure of R&D expenditure

Table 10.3 shows the number of companies disclosing an amount relating to R&D for the current year and also the comparative figure for the previous year. The overall trend is for the percentage of companies disclosing R&D amounts to increase. The first noticeable jump is in the 1988 accounts which could be explained as a response to the publication in June 1987 of ED 41. The percentage of public limited companies disclosing R&D amounts in their 1990 accounts is of interest; only 79 per cent of companies were complying with SSAP 13 (revised). This is a maximum estimate of the rate of compliance as any category B companies would add to the number of non-compliers. However, the scale of the non-compliance in value terms is likely to be much less as it is probably companies spending very little on R&D which are not reporting their expenditure; one company specifically states that its R&D expenditure is not material. Where the amounts disclosed in Table 10.3 relate to amortized development expenditure disclosure of at least the current year's figure would be required by the original version of SSAP 13. Policy decisions as to whether to write off development expenditure or carry it forward are discussed later.

Table 10.4 shows the place of disclosure of the R&D amounts for expenditure written off as incurred. Disclosure of amortized development expenditure sometimes appeared only in a note to the balance sheet. Some companies carrying development expenditure as an intangible asset reported movements in intangible assets in aggregate only, thus hiding the write-off of development expenditure as a separate item. The numbers in Table 10.4 show a pattern which fits neatly with the change in reporting requirements. In the early years the only requirement relating to R&D written off as incurred was the requirement to say something in the directors' report (schedule 7 para 6 (c) Companies Act 1985) and for 1985–87 the most popular place to disclose R&D amounts was the directors' report. The companies responding early to the revision of SSAP 13 appear to have begun disclosing R&D amounts in notes to the profit and loss account, and compliance with the revised version of SSAP 13 in 1989 and 1990 is evidenced by the big jump in numbers of companies reporting amounts particularly as a note to the profit and loss account. SSAP 13 applies only to accounts commencing on or after 1 January 1989 so for some 1989 accounts compliance would not be required, row 1989b shows the numbers for accounts where compliance was required. Accounts in row 1989a were released after the publication of SSAP 13 (revised) but covered periods commencing before 1 January 1989, disclosure of R&D expenditure in these accounts is therefore voluntary but may have been influenced by the revised SSAP. Table 10.4 also reveals that in 1990 there were five companies where disclosure

Table 10.3 Disclosure of R&D amounts

Year	*Number of accounts available (out of a possible 168)*	*Disclosure of R&D expenditure* — *This year* — *Number disclosing (of which (x) = disclosure of amortized development expenditure)*	*This year* — *% disclosing*	*Comparative figure* — *Number disclosing*	*Comparative figure* — *% disclosing*
1985	87	19 (4)	21.84	12	13.79
1986	102	25 (4)	24.51	21	20.59
1987	111	28 (4)	25.23	21	18.92
1988	120	39 (7)	32.50	29	24.17
1989	147	85 (4)	57.87	79	53.74
1990	81	64 (4)	79.01	58	71.60

Table 10.4 Place of disclosure (comparative year's figures in parentheses)

Year	*Directors' report only*	*P&L account only*	*Note to P&L account only*	*Directors' report and note to P&L account*	*Directors' report and P&L account*	*Total*
1985	8 (4)	2 (2)	3 (4)	2 (1)	0 (0)	15 (11)
1986	9 (8)	3 (3)	5 (6)	4 (3)	0 (0)	21 (20)
1987	9 (5)	2 (2)	8 (8)	5 (5)	0 (0)	24 (20)
1988	11 (5)	3 (3)	11 (13)	7 (5)	1 (1)	32 (27)
1989a	7 (4)	1 (1)	35 (36)	7 (4)	0 (0)	50 (45)
1989b	3 (3)	5 (5)	19 (20)	4 (3)	0 (0)	31 (31)
1990	5 (3)	2 (2)	46 (47)	7 (4)	0 (0)	60 (56)

of R&D expenditure appeared only in the directors' report. This is a form of failure to comply with SSAP 13 as disclosure is required in the company accounts.

The other possible pattern in voluntary disclosure was according to industry classification. This was investigated in two ways: using the survey sample of published accounts and using Datastream accounts data. If industry classification was a major influence on voluntary disclosure of R&D expenditure, a distinct pattern should have emerged with voluntary disclosures concentrated in certain industries and absent from others. Neither sample produced this result; in most industries some but not all companies chose to disclose prior to the revision of SSAP 13.

Compliance with disclosure requirements

Schedule 7 para 6 (c) of the Companies Act 1985 requires an indication in the directors' report of the activities of the company in the field of R&D. Two aspects of compliance with this requirement were investigated: firstly, of the companies known to perform R&D, how many were mentioning their R&D activities in the directors' report; and secondly, how were companies interpreting the requirement? Table 10.5 shows that the rate of compliance has been consistently low although it has been increasing over the years 1985 to 1990. It is perhaps surprising that so many companies should give an indication elsewhere in their accounts that R&D is performed and yet fail to comply with this legal requirement.

Any reference to R&D activity no matter how short, bland or uninformative has been counted as compliance in compiling Table 10.5. Some companies used the same wording each year, so later sets of accounts gave no additional information on R&D. Where the text was repeated from year to year it tended to be a short statement of one or two sentences, to be very general and to give no indication of the scale of the R&D activity or its growth, for instance: 'It is the group's policy to commit sufficient funds to enable it to keep abreast of all product, process, market and system developments in the field in which it operates.' Table 10.6 shows the extent to which companies repeat the R&D information in the directors' report from year to year. Another way in which a very brief reference to R&D in the directors' report can fulfil the schedule 7 para 6 (c) requirement is by a reference to other pages of the annual report. This allows companies where R&D activity is reported in more detail elsewhere in the annual report to avoid repetition. The final two columns of Table 10.6 exclude these companies from the 'repeaters'. Even when these companies are excluded, the final column of Table 10.6 shows a significant proportion of companies making a reference to R&D

Table 10.5 Compliance with schedule 7 para 6 (c) Companies Act 1985 by reference to R&D in directors' report

Year	*Number of accounts examined*	*Reference present*		*Reference not present*	
		Number	*%*	*Number*	*%*
1985	87	45	51.72	42	48.28
1986	102	57	55.88	45	44.12
1987	111	67	60.36	44	39.64
1988	120	75	62.50	45	37.50
1989	147	91	61.90	56	38.10
1990	81	53	65.43	28	34.57

Table 10.6 Repetitions of text in directors' report

Year	*(a) Number of accounts with R&D reference*	*(b) Cases in col. (a) where accounts available for previous year*	*(c) Cases in col. (b) where text is repeated*	*(d) Percentage of repeats c/b* 100*	*(e) Exclude cases where text refers to other pages*	*(f) Percentage of repeats e/b* 100*
1986	57	42	27	64.29	21	50.00
1987	67	62	40	64.52	27	43.55
1988	75	63	44	69.84	32	50.79
1989	91	74	59	67.57	38	51.35
1990	53	34	24	70.59	16	47.06

activity in the directors' report repeating this reference year after year. As expected, it was the companies where R&D amounts were voluntarily disclosed that also provided more detailed statements in the directors' reports.

Compliance with SSAP 13 (revised)

The survey revealed that some 17 companies failed to implement the revised accounting standard in their 1990 accounts and a further 8 companies reporting at 31 December 1989 also failed to disclose R&D expenditure. Failure to comply with an accounting standard should be indicated in the audit report and therefore the audit reports of these 25 companies were examined. All 25 sets of accounts were given unqualified audit reports with no mention of the failure to disclose. As pointed out earlier these 25 instances of failure to comply are cases where the company has itself made identification possible by indicating that R&D activity is undertaken either by stating an accounting policy on R&D or by making a reference to R&D activity in the directors' report. Three companies acknowledged that R&D expenditure was not being disclosed as required. Triplex Lloyd stated in the 1990 directors' report:

> Improvements in technology and products are regarded as an integral part of the Group's development and customer assurance programme. Amounts spent on research and development expenditure are therefore not identifiable in a form required by SSAP 13, the accounting standard on research and development.

Wagon Industrial's 1990 directors' report contained a remarkably similar statement:

> Improvements in technology and products are regarded as an integral part of the Group's development and customer assurance programmes. As such the total amount of Research and Development expenditure charged in the profit and loss account during the year is not available as required by Statement of Standard Accounting Practice Number 13 Accounting for Research and Development.

Perhaps the similarity can be explained by the fact that both companies had audit reports signed KPMG Peat Marwick McLintock, Birmingham. However, the reason for non-compliance is itself of interest. The definition of R&D expenditure used in SSAP 13 (both versions) is the OECD definition, appearing in the Frascati Manual. This definition has been criticized as being biased towards scientific, laboratory-based work. As the UK economy moves away from manufacturing industries with centralized R&D functions towards industries, particularly in the service sector, where R&D activities are increasingly operationally integrated, the definition is becoming progressively less relevant. Reported non-compliance is one solution to these problems. R&D activity was also reported under non-standard headings which may also be a response to definitional difficulties, for instance 'product development', a tighter definition than 'development'; 'design and development' and 'testing and development', both broader definitions than 'development'.

A different reason for non-compliance is noted in Brammer's 1989 directors' report:

> The companies within the group are not normally engaged in research, but development activities are carried out in pursuit of new products and also to improve product quality, performance, competitiveness and profitability. This expenditure is not material in relation to the size of the group.

Industries where R&D functions are formalized and laboratory based are not represented amongst the non-compliers. Materiality and/or the cost of separating R&D expenditure from other integral expenditure could be plausible reasons for failure to comply. However, it remains the case that only the three companies quoted above did give a reason for non-compliance.

Accounting policies

Disclosure of accounting policies is required by SSAP 2 for items which are judged material or critical in determining profit or loss for the year and in stating the financial position of the company. Immediate write off is required by SSAP 13 (original and revised versions) for development expenditure not fulfilling the specified criteria and all research expenditure. This means that for most of the expenditure covered by SSAP 13 there is no policy choice available and disclosure of policy may therefore seem superfluous. However, where there is any expenditure on development which could be carried forward or written off immediately, a policy choice must be made and disclosed if this item is 'judged material or critical'.

In practice most companies in the survey sample made one brief policy statement referring to R&D expenditure generally and in the vast majority of cases the policy was immediate write-off of both research and development expenditure. Table 10.7 shows the pattern of policy disclosure. Where no policy is disclosed this may be because R&D expenditure is not material or because the company never incurs expenditure which could be carried forward and therefore never has to choose a policy. It is notable that very few companies fail to disclose a policy.

The small number of companies carrying forward qualifying development expenditure can also be seen in Table 10.7. Under SSAP 13 (original version) a policy of immediate write-off of all R&D expenditure made complete secrecy concerning R&D spending possible whereas carrying forward qualifying development expenditure would mean partial disclosure of R&D spending. Other reasons for the small number of companies carrying forward development expenditure are that few projects are undertaken that would qualify for carry forward and that companies consider the benefits, if any, of deferring development expenditure to be outweighed by the effort needed to identify qualifying expenditure. Benefits of carrying forward development expenditure include signalling that this expenditure is thought of as an investment with a positive net present value and allowing profits to be smoothed, especially where development expenditure fluctuates substantially from year to year.

Under SSAP 13 (revised) immediate write-off loses the benefit of secrecy. If there are benefits in carrying forward development expenditure where possible then the revision of SSAP 13 should have encouraged

Table 10.7 Accounting policies on R&D

Year	*Number of accounts examined*	*Cases where no policy disclosed*	*Immediate write-off of research is indicated*	*Carry forward of development is indicated*
1985	87	9	78	5
1986	102	8	94	5
1987	111	8	103	7
1988	120	6	111	10
1989	147	9	136	15
1990	81	4	75	11

policy changes with more carrying forward of qualifying expenditure after the revision. For 1989 and 1990 the number of companies disclosing a policy of carrying forward development expenditure as a percentage of the number of accounts examined does indeed increase, but the overall number of companies carrying development expenditure in their balance sheets remains small. Whitecroft, Photo-Me, Siebe and Pittard Garnar all changed their accounting policy to allow development expenditure to be carried forward in the year when the revision of SSAP 13 was implemented.

Qualitative aspects of R&D disclosure

In addition to disclosure of R&D expenditure within the statutory part of the annual report, some companies repeated the R&D expenditure figure in the financial highlights, the review of operations or a five-year financial summary. Extra disclosures of R&D amounts in the 'glossy' part of the report where the directors are more obviously trying to boost the company's image can be taken as indicating a belief that the R&D figures are good news for shareholders. Reporting in the non-statutory part of the document can also allow the figures to create a bigger impact by the use of graphs, pie charts or bar charts; for instance Reuters used bar charts for their five-year summary statistics and selected R&D expenditure to be reported in this way in 1989.

The survey also noted the amount of text devoted specifically to describing R&D activities, as it was assumed that more text implied a greater emphasis on R&D activity as a means of promoting the company's image. Ten companies were found to publish significant amounts of text (more than one paragraph) on the subject of R&D. For these ten the average amount of text devoted to R&D in each report was 2 pages, the maximum amount being 7 pages. Nine of the ten were amongst the companies voluntarily disclosing R&D expenditure pre-1989.

The sort of information being given about R&D effort was also of interest. Sometimes R&D was given special treatment in only one year. For instance, in 1985 GKN used the following quotation on the front cover of the annual report:

> Underpinned by a substantial research and development programme specialisation in selected business areas will continue to create exciting new opportunities in world markets.

In 1990 BOC commissioned a survey to evaluate what people thought of BOC, then ran a television advertising campaign describing itself as 'A world wide company that patents new inventions at the rate of one every four days', and commissioned a follow-up survey after this campaign. The 1990 annual report includes pictures and words from the advertisement, a description of the purpose of the campaign and the results of the before and after surveys. The percentage of target audience agreeing that BOC is committed to R&D rose from 35 per cent before to 49 per cent after. This is an unusual and interesting instance of a company including R&D effort as one of the main images it wishes to impress on its 'target audience', in this case 'business and other opinion leaders'.

Another feature of the company reports which were examined was the increasing use of a short mission statement repeated each year. The inclusion of references to R&D in a mission statement clearly indicates that R&D is thought to be an important activity which will be well received by the shareholders. Wellcome's statement is an example of this persistent emphasis on R&D.

> Wellcome is an international group devoted to the research, development and marketing of products for the promotion of human and animal health. Its origins go back more than a hundred years. Today it operates in all the world's major pharmaceutical markets and has manufacturing operations in more than 20 countries. Worldwide the group employs some 21,000 people, of whom 17 per cent are engaged in the group's research and development estrablishments. [Figures are from the 1988 report]

Glaxo, another pharmaceutical company, also uses this type of statement: 'Glaxo is an integrated research based group of companies whose corporate purpose is the discovery, development, manufacture and marketing of safe, effective medicines of the highest quality.'

CONCLUSION

This chapter has explored the theory and practice of R&D disclosure in annual reports. In the simplest theoretical models full disclosure is predicted and therefore explanations are required for less-than-full disclosure. In the case of R&D explanations for non-disclosure can be provided by managerial motives if the market is not efficient and in value-maximizing models by preparation costs and proprietary costs. Proprietary costs depend on the threat of entry by potential competitors and competition from existing rivals. From comments made on ED 14 it is clear that the directors of some UK companies believed proprietary costs to be significant. The two important findings of the survey of company reports were that there was evidence of a significant number of companies failing to comply with SSAP 13 and that the revision of SSAP 13, a revision which changed only disclosure requirements, appears to have caused some firms to have changed their accounting policy. The diversity found in the survey, in terms of the level, positioning and nature of R&D disclosures was notable. The lack of any distinct pattern of disclosure according to industry classification suggests that firm-specific factors rather than industry norms may have influenced the disclosure decision.

REFERENCES

Darrough, M.N. (1993) 'Disclosure Policy and Competition: Cournot vs. Bertrand', *The Accounting Review*, 68, (3), 534–561.

Darrough, M.N. and Stoughton, N.M. (1990) 'Financial Disclosure Policy in an Entry Game', *Journal of Accounting and Economics*, 12, 219–243.

Dye, R.A. (1986) 'Proprietary and Nonproprietary Disclosures', *Journal of Business*, 59, (2), 331–366.

Dye, R.A. (1990) 'Mandatory Versus Voluntary Disclosures: The cases of financial and real externalities', *The Accounting Review*, 65, 1–24.

Fishman, M.J. and Hagerty, K.M. (1989) 'Disclosure Decisions by Firms and the Competition for Price Efficiency', *Journal of Finance*, 44, (3), 633–646.

Fishman, M.J. and Hagerty, K.M. (1990) 'The Optimal Amount of Discretion to Allow in Disclosure', *Quarterly Journal of Economics*, 105, 427–444.

Gray, R.H. (1985) *Accounting for R&D: A Review of Experiences with SSAP 13*, Research Board of the Institute of Chartered Accountants in England and Wales Report.

Grossman, S. (1981) 'The Information Role of Warranties and Private Disclosure about Product Quality', *Journal of Law and Economics*, 24, 461–483.

Grossman, S. and Hart, O. (1983) 'An Analysis of the Principal-agent Problem', *Econometrica*, 51, 7–45.

Hope, A.J.B. and Gray, R.H. (1982) 'Power and Policy Making: The development of an R&D standard', *Journal of Business Finance and Accounting*, 9, (4), 531–558.

Horwitz, B. and Kolodny, R. (1980) 'The Economic Effects of Involuntary Uniformity in the Financial Reporting of R&D Expenditures', *Journal of Accounting Research*, 18, Supplement, 38–74.

House of Lords Select Committee on Science and Technology, First Report (Civil Research and Development), 1986.

MacArthur, J.B. (1988) 'An Analysis of the Content of Corporate Submissions on Proposed Accounting Standards in the UK', *Accounting and Business Research*, 18, 213–226.

Manne, H.C. (1965) 'Mergers and the Market for Corporate Control', *Journal of Political Economy*, 73, 110–120.

Milgrom, P. (1981) 'Good News and Bad News: Representation theorems and application', *Bell Journal of Economics*, 12, 380–391.

Myers, S.C. and Majluf, N.S. (1984) 'Corporate Financing and Investment Decisions when Firms have Information that Investors do not have', *Journal of Financial Economics*, 13, 187–221.

Newman, P. and Sansing, R. (1993) 'Disclosure Policies with Multiple Users', *Journal of Accounting Research*, 31, (1), 92–112.

Nixon, B. (1991) *Accounting for Research and Development: The Need for a New Perception*, Report for the Board of Chartered Accountants in Business.

Verrecchia, R.E. (1983) 'Discretionary Disclosure', *Journal of Accounting and Economics*, 5, 179–194.

Verrecchia, R.E. (1986) 'Managerial Discretion in the Choice Among Financial Reporting Alternatives', *Journal of Accounting and Economics*, 8, 175–195.

Verrecchia, R.E. (1990) 'Information Quality and Discretionary Disclosure', *Journal of Accounting and Economics*, 12, 365–380.

Whittington, G. (1989) 'Accounting Standard Setting in the UK after 20 years: A critique of the Dearing and Solomons reports', *Accounting and Business Research*, 19, 195–205.

11

R&D IN UK QUOTED COMPANIES: THE EFFECTS OF DISCLOSURE AND FINANCE

Jonathan Seaton and Ian Walker[1]

INTRODUCTION

Research and Development (R&D) is usually a risky and long-term form of investment and there is considerable evidence that the stock market undervalues R&D capital. A number of reasons have been put forward to explain this phenomenon and most of these relate to credit market failures arising from the nature of R&D. The arguments are often based on the idea that there may be a *lemons premium* that arises because markets have inferior information to the firm. The lemons premium raises the cost of capital to the firm from the external credit market – indeed, firms may be reluctant to reveal technical information to the market because they would then find it difficult to exclude other firms from benefiting from that information.

These arguments motivate the idea that R&D intensive firms may be less likely to be reliant on external finance. Moreover, there are arguments that suggest that the composition of external finance may be affected. For example, imperfect information may prompt banks to demand collateral for loans and R&D capital may, by its nature, not be sufficiently tangible to satisfy this demand so that R&D intensive firms rely less on debt and more on equity. On the other hand there may be a bankruptcy constraint which is more likely to bind for firms which engage in high risks – to overcome this firms, which believe they are good risks, may attempt credibly to signal this to the market by adopting a high debt financial policy. This argument would suggest that R&D intensive firms deliberately adopt high debt policies. That is, the relationship between R&D intensity and the debt/equity ratio of firms is not as clear-cut.

Indeed, Board *et al.* (1993) have investigated the relationship between gearing and R&D (in a multivariate framework which controls for size differences) and they find a statistically significant negative relationship in the UK. However, their paper assumes that R&D is exogenous and looks only at a selected sample of firms which record positive amounts of R&D. In earlier work (Seaton and Walker (1993)) we investigate the relationship between financial variables and R&D in a simultaneous equations framework using limited dependent variable techniques to overcome the problems associated with having large numbers of firms recording no R&D. We find that R&D intensity is negatively related to the probability of being externally financed and, conditional on external finance, is negatively related to the probability of being debt financed.

Thus, there seems to be some evidence that high R&D firms face higher costs of capital in external markets. In light of this companies may feel penalized by disclosing R&D activity and new R&D investment. While it is common to argue that better information will improve the operation of markets, second best considerations may undermine this case. That is, if the credit market suffers from some market failure associated with the financing of high technology firms it may, in fact, be better for firms to provide less information rather than more. Indeed, Black and Tonks (1991) construct a theoretical model where there is a potential take-over threat so that firms prefer not to disclose information that increases the variance in their share price.

The new Statement of Standard Accounting Practice SSAP 13 (revised) requires publication of expensed R&D for accounting years ending on or after 1st January 1989. This allows us to examine whether the compulsory disclosure of R&D information has had any impact on the extent to which R&D is sensitive to the financial structure of the firm.

The case normally made for compulsory disclosure is that it provides more information for the credit market to base decisions on. That is, disclosure would improve the efficiency of the market. Moreover, since compulsory disclosure may make raising external finance more difficult or expensive this may, for given internal funds, reduce the level of R&D conducted. However, these are first best arguments and there may be grounds for believing that making disclosure compulsory deprives firms of using a valuable signal which allows the market to distinguish between good and bad risks.

Thus, there are three questions that we attempt to address: does the method of finance affect R&D; has compulsory disclosure affected this relationship; and did compulsory disclosure have any impact on the level of R&D undertaken?

The chapter uses a balanced panel of 457 UK quoted companies over the period 1983 to 1990. The econometric modelling takes account of the limited dependent nature of R&D – that is, many companies record no R&D expenditure – and attempts to account for non-disclosure prior to SSAP 13 by comparing the model of R&D estimated on the post-SSAP 13 data with the observed behaviour prior to SSAP 13.

Section 2 briefly highlights the main theoretical arguments that have been advanced in the literature. Section 3 describes the main features of the data and the econometric methodology. The main findings support our suspicion that compulsory disclosure could have a detrimental effect on R&D by making it more difficult for firms to signal their quality to the financial markets. Section 4 concludes the chapter with some discussion of the results and some directions for future research.

FINANCE AND R&D

Modigliani and Miller (1958) demonstrated that under certain conditions, the financial structure of a firm is irrelevant to its real behaviour, i.e. behaviour with respect to employment, output and investment. Thus it is the violation of these conditions that generates any interaction between financial and real decisions. Here we are particularly interested in the financing pattern of firms who engage in R&D investment expenditure. A firm can resource an investment project either *internally* or *externally*. Internal finance is typically defined as cash flow or retained profits, although Fazzari and Petersen (1993) suggest an extension of this definition to include working capital. External finance can be disaggregated into *debt* and *equity* finance. Equity gives legal ownership for shareholders of the company's assets and a proportion of the company's future profits (dividends). Debt gives debt holders the principal amount at maturity, plus periodical fixed interest payments.

Thakor (1993) looks at the dynamic investment policies of firms under asymmetric information, where managers seek to maximize the wealth of existing shareholders. Investment projects are divided into late bloomers and early winners with less overall, but high initial payoffs. One can think of late bloomers as being R&D projects. Thakor's (1993) model suggests that firms, working to maximize current shareholder wealth, may forgo valuable long-term projects in favour of less valuable short-term projects.

Myers and Majluf (1984) argued that debt would be preferable to equity finance by undervalued firms. Although Narayanan (1988) agrees with the conclusion, the result was achieved by assuming the existence of lemons and risky investment. An advantage of debt finance cited by Narayanan (1988) is that where managers have knowledge of their own firm's high quality they can use risky debt to provide a credible signal to financial markets, whilst poor firms would not. This acts as a barrier to entry for inferior firms and is beneficial for the high quality firms because they are valued at the (now higher) market average. Narayanan (1988) concludes that if they issue risk-free debt no *lemon* enters the market, and, risky or not, debt is always better than equity.

Current shareholders may see debt as a preferable source of new financing. Maloney, McCormick and Mitchell (1993) investigate whether more debt implies better managerial decision-making, and their empirical work appears to support this view. Debt finance may be in the interest of shareholders since there may be incentive problems when a firm is wholly equity financed. Bankruptcy costs may give an added spur to managers. Since lenders may have the power to withdraw funds from the firm, this may provide better discipline to managers than does the voting rights of shareholders.

One further argument for firms preferring debt to equity comes from certain tax advantages debt may have. In a perfect financial market the costs of different forms of finance would be identical. However, taxation would distort this result. Modigliani and Miller (1963) suggested that if debt is tax deductible it might become the preferred method of financing. For further discussion of these issues see Miller (1977), DeAngelo and Masulis (1980), and Fazzari, Hubbard and Petersen (1988a, 1988b) who have considered the interaction of corporate and individual tax systems.

Unlike Myers and Majluf (1984) who suggested that internal finance is preferred to debt and debt to equity, Board, Delargy and Tonks (1993) argue that equity may be preferable to debt since, for R&D investing companies, the cost of debt may be unusually high. Similarly for R&D companies the asymmetric information problem is likely to be much higher than non-R&D companies. They also expect new R&D intensive firms to prefer equity to debt finance. This is because R&D produces uncertain cash flows and often ones with very low levels of initial cash flow. This would mean periodical interest payments would be hard to cover. On the supply side, the potential creditors would not be willing to take such risks at first, without a large premium. Moreover, they would find that loans could be hard to secure against R&D assets, which may be undervalued by the market. They also suggest that more mature large diversified companies should be able to use their assets to secure debt, and therefore may make greater use of debt rather than equity finance; whereas equity may be preferred for small undiversified companies.

A highly geared firm presents a greater risk for equity holders and creditors since there is greater chance of bankruptcy. If a firm is in financial distress, then meeting interest as well as repayment of the principal may be more difficult. To compensate for potential costs of bankruptcy and liquidation debt holders would require higher returns on debt. Linked to this problem is the problem of agency costs which can arise because debt is often of limited liability nature so managers may be tempted to overburden themselves with it, against the interests of the creditors. To protect themselves, creditors may put restrictions on firm behaviour – that is impose agency costs. Jensen and Meckling (1976) argue that conflicts derived from this agency problem may lead to higher costs of external finance, through monitoring. That is, outsiders react by attempting to control management's behaviour through audits, budget restrictions, and compensation systems designed to align management interests with shareholder interests.

Fazzari and Athey (1987) suggest that asymmetric information on loan quality may lead to some borrowers being prevented from obtaining loans at the prevailing cost of capital. This is because firms have an incentive to give an optimistic picture of their investment plans and financial condition. They also may be reluctant to release sensitive information and it may be costly for outsiders fully to determine the financial shape of a company. However, Ross (1977) suggests company managers are indifferent between forms of external finance, though they may use them as signalling devices.

In a similar fashion Leland and Pyle (1977) argue that quality companies signal their worth to potential investors in a world of asymmetric information. Borrowers of funds have the incentive to talk up their investments and plans, whilst verification of the true projects may be very difficult or extremely costly. They speculate that it is the entrepreneur's willingness to invest in his or her own projects that acts as a signal to project quality. They state that this would mean that the company value would be an increasing function of the share of it held by the entrepreneur. The availability of internal finance reduces the prospect of being rationed by external finance. They also argue that a further signal that companies can give to the credit markets is whether they are willing to fund projects internally.

Financial market constraints could appear in two ways. Firstly, firms face credit rationing which may limit the number or size of investment projects which they are able to finance. Secondly, credit rationing may not occur but firms may still face a higher cost of capital which leads them to engage in lower investment. That is, firms may face quantity constraints or higher prices. Fazzari, Hubbard and Petersen (1988a) argue that small and medium-sized companies are unlikely to gain access to large debt markets. Outside the US Fortune 500 they may have to get bond finance through private placements which often put constraints upon certain financial variables within the firm, for example working capital, dividend payments, equity, etc. Secondly, periods of tight credit may mean smaller firms may be denied credit whilst larger, safer, *better quality*, companies get funded.

This section has shown that a large literature has grown up over the last two decades, attempting to identify whether and why companies prefer internal to external finance and debt or equity. The essence of the argument can be captured in Figure 11.1 which depicts the relationship between the marginal costs of funds and the level of funding presumed by the pecking order literature. The cost of *internal* finance is the opportunity cost of not investing those funds in the market, r^i. For funding in excess of the available internal finance, F_o, the marginal

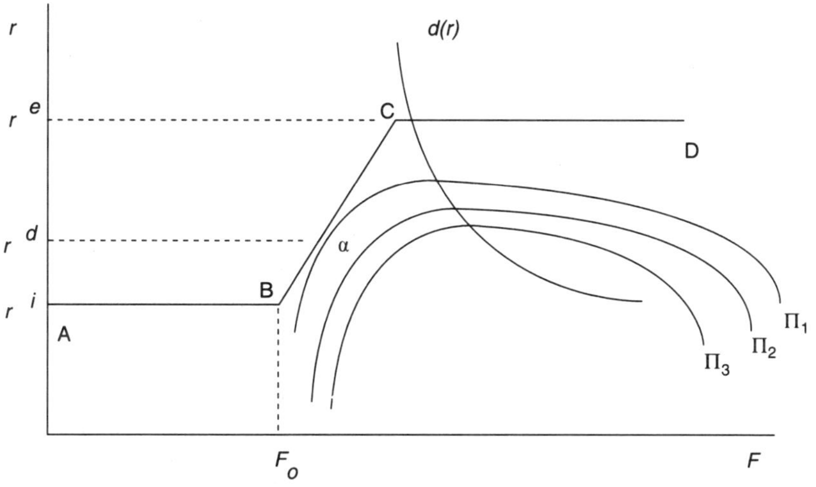

Figure 11.1 The financial pecking order

cost is that associated with the next cheapest form, say debt, r^d. This marginal cost may rise with the level of debt. However, there will come a point where further debt is more expensive than the cost of issuing equity, r^e. Thus the supply curve of funds may be given by ABCD. The inverted U shaped curves (Π_1, Π_2, Π_3) represent iso-profit lines for the firm, where the direction of increasing profit, i.e. $\Pi_1 < \Pi_2 < \Pi_3$, is down the finance demand curve, $d(r)$, since finance is an input and the firm's profit function is a decreasing function of input prices. The shape of the iso-profit lines reflects the fact that the demand function $d(r)$ is defined as the profit-maximizing level of finance at any interest rate r (that is, if ABCD were a horizontal line).

The firm will maximize profits at the point on the supply of funds curve corresponding to the highest iso-profit curve, i.e. at point α. Note that α corresponds to the point where the firm uses its available internal finance and some debt. However, a firm which faces a severe lemons problem, perhaps because it is a highly R&D intensive firm, would find that the supply curve would be steep, as in Figure 11.2 (ABC′B′), so that the equilibrium would be more likely to occur at β, the point where investment is limited to the available internal finance because external finance is so expensive at the margin.

THE EMPIRICAL MODEL

The essence of the phenomena that we wish to capture can be expressed as follows. Post-SSAP 13 we assume that R&D expenditure, y_1, is determined via the following Tobit equation

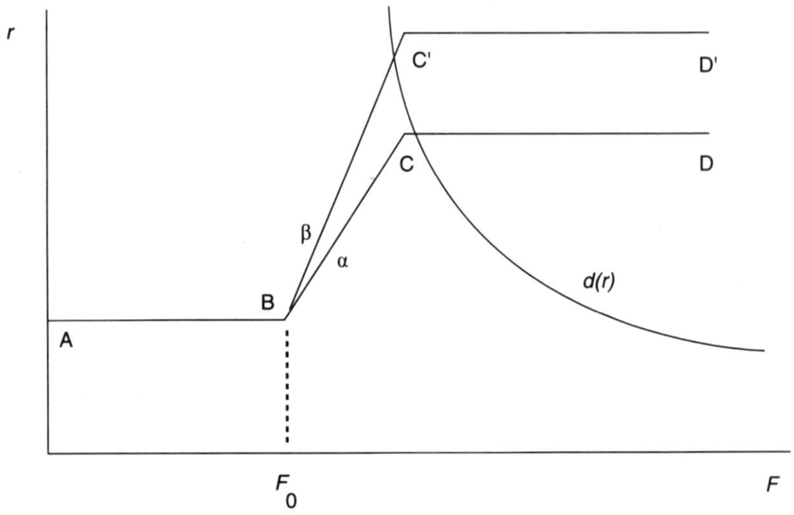

Figure 11.2 The financial pecking order with higher costs

$$y_1^* = X\beta + \varepsilon_1,$$

where y_1^* is the latent variable corresponding to y_1 such that $y_1^* = y_1$ if $y_1 > 0$ and X contains financial and other variables. This is a Tobit model reflecting the fact that many companies in our data engage in no R&D spending. However, prior to SSAP 13 we assume that observed R&D expenditure is determined in the following selection model

$$y_1^* = X\gamma + u_1,$$

where $y_1^* = y_1$ if $y_1.y_2 > 0$ and y_2 is a variable indicating whether voluntary disclosure occurred. That is, R&D is only observed for firms that engage in R&D ($y_1 > 0$) *and* choose to disclose it ($y_2 > 0$). Moreover, y_2 may directly affect the level of R&D that is conducted. The difficulty here is that y_2 is an endogenous variable if firms have an incentive not to reveal information to financial markets that may lead to them facing a lemons premium in the market. To overcome the simultaneity in the relationship between y_1 and y_2 we need an instrument for y_2. That is, we need

$$y_2^* = Z\delta + \nu,$$

where y_2^* is the latent variable corresponding to y_2 and Z is a matrix of instrumental variables. While this model is identified by the assumptions about the functional forms this should not be regarded as a satisfactory solution, not least because the explanatory power of the vector Z is likely to be modest. There are two ways in which to provide non-parametric identification in this model. First one could impose equality in the coefficients on the X's across the pre- and post-SSAP 13 data, i.e. $\gamma = \beta$. That is, we could exploit the fact that $y_2 = 1$ in the post-SSAP 13 data. Alternatively, identification requires that Z contains at least one variable that is not contained in X. While both methods impose normality, the former method seems likely to be more efficient since it uses both pre- and post-SSAP 13 data simultaneously. Moreover, the latter method requires that we have a valid instrument in the data and it is difficult to envisage a variable which is correlated with disclosure that is not also correlated with the level of R&D. Thus, there are no natural exclusion restrictions that suggest themselves. However, here we present results where identification is achieved by the functional form restrictions. Further work will investigate the sensitivity of the results.

The panel of company accounts data is extracted from Datastream International. The sample consisted of all manufacturing company accounts which reported annually from 1983 to 1990 with positive sales. A small number of companies were excluded because of missing values and extreme values for certain variables, profit, debt, etc. leaving a panel of 451 companies over an eight-year period (3,608 data points).

Figures 11.3 and 11.4 show the distribution of the sample compared with the US data reported in Bound *et al.* (1984: 32), and shows a fairly close comparison between the UK and US data. However, our sample tends to have a greater proportion of large R&D to sales ratios, hence a steeper slope to the line of fit.

Figures 11.5 and 11.6 present a breakdown by type of finance and disclosure period (pre SSAP 13 and post-SSAP 13) for companies who have never undertaken R&D (non-R&D), those who are new disclosers in 1989/90 (Invol: involuntary disclosers) and those who have disclosed

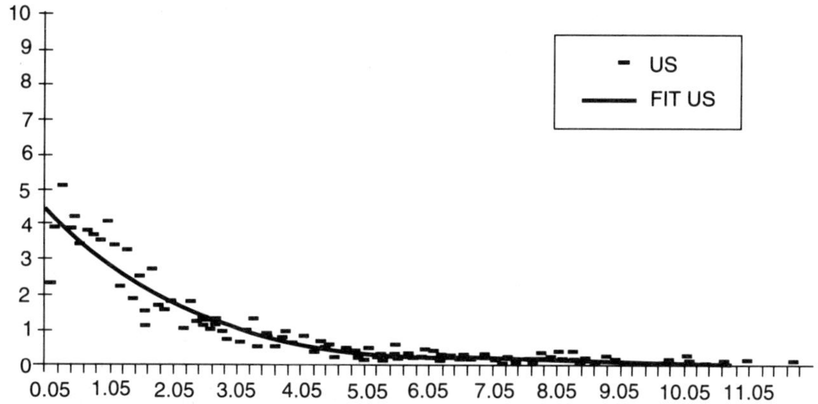

Figure 11.3 R&D sales by proportion of firms, USA, 1976
Source: Bound *et al.* 1984

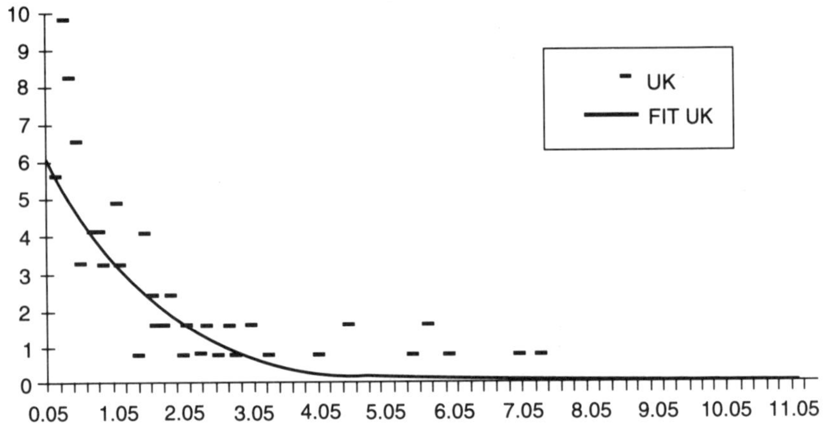

Figure 11.4 R&D sales by proportion of firms, UK, 1990

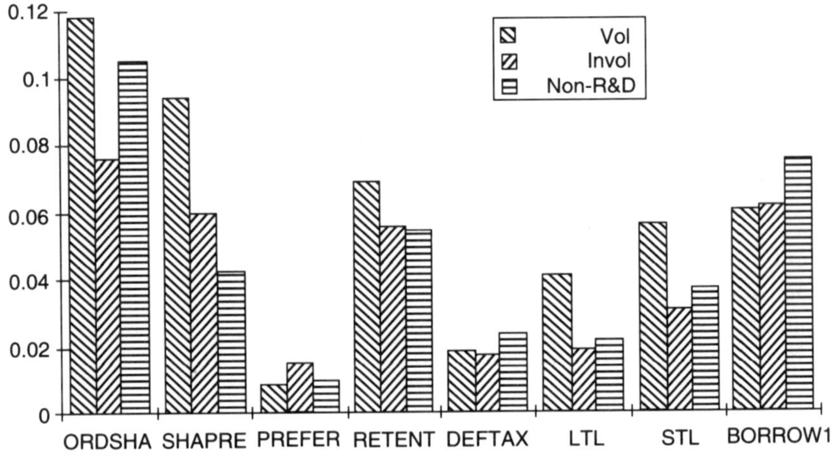

Figure 11.5 Average proportion of finance type over sales pre-SSAP 13 (1983–1988)

R&D within the sample period 1983 to 1988 (Vol: voluntary disclosers). In our sample of 451 companies 55 were voluntary disclosers, 82 were involuntary disclosers and 314 were firms who did not report R&D from 1983 to 1990.

Figure 11.5 illustrates the group (Vol, Invol, Non-R&D) average of finance type/sales ratios. In size terms ordinary share capital (OrdSha) and borrowing for less than one year (Borrow1) are very dominant. At the other extreme deferred tax (DefTax) and preference shares (Prefer) play a less important role in the financial structure of the firms sampled. The share premium (ShaPre), retentions (Retent), short-term

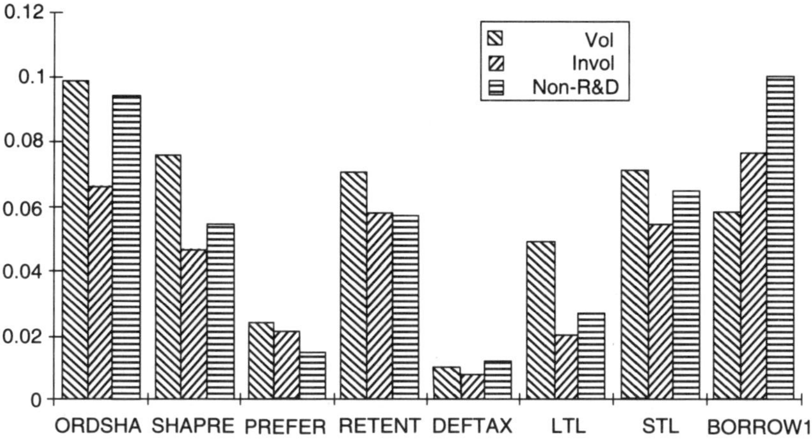

Figure 11.6 Average proportion of finance type over sales post-SSAP 13 (1989/90)

loans (STL) and long-term loans (LTL) represent the middle ground in this breakdown.

The major differences between voluntary and involuntary disclosers both pre- and post-SSAP 13 occur in OrdSha, ShaPre, Prefer, LTL and STL. The move from pre- to post-SSAP 13 increased the differences in ShaPre, LTL, and especially Borrow1, but they became closer for STL, Retent, and Prefer.

The differences of finance pattern between non-R&D and R&D companies are much lower. Major differences occur in DefTax, ShaPre, Borrow1 and OrdSha. However, comparing the pre- and post-SSAP 13 data the non-R&D and R&D companies edge closer together except for Borrow1 and Prefer.

These results seem to point out that R&D firms appear more similar now than they did pre-SSAP 13 to non-R&D companies. But at a more disaggregated level, voluntary disclosers are different to involuntary disclosers and are becoming more so in some areas of finance, particularly for Borrow1 and LTL.

Further statistical analysis was made to determine these differences in a more rigorous way using probit analysis taking account of other characteristics, for example industry group and time effects.

Table 11.1 shows two probit equation estimates for the impact of financial variables on the probability of being an R&D rather than a non-R&D firm. The first column gives the pre-SSAP 13 estimates whilst the second column displays the post-SSAP 13 estimates. These suggest R&D and non-R&D firms seem to have less significant difference in finance terms post-SSAP 13, the only significantly different term being

Table 11.1 R&D versus non-R&D companies

Variable	*Pre-SSAP 13 estimates*	*Post-SSAP 13 estimates*
Constant	−0.7693 (−9.208)	−0.7821 (−6.679)
OrdSha	−1.0615 (−3.759)	−0.7736 (−1.381)
ShaPre	1.2970 (6.323)	0.4219 (1.029)
Prefer	0.1268 (0.220)	1.4852 (1.940)
Retent	2.2435 (3.578)	0.5930 (0.569)
DefTax	−6.3638 (−6.067)	−2.8816 (−1.114)
ConvLo	−2.9962 (−1.856)	−1.5264 (−1.166)
LTL	1.7085 (3.850)	1.2075 (1.876)
STL	−0.0119 (−0.038)	0.0498 (0.147)
Borrow1	−1.0930 (−2.973)	−1.4962 (−2.620)
Young	0.1890 (1.953)	0.2195 (1.328)

Notes: The dependent variable is unity if the firm has announced R&D from 1983 to 1990, zero otherwise. Dummy variables were used for industry group and year, t-statistics in brackets. Young equals unity if a firm is recorded as having less than 10 years of accounts, otherwise zero.

Table 11.2 Of R&D firms, voluntary versus involuntary disclosers

Variable	*Pre-SSAP 13 estimates*	*Post-SSAP 13 estimates*
Constant	−0.5179 (−3.229)	−0.3908 (−1.610)
OrdSha	2.1916 (3.839)	3.0564 (2.225)
ShaPre	−0.4067 (−1.182)	−1.8778 (−1.738)
Prefer	−4.1095 (−3.005)	0.6563 (0.448)
Retent	0.8110 (0.709)	2.6486 (0.945)
DefTax	−1.9752 (−0.912)	−0.3182 (−0.052)
ConvLo	−7.8161 (−1.890)	1.7493 (0.309)
LTL	8.1496 (5.438)	6.2385 (3.189)
STL	1.4510 (1.231)	−0.6749 (−0.520)
Borrow1	−0.4122 (−0.487)	−2.7214 (−2.065)
Young	0.0825 (0.512)	0.1120 (0.405)

Notes: Dependent variable equals unity if voluntary disclosure, zero if involuntary disclosure, sample consists of all R&D announcing firms. Dummy variables were used for industry group and year, t-statistics in brackets. The bivariate probit model with selection, Greene (1992: 466), would seem a more appropriate model, however with identical variables in each equation we used single equation probit.

DefTax, which is a very small component of finance. However, before 1989, these companies did appear to display some differing characteristics, especially for retained earnings, convertible loans and deferred taxation.

If we select the sample of R&D firms, and analyse which factors, in finance terms, identify the differences between the voluntary and involuntary disclosers we find that some do appear. Table 11.2 shows that the main differences pre-SSAP 13 are in shares, ordinary and preference as well as in long-term loans. Post-SSAP 13 borrowing becomes one of the

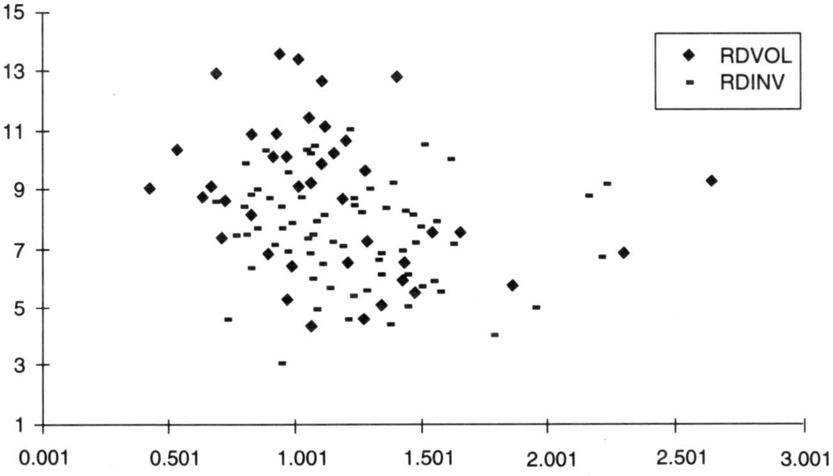

Figure 11.7 Sales v. R&D (voluntary/involuntary firms)

major divisive characteristics, as well as retained earnings. Voluntary disclosers of the past are taking proportionately less borrowing within one year and are using more retained earnings than the non-disclosers.

Figure 11.7 shows the relationship between R&D and sales over working capital for firms which disclose prior to SSAP 13 compared to those that do not disclose. There does not appear to be much difference in the scatter of points except that the voluntary disclosers appear to be more spread out. The relationship altogether seems to be negative. Size of firm also seems to be an important distinguishing characteristic, non-R&D firms have an average of 3,038 employees, involuntary disclosers a larger 8,424 whilst the voluntary disclosers have on average 20,616.

Figure 11.8 shows the relationship between R&D and profits for firms which disclose prior to SSAP 13 compared to those that do not disclose. Again there is little difference except the voluntary disclosers distribution is higher.

Figure 11.9 shows the relationship between R&D and debt/equity ratio for firms which disclose prior to SSAP 13 compared to those that do not disclose. The voluntary disclosure companies each year have a greater DE ratio than the other two groups.

The analysis of investment under finance constraints has generated a large degree of interest recently, for example Bond and Meghir (1994), but there is very little previous UK work either on R&D itself, or on the implications of disclosure. Belcher (1994) analyses the determinants of disclosure but does not consider modelling R&D itself. Board, Delargy and Tonks (1993) examine the link between R&D and the debt equity

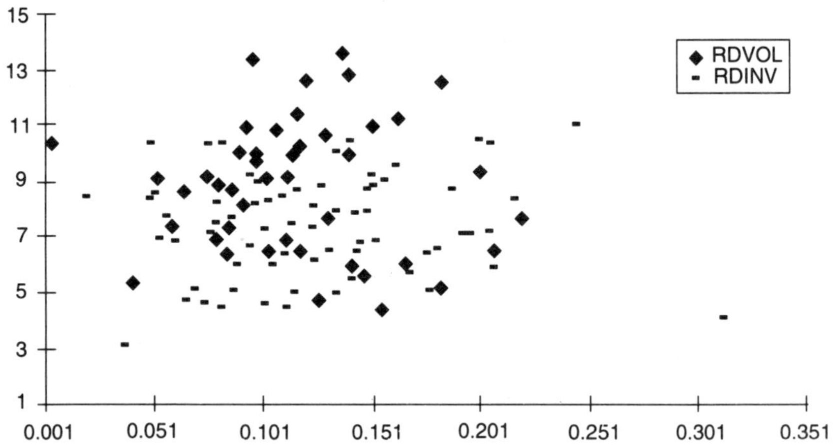

Figure 11.8 Profits v. R&D (voluntary/involuntary firms)

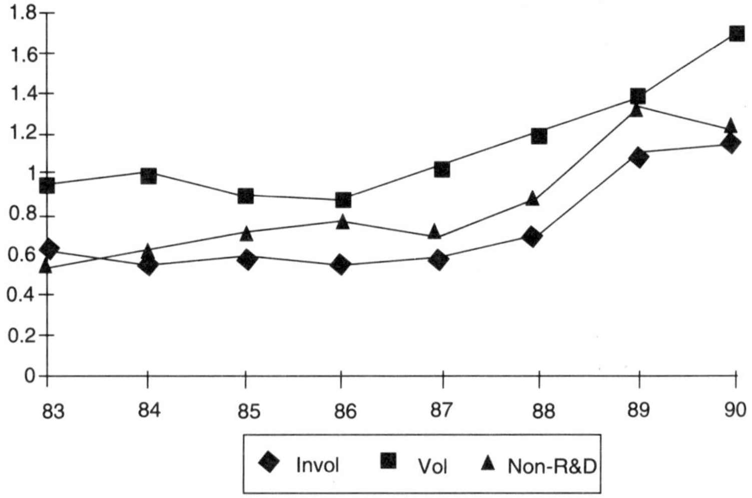

Figure 11.9 Debt/equity ratio v. R&D (voluntary/involuntary firms)

ratio for the UK and the USA. However, they do not consider the disclosure issue and simply use a, presumably non-random, sample of firms which disclose for their analysis. Their results show marked differences between pre- and post-SSAP 13 observations which may be a reflection of selection bias in the use of a sample of firms which disclose.

Unlike Board *et al.* the focus of our analysis is R&D and its disclosure, and here we treat financial variables as exogenous. Future work will investigate the extent to which this is valid and will consider simultaneous modelling.

Table 11.3 Tobit estimates – R&D equation

Variable	*Tobit (select) pre-SSAP 13 estimate*	*Tobit post-SSAP 13 estimate*
Constant	−0.08695 (−9.636)	−0.03350 (−5.089)
OrdSha	−0.03339 (−1.208)	−0.03371 (−1.521)
ShaPre	0.02625 (1.078)	−0.01423 (−0.679)
Prefer	−0.14479 (−1.352)	0.03577 (1.598)
Retent	0.19549 (4.487)	0.11263 (3.164)
DefTax	−0.44054 (−3.401)	−0.13922 (−1.480)
ConvLo	−0.33154 (−1.383)	−0.06086 (−0.711)
LTL	0.13478 (2.701)	0.08402 (3.016)
STL	−0.03699 (−0.896)	−0.00764 (−0.571)
Borrow1	−0.16895 (−3.897)	−0.01813 (−1.032)
Young	0.01211 (1.755)	0.00941 (1.888)

Notes: Dummy variables were used for industry group and year, t-statistics in brackets.

The dependent variable in our analysis is the ratio of R&D to sales, since we need to scale the variables to account for size. The explanatory variables are inspired by theories of investment in the literature. Profit, Π, is included to capture potential credit market failure. Financial variables are also included on credit market failure grounds. All variables are deflated by sales to scale the variables.

The results are given in Table 11.3. Column 1 is the results of the Tobit Selection applied to the pre-SSAP 13 data. Column 2 is the simple Tobit for post-SSAP 13 data. There is a striking similarity between both columns of results. Both indicate that R&D companies are constrained internally (positive and significant sign on Retent) and also that long-term loans, LTL, gives a positive push to R&D investment. All other significant financial variable signs are negative implying that more finance in these areas is bought by a reduction in R&D. Financial structure does appear to affect the proportion of R&D.

The number of significant variables has dropped as we move to the post-SSAP 13 period. Secondly, most of the coefficients have reduced in size. This could imply that although the financial markets are not perfect, they are tending that way. The results also indicate the future direction of that change, that is, internal finance restrictions might be eased by cheaper and more abundant provision of long-term loans.

CONCLUSION

This chapter has considered the relationship between the financial decisions of firms, the disclosure of R&D spending and the level of R&D. The motivation for the analysis is a fear that the changes in UK disclosure rules in company accounts, which came into effect in

1990, might exacerbate any failure in the financial system to provide appropriate funding for R&D.

The methodology involves estimating the relationship between R&D and a set of explanatory variables which included sales, profits and financial variables. This relationship was estimated using econometric methods that deal with the observations that record no R&D, and took account of the potential endogeneity of R&D disclosure prior to the change in the accounting rules. The results support the view that R&D is *still* sensitive to the availability of internal finance following compulsory disclosure. However, the sensitivity of R&D to financial variables appears to be diminishing.

Table 11.2 showed that the differences between voluntary and involuntary disclosers were in the main caused by retentions and long-term loans. That is, the involuntary disclosers do not suffer market failure to the degree that voluntary disclosers do. This means our post-SSAP 13 results suggest less market failure due to the impact of disclosure on R&D firms as a whole, simply because the new disclosers counterbalance the market failure experienced by voluntary disclosers.

One possible reason why the involuntary disclosers did not disclose is because they would not gain or lose to a large extent by disclosing to the financial markets, but their main cost is news getting to their competitors. The voluntary disclosers on the other hand, gained in some way by announcement, perhaps credibility within the industry, but the loss for them is higher finance costs and internal finance constraints.

Our results also indicate that one main difference between voluntary and involuntary disclosers post-SSAP 13 is that voluntary disclosers respond more to long-term debt. Further higher R&D investment in UK quoted companies could according to our results be increased by improved access to cheaper less risky long-term debt to counter the difficulties with risky, long-term investment in R&D.

There are a number of weaknesses to our analysis which remain to be addressed. Firstly, we do not control for *fixed effects* which requires that we exploit the panel nature of the data. There are considerable difficulties in extending the limited dependent modelling in this direction but recent research (by Labeaga (1992) on tobacco expenditures) has suggested computationally tractable methods. Secondly, we have assumed that the method of financing is exogenous and there is some evidence (Seaton and Walker (1993)) which suggests that this is not the case – at least in the post-SSAP 13 data. The difficulty here is overcoming the lack of any obvious exclusion restrictions with which to identify such a simultaneous model. Finally, the analysis needs to be extended to exploit more recent data to ensure that the effects identified here are not a coincidence of timing.

NOTE

1 We are grateful to the ESRC for financing this project under the Functioning of Markets Initiative grant No. W102251012. Alice Belcher, Colin Bladen-Hovell and Mike Devereux made useful comments and gave assistance with the data used in this project. We would also like to thank the participants of the University of St. Andrews Economics workshop, especially Gavin Reid, Felix FitzRoy and Bill Nixon for their helpful suggestions on an early draft of this paper. Any errors and omissions remain the sole responsibility of the authors.

REFERENCES

Belcher, Alice (1994) 'The Decision to Disclose R&D Expenditure: UK Companies 1980–1989', mimeo of paper given at University of Keele Conference.

Black, Jane and Ian Tonks (1991) 'The Decision to Disclose Research and Development Expenditure in the Presence of a Take-over Threat', mimeo copy.

Board, John, P.J. Robert Delargy and Ian Tonks (1993) 'R&D Intensity and Firm Finance', Chapter 14, in *New Technologies and the Firm*, Peter Swan (ed.), Routledge, pp. 321–342.

Bond, Stephen and Costas Meghir (1994) 'Dynamic Investment Models and the Firm's Financial Policy', *Review of Economic Studies*, vol. 61, pp. 197–222.

Bound, John, Clint Cummins, Zvi Griliches, Bronwyn H. Hall and Adam Jaffe (1984) 'Who Does R&D and Who Patents', Chapter 2, in *R&D, Patents and Productivity*, Zvi Griliches (ed.), University of Chicago Press.

DeAngelo, H. and R. Masulis (1980) 'Optimal Capital Structure under Corporate and Personal Taxation', *Journal of Financial Economics*, vol. 8, no. 1, pp. 3–29.

Fazzari, Steven M. and Michael J. Athey (1987) 'Asymmetric Information, Financing Constraints, and Investment', *The Review of Economics and Statistics*, pp. 481–487.

Fazzari, Steven M., R. Glenn Hubbard and Bruce C. Petersen (1988a) 'Financing Constraints and Corporate Investment', *Brookings Papers on Economic Activity*, pp. 141–206.

Fazzari, Steven M., R. Glenn Hubbard and Bruce Petersen (1988b) 'Investment, Financing Decisions, and Tax Policy', *American Economic Review, Papers and Proceedings*, vol. 78, no. 2, pp. 200–205.

Fazzari, Steven M. and Bruce C. Petersen (1993) 'Working Capital and Fixed Investment: New Evidence on Financing Constraints', *The RAND Journal of Economics*, vol. 24, no. 3, pp. 328–342.

Greene, William H. (1992) *LIMDEP version 6.0 User's Manual and Reference Guide*, Econometric Software Inc.

Jensen, M.C. and W.H. Meckling (1976) 'Theory of the Firm: Managerial Behaviour and Ownership Structure', *Journal of Financial Economics*, vol. 32, pp. 371–387.

Labeaga, Jose M. (1992) 'A Dynamic Panel Data Model with Limited Dependent Variables: An Application to the Demand for Tobacco', *Fundacion Empresa Publica, Documento de Trabajo*, No. 9210.

Leland, Hayne E. and David H. Pyle (1977) 'Informational Asymmetries, Financial Structure, and Financial Intermediation', *The Journal of Finance*, vol. 32, no. 2, pp. 371–387.

Maloney, Michael T., Robert E. McCormick and Mark L. Mitchell (1993) 'Managerial Decision Making and Capital Structure', *Journal of Business*, vol. 66, no. 2, pp. 189–217.

Miller, M.H. (1977) 'Debt and Taxes', *Journal of Finance*, pp. 261–275.

Modigliani, Franco and Merton H. Miller (1958) 'The Cost of Capital, Corporation Finance and the Theory of Investment', *The American Economic Review*, vol. 48, no. 3, pp. 261–297.

Modigliani, Franco and Merton H. Miller (1963) 'Corporate Income Taxes and the Cost of Capital: A Correction', *The American Economic Review*, pp. 433–443.

Myers, Stewart C. and Nicholas S. Majluf (1984) 'Corporate Financing and Investment Decisions when Firms have Information that Investors do not have', *Journal of Financial Economics*, vol. 13, pp. 187–221.

Narayanan, M.P. (1988) 'Debt versus Equity under Asymmetric Information', *Journal of Financial and Quantitative Analysis*, vol. 23, no. 1, pp. 39–51.

Ross, S. (1977) 'The Determination of Financial Structures: The Incentive Signalling Approach', *Bell Journal of Economics*, pp. 23–40.

Seaton, Jonathan and Ian Walker (1993) 'Corporate Research and Development in the UK: Spillovers and Credit Market Failure', University of St. Andrews, Dept of Economics, Discussion Paper Series, No. 9310.

Thakor, Anjan V. (1993) 'Information, Investment Horizon, and Price Reactions', *Journal of Financial and Quantitative Analysis*, vol. 28, no. 4, pp. 459–482.

12

THE DECISION TO DISCLOSE R&D EXPENDITURE

Alice Belcher

1 INTRODUCTION

In January 1989 the Statement of Standard Accounting Practice (SSAP) 13 Accounting for Research and Development (R&D) was revised and for the first time UK companies were required to disclose their expenditure on R&D. SSAP 13 was originally issued in December 1977 following two exposure drafts, EDs 14 and 17 dated January 1975 and April 1976 respectively. ED 14 required immediate write-off of all R&D expenditure and required disclosure of the amount written off. But, 'the ASC changed its position on the issues of accounting treatment and disclosure of R&D because of the wishes of industry – particularly the aerospace industry' (Hope and Gray, 1982: 551). So when SSAP 13 (original version) was issued it allowed companies to choose to carry forward qualifying development expenditure and required disclosure of the amounts relating to the deferred development account only.

SSAP 13 was reviewed by an ASC working party and Gray (1985) found, in a commissioned report, that disclosure was favoured by analysts and auditors and not particularly resisted by the companies. Pressure for SSAP 13 to be revised so as to require disclosure of R&D expenditure came from another source in 1986/87. Arguments concerning the importance of R&D activity to the economy had been brought to the attention of Parliament on more than one occasion and the House of Lords Select Committee on Science and Technology stated in its first report in 1986 that companies should be required to disclose R&D expenditure. This was an indication that if the accounting standard was not revised then a requirement for disclosure would appear in company law. The Accounting Standards Committee published ED 41 in June 1987 and this can be seen as a direct response to the possibility of legislation. Nixon (1991) describes the political urgency of the revision in some detail. It meant that the pressure from companies which helped ED 14 evolve into the original SSAP 13 was unlikely to have the same impact when ED 41 was published.

The regulatory history of accounting for R&D in the UK shows that from 1977 the accounting treatment of R&D was subject to an accounting standard, but from 1977 to 1989 the disclosure of R&D written off immediately (most R&D expenditure) was voluntary not mandatory. This chapter models the decision by UK companies to disclose R&D expenditure in the period 1980 to 1989 using a limited dependent variable model. The dependent variable takes the value one when R&D expenditure is disclosed in a set of accounts, and zero otherwise. Disclosure hypotheses are discussed in section 2. The choice of model and estimation are explained in section 3. The data is described in section 4. The results are presented in section 5 and section 6 is a summary and conclusion.

2 DISCLOSURE HYPOTHESES

The nine hypotheses set out below draw on the insights of the theoretical information economics models but set them in the context of practical accounting and relevant regulatory developments. A more detailed discussion of the theory of R&D disclosure can be found in Chapter 10 of this volume.

Hypothesis 1

For most companies a decision to disclose voluntarily prior to the 1989 change in SSAP 13 was effectively a decision to begin disclosing with the expectation that disclosure would continue in later years. Reporting of R&D expenditure on an *ad hoc* basis only in years when the directors believe it will be perceived as good news presents difficulties, at least if the expenditure figure appears in the audited accounts, as truth and fairness may require consistency from year to year. This can be put into a theoretical framework by saying that once R&D expenditure has been disclosed there is a political cost of changing back to non-disclosure. A look at the data shows that, in the vast majority of cases, once a series of R&D expenditure figures begins to appear for a particular company it continues to be reported in later years. The first hypothesis is, therefore, that the disclosure of R&D expenditure in the previous set of accounts would have a strong positive influence on disclosure in the current set of accounts.

Hypothesis 2

A second hypothesis relates to the increasing political pressure for disclosure to become mandatory. The steady political push for the mandatory disclosure of R&D expenditure leading eventually to the revision of SSAP 13 meant that the likelihood that disclosure would eventually be forced increased over the period up to 1989. Specific pieces of political news which could have influenced the probability of forced disclosure include the House of Lords Select Committee on Science and Technology firstly investigating the reporting of R&D and then indicating the need for more disclosure in annual reports; the concern of the accounting bodies following the report of the House of Lords Select Committee; the publication of ED 41 and the publication of SSAP 13 (revised). The second hypothesis is that the increasing probability of being forced to disclose caused more voluntary disclosures to be made either because disclosure was seen as virtuous or because companies preferred to begin disclosing R&D expenditure at a time of their choosing, possibly in an annual report containing good news which could offset any bad news contained in the R&D figure, rather than be forced to begin disclosing at a time set by an outside agency. A variable was needed to capture the increasing probability of disclosure being forced. If it is assumed that this probability increases linearly with time, then a variable which simply measures the number of years from the annual report to the 1989 change in SSAP 13 can be used. This variable decreases as the probability of forced disclosure increases and a negative coefficient was, therefore, expected.

Hypothesis 3

The third hypothesis is that the decision to disclose is influenced by industry norms. The disclosure decisions of all firms in an industry will help to shape the market's view of one particular firm's policy on disclosure by setting industry norms. For some industries the disclosure of R&D expenditure could become part of a lexicographic ordering of supplementary information (Fishman and Hagerty, 1990). Patenting behaviour also seems to be influenced by industry norms with some industries using patents to appropriate the benefits of R&D activity and other industries preferring to use secrecy as the method of appropriation. The evidence on disclosure in the period 1985 to 1990 suggests that an industry classification would not be particularly helpful in predicting disclosure (see Chapter 10 of this volume). However, the hypothesis was thought to be worth testing. An industry effect is also suggested in hypothesis 6. Industry dummy variables were used to test hypothesis 3.

Hypothesis 4

The attention of financial analysts may motivate companies to disclose more information of all types (Fishman and Hagerty, 1989). This follows from the theoretical models of information economics where non-disclosure is seen as indicating bad news so full disclosure is always made voluntarily. However, the hypothesis here has the added dimension that the market's power to influence disclosure in this way is stronger when the company knows that analysts are studying all the information it releases very closely or when companies are competing for the attention of traders. The fourth hypothesis is that disclosure is influenced by the company's visibility in the market with more disclosure expected of the more visible firms. Two proxies for visibility were used. Visibility was thought to increase with size, also trading volume was thought to indicate visibility and a dummy variable taking the value one for an alpha stock and zero otherwise was, therefore, used as the second proxy.

Hypothesis 5

The materiality of the amount of R&D expenditure may also influence the decision to disclose. Better quality information increases disclosure (Verrecchia, 1990). Quality of information is linked to its ability to help in the valuing of future cash flows. Information about R&D expenditure is likely to be more important in valuing future cash flows as materiality increases. Where R&D expenditure is not disclosed it is not possible to measure its materiality. The ratio R&D:sales for the first forced announcement was used as a measure of materiality for each company. This variable was therefore constant over time for each company.

Hypothesis 6

Disclosure may be influenced by the costs of producing the information. Where costs are significant they may outweigh any potential benefits of disclosure. Costs could include the costs of identifying R&D expenditure as distinct from other expenditure. If R&D activity is an integral part of the production process of the company, identification of R&D expenditure may be very difficult, possibly involving allocation of joint costs between production and R&D, such allocations always being subject to criticism on the grounds that the bases for allocation are arbitrary. The costs also include the costs of organizing or re-organizing the company's accounting systems to record separately the costs identified as R&D. If the R&D expenditure figure is to appear in the audited accounts then it will have to be audited and this will add to the audit costs. The sixth hypothesis is that disclosure is influenced by the costs of producing the R&D expenditure figure. These costs cannot be observed. It is likely that they will depend on the company's accounting system, so the larger the company the more sophisticated its accounting system is likely to be and thus the smaller the marginal costs involved in calculating R&D expenditure are likely to be. For larger companies the marginal cost of having R&D expenditure audited is also likely to be smaller. The size variable in the model is used to test this hypothesis in addition to testing the fourth hypothesis concerning visibility. The costs and visibility arguments both predict more disclosure to come from larger companies. Another factor determining the costs of production of the R&D expenditure figure is the separateness of R&D activity. This in turn is likely to be determined by industry. Indeed the industry norms suggested in the third hypothesis could themselves be partly influenced by preparation costs. Preparation costs are also more likely to discourage disclosure where they are large in relation to the size and materiality of the R&D expenditure likely to be reported. This means that the materiality variable used to test the fifth hypothesis will also pick up a third aspect of preparation costs. The expected sign of the coefficient on materiality is the same under this hypothesis with disclosure being discouraged less as materiality increases.

Hypothesis 7

This hypothesis concerns proprietary costs. Proprietary costs are associated with competition and potential competition. There are, however, conflicting theories of how current industrial structure could affect proprietary costs (see Verrecchia, 1983 and Newman and Sansing, 1993). The approach taken here is that R&D activity is associated with positioning. Its purpose is to give the company an advantage over others in the same industry. Companies in a relatively strong position are more likely to disclose their expenditure and so deter competitors. One test of the hypothesis that proprietary costs influence disclosure is to test whether companies whose R&D:sales ratio is large relative to the industry average are more likely to disclose R&D expenditure. Another threat which can be seen as a proprietary cost is the threat of take-over. Small firms engaging in R&D activity are often take-over targets for larger firms because they see a take-over as a method of purchasing the smaller firm's R&D effort cheaply. Smaller firms may therefore seek to hide the size of their R&D activity.

Hypothesis 8

A managerial motive for the disclosure of R&D is the prestige of R&D as an activity. Prestige could increase with the materiality of R&D expenditure or with the size of R&D activity relative to the industry average. The hypothesis is that if either of these measures increases disclosure will increase.

Hypothesis 9

One other hypothesis which was tested was that the first disclosure of R&D expenditure was made at a time when the company had some other good news to disclose. There are two reasons why companies would choose a 'good news year' to begin their R&D series. Firstly, managers may have believed that the R&D expenditure figure was itself good news but have been unsure how it would be received by the market and so coupled the first disclosure with good news. Secondly, if disclosure was viewed by managers as a bad thing but ultimately inevitable (this would apply mostly to the years 1987–89), companies were likely to begin disclosing voluntarily at a time when there was some compensating good news to balance the expected negative market reaction to the R&D expenditure. In order to test this hypothesis which relates only to first disclosures in a series, a 'first disclosure' dummy variable was first constructed and this was then multiplied by a 'good news' variable. One possible piece of good news is an increase in profits or profitability; the change in the profit/sales ratio was chosen as the 'good news' variable. This is a hypothesis which explicitly refers to management's expectations of the market's response to the release of R&D information and provides a link with the work in the following two chapters. Table 12.1 shows the various hypotheses and variables used in the model with the predicted signs for the coefficients. Because some of the variables are associated with more than one hypothesis the tests performed are of joint hypotheses.

3 THE CHOICE OF MODEL AND ITS ESTIMATION

The hypotheses set out above concern the decision to disclose. It has already been stated that the dependent variable in this model of

Table 12.1 Hypotheses and variables used in the logit model showing the predicted sign for the coefficients

	Hypothesis								
Variable	*1*	*2*	*3*	*4*	*5*	*6*	*7*	*8*	*9*
Lagged dependent	+ve								
Time to 1989		−ve							
Industry dummies			?			?			
Firm size				+ve		+ve	+ve		
Alpha stock				+ve					
Materiality of R&D					+ve	+ve		+ve	
Relative materiality of R&D							+ve	+ve	
Good news with first disclosure									+ve

accounting choice is a dichotomous variable taking the value one when R&D expenditure is disclosed, and zero otherwise. There are several models which can be applied to this type of data. Four models are commonly discussed: discriminant analysis; the linear probability model, the logit model and the probit model (see Amemiya, 1981 and Maddala, 1983, 1988, Chapter 8 and 1991). The logit model was chosen as the most appropriate technique, but the probit model was also estimated for comparison.

The logit and probit models are very similar; Cramer gives a short history of the development of the two models (Cramer, 1991: 39–42). They fit curves lying in the range nought to one and can both be written in the form

$$y_i^* = \beta_0 + \sum_{j=1}^{k} \beta_j x_{ij} + u_i \tag{1}$$

where y_i^* is not observed. It is commonly called a latent variable. What is observed is the dichotomous variable y_i which is defined by

$$y_i = \begin{cases} 1 \text{ if } y^* > 0 \\ 0 \text{ otherwise} \end{cases} \tag{2}$$

The notation used is taken from Maddala (1988: 272). The logit and probit models differ only in the specification of the error term u in (1). For the logit model the cumulative distribution of the error term is logistic, hence the model's name. For the probit model the errors follow a normal distribution. These two distributions are very close to each other except in the tails. There is, therefore, very little to choose between the two unless the data is concentrated in the tails. An extremely large sample is usually required to distinguish between them statistically. This applies to the dichotomous model; in multivariate models the logit and probit models differ more substantially (Amemiya, 1981: 1488). In order to compare the results of the two models the logit estimates should be multiplied by 0.625 (Maddala, 1988: 273).

The main arguments in favour of the logit and probit models are, firstly, they do not require the explanatory variables to be normally distributed. Stone and Rasp (1991) found logit test statistics to be biased for non-normal explanatory variables in small samples but concluded that even for samples as small as 50, logit rather than OLS may be the preferable model for accounting choice studies. The sample for this study (1,774 observations) is not small. Secondly, they do not produce estimated values for probabilities outside the range 0 to 1 (a problem with the linear regression model, see Cramer, 1991: 7).

W.H. Greene's LIMDEP program was used for the estimation of the models. A choice of algorithms is available for computing maximum likelihood estimates in this program. Newton's method was used as this is recommended for large samples and convergence was not found to be a problem in any of the models estimated. LIMDEP was developed initially as an easy to use Tobit estimator and is named after LIMited DEPendent variable models. This made it an ideal program for the estimation of the decision to disclose model.

4 DATA USED

Data was gathered from Datastream where R&D expenditure is recorded, if reported, from 1980 onwards. The population of all annual reports can be divided into three groups: those of companies which perform no R&D; those of companies performing R&D but not reporting their R&D expenditure; and those of companies performing R&D and reporting R&D expenditure. In order to model the decision to disclose it was important to ensure that companies in the first group (non-performers) were excluded from the sample. From 1989 onwards SSAP 13 required disclosure of R&D expenditure. The number of companies reporting R&D expenditure showed a large increase at that time. It has been assumed in this study that companies reporting R&D expenditure post-1989 were performing R&D in any accounting periods appearing in Datastream in the period 1980 to 1989 whether they reported it or not. This was one way of identifying non-disclosers. It is acknowledged that an assumption is required and that companies not complying with SSAP 13 (revised) are excluded from the sample. However, the problem of non-performers and non-disclosers has been set out and the assumption used here is felt to be reasonable as two characteristics of R&D activity are that the barriers to entry are significant and that it tends to be long term. As companies can be identified as performing R&D only if they were in existence after 1989, there could be some attrition bias in the sample. It is difficult to estimate the extent of such a bias.

This model uses pooled time-series and cross-section data. Companies reporting R&D post-1989 and having accounting data available on Datastream were first identified. A data set including the relevant accounting variables for all accounting periods recorded by Datastream for those companies was then established. The model covers only the period 1980 to 1989 as R&D expenditure was not recorded by Datastream before 1980 and post-1989 disclosure was no longer voluntary. Annual reports covering accounting periods ending in 1989 were included only where the accounting period commenced before January 1989 and, therefore, the report was not subject to the revised disclosure rules of SSAP 13 which were implemented for accounting periods commencing on or after 1 January 1989. This ensured that voluntary disclosures dated 1989 were included and 1989 disclosures forced by the revision of SSAP 13 excluded. Having established a sample of companies which performed R&D, but did not always report R&D expenditure, the dependent variable was set to one for observations where R&D expenditure was reported and zero in other cases.

The independent variables requiring the use of company accounts data were constructed from Datastream accounting variables. Industry dummy variables were based on the industrial classification reported in the R&D scoreboard and their numbering follows the numbering of the industries in the scoreboard. This classification was used because it resulted in a reasonably small number of dummy variables whilst preserving an adequate level of disaggregation. Table 12.2 gives the definitions of the independent variables together with their means and standard deviations.

Table 12.2 Independent variables: definition and descriptive statistics

Variable	*Definition*	*Mean*	*Standard deviation*
D1	Dummy for aerospace industry	0.0248	0.1555
D2	Dummy for automotive industry	0.0462	0.2100
D3	Dummy for chemicals industry	0.0653	0.2472
D4	Dummy for conglomerates	0.0377	0.1906
D5	Dummy for consumer products industry	0.0541	0.2263
D6	Dummy for electrical and electronics industry	0.1747	0.3798
D9	Dummy for food industry	0.0507	0.2195
D11	Dummy for general manufacturing	0.2621	0.4399
D12	Dummy for health care industry	0.0535	0.2251
D13	Dummy for housing and construction industry	0.0716	0.2560
D14	Dummy for leisure industry	0.0445	0.2063
D15	Dummy for metals and mining industry	0.0315	0.1748
R&D Lag	The lagged dependent variable	0.1640	0.3704
Time to 1989	Time from the year of disclosure to 1989 measured in years	3.6849	2.3738
Size	Measured as capital employed	542,780	193,080
ALPHA	Dummy taking the value 1 for an alpha stock and zero otherwise	0.2175	0.4127
RDS	Materiality of R&D expenditure *R&D:S*ales ratio for the first forced announcement by each company	0.0190	0.0263
EREL	Materiality of R&D *E*xpenditure *REL*ative to industry (RDS/industry average R&D:sales ratio)	0.0072	0.1289
FDP	Dummy variable taking the value 1 for *F*irst *D*isclosures and zero otherwise multiplied by the change in the *P*rofit:sales ratio	0.0004	0.0125

Table 12.3 Cross-correlation coefficients for the independent variables

	R&D Lag	*Time to 1989*	*Size*	*ALPHA*	*RDS*	*EREL*	*FDP*
R&D Lag	1.000						
Time to 1989	−0.216	1.000					
Size	0.301	−0.032	1.000				
ALPHA	0.234	0.053	0.464	1.000			
RDS	0.319	−0.125	0.0004	0.060	1.000		
EREL	0.050	0.297	0.009	−0.011	0.259	1.000	
FDP	0.132	−0.602	0.026	−0.021	0.053	−0.094	1.000

Table 12.3 shows the cross-correlation coefficients for the independent variables excluding the industry dummies. Most of the correlation coefficients are close to zero. Size and ALPHA are relatively highly correlated with a coefficient of 0.464. As they are included as alternative measures of visibility, this result was expected. The collinearity was not sufficient to prevent convergence and both variables were retained in the model. The result that time to 1989 and EREL are positively correlated is in line with the general proposition that a high R&D:sales ratio relative to the company's industry encourages early disclosure. A pattern of companies with high relative materiality beginning to disclose early and continuing to do so with other companies beginning to disclose later would produce this positive correlation. FDP and Time to 1989 show the highest degree of correlation (−0.602). FDP takes the value zero except when the disclosure is the first one for the particular company. For any one company a plot of FDP against Time to 1989 consists of a set of observations which are all on the horizontal axis except the one for the year of first disclosure. With the vast majority of points for the whole sample therefore lying on the axis the high degree of correlation would be expected. Again this correlation did not prevent convergence and the two variables were retained.

5 RESULTS

Table 12.4 shows the results of a logit model of the decision to disclose R&D expenditure. Industry classifications included were 1 aerospace, 2 automotive, 3 chemicals, 4 conglomerates, 5 consumer products, 6 electrical and electronics, 9 food, 11 general manufacturing, 12 health care, 13 housing and construction, 14 leisure and 15 metals and mining. The industry group omitted was the one representing all other classifications. The individual coefficients on the industry dummies which have been included were not significantly different from zero. However, as the individual results for these dummies depended on which industry was omitted in the creation of the dummy variables, the test was of the joint

Table 12.4 Logit model of the decision to disclose

Variable	*Coefficient*	*t-statistic*
Constant	−2.7009	−6.310***
D1	−0.0507	−0.710
D2	0.7063	−1.204
D3	0.0931	0.162
D4	−0.8934	−1.126
D5	−1.3013	−1.629
D6	−0.3405	−0.681
D9	−0.2225	−0.387
D11	−0.0969	−0.221
D12	−0.9214	−1.282
D13	−0.3494	−0.578
D14	−0.4107	−0.656
D15	−0.5329	−0.632
R&D Lag	5.2167	18.621***
Time to 1989	−0.1914	−3.424***
Size	0.2217E-06	2.958***
ALPHA	0.6296	1.983**
RDS	11.134	2.164**
EREL	16.704	1.751
FDP	33.598	3.875***

Notes: Variables are defined in Table 12.2 above
Number of observations = 1,774
Number of companies = 259
***, ** and * indicate significance at the 1 per cent, 5 per cent and 10 per cent levels respectively

significance of all the dummies and the intercept term. A Wald test of the joint significance of the industry variables produced a negative result; they were not jointly significant even at the 10 per cent level of significance.

R&D lag is the variable used to test the first hypothesis. It is the lagged value of the dependent variable, but as the sample is a pooling of cross-section and time-series data the use of this variable involves the loss of the first observation for each company. This is almost always the loss of an observation where R&D is not disclosed. The coefficient is significantly positive as predicted by hypothesis 1. Time to 1989 is the variable used to test the second hypothesis and measures time in years, its mean value being 4.3. The coefficient is significantly negative as predicted by hypothesis 2. Size measured in terms of capital employed and the coefficient is significantly positive. This supports hypotheses 4, 6 and 7 concerning visibility, preparation costs and the threat of take-over. Alpha is a dummy variable indicating an alpha-rated stock, its coefficient is significantly positive at the 5 per cent level of significance. This gives further support to hypothesis 4. RDS is the R&D:sales ratio for the first forced announcement made by the company. It therefore takes the same value for all observations for a particular company but varies across companies. The coefficient is significantly positive at the 5 per cent significance level. This is in line with hypotheses 5, 6 and 8 concerning the quality of information, preparation costs and prestige respectively. EREL is the materiality of R&D expenditure for the company as measured by RDS divided by the industry average R&D:sales ratio. The coefficient is only significantly different from zero at the 10 per cent level but is positive as expected under hypothesis 7. FDP is the variable created to test hypothesis 9 that there is a timing effect in the first disclosure of R&D. It is an interactive dummy variable taking the value one when the disclosure is the first and zero otherwise, multiplied by a 'good news' variable measured as the change in the profit:sales ratio from the previous period. The coefficient is significantly positive at the 1 per cent level of significance which supports the hypothesis that first disclosures are influenced by the availability of other good news.

Table 12.5 shows the actual and predicted outcomes for the logit model reported in Table 12.4. The overall predictive accuracy of the model is 95 per cent and its accuracy in predicting disclosure is 80 per cent. Although termed *predictive* accuracy this amounts to a measure of the goodness of fit of the model. The probit model for the same set of variables was also estimated and the results are shown in Table 12.6. The logit coefficient multiplied by 0.625 is shown for comparative purposes. The predictive accuracy of the probit model is slightly lower than that of the logit model, the overall accuracy being again 95 per cent but the accuracy in predicting disclosure falling to 78 per cent. The fall in predictive accuracy when considering the prediction of disclosure is due to the unbalanced nature of the sample with 347 disclosures and 1,427 non-disclosures. McFadden's R^2 (see McFadden, 1974 and Maddala, 1988: 279) is 0.626 for the logit model and 0.619 for the probit model, again indicating a slightly better fit for the logit model.

The model was tested for stability in three ways, by creating a sub-sample, by looking at the results over time and by looking for differences in predictive accuracy attributable to the size of the company. The last test amounts to a simple test for heteroscedasticity, more sophisticated

Table 12.5 Frequencies of actual and predicted outcomes

Actual	*Predicted*		*Total*
	0	1	
0	1407	20	1427
1	69	278	347
Total	1476	298	1774

Table 12.6 Probit model of the decision to disclose

Variable	*Coefficient*	*t-statistic*	*Logit coefficient* × *0.625 for comparison*
Constant	−1.460	−7.204***	−1.688
D1	−0.0787	−0.216	−0.0317
D2	0.3159	−1.110	0.4415
D3	0.0320	0.120	0.0582
D4	−4.3333	−1.205	−0.5584
D5	−0.5316	−1.510	−0.8133
D6	−1.5887	−0.674	−0.2128
D9	−1.2290	−0.438	−0.1391
D11	−0.0571	−0.274	−0.0691
D12	−0.4813	−1.428	−0.5759
D13	−0.1903	−0.663	−0.2184
D14	−0.1622	−0.552	−0.2567
D15	−0.2160	−0.590	−0.3331
R&D Lag	2.8819	21.154***	3.2604
Time to 1989	−0.1005	−3.845***	−0.1196
Size	0.1260E-06	2.941***	0.1385E-06
RDS	5.7508	2.355**	6.9588
EREL	8.007	1.689*	10.44
ALPHA	0.2763	1.801*	0.3935
FDP	6.493	3.098***	20.999

Notes: Variables are defined in Table 12.2 above
Number of observations = 1,774
Number of companies = 259
***, ** and * indicate significance at the 1 per cent, 5 per cent and 10 per cent levels respectively

tests not being available using LIMDEP for panels of more than five years of data.

Table 12.7 shows the result of grouping the sample by company size. The predictive accuracy does not appear to be related to the size of the company. Accuracy in predicting disclosure is greater for the largest group of companies, but overall accuracy falls for this same group. There is no evidence of any problem of heteroscedasticity.

Table 12.8 shows the predictive accuracy of the model over time. Whilst it is clear that the model performs better in some years than others there is no obvious pattern in this performance. 1989 is the year of lowest overall accuracy which could be due to some disclosures being technically voluntary as judged by the implementation date for the revised version of SSAP 13 but directly caused by the publication of the SSAP in its revised form. The political pressure to disclose may not have been linear as assumed by the variable Time to 1989 but could have increased significantly when the revised SSAP was published.

A hold-out sample was also used to test the stability of the model. This was constructed as a stratified sample so that its distribution by size of

Table 12.7 Size and predictive accuracy

Size range (quartiles)	*Overall accuracy* %	*Predicting disclosure* %
Q1	0.95	0.78
Q2	0.95	0.74
Q3	0.97	0.78
Q4	0.92	0.84

Table 12.8 Predictive accuracy over time

Year	*Overall accuracy* %	*Predicting disclosure* %
1981	0.99	0.86
1982	0.97	0.69
1983	0.94	0.62
1984	0.95	0.76
1985	0.97	0.93
1986	0.98	0.95
1987	0.95	0.84
1988	0.94	0.84
1989	0.85	0.65

company and over time was close to that of the full set of observations. The distribution of observations over time is shown in Table 12.9 for both the estimation sample and the hold-out sample. The overall sample was based on companies known to be performing R&D in 1989. Some of those companies entered Datastream's records after 1980, usually by becoming a listed company after that date. This accounts for the increasing numbers of observations up to 1988. The fall in the number of observations for 1989 is due to the implementation date for SSAP 13 (revised) which effectively meant that there was no decision to disclose for accounts dated 31 December 1989 as at that point disclosure became mandatory, other 1989 accounts were, however, included in the sample.

It can be seen from Table 12.9 that the hold-out sample fairly reflected the estimation sample over time and this was also the case in terms of company size. The results for the hold-out sample were an overall predictive accuracy of 93 per cent which compares with 95 per cent for the estimation sample and a predictive accuracy for disclosure of 76 per cent compared with 80 per cent for the estimation sample.

One other aspect of the model was tested. The use of the lagged dependent variable is obviously very important in the model. Its coefficient has a t-statistic of 18.621 which is higher than that of any of the other variables. If one variable appears to be predominant, the additional contribution of the other variables may be in question. The other

Table 12.9 Distribution of observations by time

Year	*Estimation sample* *number*	%	*Hold-out sample* *number*	%
1981	92	5.2	9	5.1
1982	187	10.5	19	10.7
1983	200	11.3	20	11.2
1984	206	11.6	21	11.8
1985	216	12.2	21	11.8
1986	222	12.5	23	12.9
1987	238	13.4	23	12.9
1988	255	14.3	26	14.6
1989	158	9.0	16	9.0
Total	1,774	100	178	100

variables, excluding the industry dummies, all have coefficients which are significantly different from zero at least at the 10 per cent level, and three of the other variables (Time to 1989, size and FDP) have coefficients which, like RDL, are significant at the 1 per cent level. These t-statistics would seem to both justify the inclusion of the other variables and testify to their contribution to the model. Two other ways of showing their value would be to exclude them from the model and then compare the goodness of fit and predictive accuracy of a model using only the lagged dependent variable and the full model estimated above. When this was done the measure of goodness of fit (McFadden's R^2) fell from 0.626 to 0.561. The overall predictive accuracy was affected very little, falling from 95 per cent to 93 per cent, but the accuracy in predicting disclosure fell more significantly from 80 per cent to 73 per cent. This shows that the other variables in the model do have a significant contribution to make and that their contribution is particularly valuable in predicting more of the instances of disclosure.

6 SUMMARY AND CONCLUSION

The logit model of the decision to disclose R&D expenditure estimated in this chapter shows good predictive accuracy and supports most of the nine hypotheses put forward. The first hypothesis was that for reasons of consistency in presentation of accounts the lagged dependent variable would have a strong influence on the decision to disclose R&D expenditure for any particular period. This hypothesis was very strongly supported by the highly significant coefficient on the lagged dependent variable when the model was estimated.

The second hypothesis was that the decision to begin disclosing R&D voluntarily was encouraged by the increasing probability that disclosure would become mandatory. The increasing political pressure for mandatory disclosure was captured by the variable Time to 1989 which simply measured the number of years between the observed set of accounts and the year of implementation of SSAP 13 (revised). The second hypothesis was strongly supported by a highly significant and negative coefficient on this variable.

The third hypothesis was that firms in particular industries would disclose R&D more readily than firms in other industries. This hypothesis was based on two ideas, one being that whole industries could have particular attitudes to the disclosure of R&D which could parallel their patenting behaviour and so set industry norms for disclosure. The other idea was that if information was ordered lexicographically the position of R&D in that ordering could be similar for firms in the same industry but differ between industries. These ideas seemed plausible, but when industry dummy variables were included in the model they showed no significance individually and a Wald test revealed that they were not jointly significant even at the 10 per cent level of significance.

The fourth hypothesis was that companies competing for the attention of analysts would disclose more information generally and R&D expenditure would, therefore, be more likely to enter the list of items to be disclosed by these companies. Under this hypothesis disclosure is associated with visibility. Two variables were used to capture a company's visibility, size and a dummy set to one for alpha rated shares and zero otherwise. The size variable appears in two other hypotheses. The alpha dummy is used only to test this hypothesis. The result for the alpha dummy variable was that the coefficient was significantly different from zero at the 5 per cent level of significance. This is good evidence that visibility in the market influences disclosure. The size variable was even more highly significant but this result supports not only the visibility hypothesis but also hypotheses six and seven below. Overall the evidence in favour of a visibility effect seems strong.

The fifth hypothesis was that better quality information promotes disclosure. Materiality was used as a proxy for quality. The coefficient on the materiality variable was significantly different from zero at the 5 per cent level of significance. However, as a positive relationship between materiality and disclosure is also predicted by hypotheses 6 and 8 this is again a joint test.

The sixth hypothesis concerned the costs of preparing and auditing the R&D expenditure figure. As costs increase disclosure was hypothesized to be discouraged. Preparation costs were thought to decrease with size of the company and the materiality of the R&D figure and possibly to be associated with the company's industry group. Results for size and materiality support this hypothesis but the industry dummies do not.

The seventh hypothesis concerned the proprietary costs of disclosure. These were thought to be important in the decision to disclose R&D

because of the special characteristics of the information being disclosed, in particular its commercial sensitivity. It was argued that proprietary costs were likely to be associated with a company's position in its industry and so a variable measuring the materiality of the company's R&D expenditure relative to that of its industry was used to test this hypothesis (EREL). The coefficient on EREL was significant at the 10 per cent level. Size was also used to test this hypothesis on the basis that small firms were more likely to become take-over targets if they disclosed their R&D expenditure. The evidence of the size variable taken together with the positioning variable support this hypothesis.

The eighth hypothesis was the only one based on managerial motives rather than a value-maximizing approach. It was that managers would want to report R&D activity as a matter of prestige and prestige would be related to either the materiality of R&D expenditure or its materiality relative to other companies in the same industry. Both these variables are associated with other hypotheses and have significant coefficients with the expected sign to support this and the other suggested hypotheses.

The final hypothesis was that the first disclosure of R&D would be subject to much uncertainty about the market's reaction to it. Managers would, therefore, try to couple the first disclosure with good news elsewhere in the accounts. A 'good news' variable was therefore constructed and used with an interactive dummy variable set at one for first disclosures and zero otherwise. The coefficient on this variable was significantly different from zero at the 1 per cent level of significance. This is an important result of the model and the evidence for this hypothesis seems unequivocal as the variable used here tests only this hypothesis.

In conclusion, this chapter has presented a logit model of decision to disclose R&D expenditure which performed well in terms of predictive ability, goodness of fit, stability and lack of problems of heteroscedasticity. It also supported eight of the nine hypotheses put forward although this must be qualified to some extent by the fact that several of the t-tests are of joint hypotheses. The major results were that proprietary costs influenced the decision to disclose and that the association of the first disclosure with other 'good news' was shown to be strong.

REFERENCES

Amemiya, T. (1981), 'Qualitative Response Models: A Survey', *Journal of Economic Literature*, 19, 1483–1536.

Cramer, J.S. (1991), *The Logit Model: An Introduction for Economists*, (Edward Arnold).

Darrough, M.N. and N.M. Stoughton (1990), 'Financial Disclosure Policy in an Entry Game', *Journal of Accounting and Economics*, 12, 219–243.

Fishman, M.J. and K.M. Hagerty (1989), 'Disclosure Decisions by Firms and the Competition for Price Efficiency', *Journal of Finance*, 44, (3), 633–646.
Fishman, M.J. and K.M. Hagerty (1990), 'The optimal amount of discretion to allow in disclosure', *Quarterly Journal of Economics*, 105, 427–444.
Gray, R.H. (1985) *Accounting for R&D: A Review of Experiences with SSAP 13*, Research Board of the Institute of Chartered Accountants in England and Wales Report.
Hope, A.J.B. and R.H. Gray (1982), 'Power and Policy Making: The development of an R&D Standard', *Journal of Business Finance and Accounting*, 9, (4), 531–558.
House of Lords Select Committee on Science and Technology, First Report (Civil Research and Development), 1986.
McFadden, D. (1974), 'The Measurement of Urban Travel Demand', *Journal of Public Economics*, 303–328.
Maddala, G.S. (1983), *Limited-Dependent and Qualitative Variables in Econometrics*, (Cambridge University Press).
Maddala, G.S. (1988), *Introduction to Econometrics*, (Macmillan).
Maddala, G.S. (1991), 'A Perspective on the Use of Limited-Dependent and Qualitative Variables Models in Accounting Research', *The Accounting Review*, 66, (4), 788–807.
Manne, H.C. (1965), 'Mergers and the Market for Corporate Control', *Journal of Political Economy*, 73, 110–120.
Newman, P. and R. Sansing (1993), 'Disclosure Policies with Multiple Users', *Journal of Accounting Research*, 31, (1), 92–112.
Nixon, B. (1991), *Accounting for Research and Development: The Need for a New Perception*, Report for the Board of Chartered Accountants in Business.
Stone, M. and J. Rasp (1991), 'Trade-offs in the Choice Between Logit and OLS for Accounting Choice Studies', *The Accounting Review*, 66, (1), 170–187.
Verrecchia, R.E. (1983), 'Discretionary Disclosure', *Journal of Accounting and Economics*, 5, 179–194.
Verrecchia, R.E. (1990), 'Information Quality and Discretionary Disclosure', *Journal of Accounting and Economics*, 12, 365–380.

13

THE IMPACT OF R&D KNOWLEDGE ACCUMULATION ON WAGES

Evidence from European Corporations

Stephen Machin and John Van Reenen

1 INTRODUCTION

The recent explosion of work on the changes in the structure of wages in various countries has emphasized the potential role for changes in technology (however defined) to shape the evolution of wages.[1] Many authors have argued that because the bulk of the observed change in the structure of wages and employment appear to have occurred within industries or within various demographic groups that this rules out other hypotheses that could predict changes in labour market structure (e.g. the within-industry finding suggests that the rise in international competition, which is essentially an across-industry phenomenon, is relatively unimportant).[2]

The appropriate interpretation of these findings, and any associated policy implications, are severely limited by a number of features of the reported results. Firstly, 'technology' is often merely taken to be the unexplained residual component that cannot be picked up by various observables (see, for example, Bound and Johnson (1992), who treat technical change as the residual from a production function). Secondly, even where more concrete measures are available they are often poorly measured or suffer from problems of unrepresentativeness. Thirdly, whilst some have tried to draw international comparisons (e.g. Freeman and Katz, 1994) it is often the case that comparisons may be marred by data differences and concepts across countries.

In this chapter we attempt to provide a more systematic investigation of the relationship between wages and technology by using firm-level data across four European countries. To model technology effects, we use an observable firm-level indicator that has been commonly used in industry-level work, research and development expenditure (R&D), and we try to circumvent the well-known problems of disclosure associated with this variable by exploiting cross-country differences in accounting standards related to disclosure of R&D information in company accounts.

The results that we report suggest that both tangible and intangible capital tend to have a positive and significant effect in raising average wages. The selection equation is successful in relating changes in accounting regimes to disclosure probabilities. Selectivity bias is a problem, but its main effect is in correcting the downward bias on physical capital rather than R&D intensity. R&D appears to have the strongest effect on firm-level real wages in Germany and the weakest effect in French corporations.

The structure of the remainder of the chapter is as follows. In the next section we consider what has happened to wages and R&D in the countries that we study (the United Kingdom, France, Germany and Italy) and draw comparisons with a larger number of countries. We also discuss in some detail the disclosure procedures for reporting R&D in company accounts in the four countries on which we base our micro-economic analysis. In Section 3 the modelling procedure is discussed; emphasis is placed on the way in which non-disclosure of R&D information can be corrected for in the equations that we intend to estimate. Some descriptive material on the data is also given. Section 4 presents a set of firm-level wage equations where wages are modelled as a function of R&D intensity and considers international differences in the estimated wage–technology relation. Section 5 offers some concluding remarks.

2 WAGES, R&D AND THE DISCLOSURE OF R&D DATA ACROSS COUNTRIES

Table 13.1 gives aggregate statistics for wages and R&D in our four countries. R&D intensity has been rising across all countries, although there are clear differences. Italy has the lowest R&D per worker and

Table 13.1 R&D per employee and average wages by country

	France	*Germany*	*Italy*	*UK*
Real R&D per employee in manufacturing				
1970	0.78	0.94	0.31	0.52
1980	1.24	1.62	0.49	1.18
1990	2.60	2.77	1.42(1989)	2.06
Average real hourly compensation in manufacturing (1970 = 1)				
1970	1	1	1	1
1980	1.610	1.595	1.608	1.472
1990	1.887	2.052	1.932	1.763

Notes: 1 R&D source: OECD STAN/ANBERD Database
2 Wages source: Table 1413, *Statistical Abstract of the United States*, 1993

Germany the highest. In terms of wages all four countries experienced average real wage growth in the 1970s and 1980s, although it is evident that real hourly compensation grew less strongly in the UK than in the other three countries. The highest level of real wage growth occurred in the former West Germany, especially in the 1980s.

Any investigation of the impacts of R&D spending in European corporations is faced by an immediate problem. Accounting regimes differ widely in their requirements on what information companies have to give in the accounts regarding R&D spending. This is readily seen from the accounts: many firms have given no information whatsoever regarding their R&D spending.

Figure 13.1 plots the disclosure rates for each of countries in the dataset between 1983 and 1990. Because the reasons for the failure to disclose may be correlated with some of the variables in our wage equations it is necessary to correct for this potential selectivity bias. This then leads to the question of what can identify the selectivity equation from the wage equation, as most of the candidate instruments could legitimately be thought of as being in both equations.[3] Our proposal is to use changes in the accounting practices across different countries over time as identifying instruments. It is therefore necessary to give a brief description of the disclosure requirements and how they vary across and within countries.

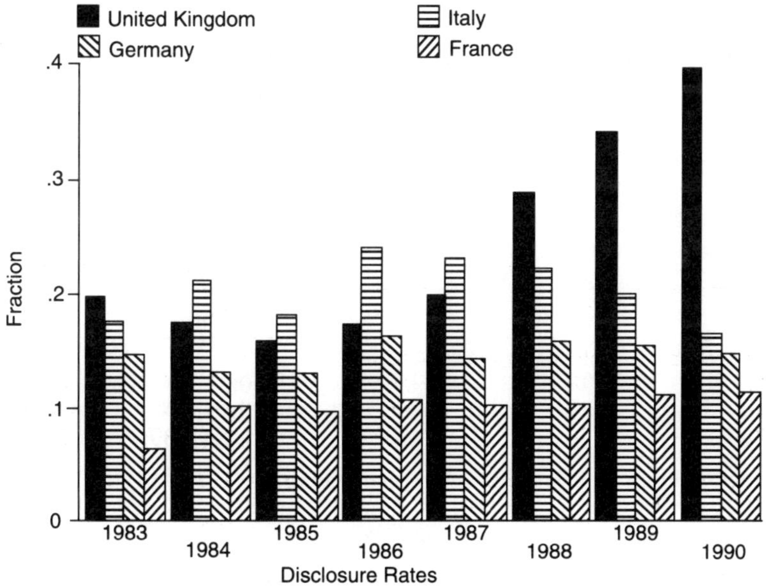

Figure 13.1 Disclosure rates across countries
Source: Standard and Poor

There has been a general pressure from the European Community through the 1980s to harmonize accounting practices in general and improve R&D disclosure. This has been embodied primarily in the Fourth EC Directive which prescribes principles for European accounting and layouts for the balance sheet and profit and loss sheet. This Directive has been adopted by the countries in our dataset, but at different speeds and with national differences over the coverage and form of R&D disclosure. This has been spurred by fears that Europe's declining international competitiveness may be linked with its relatively poor technological position. Although European countries have been generally increasing their R&D intensities, they have been massively outstripped by Japan and during the 1980s, by the USA.

Some of the most dramatic changes in R&D accounting practices have occurred in the UK. When setting up their accounts, companies conventionally follow the Statement of Standard Accounting Practices (SSAP). SSAP 13 deals with R&D and was heavily revised in January 1989 to make disclosure of R&D spending mandatory for all 'large' companies. To qualify as large a company had to meet two of the following three criteria: turnover exceeds £80m, average numbers employees exceeds 2,500 and balance sheet total exceeds £39m. The original version of SSAP 13 (1977) required the disclosure only of R&D which had been capitalized and carried forward. In 1985 this was tightened in a very minor way by the Companies Act (1985) requiring an indication of the companies' activity in R&D in the directors' report. Political pressure from the House of Lords Select Committee on Science and Technology resulted in the publication of Executive Draft 41 (ED 41) in June 1987 recommending mandatory disclosure. This was eventually made law in 1989.[4] The UK regime is now on a par with the FAS documents in the USA which have required full R&D disclosure since 1974, and this is reflected in the proportion of firms disclosing positive R&D (about 40 per cent in our dataset in both countries).

In Germany accounting rules are mainly incorporated in the third book of the Commercial Code. In 1985 three EC Directives were incorporated into German law completely changing the regulatory system. After 1987 large corporations were required to make a financial statement regarding R&D,[5] and there were lesser requirements on smaller firms. The size criteria were two of the three following (for two consecutive years): sales greater than DM32m, employees greater than 250 and balance sheet total in excess of DM15.5m. Unfortunately, the requirement for full disclosure extends only to the supervisory board and major creditors and does not force firms to give information to all parties.

In Italy R&D expenditures are not defined by the civil code (like Germany) or the accounting standards issued by the representative body of the accounting profession (like the UK). However, in 1986, the Decree of the President of the Republic (12.2.86, article 74) modified disclosure practices to make corporations give information on R&D activities and expenses in the directors' report.

In France generally accepted accounting principles are derived from the General Accounting Plan based on the Fourth EC Directive. This was effective from the beginning of 1983. Nevertheless France has probably the weakest disclosure requirements of all four countries.

In short, there has been considerable variation within the general trend to greater openness in R&D reporting across time and countries. It is extremely important to notice that there have been changes in disclosure requirements that have varied across countries and within countries, the latter mainly operating through the fact that disclosure criteria were made tighter for (relatively) larger corporations. These changes in accounting practices can be used as instruments in the selectivity corrections for possible bias in the estimated wage–R&D elasticities reported below.

3 MODELLING PROCEDURE AND DATA DESCRIPTION

Modelling procedure

The theoretical framework we adopt is quite standard (e.g. Nickell and Wadhwani, 1990). Assume that average wages in a firm are determined by a bargain between managers and insider workers such that the wage is a weighted average of the outside alternative wage, W^A, and output per worker. The importance of this latter, firm-specific term, is sometimes regarded as a measure of 'insider power'. More formally write the natural log of average wages, lnW, as

$$lnW = \theta lnW^A + (1 - \theta)\ ln\ (Q/L) \tag{1}$$

where the constant returns to scale production function is of the form $Q = AL^{\alpha}K^{\beta}R^{\gamma}$ and A = neutral technical change, L = labour, K = physical capital, R = R&D expenditures. Substituting for Q gives the following simple wage equation

$$w = \theta w^A + (1 - \theta)\ a + (1 - \theta)\ \beta\ (k - l) + (1 - \theta)\ \gamma\ (r - l) \tag{2}$$

where lower-case letters denote natural logarithms (i.e. x = lnX).

The modelling procedure we adopt is the well-known two-step estimator of Heckman (1979). We first estimate a probit for whether or not a corporation disclosed its R&D expenditure. The Mills ratio calculated from these probits is then used as an extra regressor in the wage equation. Since we have a panel with potential firm-specific effects we also attempt to model this unobserved heterogeneity by using random and fixed effects techniques. More formally, write the wage and disclosure equations as follows (the vector of xs includes the factors in equation (2)).

$$w_{it} = \delta' x_{i,t-1} + \varepsilon_{it} \tag{3}$$

$$d_{i,t-1} = \psi' z_{i,t-1} + u_{i,t-1} \tag{4}$$

where the (unobserved) index of disclosure is related to our binary observed indicator in the following manner

$$\begin{aligned} disc_{i,t-1} &= 1 \text{ if } d_{i,t-1} \geq 0 \\ &= 0 \text{ otherwise} \end{aligned} \tag{5}$$

The selectivity corrected wage equation then becomes:

$$\begin{aligned} E[w_{it} \mid x_{i,t-1} \text{ if } disc_{i,t-1} = 1] &= \delta' x_{i,t-1} + \sigma\lambda_{i,t-1} \\ \text{where } \lambda_{i,t-1} &= \frac{\phi\,(\psi' z_{i,t-1})}{\Phi\,(\psi' z_{i,t-1})} \end{aligned} \tag{6}$$

In (6) λ is the inverse Mills ratio from the probit model of disclosure (ϕ and Φ are respectively the standard normal density and distribution functions). There is clearly an important question of what identifies the disclosure equation which generates the Mills ratio from the wage equation (i.e. what variables enter the z vector that do not enter the x vector). Although one can formally achieve identification through the inherent non-linearity underpinning the different error structures in (3) and (4), identifying from functional form in this way is not a robust procedure and lacks any economic foundation. As detailed above we will use variation in the accounting regulations which affect the costs of failing to disclose as additional variables in (4). These are country- and time-specific and display some within-country variance as they affect different firms in different ways (generally large firms are more affected than smaller firms). There is no obvious reason why such accounting changes should affect wage determination so they are legitimately excluded from equation (3).

A further econometric issue is the presence of unobserved firm-specific effects. If the effects are uncorrelated with the right-hand-side variables then OLS will be unbiased and efficient. If the effects are correlated, but are random across firms then a random effects model is more efficient. If there is a fixed firm-specific intercept then a random effects model will be inconsistent, so we include an extra dummy variable for every firm to capture this effect ('within-groups' estimator).[6]

As a final econometric remark, to capture country-specific effects a full set of country dummy variables were included. To capture common macro-economic shocks on wages a full set of time dummies are also included. In some specifications a set of one-digit industry dummy variables is also included. These variables should also proxy the alternative wage faced by workers.

Data description

The data that we use is drawn from Standard and Poor's Global Vantage dataset. This is an on-line facility with accounting variables for firms listed on the Stock Exchange and other large private firms. Information was extracted on employment, net assets, staff costs, sales, R&D expenditures and industry, keeping only firms who reported information on these key variables for at least four years. After removing outliers we were left with information on 385 firms, over 2,619 observations. The combined employment of these firms was, in 1990, in excess of 7.2m. The wage is calculated as the ratio of staff costs to employment. All nominal figures were converted into US dollars using the exchange rate prevailing in the last month of the accounting year. The dollar figure was then deflated by the US consumer price index.

Sample characteristics for the unbalanced and balanced panel are in Table 13.2. Note that these are predominantly large and multinational firms who are the key players in privately funded European R&D. Figure 13.2 shows average wages over time in these corporations. Average wages are generally lower in UK firms and higher in German firms, but there has been a general upward movement throughout the sample period, especially amongst R&D disclosers (Figure 13.3). Similarly, as Figure 13.4 shows, average R&D per worker has risen across all four countries, which is consistent with the aggregate figures given above in Table 13.1.

Table 13.2 Sample characteristics

	Number of firms	*Rate of disclosure of R&D*	*Ln (real wage) in $*	*Ln (real wage) in $ if disclose R&D*	*R&D per employee ($1000 per employee)*
France: All	121	.103	2.776	2.660	2.698
France: Balanced	55	.100	2.730	2.649	3.851
Germany: All	123	.146	2.850	2.815	3.563
Germany: Balanced	77	.153	2.845	2.763	3.263
Italy: All	40	.206	2.853	2.835	3.436
Italy: Balanced	16	.281	2.758	2.793	2.152
UK: All	101	.241	2.320	2.385	1.974
UK: Balanced	63	.278	2.292	2.391	2.388
All Companies	385	.160	2.676	2.617	2.748
All Companies: Balanced	211	.186	2.643	2.591	2.845

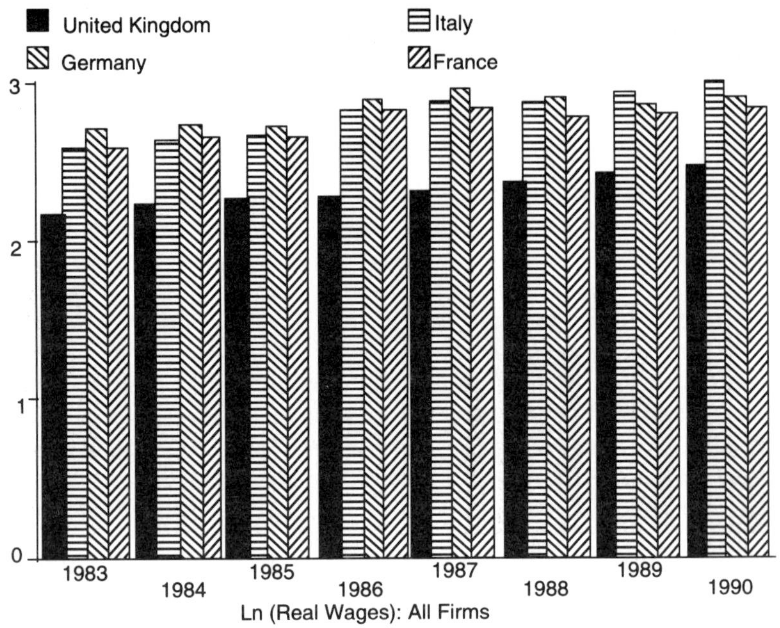

Figure 13.2 Average real wages: all firms

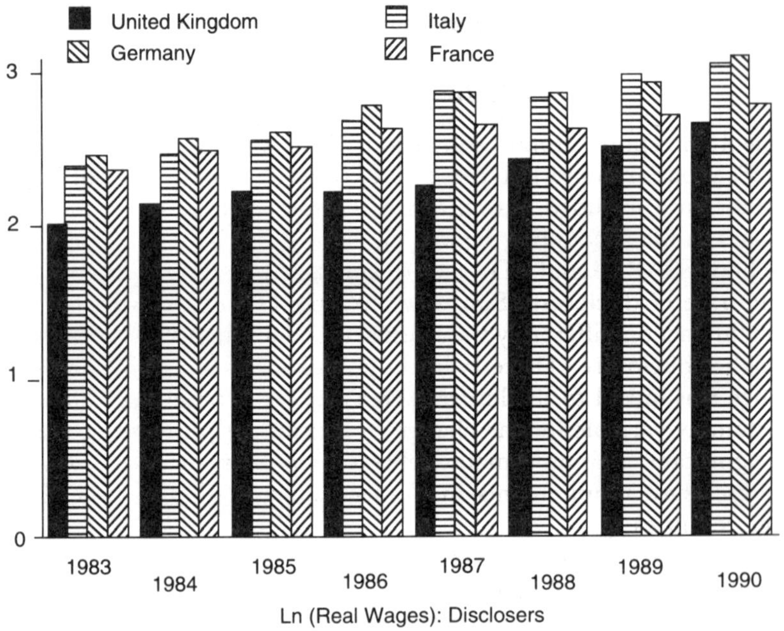

Figure 13.3 Average real wages: firms who disclose R&D

Figure 13.4 Average R&D per worker: firms who disclose R&D

4 FIRM-LEVEL WAGE–R&D ASSOCIATIONS ACROSS COUNTRIES

Disclosure equations

Table 13.3 reports probit estimates of R&D disclosure equations. Two specifications are reported, the difference being whether or not industry dummies are included. As expected the variables intended to capture changes in the accounting regime all attract positive coefficients. In the UK both SSAP 13 and ED 41 were associated with significant increases in the rate of disclosure. Similarly, the other change that had a differential impact on differently sized firms, the 1987 change in Germany, led to higher disclosure. There is (slightly weaker) evidence that the Italian change was linked to disclosure increases. The estimated coefficient on the dummy variable for the change in accounting practices in France is not significant. This presumably reflects the point made in Section 2 that the disclosure requirements in France appear rather weaker than in other countries.

Hence, there is some strong evidence that changes made to the accounting standards regarding disclosure have a significant effect on disclosure rates. These estimated models are used to construct the inverse Mills ratio to correct for selection bias in our firm-level wage equations.

Table 13.3 Probit models of disclosure of R&D data in company accounts

	(1)	*(2)*
Probability of disclosure (t−1) equations		
Constant	.156 (.201)	−.035 (.213)
Germany, Commercial Code, 1987	.306 (.117)	.252 (.121)
Italy, Decree of the President, 1986	.452 (.204)	.416 (.212)
France, General Accounting Plan, 1983	.382 (.266)	.365 (.279)
United Kingdom, Consolidated Company Act 1985	.058 (.143)	.033 (.147)
United Kingdom, Exposure Draft 41, 1987	.384 (.143)	.377 (.147)
United Kingdom, SSAP 13 (revised), 1989	.542 (.184)	.616 (.189)
Ln (net assets per employee)(t−1)	−.347 (.037)	−.264 (.045)
United Kingdom	−.034 (.189)	−.131 (.197)
Germany	−.338 (.180)	−.391 (.187)
France	−.775 (.306)	−.932 (.322)
Industry dummies (7)	No	Yes
Log-likelihood	−1,017.6	−968.5
Sample size	2,619	2,619

Notes: Coefficients are estimated by probit, standard errors in parentheses

Wage equations

Table 13.4 holds the results from the wage equations. Eight specifications are reported, which differ in the functional form adopted for the R&D variable, whether correction is made for selectivity, whether industry dummies are included and whether fixed or random effects are controlled for. For each specification two alternative measures are given for R&D per worker. One is in levels and the other in natural logarithms. As there are some firms disclosing zero R&D we follow Pakes and Griliches (1984) and set the logarithm equal to zero if R&D was zero, and include a separate dummy variable.

The first two columns of Table 13.4 contain the wage equation without selectivity correction. R&D enters positively and significantly in both columns suggesting that technologically progressive firms pay their workers higher wages. As the more flexible functional form of column (2) makes evident, this operates through a sizeable wage 'penalty' for those firms performing no R&D, together with a small but statistically significant positive elasticity of the order of 0.05. This is just over half the magnitude of the elasticity of the wage with respect to physical capital. Of course, much of the R&D may be tied up in physical capital which would point to an underestimate of the wage–R&D relation. Nevertheless these results point to an important link between wages and disembodied knowledge working through the R&D variable.

In the third and fourth columns the Mills ratio is included to correct for selectivity that attracts a significant and negative coefficient. Hence,

Table 13.4 The relationship between firm wages and R&D intensity in four European countries

	No disclosure correction		*Disclosure correction*		*Disclosure correction and industry dummies*		*Disclosure correction and firm dummies*	
	(1)	*(2)*	*(3)*	*(4)*	*(5)*	*(6)*	*(7)*	*(8)*
Ln (real wage equations)								
Constant	2.208	2.283	2.281	2.345	2.337	2.358		
	(.097)	(.080)	(.103)	(.084)	(.085)	(.086)		
R&D per employee (t−1)	.019		.019		.012		.010	
	(.004)		(.004)		(.003)		(.004)	
Ln (R&D per employee) (t−1) if R&D (t−1) > 0		.050		.050		.051		.029
		(.012)		(.012)		(.012)		(.019)
Dummy variable for R&D (t−1) = 0		−.334		−.334		−.400		−.294
		(.042)		(.042)		(.078)		(.121)
Ln (net assets per employee) (t−1)	.095	.088	.132	.122	.117	.117	.139	.151
	(.026)	(.021)	(.032)	(.025)	(.020)	(.023)	(.031)	(.031)
United Kingdom	−.346	−.299	−.349	−.301	−.329	−.308		
	(.064)	(.059)	(.063)	(.058)	(.071)	(.066)		
Germany	.112	.111	.163	.157	.168	.148		
	(.070)	(.063)	(.075)	(.065)	(.074)	(.068)		
France	−.102	.004	−.026	.073	.050	.071		
	(.076)	(.070)	(.085)	(.075)	(.083)	(.078)		
Inverse Mills ratio from disclosure (t−1) probit			−.131	−.119	−.090	−.113	−.088	−.105
			(.068)	(.049)	(.037)	(.044)	(.051)	(.052)
Year dummies	Yes	Yes	Yes	Yes	Yes	Yes	Yes	Yes
Industry dummies	No	No	No	No	Yes	Yes	No	No
Firm dummies	No	No	No	No	No	No	Yes	Yes
R-squared	.631	.751	.638	.754	.727	.760	.945	.945
Sample size	395	395	395	395	395	395	395	395

Notes: 1 Random effects coefficient estimates (standard errors in parentheses) in columns (1)–(6). Fixed effects estimates in columns (7)–(8)

2 The dependent variable is Ln (real wages in 1985$)

3 The inverse Mills ration is from column (1) of Table 13.3 in columns (3), (4), (7) and (8) and from column (2) of Table 13.3 in columns (5) and (6)

the null hypothesis of no selection bias is rejected. It is interesting to note that the estimated coefficient on the R&D variable is substantially unchanged and continues to suggest a robust and positive effect between wages and previous period R&D per worker. What is affected is the physical capital variable whose coefficient rises by about 40 per cent.

Industry dummies are included in columns (5) and (6), with little effect on the overall nature of the results. The other coefficients of interest in the columns (1) to (6) specifications are the country dummies. Relative to the omitted reference country (Italy), it is very clear that the UK firms in the sample pay significantly lower wages (about 40 per cent less than Italian firms), and that German firms pay the highest wages (by about 15 per cent). This is interesting when one bears in mind that the companies included in the sample are some of the leading national corporations.

The final test is to consider what happens when we include a dummy variable for every company to control for unobserved permanent differences across firms (such as managerial quality and corporate culture). Fixed effects are used in place of random effects in columns (7) and (8). Remarkably, given the rigour of the test, column (7) points to the fact that the coefficient on R&D has fallen only marginally and remains significant. In column (8) the zero R&D intercept remains highly significant although the log linear R&D term is about half the size of the equivalent estimate in column (6) and poorly determined.

An interesting question is whether the R&D effect varies across different countries. This is difficult to test rigorously because of the relatively small number of firms we are looking at. Nevertheless, we interacted the R&D variables with the country dummies to see if there were any important differences. A clear ranking does emerge with Germany having the strongest correlation, the UK generally second and France and Italy the weakest.[7] Considering that Germany also has the highest R&D intensity, this points to an important role for R&D in wage determination in German companies compared to other European firms. One possible explanation for this is the very different industrial relations systems operating across nations. Germany and the UK have a stronger and more decentralized system of collective bargaining than in France or Italy. The absence of an explicit variable to capture these differences, however, makes deeper analysis difficult to pursue.

5 CONCLUDING REMARKS

This chapter is a first attempt to use firm-specific information on wages and R&D to shed light on the impact of knowledge accumulation and the wage structure across the four major European economies. In performing this investigation we have highlighted the need to control for different R&D disclosure practices in the different countries as this is a potential source of selectivity bias. Using the variance over time and place in accounting regimes to identify the disclosure equation it was shown that disclosure rates have reacted to these changes. In terms of wage determination, selectivity appears to bias downwards the elasticity between wages and net assets, but not between wages and R&D.

According to the central estimates, a doubling of R&D per worker is associated with a rise in average wages of the order of 3–5 per cent. This appears to be robust to controls for unobserved heterogeneity whether modelled by random or fixed effects. This effect of R&D is weakest in France and strongest in Germany.

One plausible reason for such a correlation lies in the importance of insider power in shaping wages, and the quasi-rents generated by R&D being shared with workers. The findings suggest that these insider forces are much weaker in France than in the other EC countries, at least amongst the larger corporations considered here.

NOTES

1 Bound and Johnson (1992) is a good US example; see Van Reenen (1996) for evidence from the UK.
2 See Berman, Bound and Griliches (1993) for US evidence and Machin (1994) for UK evidence that the majority of the shift towards non-manual work has occurred within industries.
3 An identifying instrument must affect R&D disclosure probabilities without having a direct impact on the amount of R&D performed.
4 For an account of the political pressure and bargaining in the Accounting Standards Committee over the change see Gray (1985).
5 Strictly speaking 'groups' were given until 1989 to comply, although almost all did so well before then.
6 The within-groups estimator relies on the assumption that the regressors are strictly exogenous in panels with finite T. There is no dynamic feedback in the model, but it might be argued that wages will affect R&D and capital decisions in the future. The only alternative is a first differenced instrumental variable estimator. Unfortunately such models are hard to combine with companies who switch in and out of disclosure regimes.
7 For example, using a specification identical to column (5) and allowing the R&D effect to vary with country gave the following pattern of coefficients and standard error (in parentheses): Germany 0.020 (0.006); UK 0.015 (0.004); Italy 0.012 (0.006) and France −0.003 (0.006).

REFERENCES

Berman, Eli, John Bound and Zvi Griliches (1993) 'Changes in the demand for skilled labour within US manufacturing industries: evidence from the Annual Survey of Manufacturing', National Bureau of Economic Research Discussion Paper No. 4255.

Blake, J. and Amat, O. (1993) *European Accounting*, Pitman Publishing.

Bound, John and George Johnson (1992) 'Changes in the structure of wages in the 1980s: an evaluation of alternative explanations', *American Economic Review*, vol. 82, 3: 371–392.

Freeman, Richard and Lawrence Katz (1994) 'Rising wage inequality: The United States vs. other advanced countries' in Richard Freeman (ed.) *Working Under Different Rules*, New York: Russell Sage Foundation.

Gray, R. (1985) 'Accounting for R&D: a review of experiences with SSAP 13', Institute for Chartered Accountants in England and Wales.

Heckman, J. (1979) 'Selection bias as a specification error', *Econometrica*, 47: 153–161.

Machin, Stephen (1994) 'Changes in the relative demand for skills in the UK labour market', forthcoming in A. Booth and D. Snower (eds) *Acquiring Skills: Market Failures. Their Symptoms and Policy Responses*, Cambridge University Press.

Mishel, Lawrence and Jared Bernstein (1994) 'Is the technology black box empty? An empirical examination of the impact of technology on wage inequality and the employment structure', Economic Policy Institute mimeo.

Nickell, S. and Wadhwani, S. (1990) 'Insider power and wage determination', *Economic Journal*, 100.

Pakes, A. and Griliches, Z. (1984) 'Patents and R&D at the firm level: a first look', in Z. Griliches (ed.) *R&D, Patents and Productivity*, Chicago University Press.

Van Reenen, John (1996) 'The creation and capture of rents: innovation and wages in UK manufacturing firms', *Quarterly Journal of Economics*, February: 195–226.

14

REAL R&D OPTIONS

David Newton, Dean Paxson and Alan Pearson

1 INTRODUCTION

The value of R&D is an important aspect of technology enterprise development and innovation. Emphasis placed on short-term accounting returns as compared to long-term investment values implies that the R&D investment decision process may be distorted. It can be argued that the use of management accounting and control procedures based on techniques such as net present value and internal rate of return, without comprehensive modelling of possible future returns, contribute to this short-termism.

Plausibly, any trend towards decentralization within organizations accompanied by a 'contractor–customer' oriented approach with a movement away from a central support to R&D involves more, and in some cases total, emphasis on divisional profitability and on the 'bottom line'. In this case there may be further demands for R&D to focus on short-term, more narrowly defined and directly relevant projects to the neglect of the longer term, wider and more strategic approach.

Real R&D option techniques emphasize investment values which alter over time and across projects, as well as perceived investment cost and discovery value volatility. Although such option values may not be incorporated directly into the report accounts, they may assist in better resource allocation, performance evaluation and enterprise valuation in the long term.

Section 2 provides a background for some of the problems of R&D investment strategy. Section 3 reviews some of the literature for R&D real options, and presents one model for real option pricing of R&D discovery possibilities, where there is uncertainty regarding both the discovery development cost as well as the discovery potential. Illustrations are then provided of the sensitivity of R&D discovery option value to 'moneyness', volatility, and to the correlation of development costs and discovery values. Section 4 concludes that R&D valuation research is itself a valuable real option.

2 R&D INVESTMENT STRATEGY BACKGROUND

Debate on the relevance of R&D to the needs of the organization is not new. In the 1960s many were questioning the value of the more basic research undertaken in corporate or central laboratories. To many, the Rothschild Report (1971) signalled the birth of the 'contractor–customer relationship' which simply stated that customers (generally the operating divisions of the company) know what is needed and by their willingness to pay were able to control the distribution and allocation of resources. There were some who questioned this approach to R&D and, in particular, how the relationship between the contractors and the customers should be managed to ensure that the whole organization would benefit in the long term as well as in the short term.

One such person was Hubert (1970), who presented an approach to co-ordination and collaboration which drew upon the concept of relevance. He accepted that R&D could not be supported simply for its own sake, or as some people put it (less politely) for the sake of R&D people, but rather that its value and, hence, its continuing support depended upon its relevance to the organization. The starting point for deciding the allocation of resources must therefore be the objectives of the organization. In theory this would focus attention on its long-term future.

The real R&D option approach is seen as appropriate for valuing R&D within a decentralized organization or in an environment of independent R&D ventures. At the level of the R&D project interface governed by the 'contractor–customer' principle, the uncertainty parameters depend on the relationship between producers and users.

Recognizing the emergence of new technologies is sometimes difficult for end users. The role for R&D in such cases is to highlight areas where change could occur, to encourage business units to take a longer term view and to provide appropriate financial support. Set against this are desires for strong 'bottom line' performance and the difficulties in forecasting, which is in the very nature of R&D.

Consequently, business units typically call for such activity to be supported from corporate funds, especially when the outcomes of R&D might have implications for more than one strategic business unit or provide the stimulus for creating and developing new business units. This might be funded by a form of levy on profits or sales, and is reminiscent of renewal payments (or roll-overs) of option premiums for continuous 'calls' in financial option markets.

Unlike financial options, there is often a learning experience or indirect discovery value from 'failed' projects and in particular where information from these is provided early enough to prevent subsequent heavy and unnecessary expenditures. Work that falls outside specific project boundaries can also be important and of financial value to an organization. This can include the often reported 'free' or unallocated time which may be significant in many organizations. Also 'bootlegging' activities, which have been cited on many occasions as leading to highly innovative and profitable outputs, cannot be ignored as a potential source of long-term R&D project activity.

R&D must therefore be seen as a 'portfolio' of activities, with varying degrees of uncertainty, which are carried out in different types of both formal and informal structures.

3 R&D INVESTMENT APPRAISAL

The well-known financial approaches to project evaluation and selection are by no means new in the R&D field. These include the various forms of cash flow analysis including net present value and internal rate of return. The question of uncertainty has been handled by the use of simple rank indices incorporating, for example, the probabilities of technical and commercial success. Decision trees have proved to be a useful means of focusing on the stage-wise progression of R&D and highlighting the ability to stop at an early stage without the commitment of large sums of money. Monte Carlo methods have been used to simulate solutions in which the uncertainty is high regarding costs, benefits and time. It has not been difficult to demonstrate, using such models, that time is a crucial variable. When product cycles are shortening there is often justification for spending more on R&D to achieve shorter 'time to market' as this strategy may reduce the rate of return less than delaying entry. In this respect simultaneous, or concurrent, engineering of R&D discoveries are being used effectively by many organizations to increase R&D profitability. However, there are areas in which activities of a higher uncertainty and of a longer term nature may be undervalued, even when the additional benefits already mentioned are taken into account.

Real option pricing literature

The literature on R&D real options is increasingly linked with other imaginative applications of option pricing theory in corporate finance and strategy. Roberts and Weitzman (1981) developed a model of sequential R&D development and, with an optimal stopping rule, showed that some R&D investments with initially negative present values were justifiable. Weitzman, Newey and Rabin (1981) illustrated this model in evaluating synthetic fuel plants. Sick (1989) provided an extensive survey of real option models, including more complex sequential investments, with the abandonment and maintenance alternatives of

Brennan and Schwartz (1985). Dixit and Pindyck (1994) also surveyed real option models and methods, with frequent references to R&D applications.

Bjerksund and Ekern (1990) provided a practical example of the real option values of petroleum exploration and development under price and petroleum reserve uncertainty. This is perhaps most appropriate for the development stage of R&D projects, where the market and investment cost parameters are identified, but there is substantial price uncertainty. Project flexibility in terms of investment scale and timing discretion is the valuable real option. Integrating such project development models with appropriate output derivative prices is likely to enhance model reality and usefulness.

Newton and Pearson (1994) illustrated conventional option pricing analysis of R&D programmes, with otherwise negative present values. Newton, Paxson and Pearson (1994) reviewed several analytical solutions for R&D real options, including (i) barrier options (where funding for the R&D venture might be exhausted prior to development); (ii) where the R&D option is a perpetual American option (such as a continuing research laboratory), with either normally or log-normally distributed prices; (iii) where the volatility of the potential discovery value is itself stochastic; and finally (iv) where the R&D is a 'quality option' so that the holder has the right to choose among several possible (but similar) discovery developments.

Willner (1995) modelled the pure research real option as a Poisson process, where there are a series of random jumps in new discoveries. With the extensive development of exotic option pricing models as identified in Paxson (1996) with increasing complex valuation methods, including numerical solutions, there are a host of plausibly appropriate real option models for different R&D environments.

R&D investment and discovery uncertainty

One of the primary problems in valuing R&D using conventional capital budgeting is that the 'expected' returns on investments are often not easy to forecast, while the variability of investment returns may be within ranges of confidence. A 'new conventional' approach to R&D is to utilize the variability estimate as an important determinant of initial investment value, inputting some volatility forecast into an option pricing model.

There are several approaches to real option valuation, dependent on particular assumptions regarding the life, variable stability, and pay-outs on the underlying inputs and outputs. We illustrate a real R&D option where the investment can be viewed as a perpetuity, whose value follows a jointly normal diffusion process that may be correlated with that of the value of the 'R&D discovery'. A yearly renewed pure research budget would be an example of such an investment. The variability of the investment cost might differ between R&D projects near to production (low investment cost variability), those at the development stage (medium cost variability) and basic exploratory research (high cost variability). Such real options, where there are ongoing investment costs, rather than a single decision point for investment, and where both the investment cost and the present value of the discovery are risky, are modelled by various authors (see Sick (1989) and Quigg (1993)).

Suppose the investment cost (X) follows a stochastic process:

$$\frac{dX}{X} = \alpha_x dt + \sigma_x dz_x \tag{1}$$

and the value of the discovery (P) follows a similar process:

$$\frac{dP}{P} = (\alpha_p - x_2)\, dt + \sigma_p dz_p \tag{2}$$

where

α_X and α_P = the drift or growth rate of the underlying cost or value
σ_X and σ_P = the annualized standard deviation of the cost or value
dz = a Weiner process with zero drift and unit variance
x_2 is the payout on the developed discovery, and ρdt is the constant correlation between dz_X and dz_P

Other assumptions are that the drift rates of X and P can be represented as υ_x and υ_p, that is expected future cash flows under risk-adjusted probabilities, discounted at the risk-free rate, and the risk aversion coefficients for X and P are constant parameters, λ_X and λ_P

The value of such an R&D option (V(P,X) is

$$\tfrac{1}{2}\sigma_X^2 X^2 V_{XX} + \rho_{XP}\sigma_X\sigma_P XPV_{XP} + \tfrac{1}{2}\sigma_P^2 P^2 V_{PP} + \upsilon_x XV_x + \upsilon_P PV_p - iV + \beta P = 0 \tag{3}$$

where the subscripts denote partial derivatives, i = the risk-free rate, and β is considered the income on undeveloped R&D discoveries, perhaps the 'prestige' of a R&D department.

For simplification, let the ratio of discovery value to investment costs, the option 'moneyness', z = P/X; W(z) = V(X,P)/X, the relative value of the discovery option to the investment costs; and

$$\omega^2 = \sigma_X^2 - 2\rho\sigma_X\sigma_P + \sigma_P^2 \tag{4}$$

Then equation 3 is simplified as:

$$\tfrac{1}{2}\omega^2 z^2 W'' + (\upsilon_P - \upsilon_X)\, zW' + (\upsilon_X - i)\, W + \beta\, z = 0 \tag{5}$$

In solving this differential equation, assume there is a ratio of discovery value to the investment costs z^*, at which it is optimal to commence the 'discovery' production, and that there are certain other boundary conditions. The solution is:

$$V(P, X) = X(Az^{j} + k) \tag{6}$$

where

$$A = (z* - 1 - k)\,(z*)^{-j} \tag{7}$$

$$z* = \frac{j\,(1 + k)}{(j - 1)} \tag{8}$$

$$k = \frac{\beta z}{(i - \upsilon_X)} \tag{9}$$

$$j = \omega^{-2}\,(.5\omega^2 + \upsilon_X - \upsilon_P + [\omega^2\,(.25\omega^2 - \upsilon_P - \upsilon_X + 2i) + (\upsilon_X - \upsilon_P)^{2}]^{.5} \tag{10}$$

The intrinsic value of the option, that is the discovery value over the investment cost upon commencing the development or production process, is the limit of equation 6, as ω tends to zero.

$$V^I\,(X, P) = P - X \qquad z \geq (1 + k) \tag{11}$$

$$V^I\,(X, P) = \frac{\beta P}{(i - \upsilon_X)} \qquad z < (1 + k) \tag{12}$$

R&D real option sensitivities

As an illustration, it is assumed initially that the investment costs increase by 5 per cent per annum, whereas there is no increase over time in the discovery values. The discovery net operating income (not included in the discovery value, possibly the value of leading to another discovery, which value is not immediately capitalized) is 2 per cent. The volatility of investment costs and discovery values is the same at 10 per cent (standard deviation annualized), the risk aversion coefficient is 0.1 for X and P, and β is zero. The correlation of the investment and the discovery value variances is assumed to be +0.5.

The R&D real option value is shown in Table 14.1 and Figure 14.1 for initial investment costs of £100,000,000 and increasing levels of 'moneyness' (z). The investment is required in order to obtain the discovery value, rather than as a cost (called the 'exercise price' in option theory) that must be paid to exploit the discovery value. Note that the R&D real option value increases as the discovery value increases from a moneyness of 0.9 to 1.1, showing that this type of real option is in accordance with conventional option pricing theory. Even the in-the-money real R&D options ($z > 1$) have an option 'premium' over the

Table 14.1 Real R&D option discovery value and 'moneyness' (£ millions)

Option value	0.51	1.16	2.51	5.26	10.64
Cost to develop	100.00	100.00	100.00	100.00	100.00
Discovery value	90.00	95.00	100.00	105.00	110.00
Moneyness	0.90	0.95	1.00	1.05	1.10
Intrinsic value	0.00	0.00	0.00	5.00	10.00

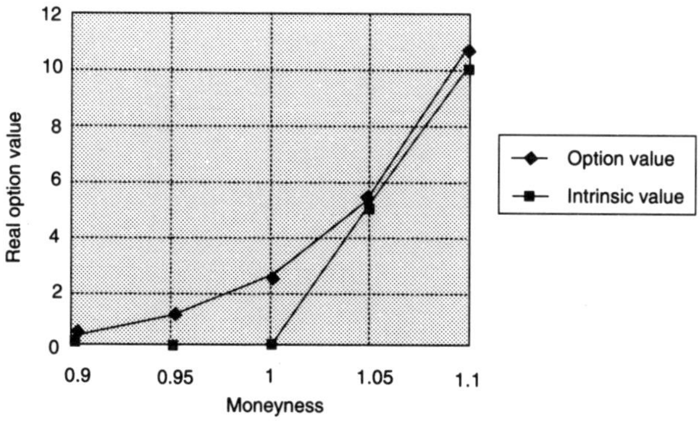

Figure 14.1 Real R&D option discovery value

intrinsic value. This table shows the value of the real option approach to capital budgeting for R&D. If the present value of the ongoing investment costs is greater than or equal to the current value of the discovery (z $\leq$ 1), a decision to cut R&D expenditure would be indicated. However, the real R&D option value shows that the R&D department should not be closed down under these conditions, since it is worth in addition some £2,500,000 at $z = 1$.

In Table 14.2 and Figure 14.2, in which $z = 1$, the investment cost volatility is held constant and the discovery value volatility (σ_P) is increased up to 30 per cent. Under otherwise the same conditions, the R&D department is worth up to an additional £11,700,000, indicating that at the margin, high volatility projects should be maintained, indeed encouraged.

Finally, Figure 14.3 shows the volatility and correlation sensitivity, as all other variables are held constant, except that the volatilities of both investment cost and discovery value are increased equally, and the correlation is increased from -1 to $+1$. The greatest real R&D option worth occurs naturally with negative correlation of cost and discovery value and high volatility. Only a myopic R&D manager would ignore such real option value patterns, although the result is contingent on the input assumed.

Table 14.2 Real R&D option: discovery volatility sensitivity (£ millions)

Option value	2.62	2.05	2.51	6.20	11.73
Cost to develop	100.0	100.00	100.00	100.00	100.00
Discovery value	100.00	100.00	100.00	100.00	100.00
Intrinsic value	0.00	0.00	0.00	0.00	0.00
Discovery volatility	0.01	0.05	0.10	0.20	0.30

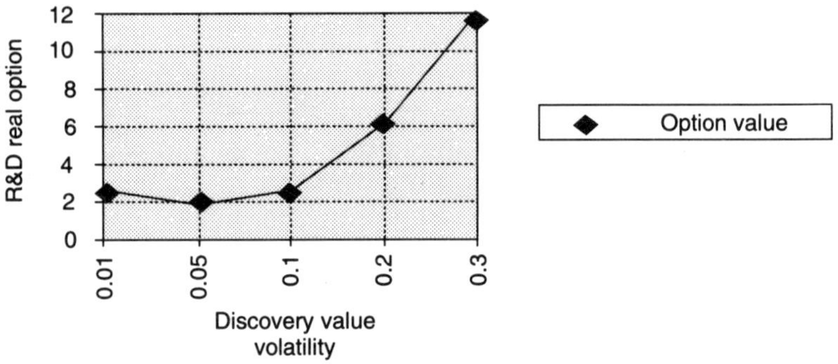

Figure 14.2 R&D option volatility sensitivity

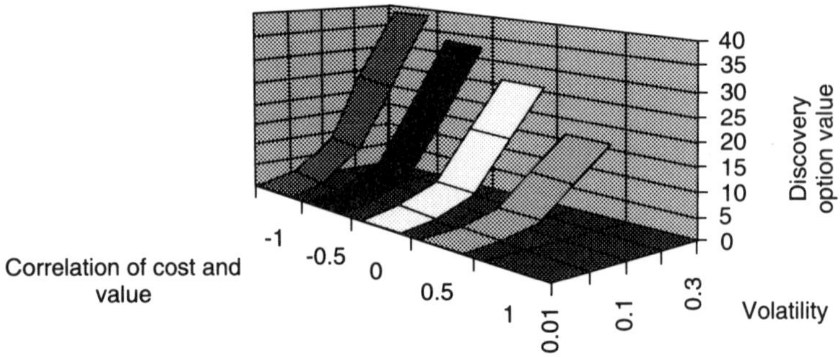

Figure 14.3 R&D option: volatility and correlation

4 R&D VALUATION RESEARCH OPTION

The literature on real R&D options is an abundant source of models for valuing R&D in different settings and with different types of projects. We are convinced that real option pricing needs further exploration as an aid to project and portfolio evaluation in R&D. In saying this we believe that it can provide additional, and useful, information inputs into the decision-making process and could be of real value in situations where the volatility is high and where it is difficult to justify expenditures using the more conventional financial approaches.

Perhaps some anti-intuitive lessons are to be learned using real R&D option models. In our illustration, R&D expenditures may be valuable even though no intrinsic value emerges, which would not normally justify a R&D budget. Also volatility of both investment cost and discovery value increases option value, since after all the actual investment may be deferred or cancelled. Finally, lower or even negative correlation between cost and discovery value (especially in the case of highly volatile investment costs and discovery value) increases the option value of R&D, a consideration not always at the forefront of R&D expenditure committees.

Possibly the option value of the above type of R&D investment appraisal research will increase with the volatility of both the underlying effort and the 'discovery value'.

REFERENCES

Bjerksund, P. and Ekern, S. (1990) 'Managing Investment Opportunities under Price Uncertainty: From "Last Chance" to "Wait and See" Strategies', *Financial Management*, 19, 3: 65–83.

Brennan, M.J. and Schwartz, E.J. (1985) 'Evaluating Natural Resource Investments', *Journal of Business*, 58, 2: 135–158.

Dixit, A. and Pindyck, R. (1994) *Investments under Uncertainty*, Princeton: Princeton University Press.

Hubert, J.M. (1970) 'R&D and the Company's Requirements', *R&D Management*, 2, 2: 69–73.

Kolbe, A.L., Morris, P.A. and Teisberg, E.O. (1991) 'When Choosing R&D Projects, Go with Long Shots', *Research-Technology Management*, January–February.

Newton, D.P. and Pearson, A.W. (1994) 'Application of Option Pricing Theory to R&D', *R&D Management*, 24, 1: 83–89.

Newton, D.P., Paxson, D.A. and Pearson, A.W. (1994) 'Seven Analytical Solutions for Real Options in R&D', MBS Working Paper, June.

Nichols, N.A. (1994) 'Scientific Management at Merck', *Harvard Business Review*, January–February: 89–99.

Pakes, A. (1986) 'Patents as Options: Some Estimates of the Value of Holding European Patent Stocks', *Econometrica*, July: 755–784.

Paxson, D. (1996) 'Exotic Options' in D. Paxson and D. Wood (eds) *Blackwell's Encyclopedia of Management*, Oxford: Blackwell Publishers.

Pearson, A.W. (1972) 'The Use of Ranking Formulae in R&D Projects', *R&D Management*, 2, 2: 69–73.

Quigg, L. (1993) 'Empirical Testing of Real Option-Pricing Models', *Journal of Finance*, 48, 2: 621–640.

Roberts, K. and Weitzman, M.L. (1981) 'Funding Criteria for Research, Development and Exploration Projects', *Econometrica*, 49, 5: 1261–1288.

Rothschild, Lord (1971) 'The Organisation and Management of Government R&D', in *A Framework for Government Research and Development*, Cmnd 4814, London: HMSO.

Sick, G. (1989) *Capital Budgeting with Real Options*, Monograph 1989–3, New

York: Salomon Brothers Center for the Study of Finance Institutions, Monograph Series in Finance and Economics, New York University.
Weitzman, M.L., Newey, W. and Rabin, M. (1981) 'Sequential R&D Strategy for Synfuels', *Bell Journal of Economics*, 12: 574–590.
Willner, R. (1995) 'Valuing Start-up Venture Growth Options', in L. Trigeorgis (ed.) *Real Options in Capital Investment: Models, Strategies and Applications*, Westport, Conn.: Praeger.

INDEX

accounting policies 218–20
accounting standards 203, 208–12, 241–2, 262–3
Accounting Standards Committee (ASC) 210–12, 241
accounting treatment 209–11
acquisitions 144
added-value 145, 146
Advisory Council on Science and Technology (ACOST) 130
aerospace industry 211, 241
Anderson, E.A. 96
annual reports 212–21
appropriability 50–1, 56–9, 169–72, 196
Arora, A. 81–2, 83, 84
Arrow, K.J. 104
attendance at work 90–1
Austin 159, 160, 161

Baltimore 158, 159
banks 128
basic technologies 190, 191
Bayer 49
biotechnology 78, 91
biotechnology industry 156–7, *see also* new biotechnology firms
Black, J. 225
Blaxter, T.J. 87–8
BOC 220–1
Boden, M. 35
Boston 158, 159, 160
bounded vision 112
Braendgaard, A. 96
Brammer 218
Bush, V. 103

Cadbury Committee 148–9
Cambridge 154, 157
Cambridge Instruments 174, 176–7
Canon 26, 43, 47, 48
capabilities 26–7, 32
capital markets 125, 126, 127–34, 140–5
cash flow 136, 145, 146, 175
chemicals industry 66
collaboration 119; external partners 91–3, 94, 144; users and producers 12–13, 189–99
Committee on the Financial Aspects of Corporate Governance 148–9
Companies Act 1985 203, 208, 216–17, 262
Companies Act 1989 208
company law 203, 208, 212, 262–3
competencies 3–4, 26, 41, 51, 111–12; characterization 43–6; development 48–50, 54–6, 59–61, *see also* core competencies
competition 86, 110–11, 189; and disclosure 207–8; and licensing 70–1, 74–5, 76
competitive advantage 12–13, 110–11, 189–92
competitiveness 106, 122
complementary assets 20; and collaboration 13, 195, 196; and core competencies 3, 43; and licensing 4, 5, 64, 66–7, 70, 72–3, 74–6
compulsory disclosure: financial variables 15–16, 225, 233, 234–5, 238; statutory requirement

203, 212, 241, 242–3, 255–6, 262–3
contracts 83–4
control 6, 92, 94, *see also* management control
Coombs, R. 81
core competence paradigm (CCP) 2–3, 25–7
core competencies 2–3, 20, 26–7, 32–6, 44, 47, 48
core products 26
corporate governance 148–9
costs: of disclosure 204, 206, 207, 208, 244–5, 256–7; of research and development 130–1
Cramer, J.S. 247
Cranfield European Enterprise Centre 128, 129
Craven, B.M. 145
creative destruction 108
creativity 145, 146; and control 6, 88–9, 92, 94; new biotechnology firms 78, 79
customers 141

debt finance 226–7
decentralization 1, 28, 29, 144
defence companies 69, 70
della Valle, F. 6, 78, 79, 81, 83, 84–5, 91, 93
Department of Trade and Industry (DTI) 133, 205
Dimsdale, N.H. 148–9
disclosure 20–1; in annual reports 212–22; and finance 14–15, 224–6, 229–38; hypotheses 16–17, 242–6, 255–7; models 13–14, 204–8, 246–55; regulatory history 203, 208–12, 241–2; and wages 17–18, 260–71
disclosure equations 267–8
discounted cash flows 136, 145, 146
discovery 276–8
discriminant analysis 247
distinctive technologies 190–1
diversification 137–8
dividends 129–30
division of labour 13, 193–4; pharmaceutical industry 5, 78, 79, 80–6, 94
DTI *see* Department of Trade and Industry
Dye, R.A. 207
dynamic scale economies 34

Eastman Kodak 44
economic growth 107–8, 121–2, 123
Economic Recovery Tax Act 1981 156
effectiveness 37–8
electronics industry 138
EMI 43
employment 164, 165–6
end-products 26
environment 122–3
equity finance 226–7
European Commission 113
European Community 101, 262–3
Exposure Draft 14 209–12, 221, 241, 243
Exposure Draft 17 209–11, 241
Exposure Draft 41 210–12, 241, 262, 267
exposure drafts 209
external finance 226–7
external links 91–3, 94, 117
external technologies 191

FAS No 2 209–11
financial analysts 131–2, 140, 142, 243–4, 256
financial control 136
financial structure: and disclosure 16, 224–40; and patenting 175–80, 185, *see also* return on capital
Fishman, M.J. 206
fixed effects models 175–80, 238
France 260, 263, 266–7, 270, 271
Fransman, M. 112
Frascati Manual 218
free-riding 179, 183–4, 185
function 192–6
fund managers 126, 127

Gambardella, A. 6, 78, 79, 81–2, 83, 84–5, 91, 93
gearing 178, 179, 180, 224–5
Germany 107, 128, 138, 181, 270, 271; disclosure 261, 262; short-term attitudes 128, 137; wages 260–1, 265, 266–7

Gilbert, R. 170, 171
GKN 220
Glaxo 87, 221
Glaxo Research and Development (GRD) 6, 9, 79, 85–93
golden shares 148
good news variable 246, 257
Goodacre, A. 131–2
Graham, M. 50
Gray, R.H. 131, 211–12
Greene, W.H. 247

Hagerty, K.M. 206
Hall, B. 130
Hamel, G. 2, 25, 26–7, 36, 44, 46–7, 51
harvesting mode 32–5, 38
Healy, P.M. 134–5
Heckman, J. 263
Henriques, I. 184
high technology clusters 10–11, 154–67
Honda 26, 47
Hope, A.J.B. 211–12
House of Lords Select Committee on Science and Technology 212, 241, 243, 262
Hubert, J.M. 274

in-house research and development 64, 66–7, 144
industrial policy 7, 114
industry norms 243, 256
infrastructure 117–18
innovation 7–8, 80–6, 107, 110–12, 115–16; appropriability 50–1, 56–9; and competitive advantage 189–90, 191–2; and corporate strategy 42–3; dynamic gains 169; evaluation of projects 145, 146; and firm size 174; linear model 5, 6–7, 79, 103–6; and market concentration 174–5; national and regional systems 117–18; public policy 101–2, 106–8, 113–14; research 108–9; and science 121–2, *see also* research and development
Innovation Advisory Board 133, 205
institutional shareholders 126, 127–30, 133–4, 140–3, 147–8, 204
intellectual property rights 13, 83–4, 193
internal finance 226
internal organization 70, 71, 76
internationalization 8, 118–21
investment 130–1
investment analysts 131–2, 140, 142, 243–4, 256
investment mode 32–5
involuntary disclosure *see* compulsory disclosure
Italy 156, 260, 262–3, 266–7, 270

Jaffee, A.B. 154, 155, 156, 162
Japan 127, 136–7, 138, 141, 165, 262
joint ventures *see* collaboration
Jorde, T. 81

Kaizen 50
Kasper 48
Klemperer, P. 170, 171
knowledge 45, 84–5, 104–5, 109, *see also* market knowledge; organizational knowledge; personal knowledge
knowledge-based economy 102
knowledge spillovers *see* spillovers
KPMG Peat Marwick McLintock 218

labour market spillover 157, 160, 164–5
Langlois, R. 118
lemons premium 224
Levin, R.C. 183
licensing 4–5, 58, 64–7, 70–6, 144
life-cycle model 191
Likert scales 68
LIMDEP 247–8
linear model of innovation 5, 6–7, 79, 81, 103–6, 107
linear probability models 247
liquidity 178, 179
logit models 247, 250–5, 257
Los Angeles 158, 159, 160

McFadden, D. 252
McKinsey Report 138
Maddala, G.S. 247
make v. buy decisions 64, 67, 70–6, 83
management control 86–91, 134–9

mandatory disclosure *see* compulsory disclosure
Mansfield, E. 65, 183
manufacturing strength 74
market efficiency 132
market knowledge 34
market share 145, 146, 147
Marston, C.L. 145
Massachusetts Institute of Technology (MIT). 154, 157
materiality 244, 256
mechanistic organizations 191–2
Metcalfe, S. 35
Ministry of Defence 69
Minnesota Innovation Research Project 115
Moody, J. 133
Mulder, K. 49

Nelson, R. 110
new biotechnology firms (NBFs) 78–9, 82–5, 91–3, 94
New York 158, 159
Newman, P. 207, 208
NIH (Not Invented Here) syndrome 4, 66–7
Nordhaus, W.D. 170

obligatory disclosure *see* compulsory disclosure
OECD 101, 108, 112, 218
organic organizations 191
organization 109
organizational knowledge 45–6, 49
organizational structure 34, 37
originality 145, 146
Ormerod, P. 148
ownership 180–3, 185

Pakes, A. 11, 170–1
patent breadth 170–1
patent families 169, 171, 175, 184–5
patent length 170
patent scope 169–72, 175, 184–5
patent width 170–1
patenting activity 11–12, 174–5; fixed effects models 175–80; and ownership 180–3
patenting process 172
patents: appropriation of returns 51, 57, 58, 243; research capability 72, 73, 74; university-based research 121, 155–6
Pavitt, K. 115
payback 136, 144–5, 146, 147
performance 90–1, 147, 192–6
performance related pay (PRP) 90–1, 134–6
personal knowledge 45–6, 49–50, 51
pharmaceutical industry 66, 67, 78–97, 138
Photo-Me 220
Pilkington 51
Pisano, G. 44, 93
Pittard Garnar 220
policy 7–8, 21, *see also* industrial policy; technology policy
Porter, M.E. 70
Prahalad, K. 2, 25, 26–7, 36, 44, 46–7, 51
prestige 245, 257
principal-agent theory 135
Prisoners' Dilemma 119
probit models 247, 252, 253, 263–4, 268
profit margins 178, 179, 180
proprietary costs 245, 256–7
proprietary information 207

Raleigh-Durham 159, 160, 161
RCA 43, 50
real option pricing theory 18–19, 273, 274, 275–6, 278–81
remuneration 204
research capability 70, 72–4, 76
research and development: definition 209; and finance 224–40; investment appraisal 274–80; management 87–90, *see also* innovation
research and development expenditure 131–2, 144, 184, 218, *see also* disclosure
return on capital 136, 145, 146, 147, 178–9
reward systems 90–1, 134–9
Rochester 159, 160, 161
Rosenberg, N. 121
Rothschild Report 274
Route 128 154

San Jose 159, 160, 161
Sansing, R. 207, 208

SBUs *see* strategic business units
Scandinavia 107, 141
Schankerman, M. 11, 170–1
Scherer, F.M. 170, 174, 177
Schon, D. 47
Schumpeter, J. 108, 110, 174
science 8, 121–2
scientific instruments industry 169
Seattle 159, 160, 161
semiconductor industry 165
Shapiro, C. 170, 171
share option schemes 135–6
shareholders 126, 127–30, 133–4, 140–3, 147–8, 204
short-termism 8–10, 125–6; capital markets influence 127–34, 139–49, 203, 205; management control systems 134–9
Shuen, A. 44
Siebe 220
Silicon Valley 154
size variable 174, 176–8, 179, 185
social framework 109–10
Sony Corporation 49, 51
Spence, A.M. 183–4
spillovers: patents 12, 178–9, 183–4, 185; research 10–11, 154–68
Standard Metropolitan Statistical Areas (SMSA) 155, 158–60, 165
Standard and Poor 265
Stanford University 154
Statement of Standard Accounting Practice (SSAP) 13 15–17, 203, 225, 248, 253, 267; accounting policies 218–20, 221; compliance 212–15, 217–18, 221; development 209–12, 241, 243, 262
Statement of Standard Accounting Practice (SSAP) 2 218
Stevenson-Wydler Technology Innovation Act 1980 156
Stoughton, N.M. 207
strategic business units 25, 27, 37
strategic management 1–5, 19–20, 28–36, 41–3, 46–61
suppliers 141

Taggart, J.H. 87–8
take-overs 125–6, 134, 141, 143, 148
Targeted Socio-Economic Research Programme 113
taxation 130, 227
Tcount variable 172, 174, 175–8, 180, 183–4
techniques 109
technocratic approach 105
technological capabilities 26–7, 32
technological change 106–8, 109, 113, 118–21
technological knowledge 104–5, 109
technological paradigm 110
technologies 3, 41, 43–6, 52–4, 60–1
technology 7, 35–6, 109–10; acquisition 65–7; and competitive advantage 190–2
Technology-Economy (TEP) programme 108, 112–13, 115
technology policy 7, 102–9, 113–14
technology strategy 64
Teece, D. 4, 44, 81, 93
Tonks, I. 225
trajectories 3, 48–50, 60
Triplex Lloyd 217
trust time 86, 90, 91
two-step estimator 263–5

United States 107, 120, 138, 181; disclosure 209–10, 262; research spillovers 10–11, 154–66
universities 144; biotechnology skills 78, 84, 85, 91–2, 94; labour market spillovers 157, 164; research spillovers 10–11, 154–7, 158–66

value-maximizing models 205–8
Vergragt, P. 49
Verrecchia, R.E. 204, 206, 207, 208
visibility 244
voluntary disclosure 15–16, 203, 204, 214–15, 217, 255–6; financial variables 233, 234–5, 238; good news variable 246; threat of entry 207–8

wage equations 268–70
wages 17–18, 164, 165–6, 259–72
Wagon Industrial 217–18
Wellcome 221
Whitecroft 220
Whittington, G. 209
Winter, S. 43, 50
working time 90–1